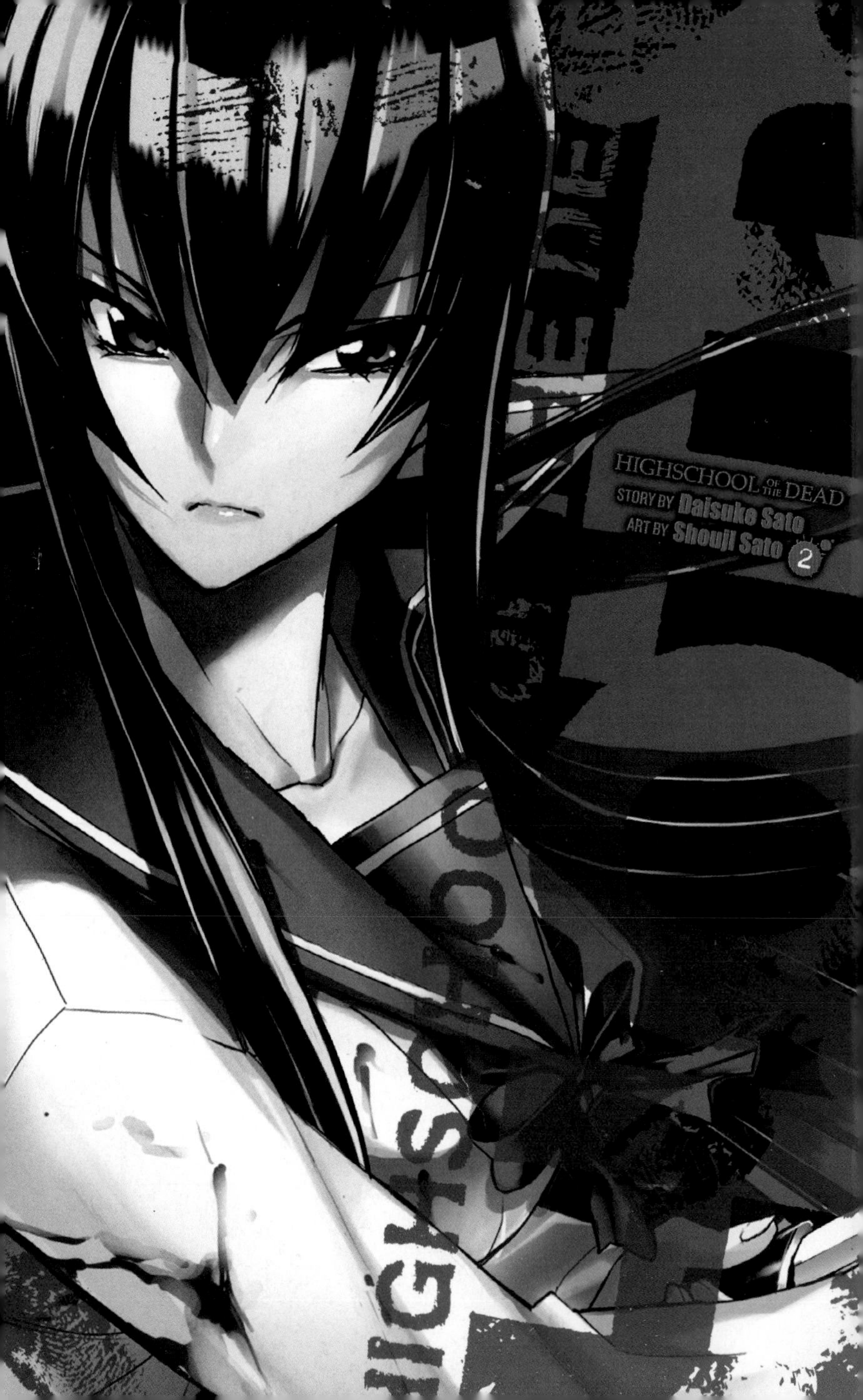
HIGHSCHOOL OF THE DEAD
STORY BY Daisuke Sato
ART BY Shouji Sato
2

CONTENTS



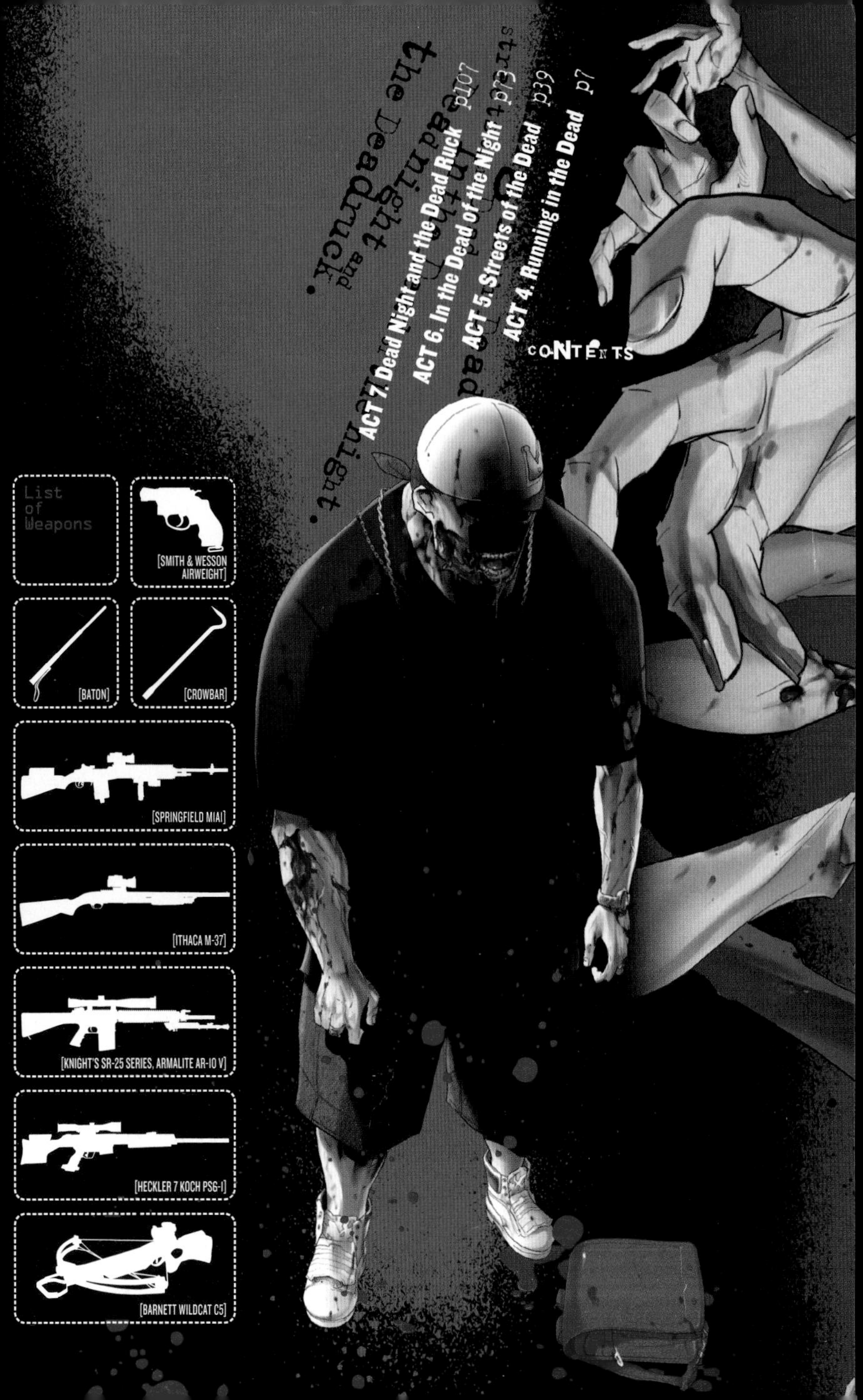

the Deadnight and the Deadruck.
List of Weapons
[SMITH & WESSON AIRWEIGHT]
[BATON]
[CROWBAR]
[SPRINGFIELD MIAI]
[ITHACA M-37]
[KNIGHT'S SR-25 SERIES, ARMALITE AR-IO V]
[HECKLER 7 KOCH PSG-I]
[BARNETT WILDCAT C5]

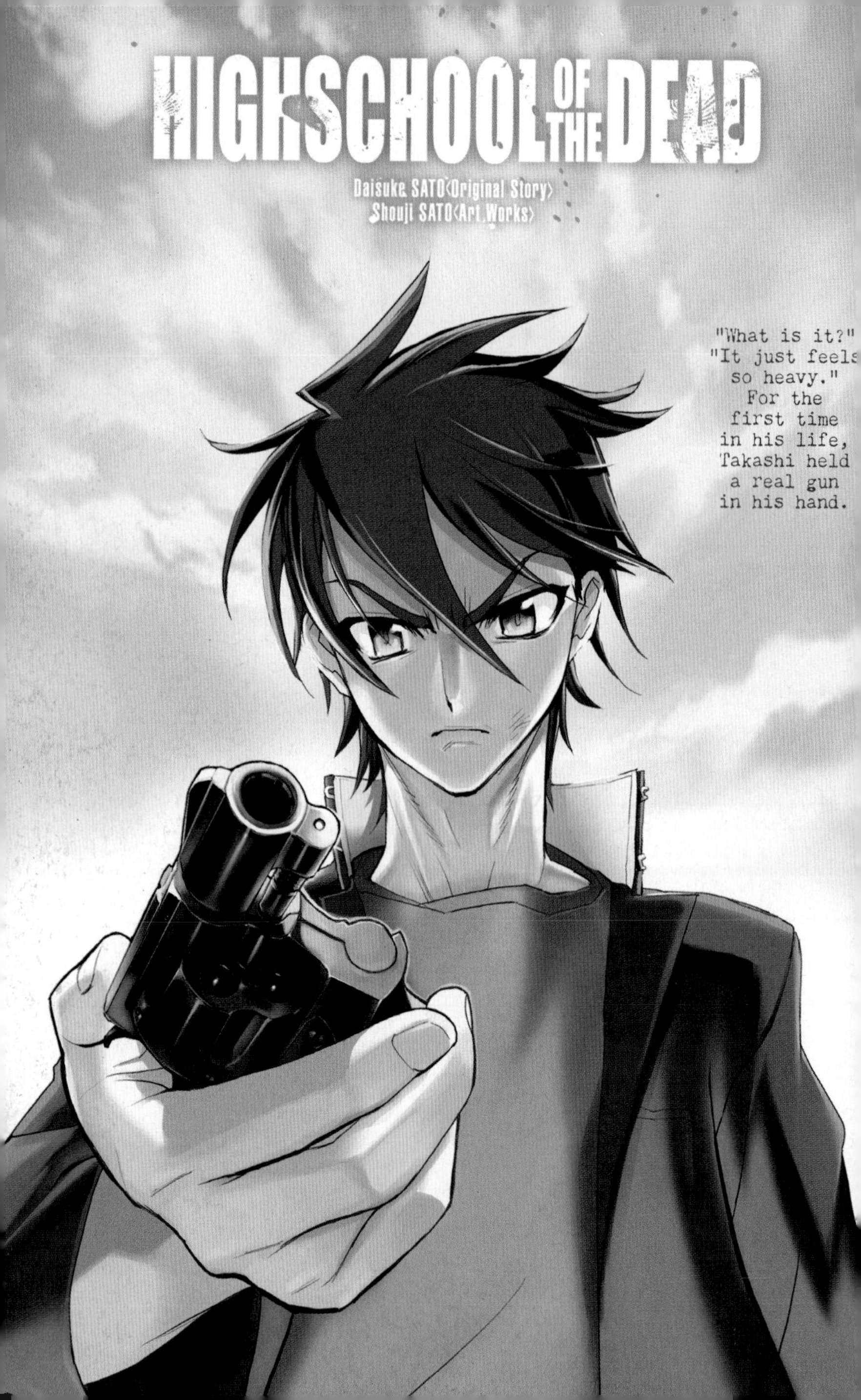
HIGHSCHOOL OF THE DEAD
Daisuke SATO<Original Story>
Shouji SATO<Art Works>
"What is it?" "It just feels so heavy." For the first time in his life, Takashi held a real gun in his hand.

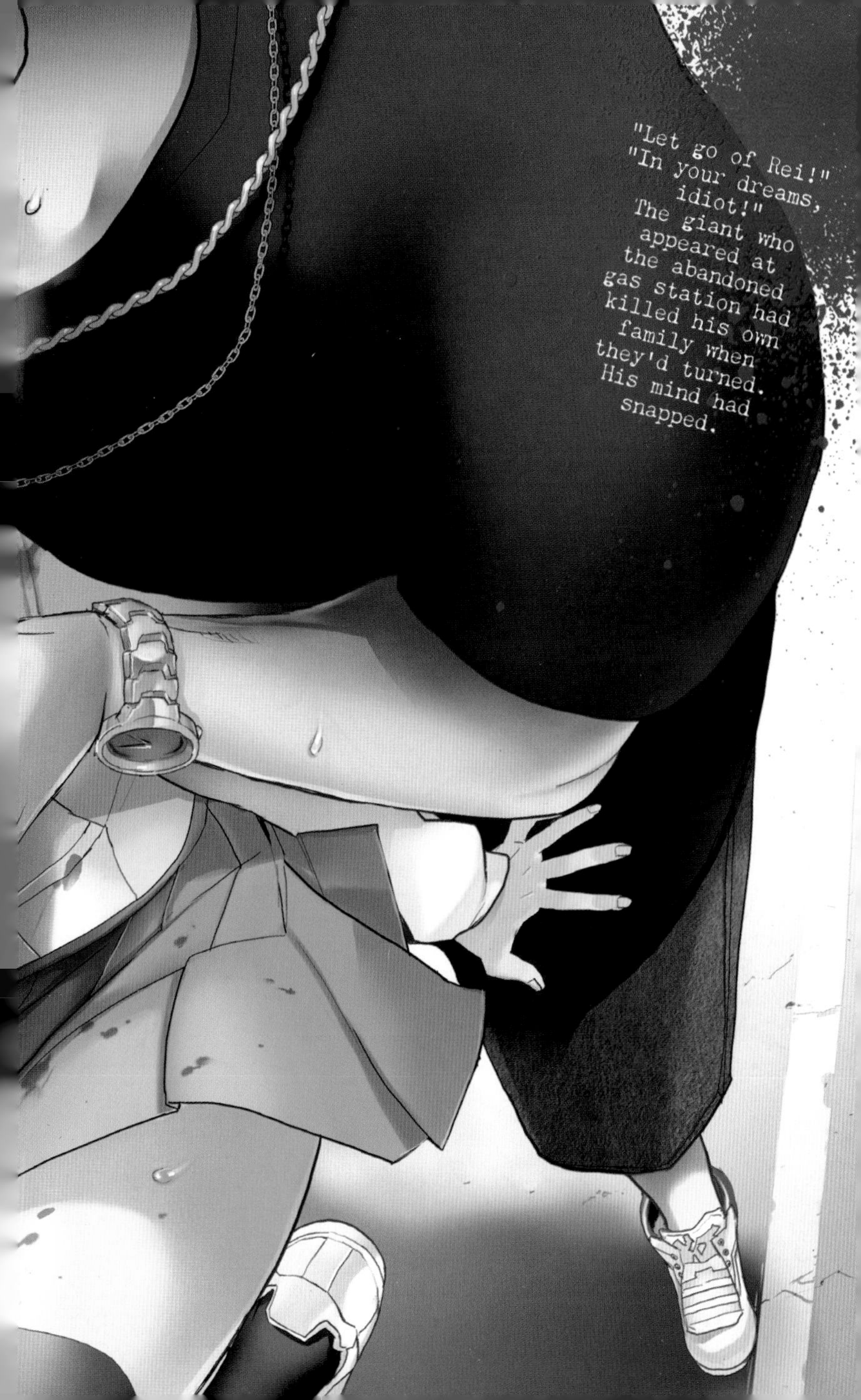
"Let go of Rei!"
"In your dreams, idiot!"
The giant who appeared at the abandoned gas station had killed his own family when they'd turned. His mind had snapped.

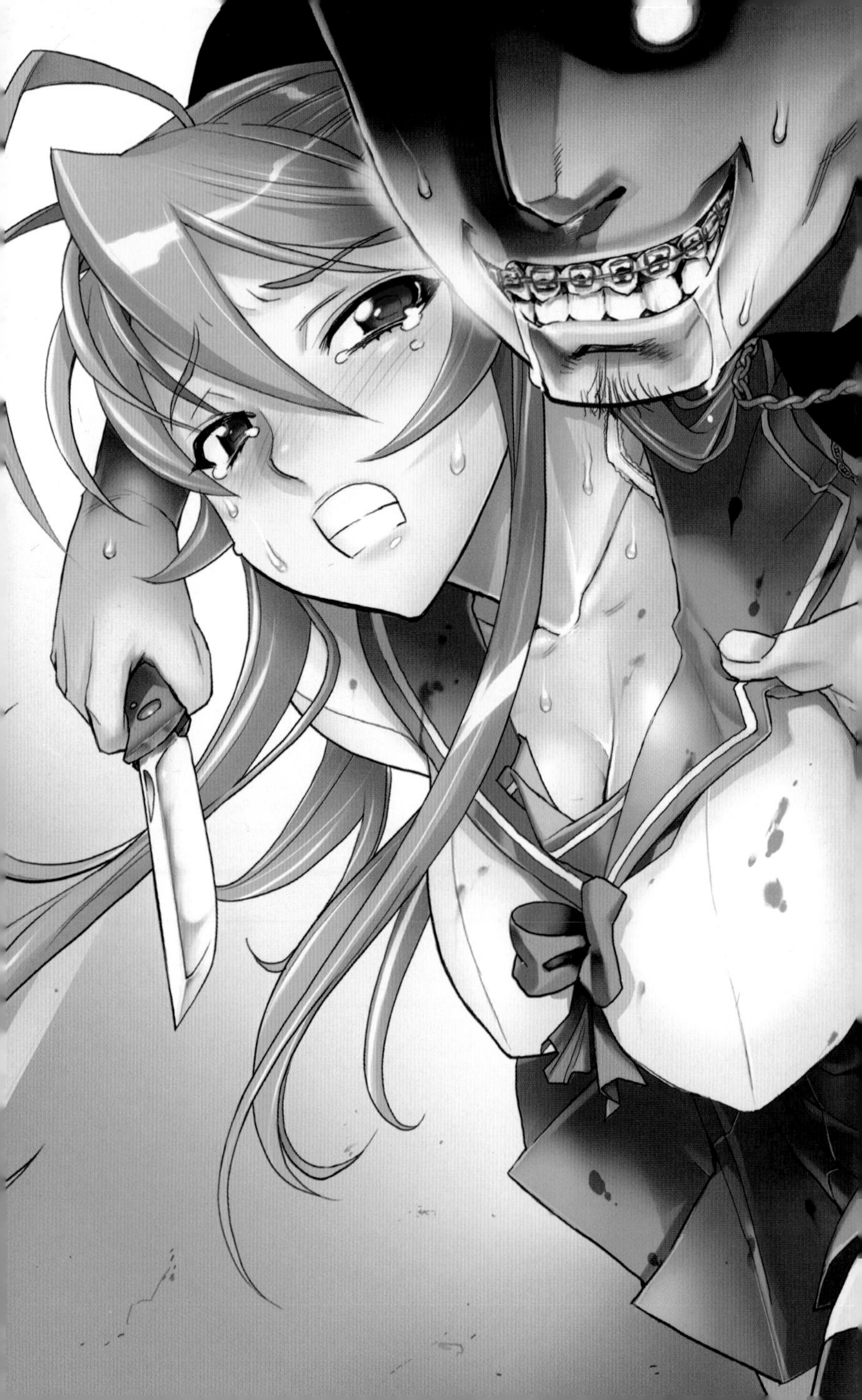

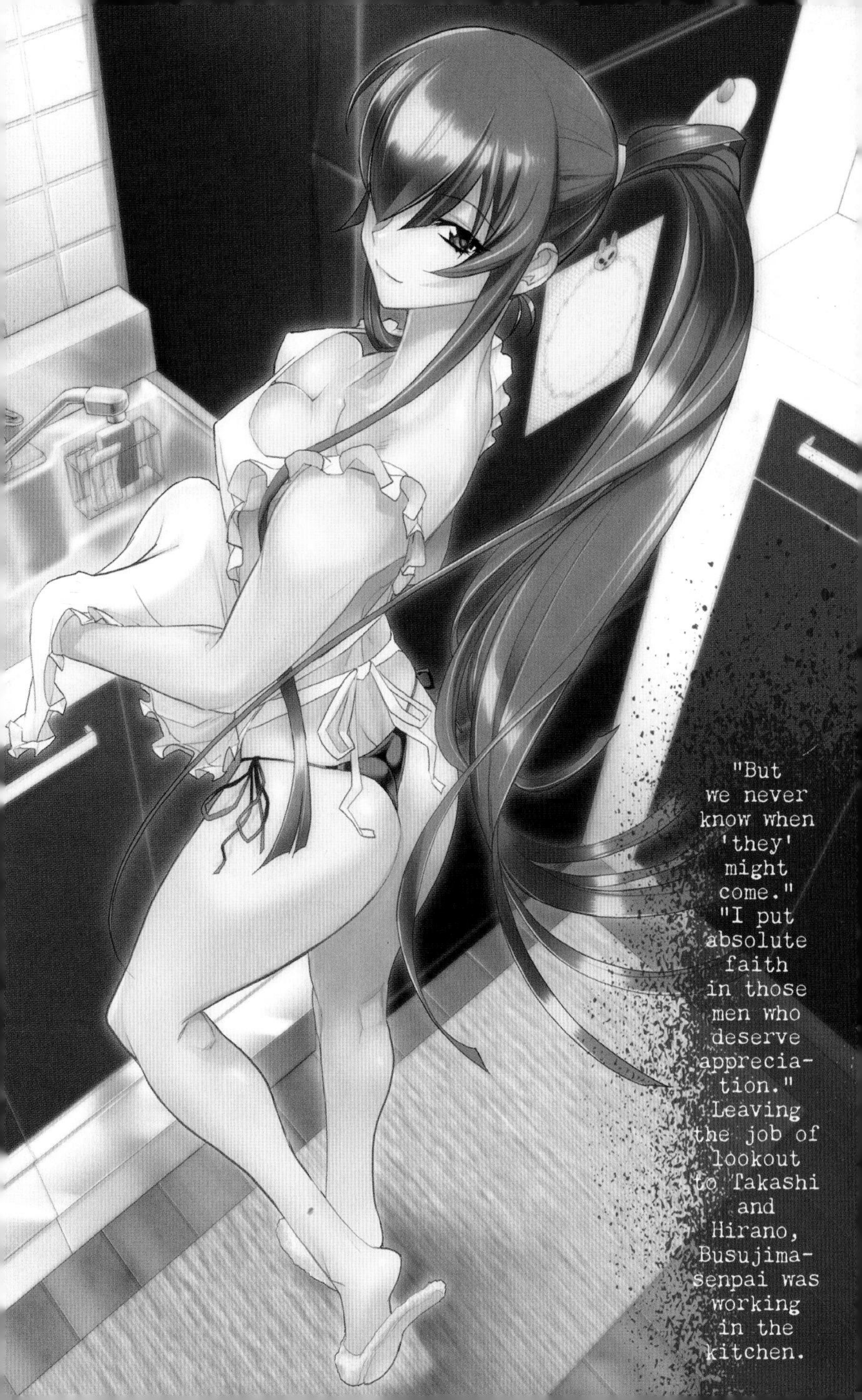
"But we never know when 'they' might come." "I put absolute faith in those men who deserve apprecia-tion." Leaving the job of lookout to Takashi and Hirano, Busujima-senpai was working in the kitchen.

# HIGHSCHOOL OF THE DEAD

## 2

STORY BY
**Daisuke Sato**

ART BY
**Shouji Sato**

**vol.1**
**outline.**

That was the day our once
peaceful world fell apart. A
second-year at the private school
Fujimi High, Takashi Komuro gets
away from "them" when they
suddenly storm his campus,
making it to the school roof along
with his best friend, Hisashi
Igou, and childhood crush, Rei
Miyamoto. However, along the way,
Igou gets bitten and dies, only
to come back as one of "them,"
forcing Takashi to put Hisashi
to rest.

Working together, Takashi and Rei
use a fire hose to clear a path
through "them," make a break from
the roof, and team up with other
survivors — namely fellow
classmates, Saya Takagi and Kouta
Hirano; a third-year master of
the sword, Saeko Busujima; and
the school nurse, Shizuka
Marikawa — ultimately escaping
from the school.

However, Shidou, a teacher
apparently sharing some bad blood
with Rei, tags along, turning the
whole situation around, and
Takashi and Rei are forced to
part ways with their friends.

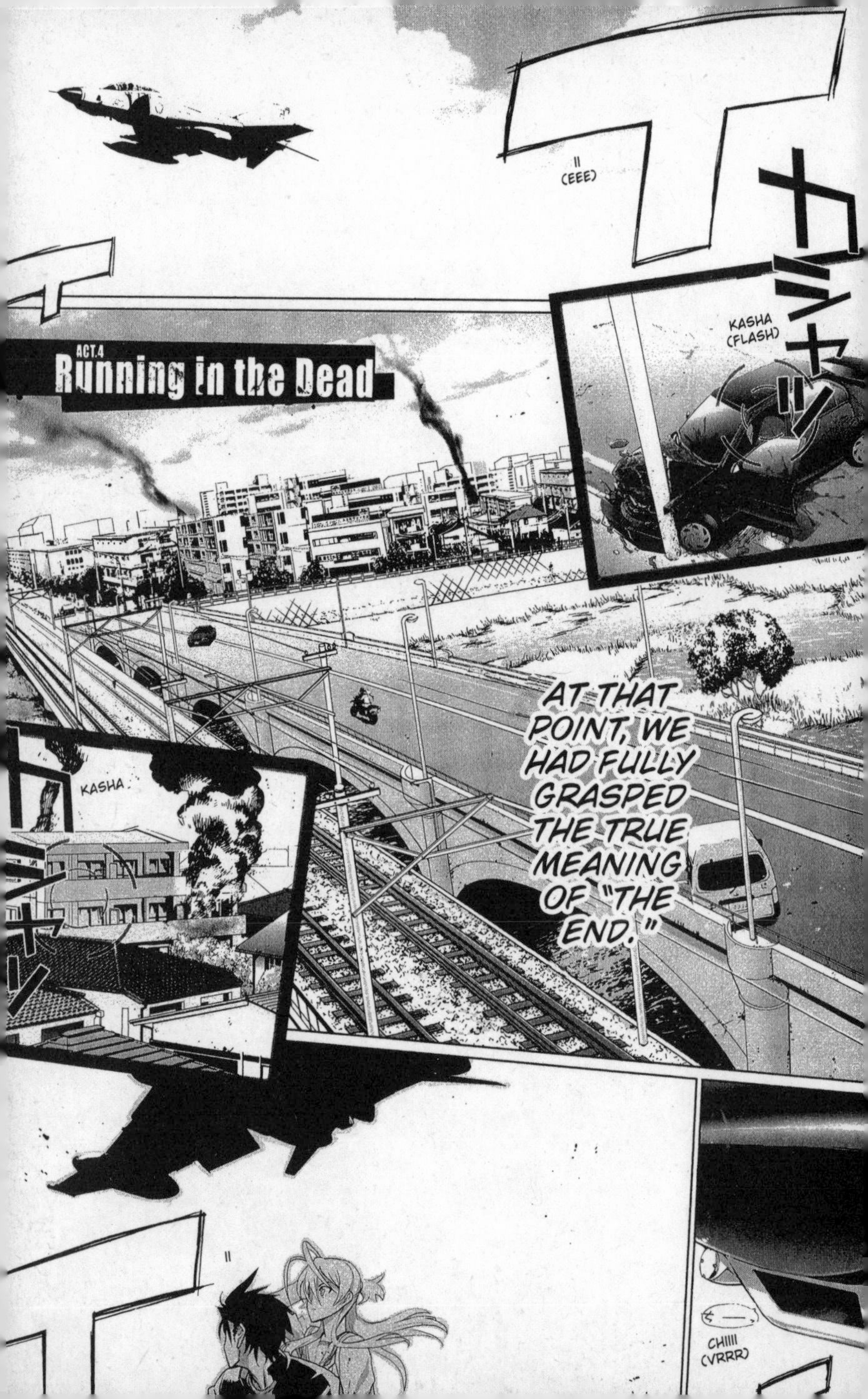

(EEE)
KASHA
(FLASH)
ACT.4
Running in the Dead
AT THAT POINT, WE HAD FULLY GRASPED THE TRUE MEANING OF "THE END."
KASHA
CHIIII
(VRRR)

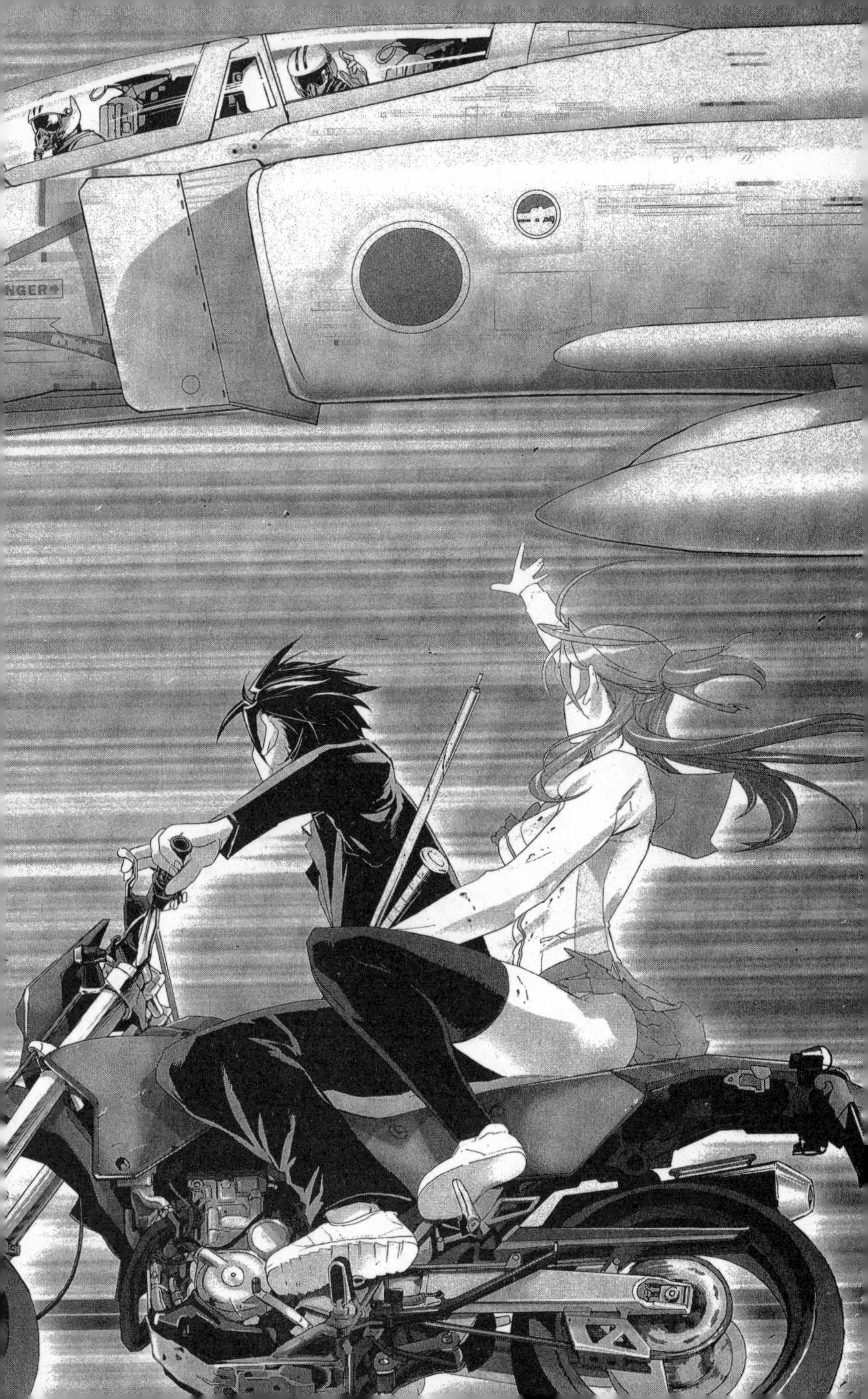

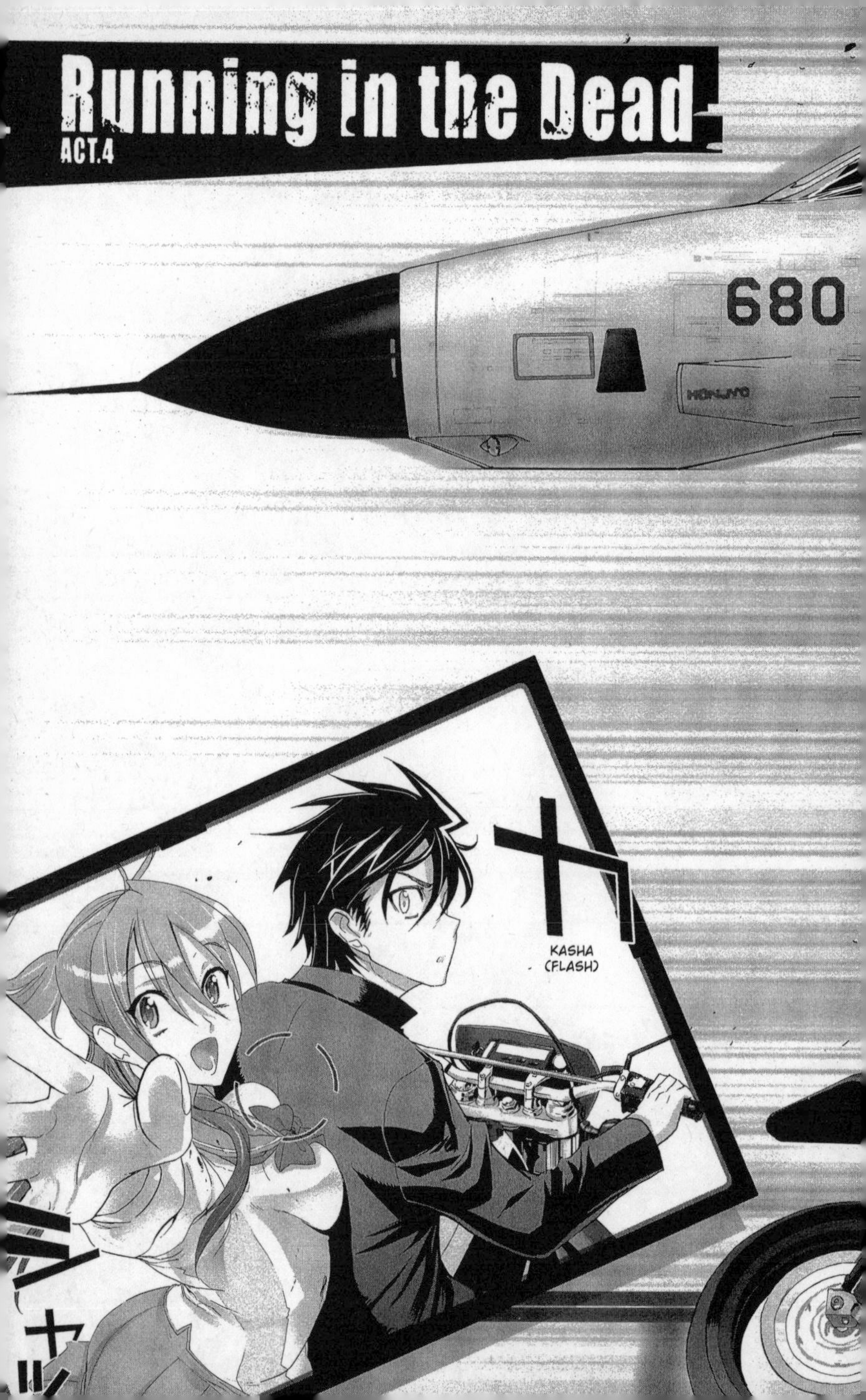
Running in the Dead
ACT.4
680
KASHA
(FLASH)

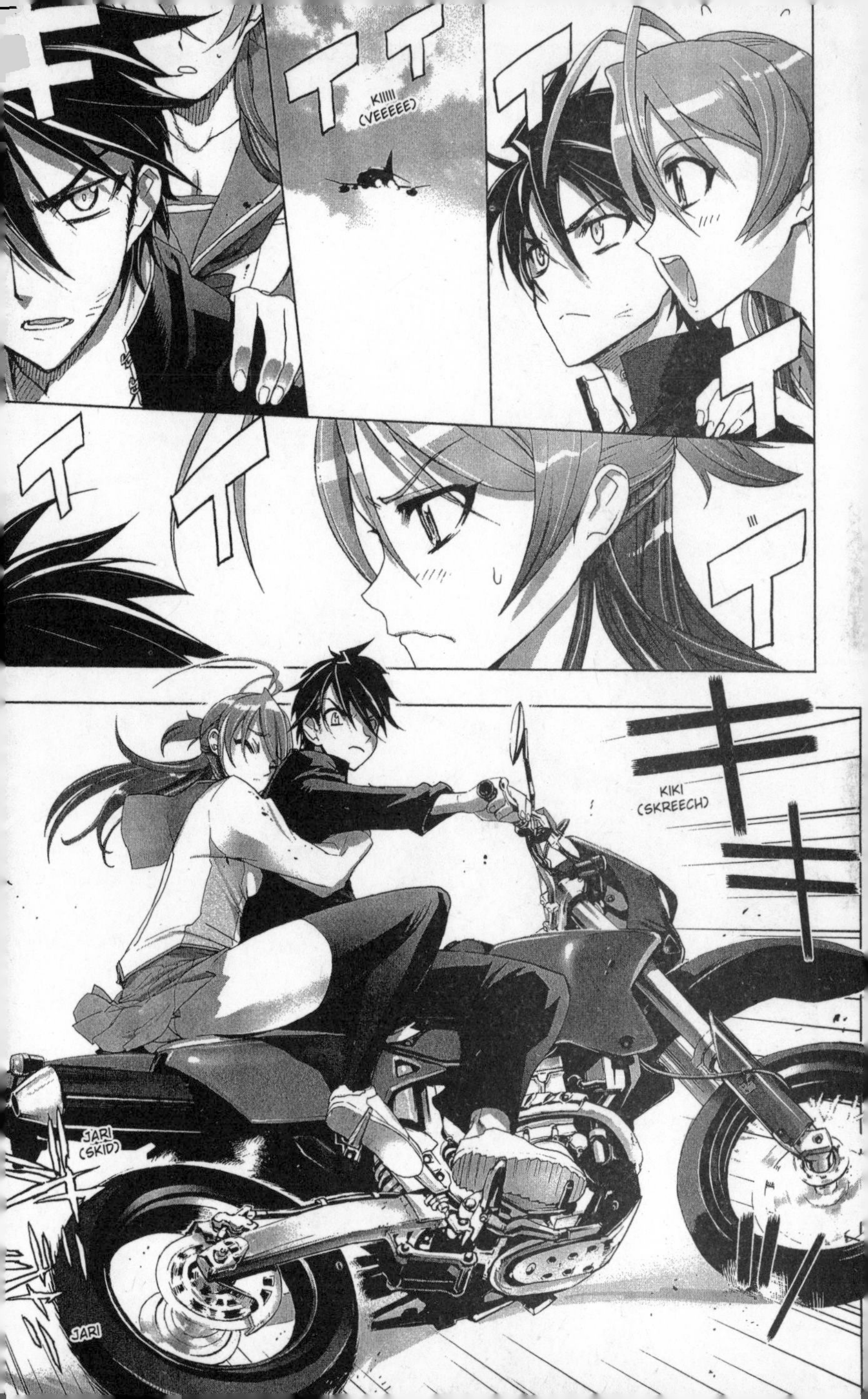
KIIIII
(VEEEEEE)
KIKI
(SKREECH)
JARI
(SKID)
JARI

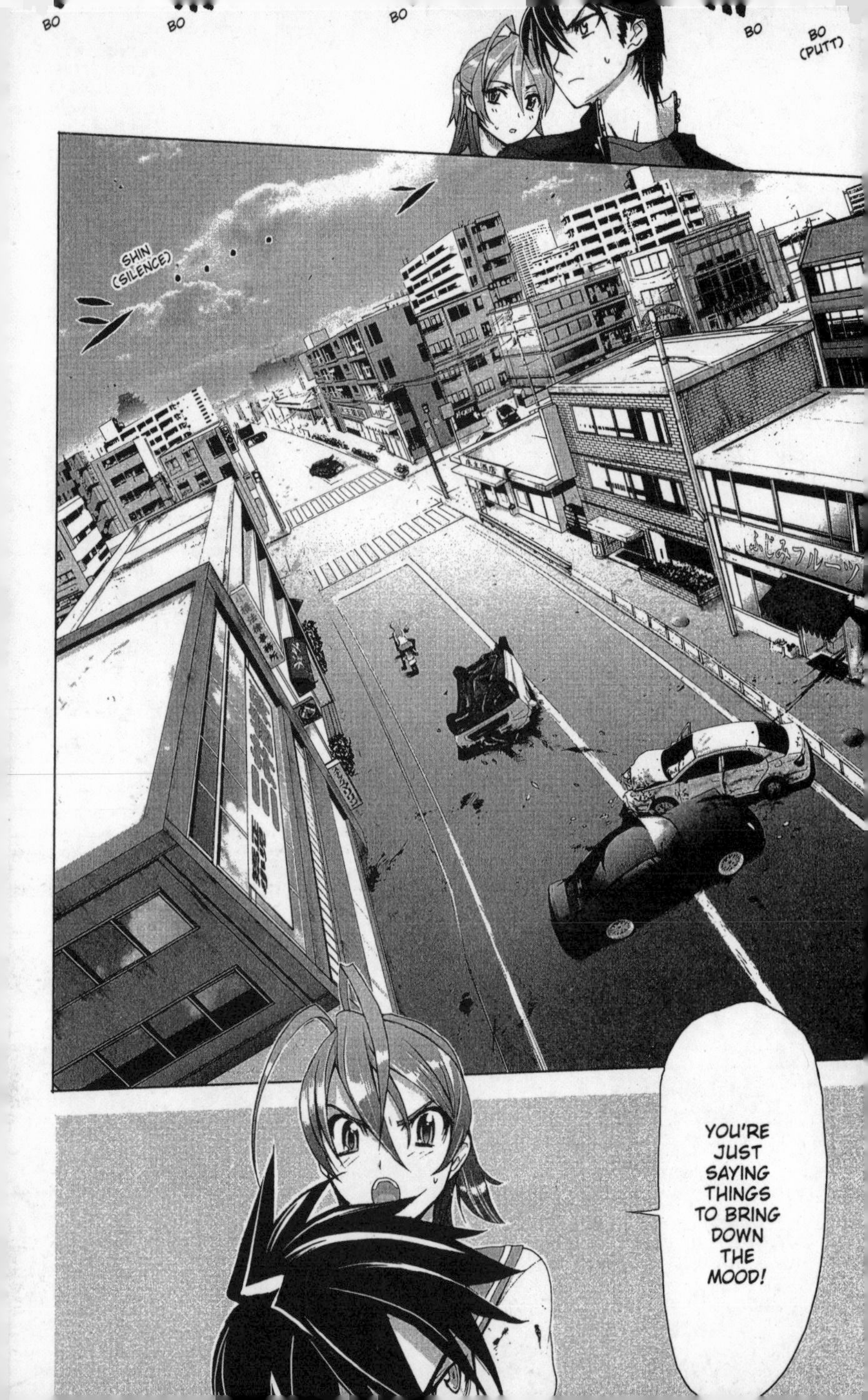
BO
(PUTT)
BO
BO
BO
BO
BO
SHIN
(SILENCE)
ふじみフルーツ
YOU'RE JUST SAYING THINGS TO BRING DOWN THE MOOD!

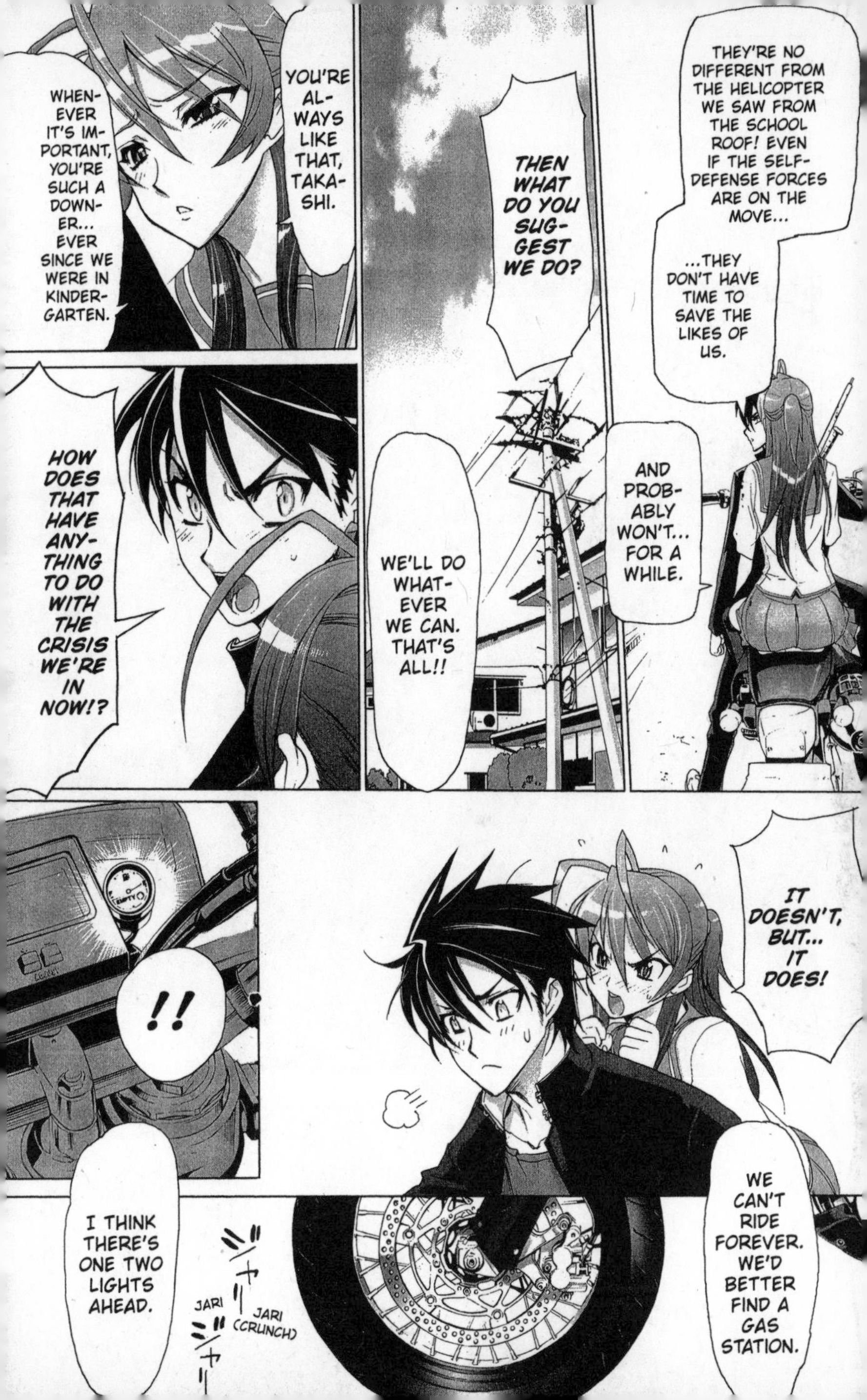
THEY'RE NO DIFFERENT FROM THE HELICOPTER WE SAW FROM THE SCHOOL ROOF! EVEN IF THE SELF-DEFENSE FORCES ARE ON THE MOVE...
...THEY DON'T HAVE TIME TO SAVE THE LIKES OF US.
AND PROBABLY WON'T... FOR A WHILE.
THEN WHAT DO YOU SUGGEST WE DO?
WE'LL DO WHATEVER WE CAN. THAT'S ALL!!
YOU'RE ALWAYS LIKE THAT, TAKASHI.
WHENEVER IT'S IMPORTANT, YOU'RE SUCH A DOWNER... EVER SINCE WE WERE IN KINDERGARTEN.
HOW DOES THAT HAVE ANYTHING TO DO WITH THE CRISIS WE'RE IN NOW!?
IT DOESN'T, BUT... IT DOES!
WE CAN'T RIDE FOREVER. WE'D BETTER FIND A GAS STATION.
!!
ジャリ
JARI (CRUNCH)
ジャリ
JARI
I THINK THERE'S ONE TWO LIGHTS AHEAD.

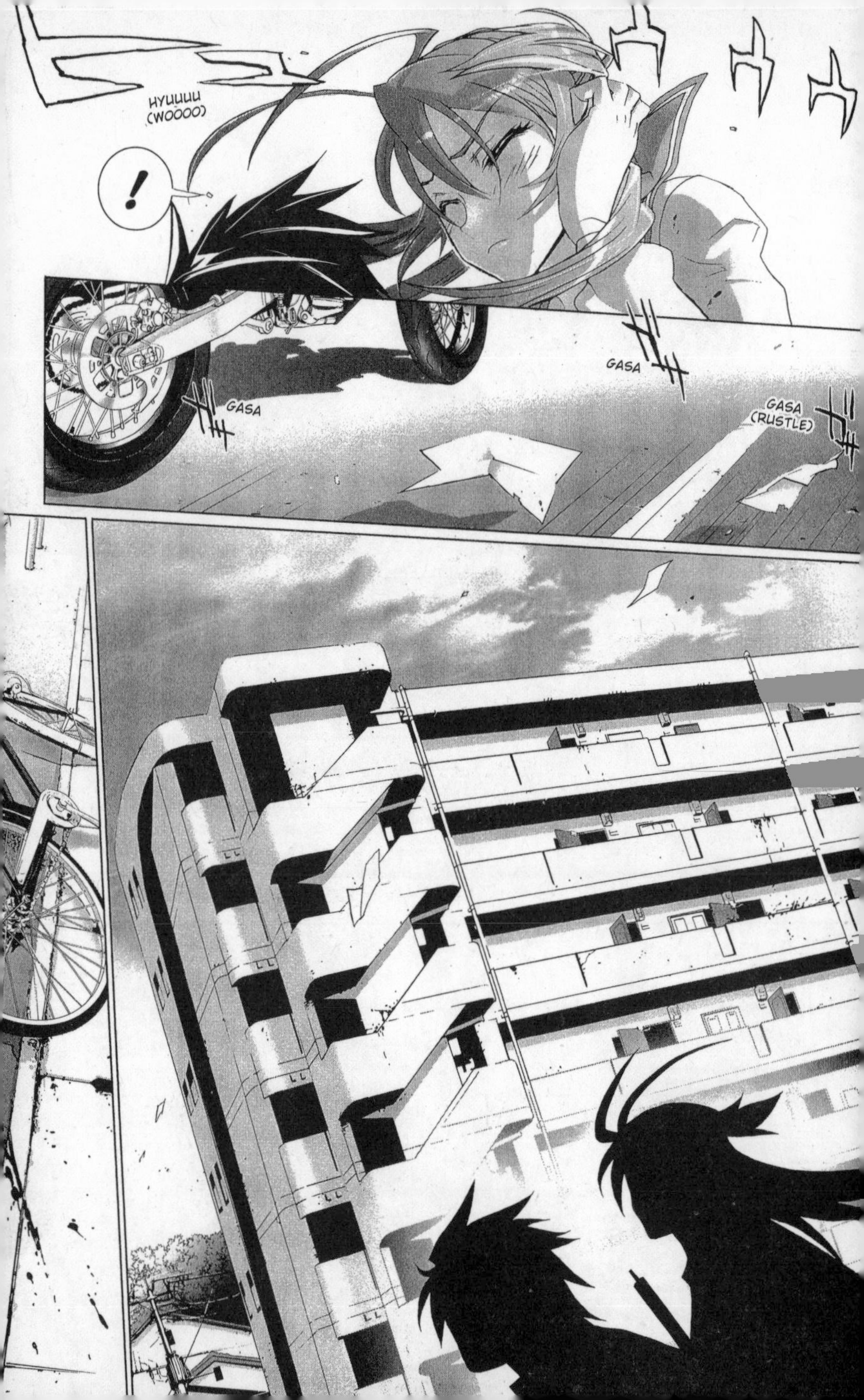
HYUUUU
(WOOOO)
!
GASA
(RUSTLE)
GASA
GASA

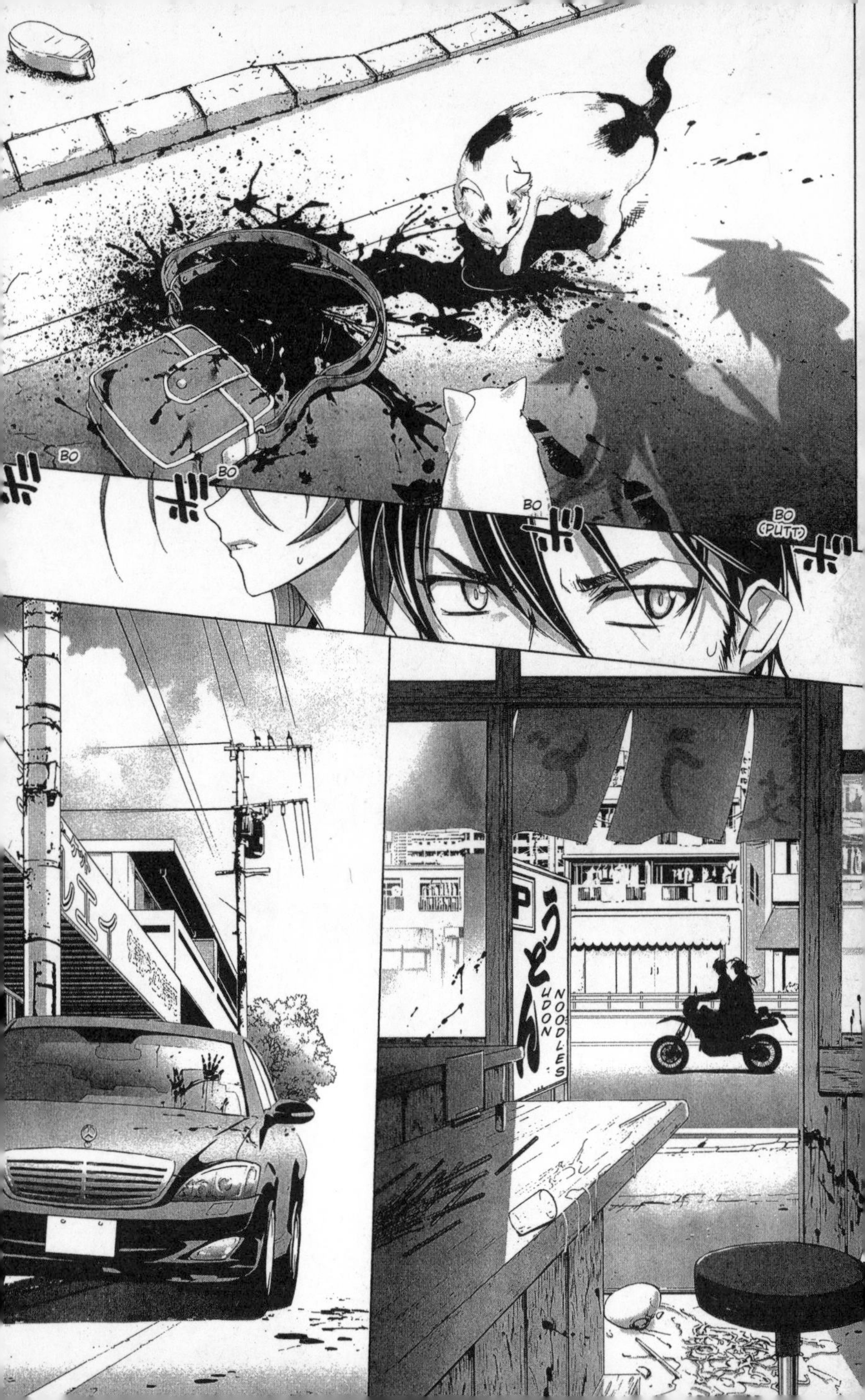
BO (PUTT)
BO
BO
BO
UDON NOODLES

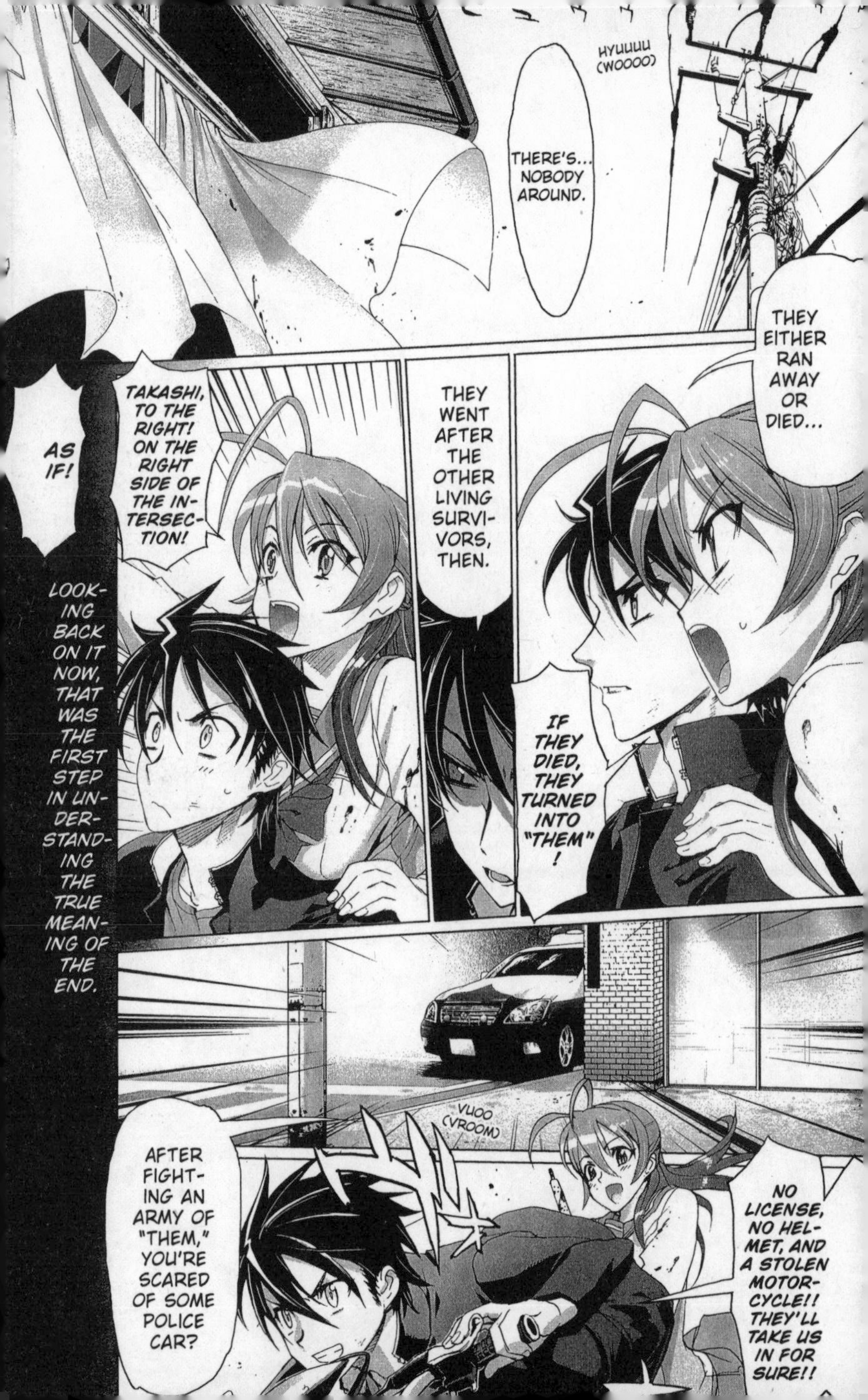
HYUUUU (WOOOO)
THERE'S... NOBODY AROUND.
THEY EITHER RAN AWAY OR DIED...
IF THEY DIED, THEY TURNED INTO "THEM"!
THEY WENT AFTER THE OTHER LIVING SURVIVORS, THEN.
TAKASHI, TO THE RIGHT! ON THE RIGHT SIDE OF THE INTERSECTION!
AS IF!
LOOKING BACK ON IT NOW, THAT WAS THE FIRST STEP IN UNDERSTANDING THE TRUE MEANING OF THE END.
VUOO (VROOM)
NO LICENSE, NO HELMET, AND A STOLEN MOTORCYCLE!! THEY'LL TAKE US IN FOR SURE!!
AFTER FIGHTING AN ARMY OF "THEM," YOU'RE SCARED OF SOME POLICE CAR?

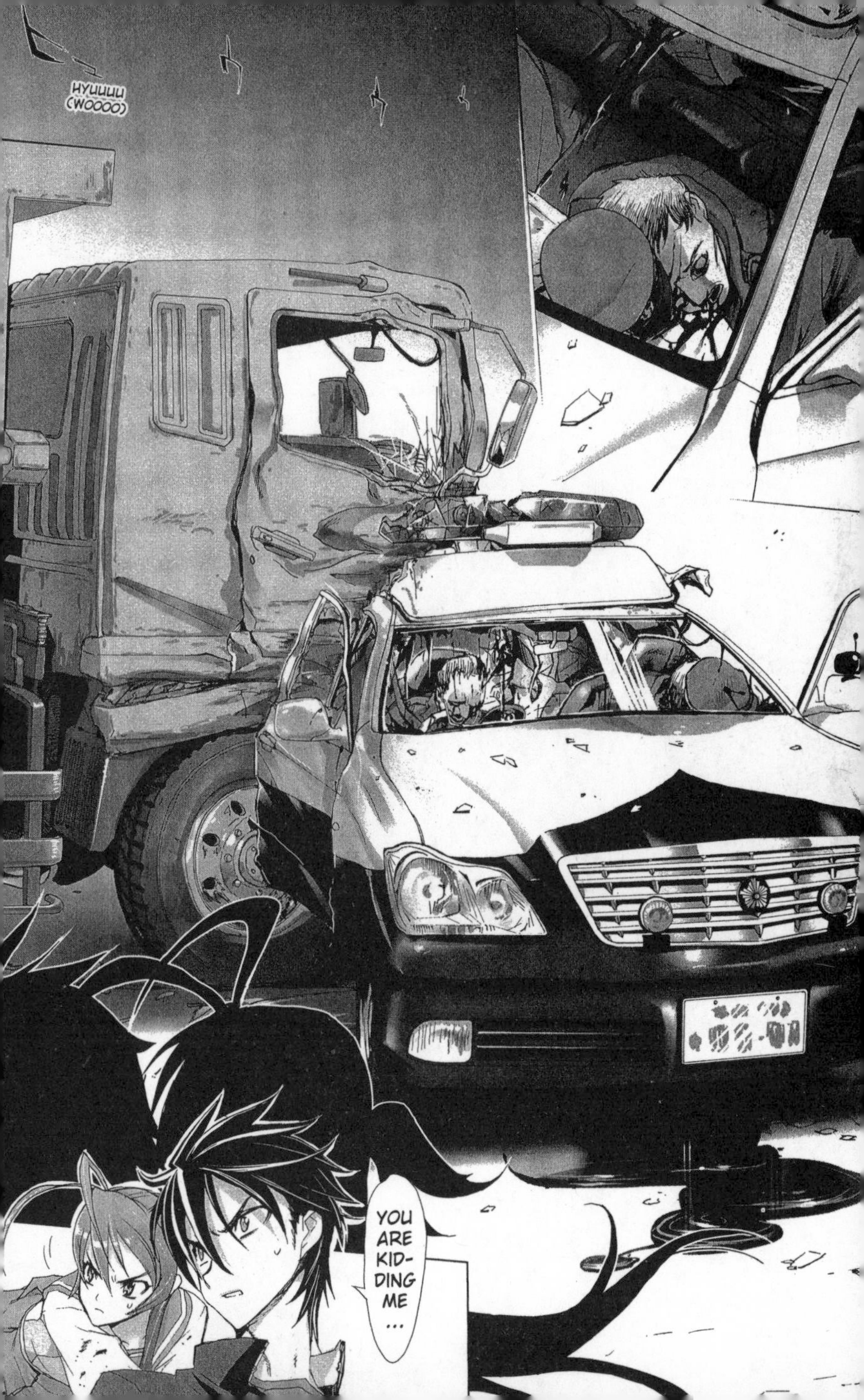
HYUUUU
(WOOOO)
YOU ARE KID-DING ME ...

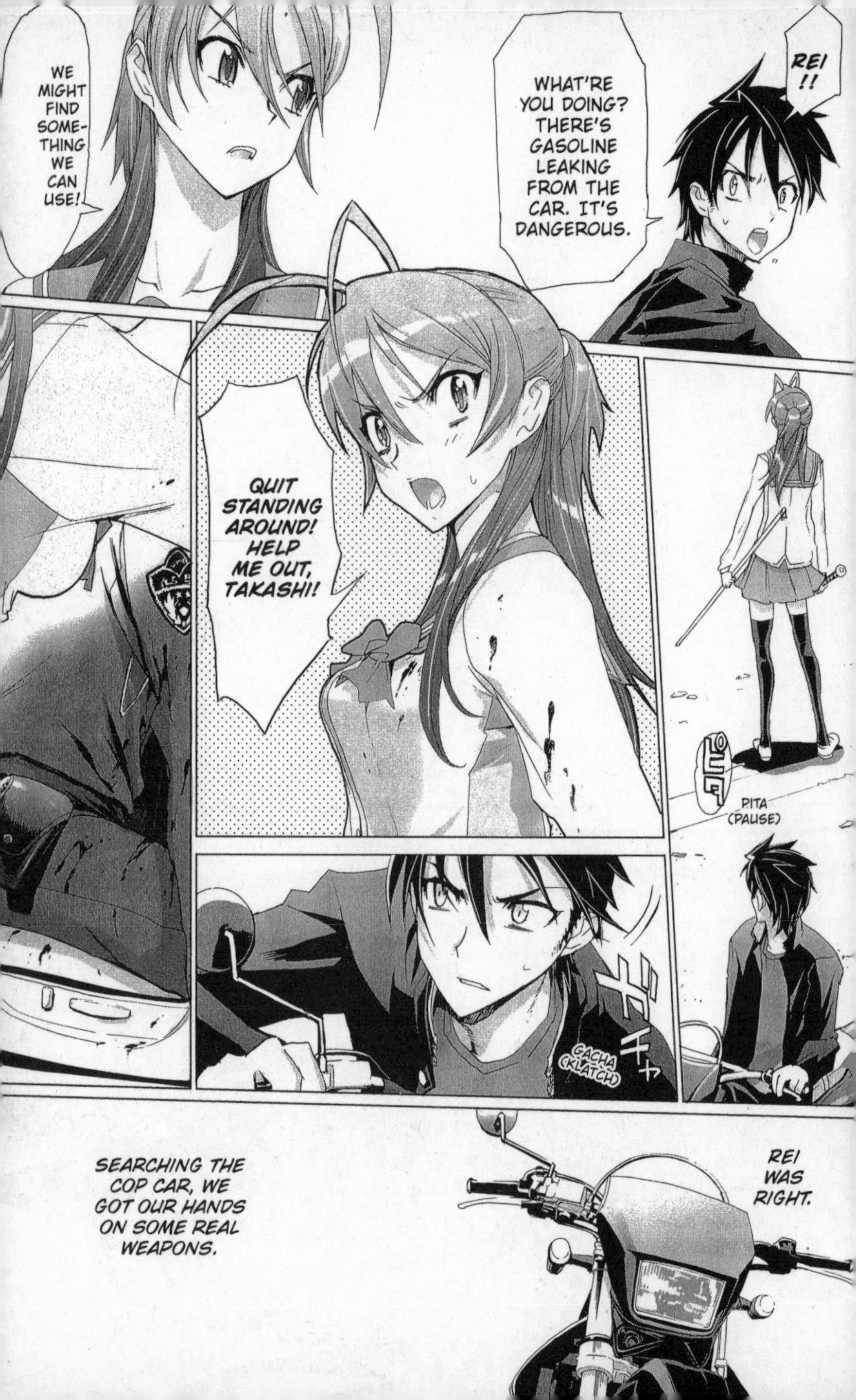
REI!!
WHAT'RE YOU DOING? THERE'S GASOLINE LEAKING FROM THE CAR. IT'S DANGEROUS.
WE MIGHT FIND SOME-THING WE CAN USE!
PITA (PAUSE)
QUIT STANDING AROUND! HELP ME OUT, TAKASHI!
GACHA (KLATCH)
REI WAS RIGHT.
SEARCHING THE COP CAR, WE GOT OUR HANDS ON SOME REAL WEAPONS.

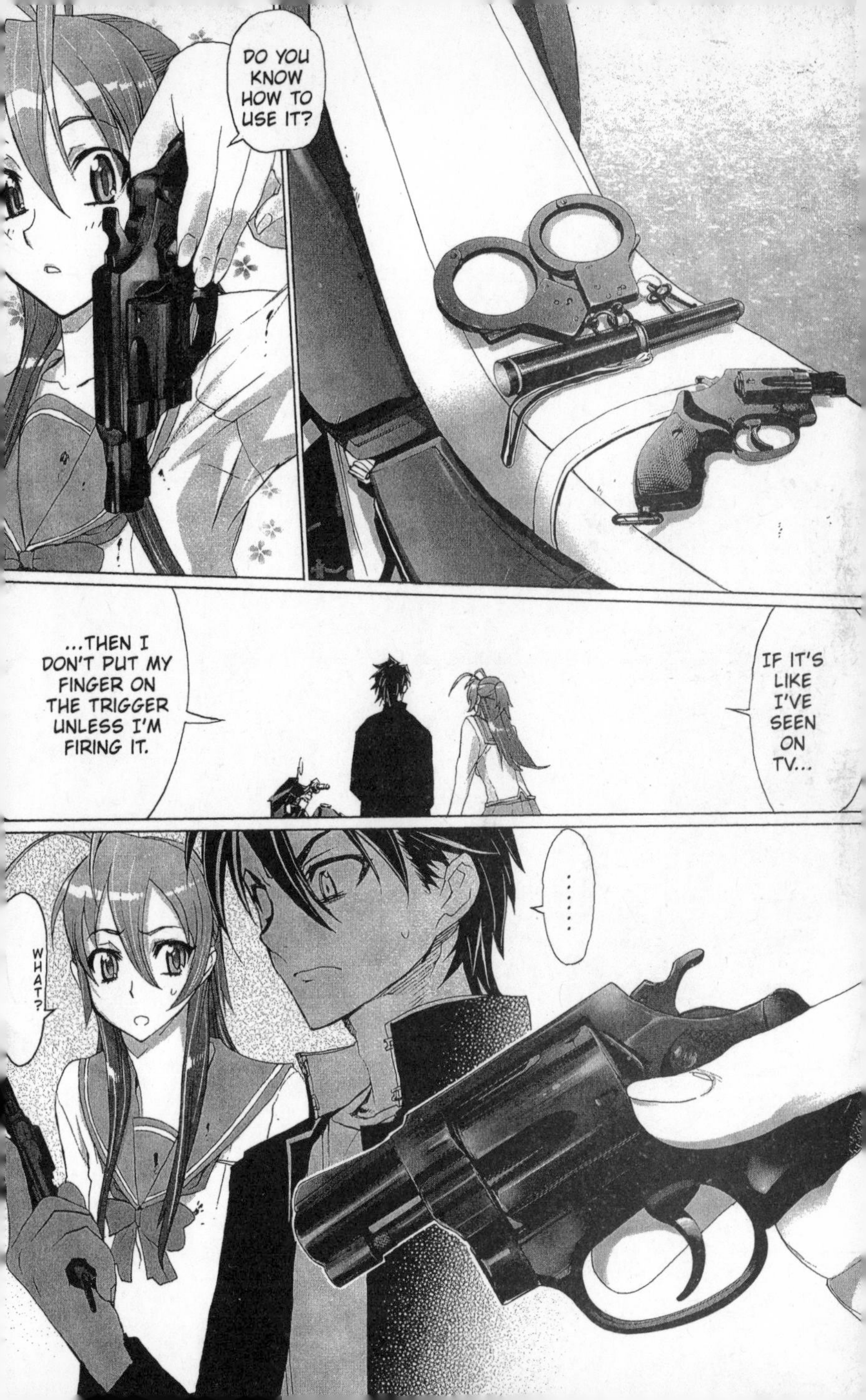
DO YOU KNOW HOW TO USE IT?
IF IT'S LIKE I'VE SEEN ON TV...
...THEN I DON'T PUT MY FINGER ON THE TRIGGER UNLESS I'M FIRING IT.
......
WHAT?

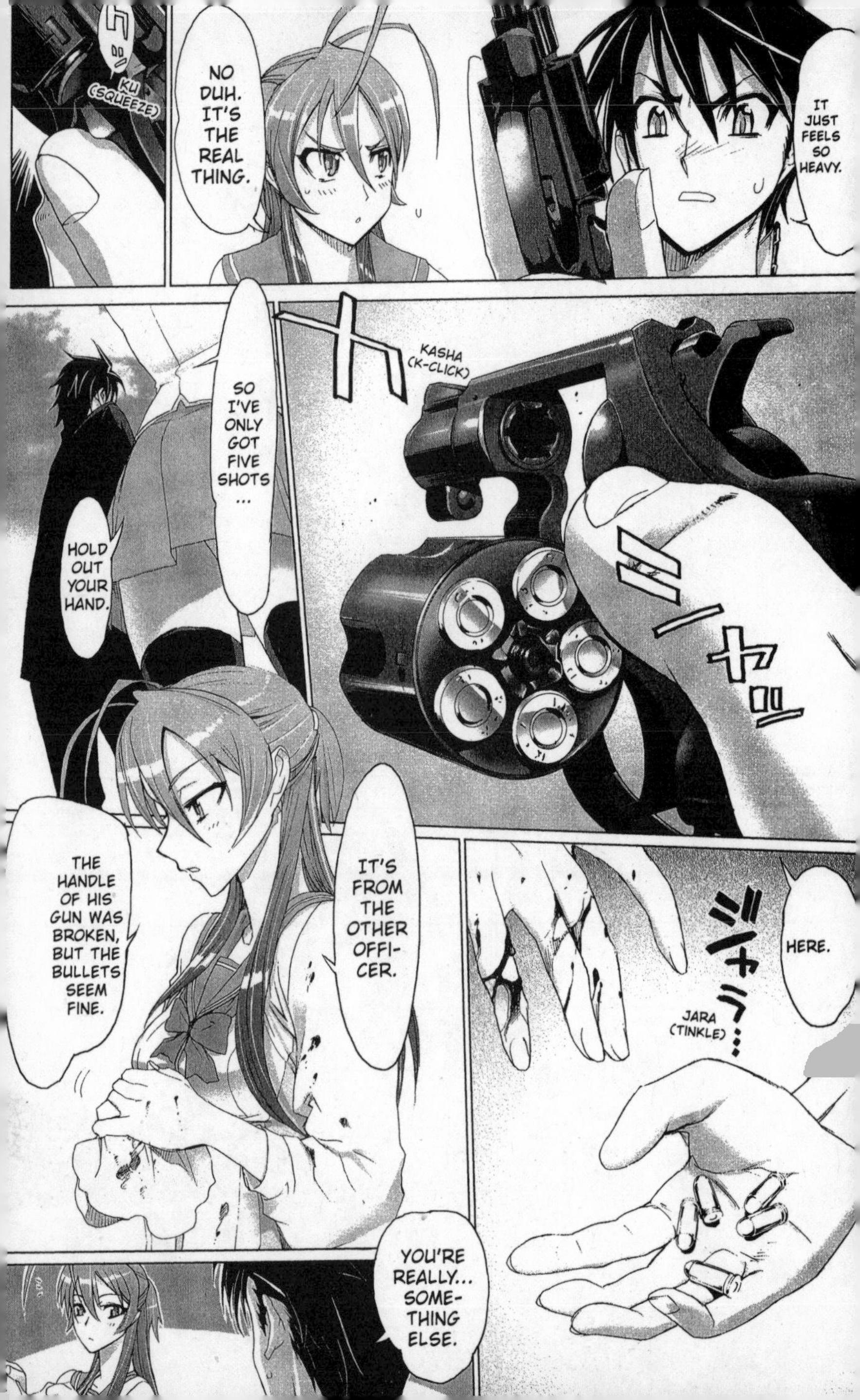
IT JUST FEELS SO HEAVY.
NO DUH. IT'S THE REAL THING.
KU (SQUEEZE)
KASHA (K-CLICK)
SO I'VE ONLY GOT FIVE SHOTS...
HOLD OUT YOUR HAND.
HERE.
JARA (TINKLE)
IT'S FROM THE OTHER OFFI-CER.
THE HANDLE OF HIS GUN WAS BROKEN, BUT THE BULLETS SEEM FINE.
YOU'RE REALLY... SOME-THING ELSE.

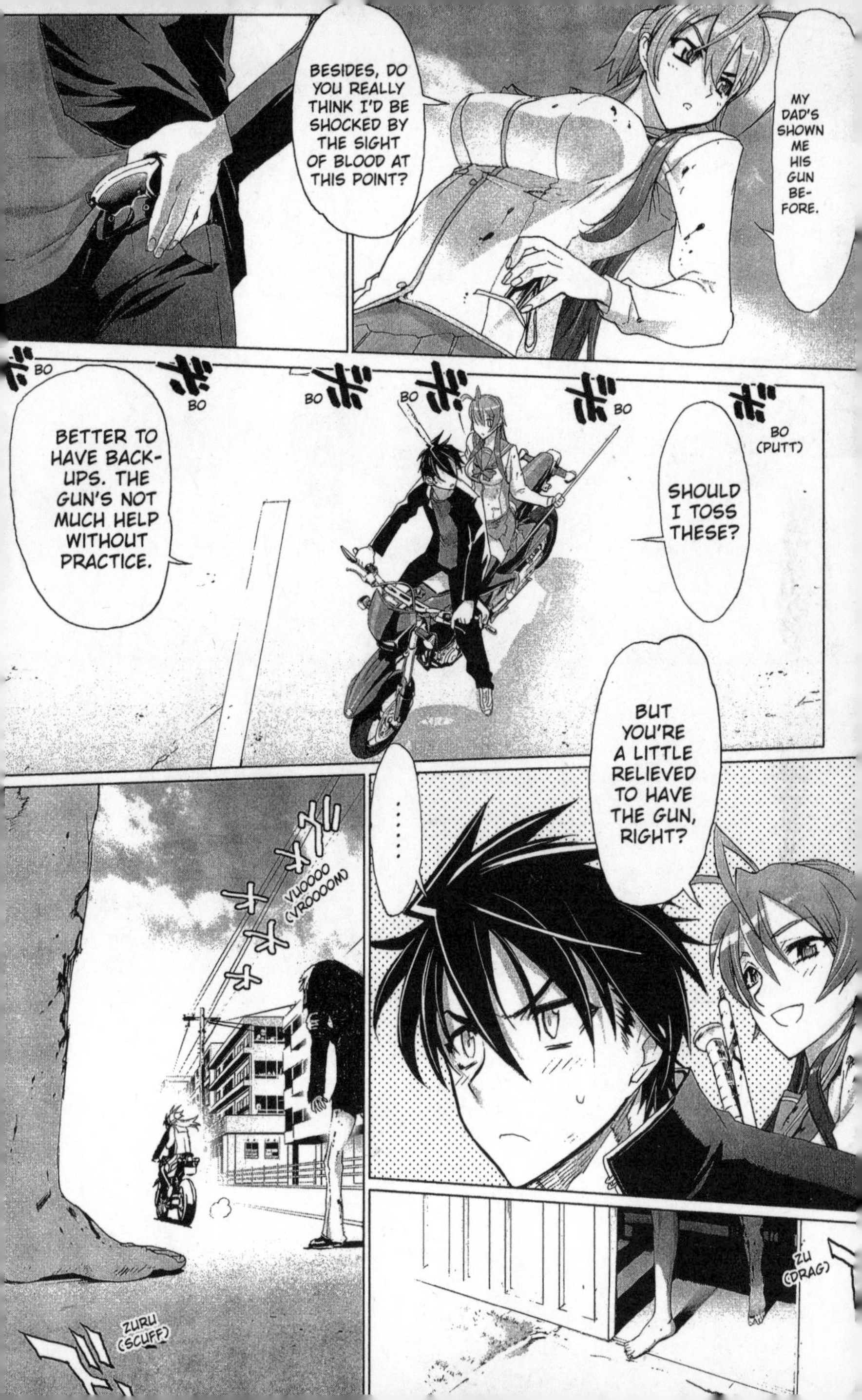
MY DAD'S SHOWN ME HIS GUN BE-FORE.
BESIDES, DO YOU REALLY THINK I'D BE SHOCKED BY THE SIGHT OF BLOOD AT THIS POINT?
BO (PUTT)
BO
BO
BO
BO
BO
SHOULD I TOSS THESE?
BETTER TO HAVE BACK-UPS. THE GUN'S NOT MUCH HELP WITHOUT PRACTICE.
BUT YOU'RE A LITTLE RELIEVED TO HAVE THE GUN, RIGHT?
......
ZU (DRAG)
VUOOOO (VROOOOM)
ZURU (SCUFF)

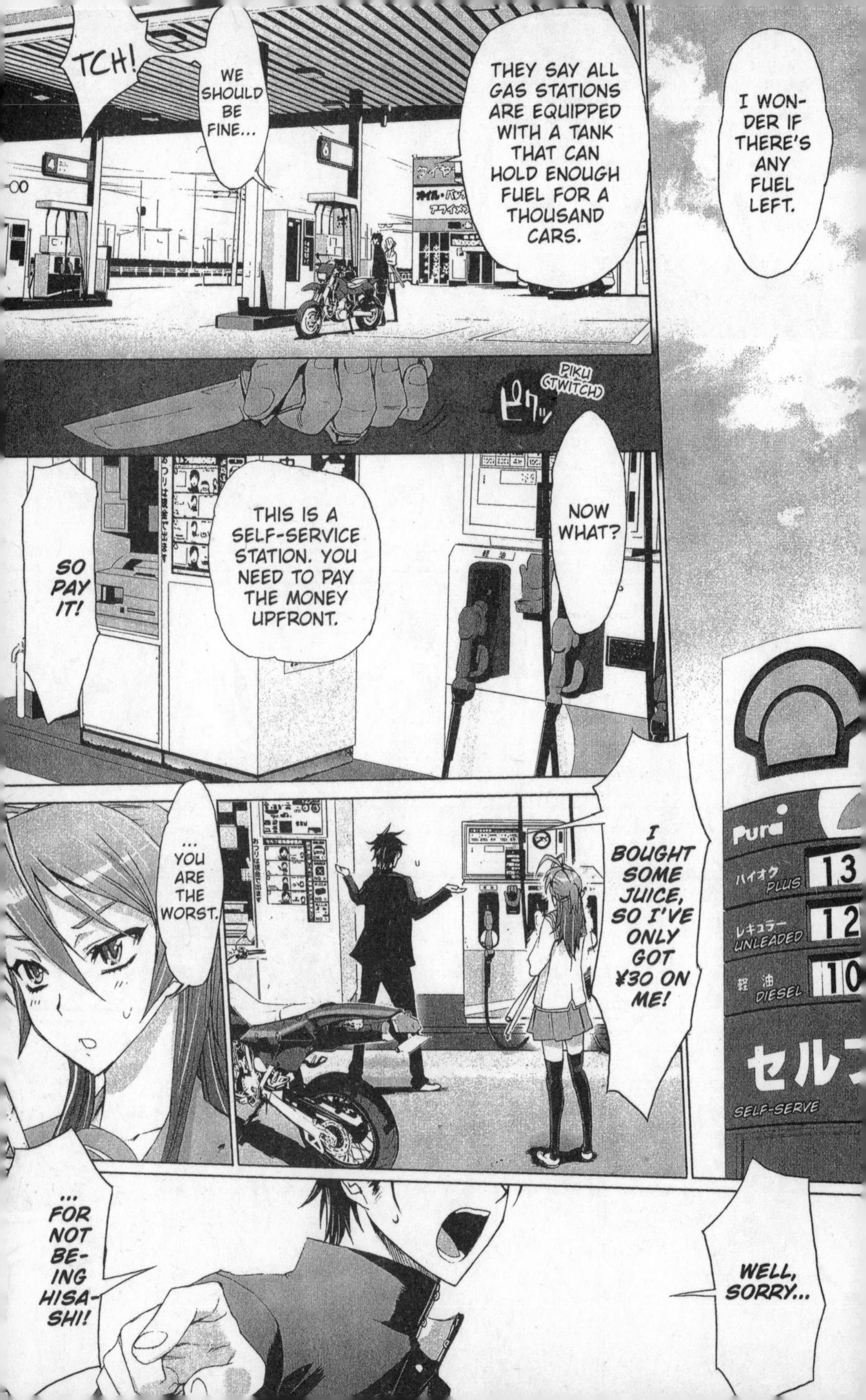
I WONDER IF THERE'S ANY FUEL LEFT.
THEY SAY ALL GAS STATIONS ARE EQUIPPED WITH A TANK THAT CAN HOLD ENOUGH FUEL FOR A THOUSAND CARS.
WE SHOULD BE FINE...
TCH!
ピクッ
PIKU (TWITCH)
NOW WHAT?
THIS IS A SELF-SERVICE STATION. YOU NEED TO PAY THE MONEY UPFRONT.
SO PAY IT!
Pura
ハイオク PLUS 13
レギュラー UNLEADED 12
軽油 DIESEL 10
セルフ
SELF-SERVE
I BOUGHT SOME JUICE, SO I'VE ONLY GOT ¥30 ON ME!
... YOU ARE THE WORST.
WELL, SORRY...
... FOR NOT BEING HISASHI!

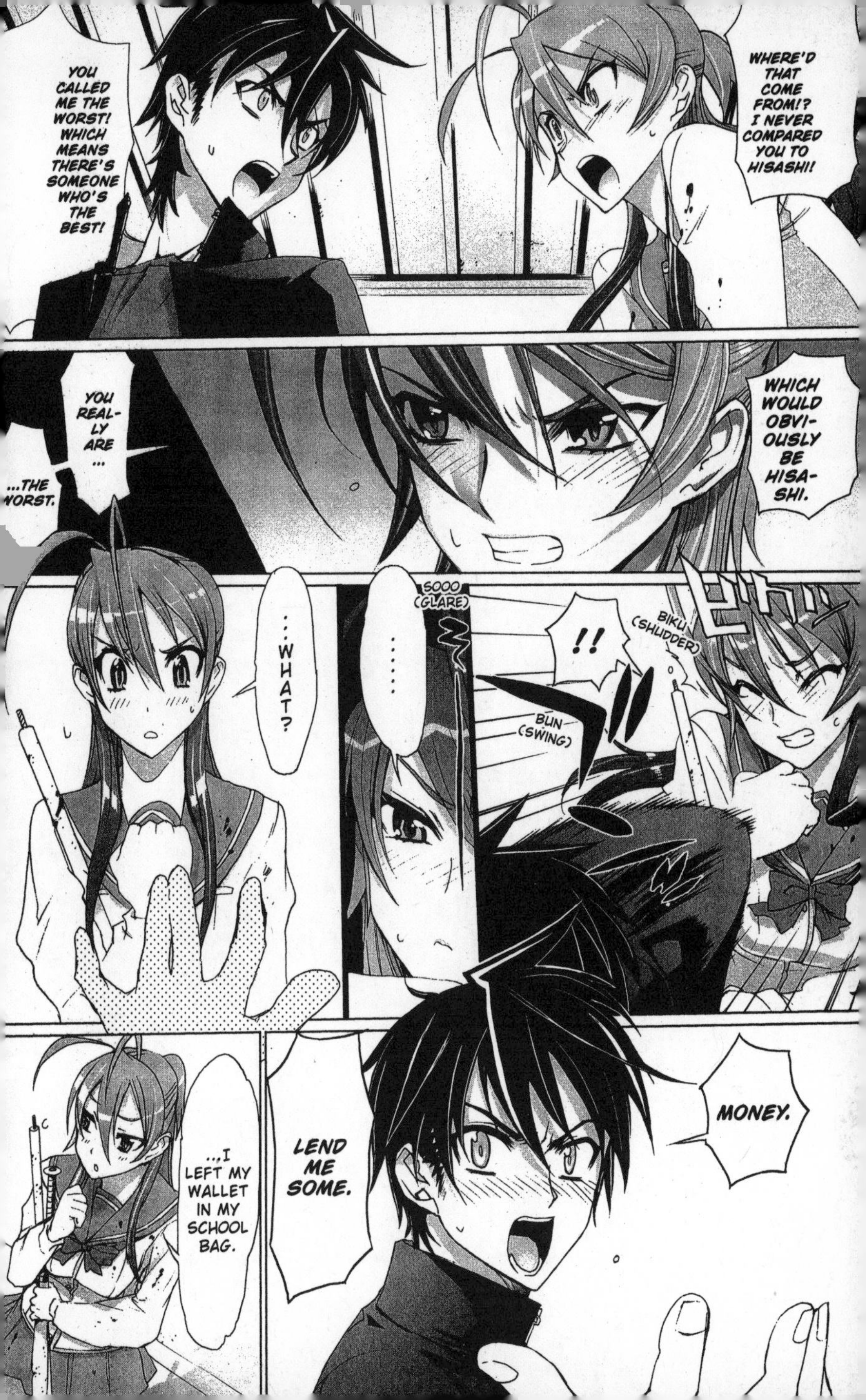
WHERE'D THAT COME FROM!? I NEVER COMPARED YOU TO HISASHI!
YOU CALLED ME THE WORST! WHICH MEANS THERE'S SOMEONE WHO'S THE BEST!
WHICH WOULD OBVIOUSLY BE HISASHI.
YOU REALLY ARE ...
...THE WORST.
BIKU (SHUDDER)
!!
BUN (SWING)
SOOO (GLARE)
......
...WHAT?
MONEY.
LEND ME SOME.
...I LEFT MY WALLET IN MY SCHOOL BAG.

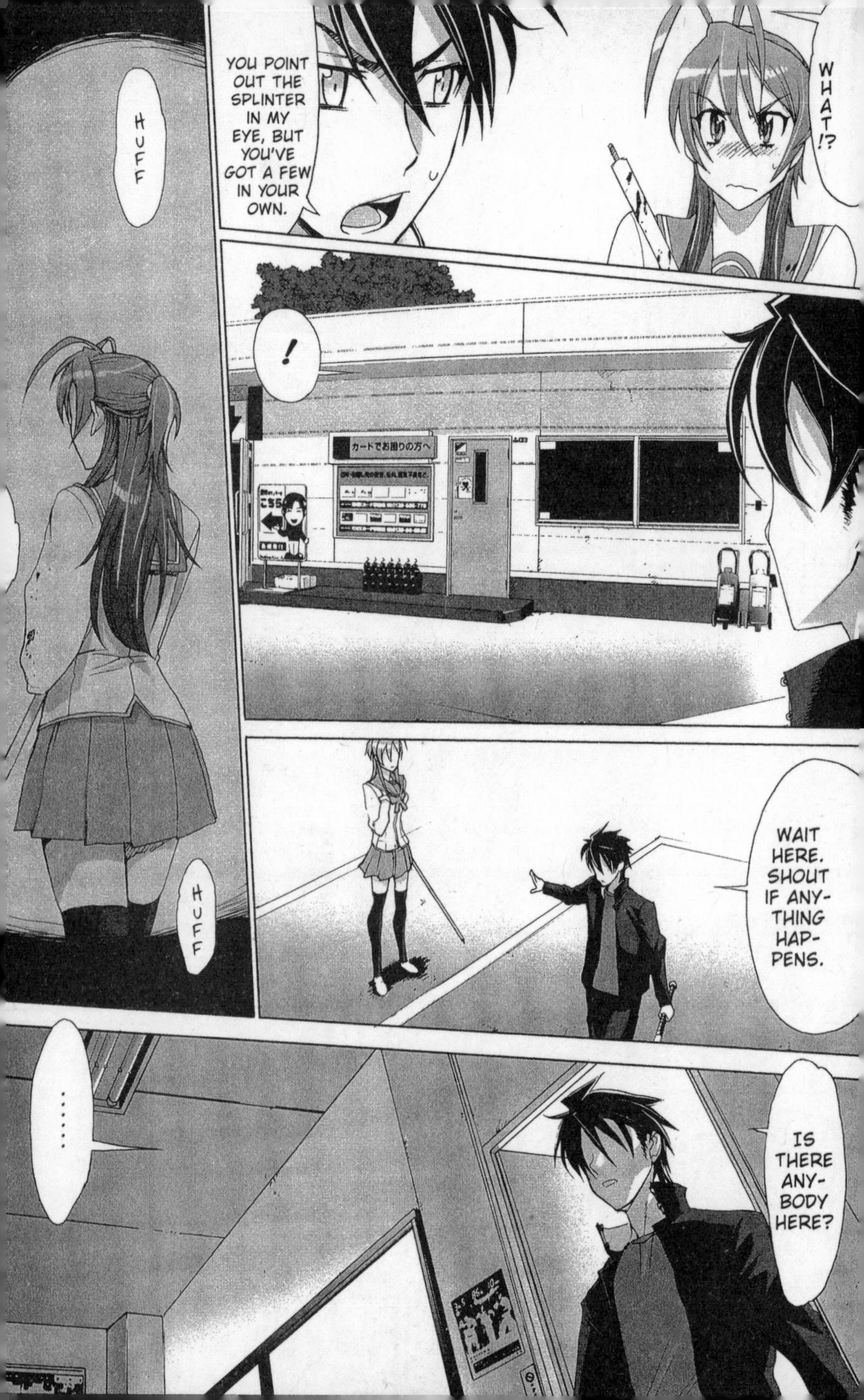
YOU POINT OUT THE SPLINTER IN MY EYE, BUT YOU'VE GOT A FEW IN YOUR OWN.
WHAT!?
!
カードでお困りの方へ
WAIT HERE. SHOUT IF ANY-THING HAP-PENS.
HUFF
HUFF
IS THERE ANY-BODY HERE?
......

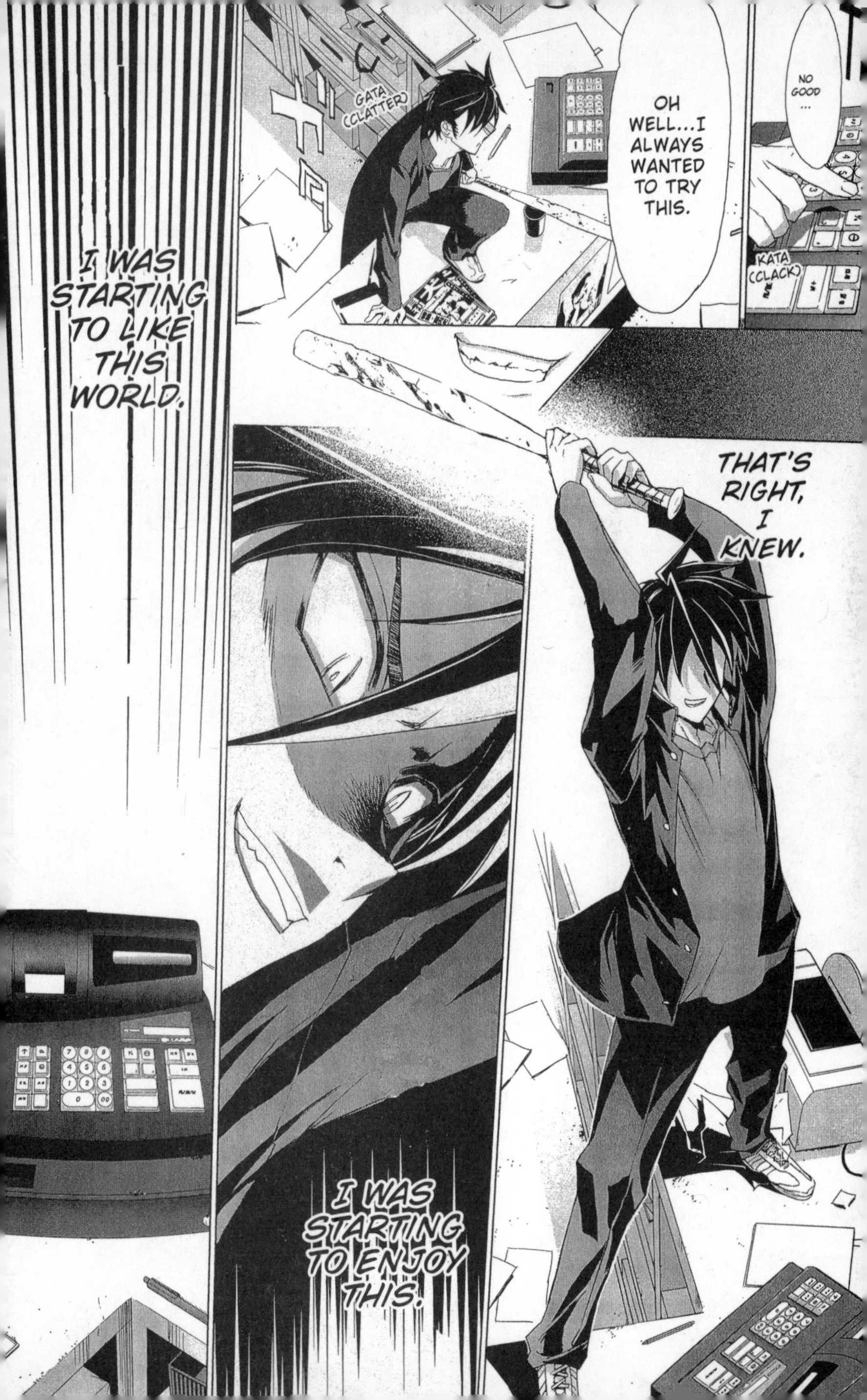
NO GOOD ...
KATA (CLACK)
OH WELL...I ALWAYS WANTED TO TRY THIS.
GATA (CLATTER)
THAT'S RIGHT, I KNEW.
I WAS STARTING TO ENJOY THIS.
I WAS STARTING TO LIKE THIS WORLD.

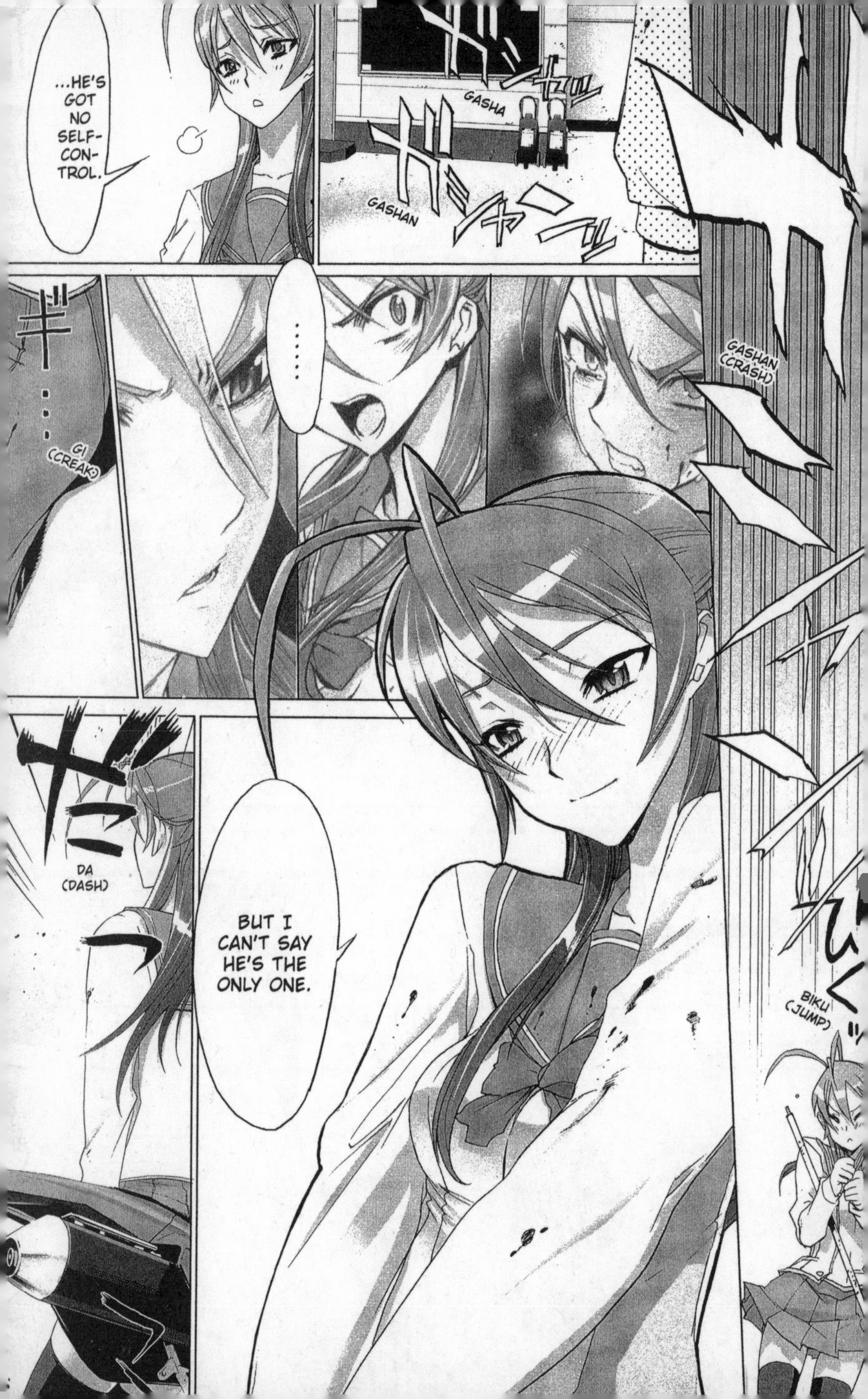
GASHA
GASHAN
...HE'S GOT NO SELF-CONTROL.
GASHAN (CRASH)
.....
GI (CREAK)
BIKU (JUMP)
BUT I CAN'T SAY HE'S THE ONLY ONE.
DA (DASH)

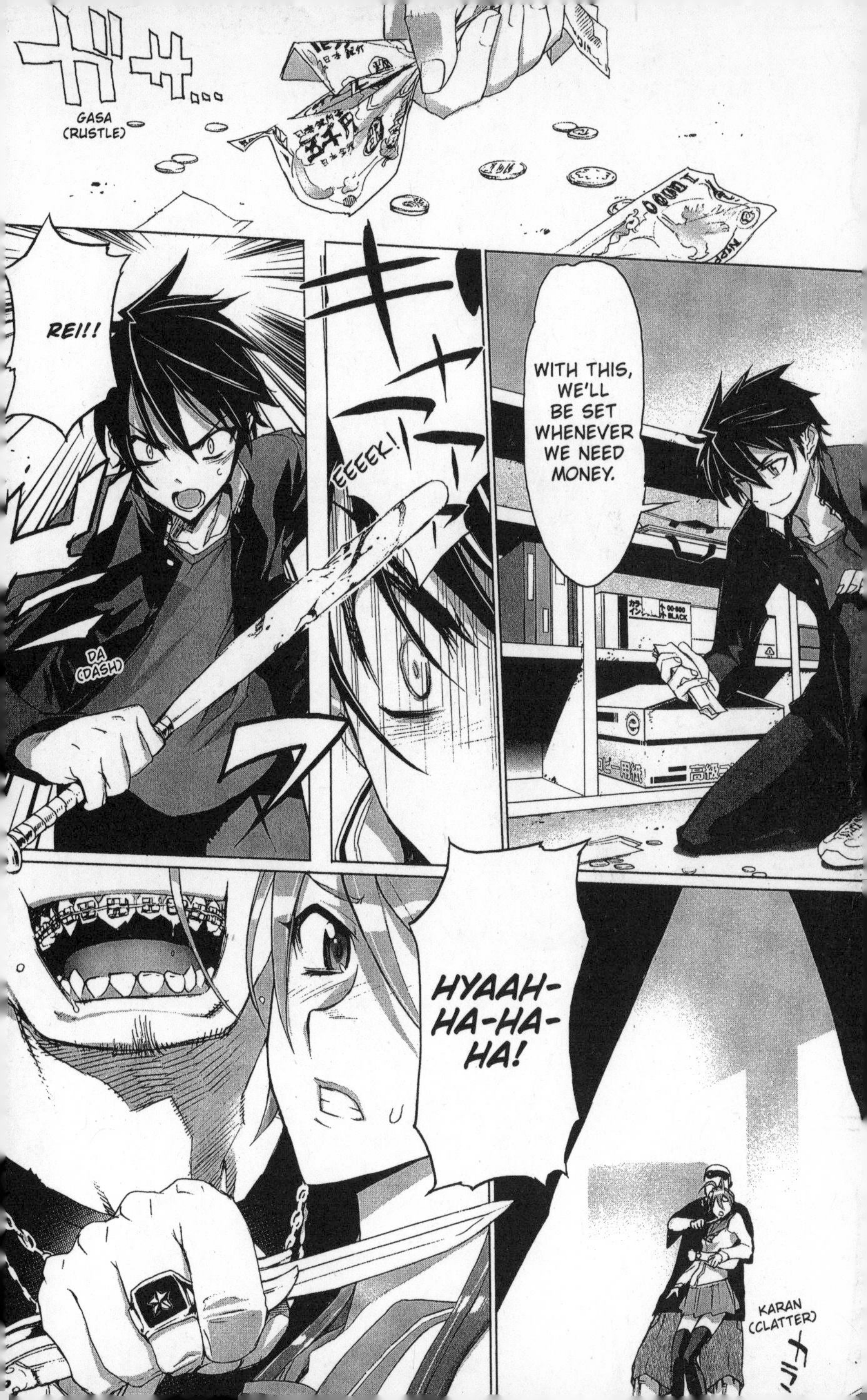
GASA (RUSTLE)
WITH THIS, WE'LL BE SET WHENEVER WE NEED MONEY.
EEEEK!
REI!!
DA (DASH)
HYAAH-HA-HA-HA!
KARAN (CLATTER)

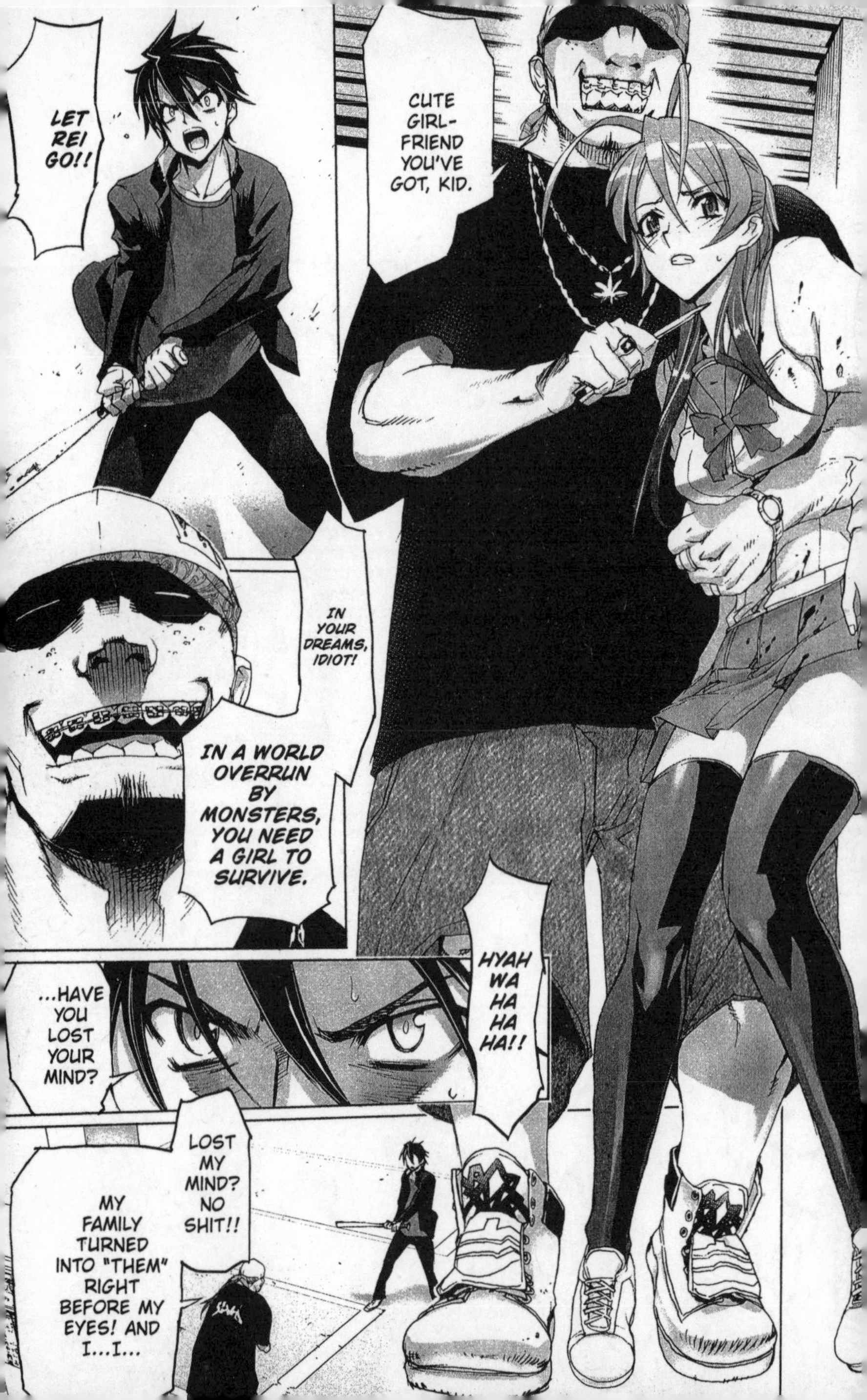
CUTE GIRL-FRIEND YOU'VE GOT, KID.
HYAH WA HA HA HA!!
LET REI GO!!
IN YOUR DREAMS, IDIOT!
IN A WORLD OVERRUN BY MONSTERS, YOU NEED A GIRL TO SURVIVE.
...HAVE YOU LOST YOUR MIND?
LOST MY MIND? NO SHIT!!
MY FAMILY TURNED INTO "THEM" RIGHT BEFORE MY EYES! AND I...I...

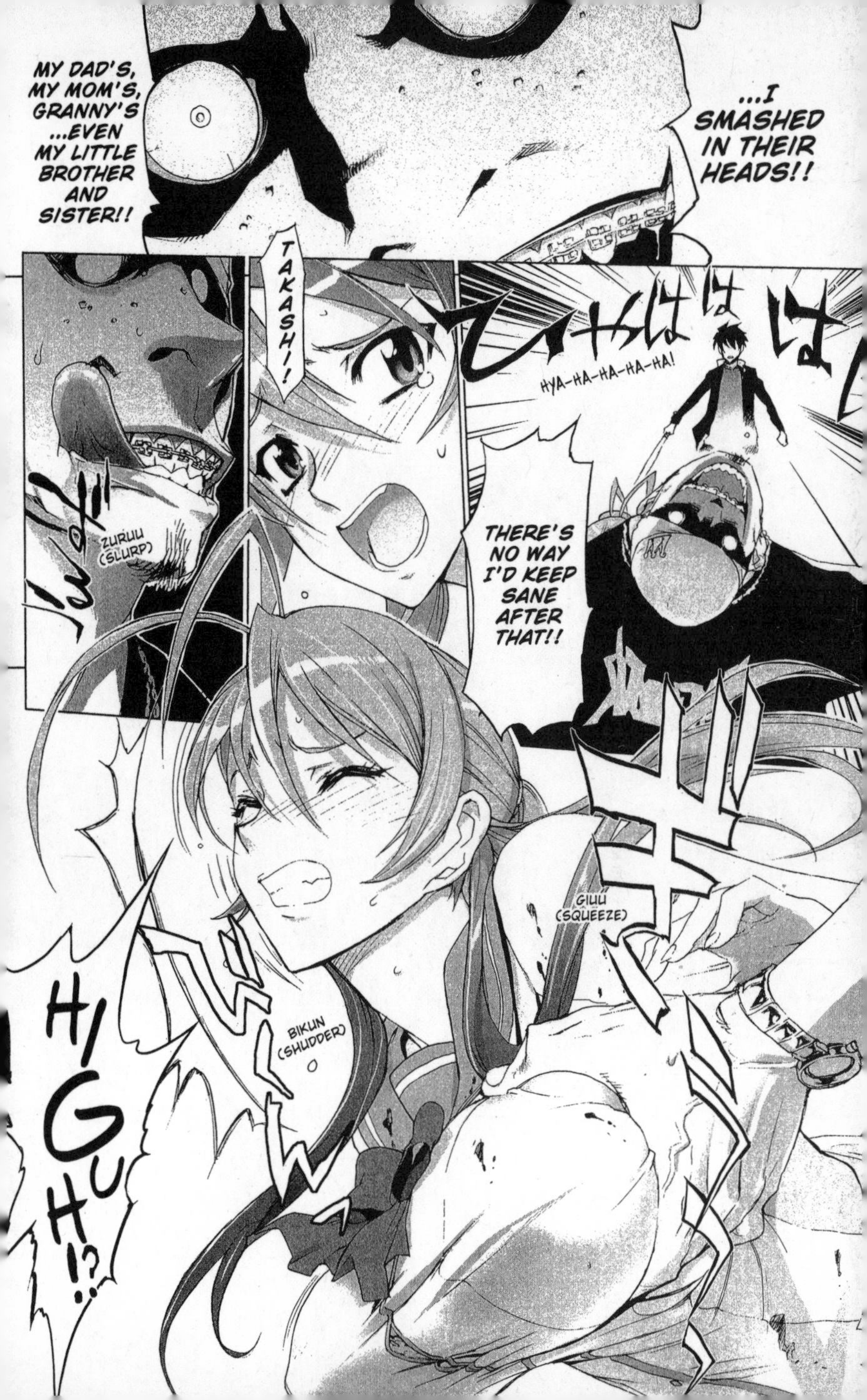
...I SMASHED IN THEIR HEADS!!
MY DAD'S, MY MOM'S, GRANNY'S ...EVEN MY LITTLE BROTHER AND SISTER!!
HYA-HA-HA-HA-HA!
TAKASHI!!
ZURUU (SLURP)
THERE'S NO WAY I'D KEEP SANE AFTER THAT!!
GIUU (SQUEEZE)
BIKUN (SHUDDER)
HIGUH!!?

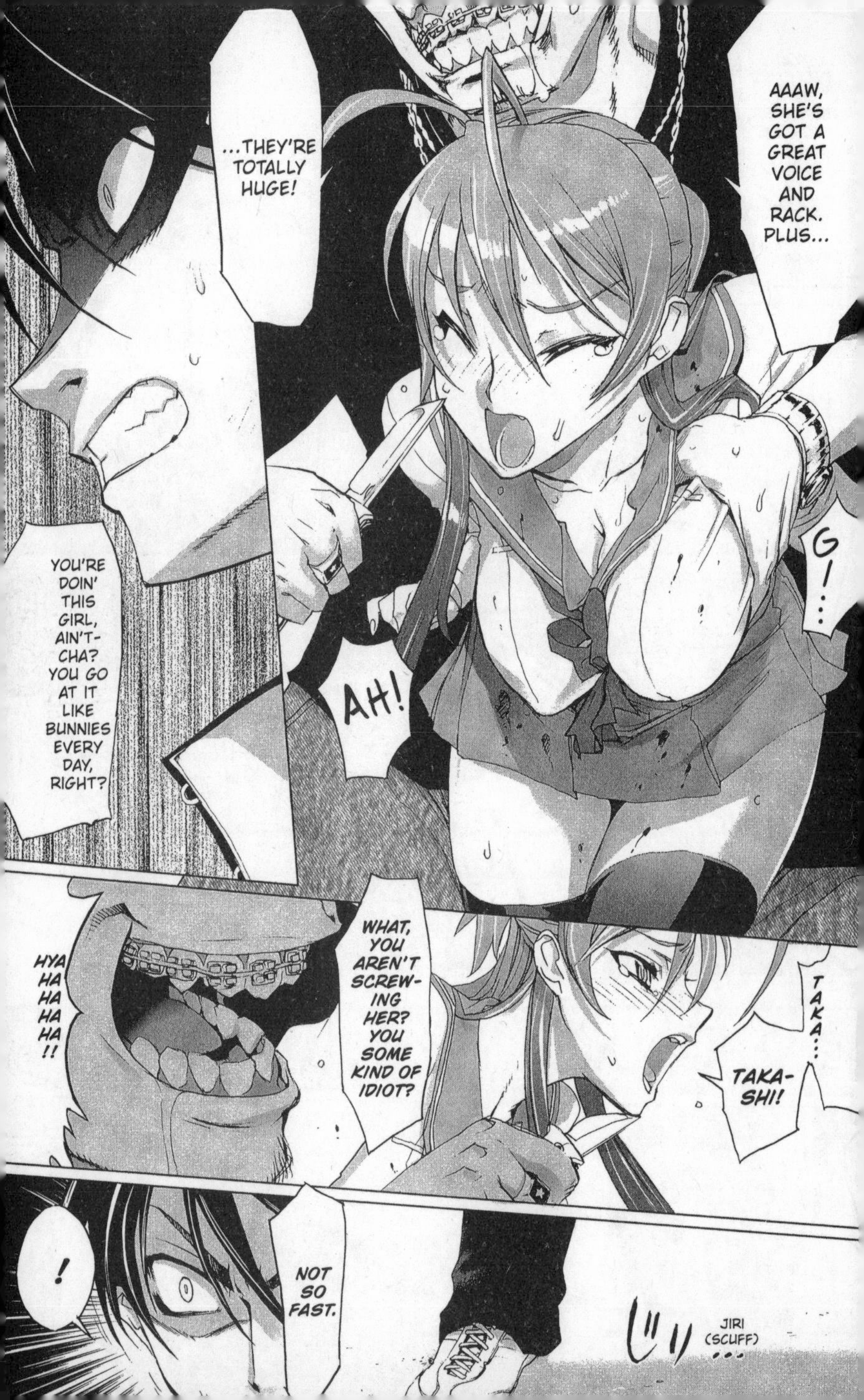
AAAW, SHE'S GOT A GREAT VOICE AND RACK. PLUS...
...THEY'RE TOTALLY HUGE!
GI...
AH!
YOU'RE DOIN' THIS GIRL, AIN'T-CHA? YOU GO AT IT LIKE BUNNIES EVERY DAY, RIGHT?
TAKA...
TAKA-SHI!
WHAT, YOU AREN'T SCREW-ING HER? YOU SOME KIND OF IDIOT?
HYA HA HA HA HA!!
JIRI (SCUFF) ...
NOT SO FAST.
!

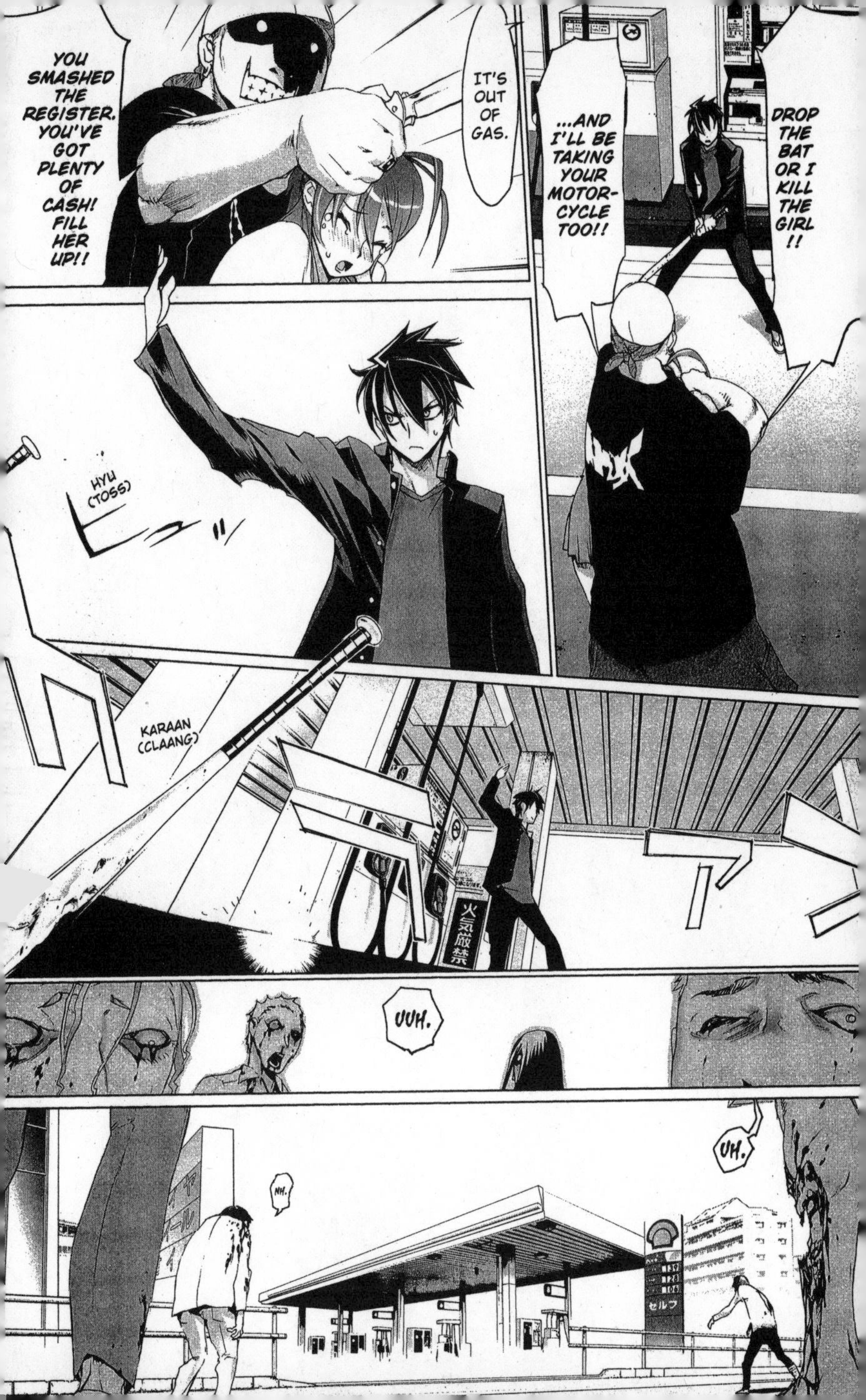
DROP THE BAT OR I KILL THE GIRL!!
...AND I'LL BE TAKING YOUR MOTORCYCLE TOO!!
IT'S OUT OF GAS.
YOU SMASHED THE REGISTER. YOU'VE GOT PLENTY OF CASH! FILL HER UP!!
HYU (TOSS)
KARAAN (CLAANG)
火気厳禁
UUH.
UH.
NH.
セルフ

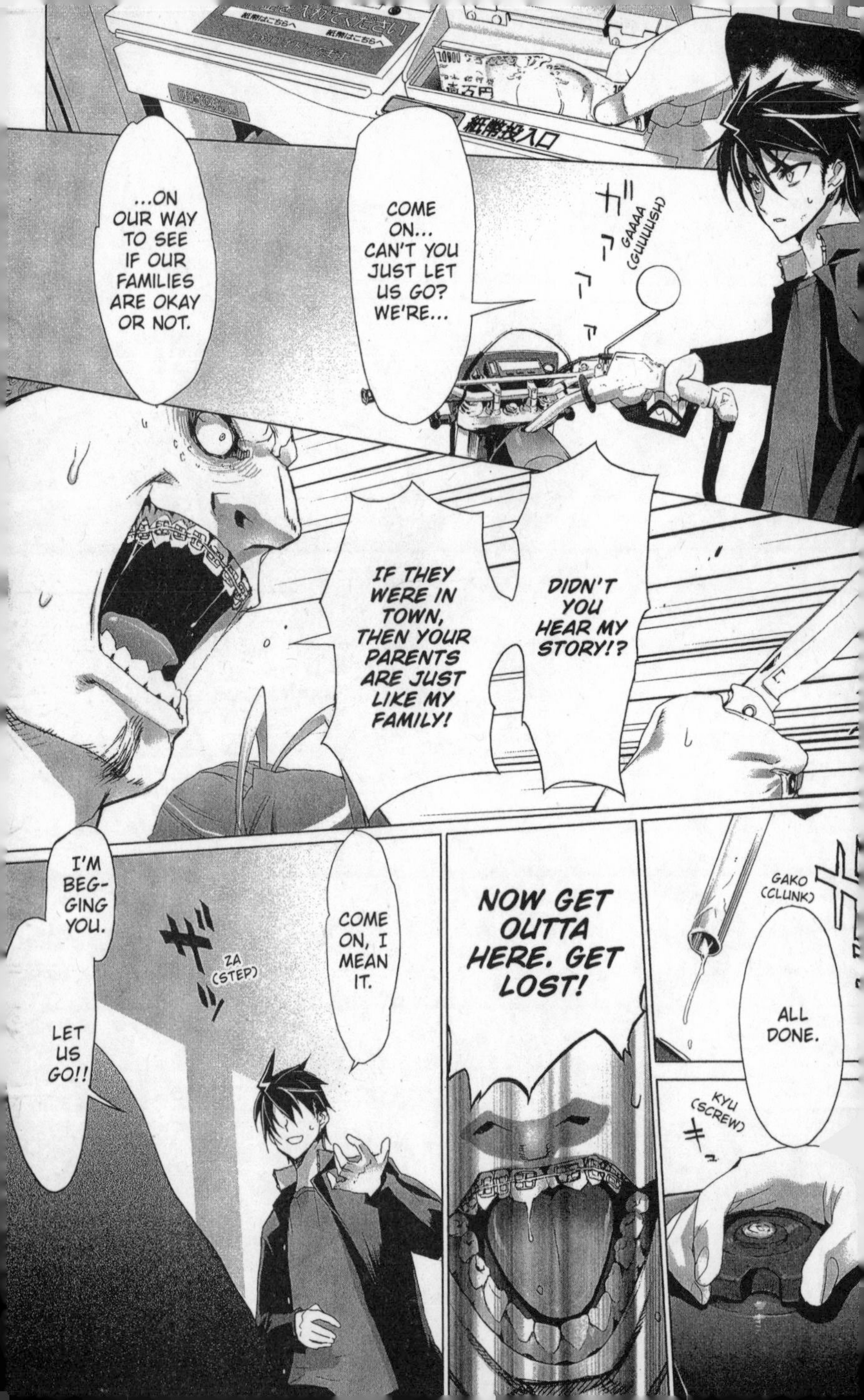
GAAAA (GUUUUSH)
COME ON... CAN'T YOU JUST LET US GO? WE'RE...
...ON OUR WAY TO SEE IF OUR FAMILIES ARE OKAY OR NOT.
DIDN'T YOU HEAR MY STORY!?
IF THEY WERE IN TOWN, THEN YOUR PARENTS ARE JUST LIKE MY FAMILY!
GAKO (CLUNK)
ALL DONE.
KYU (SCREW)
NOW GET OUTTA HERE. GET LOST!
COME ON, I MEAN IT.
ZA (STEP)
I'M BEG-GING YOU.
LET US GO!!

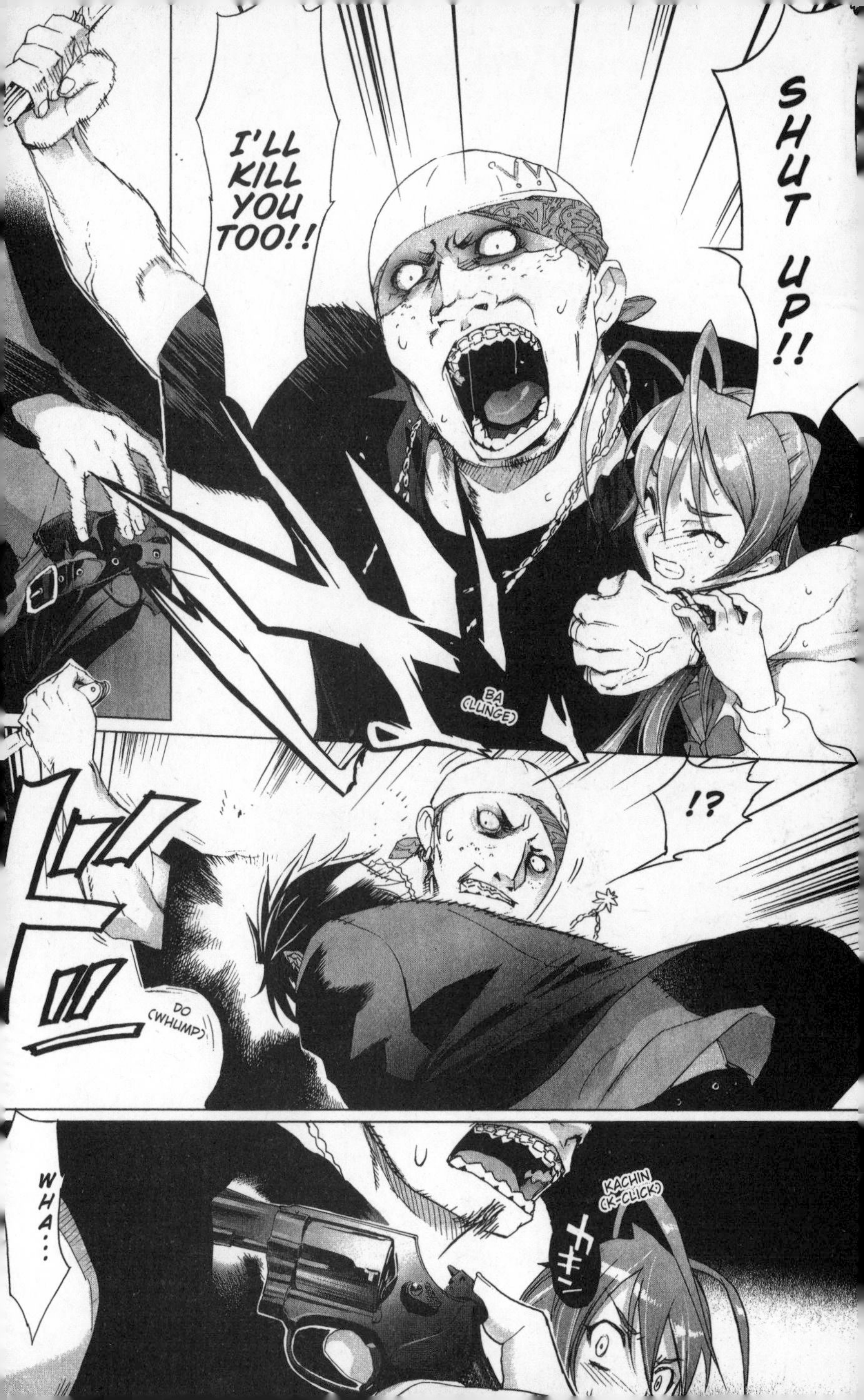
SHUT UP!!
I'LL KILL YOU TOO!!
BA (LUNGE)
!?
DO (WHUMP)
KACHIN (K-CLICK)
WHA...

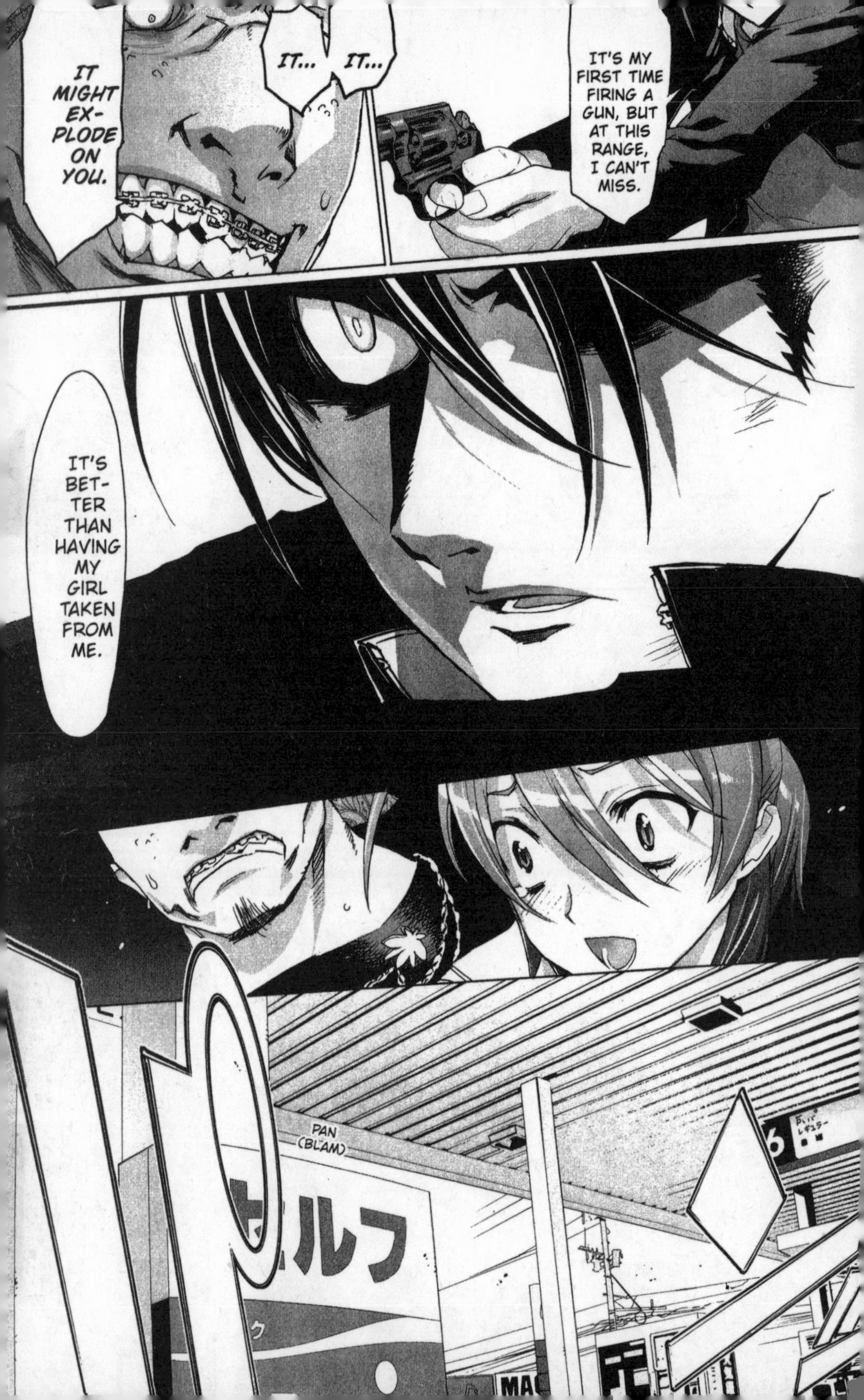
IT'S MY FIRST TIME FIRING A GUN, BUT AT THIS RANGE, I CAN'T MISS.
IT... IT...
IT MIGHT EXPLODE ON YOU.
IT'S BETTER THAN HAVING MY GIRL TAKEN FROM ME.
PAN (BLAM)

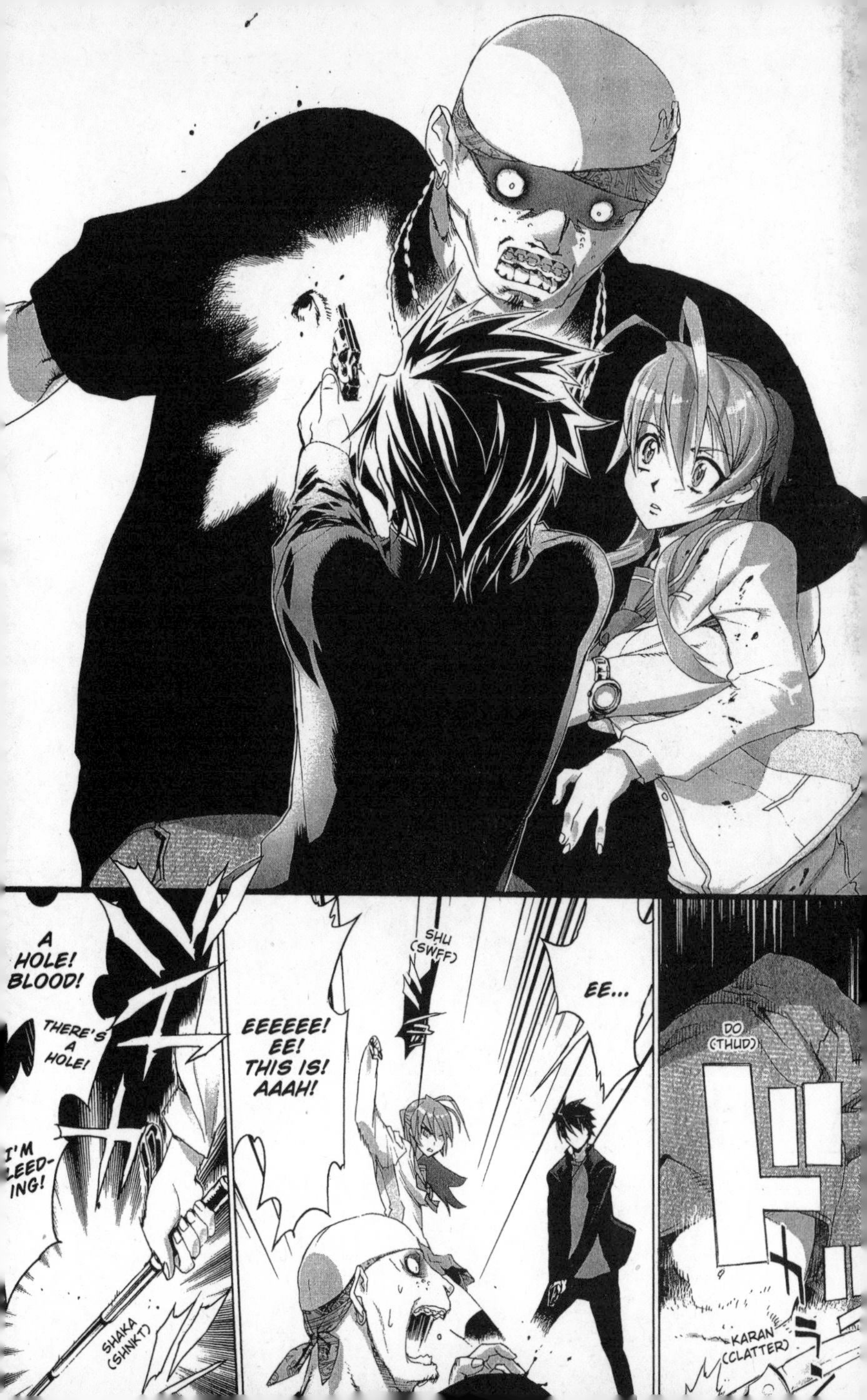
DO (THUD)
KARAN (CLATTER)
SHU (SWFF)
EE...
EEEEEE! EE! THIS IS! AAAH!
A HOLE! BLOOD!
THERE'S A HOLE!
I'M LEED-ING!
SHAKA (SHNKT)

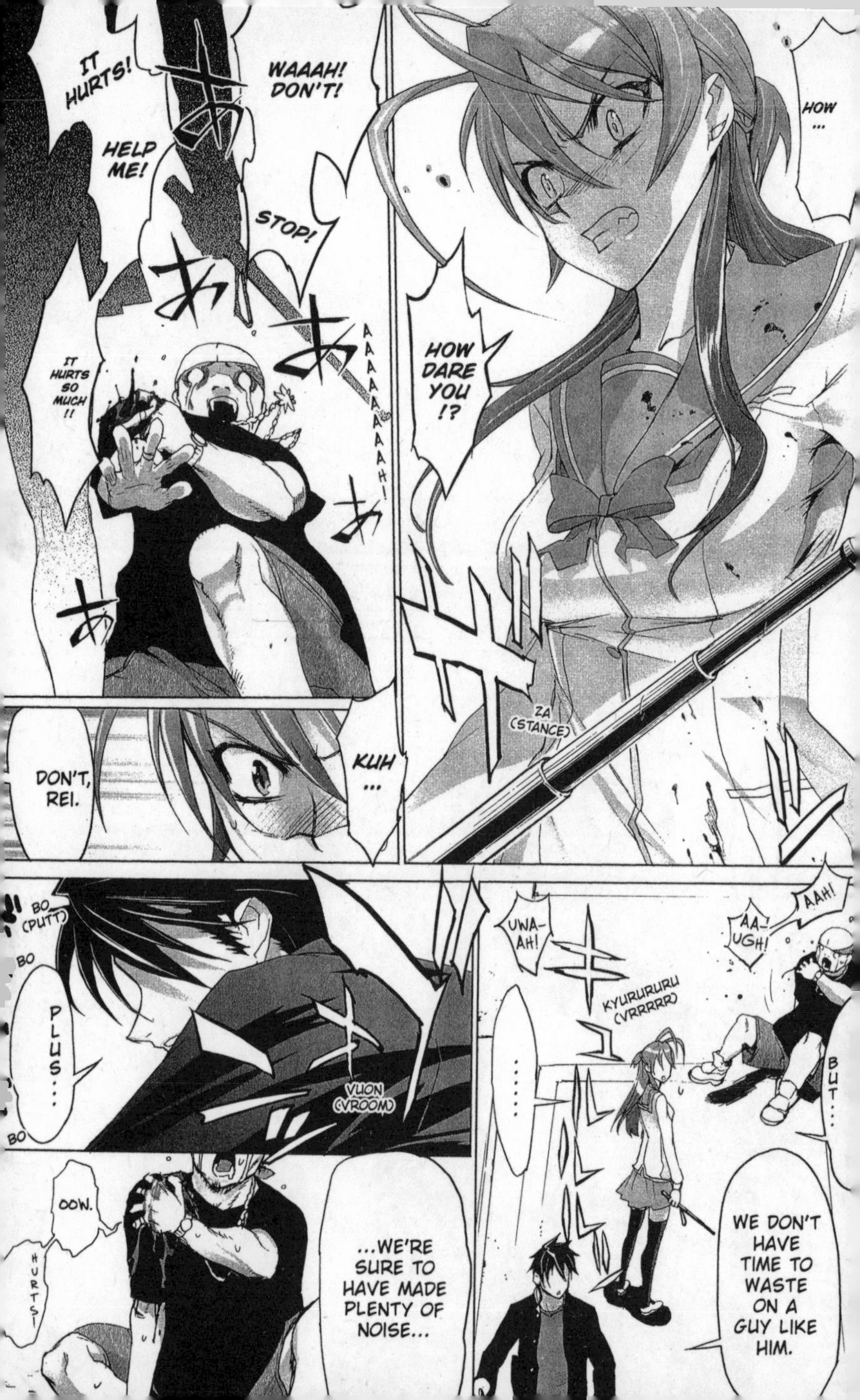
HOW...
HOW DARE YOU!?
ZA (STANCE)
WAAAH! DON'T!
IT HURTS!
HELP ME!
STOP!
AAAAAAAAAAH!
IT HURTS SO MUCH!!
KUH...
DON'T, REI.
AAH!
AA-UGH!
UWA-AH!
KYURURURU (VRRRRR)
BUT...
......
WE DON'T HAVE TIME TO WASTE ON A GUY LIKE HIM.
BO (PUTT)
BO
BO
PLUS...
VUON (VROOM)
...WE'RE SURE TO HAVE MADE PLENTY OF NOISE...
OOW.
HURTS!

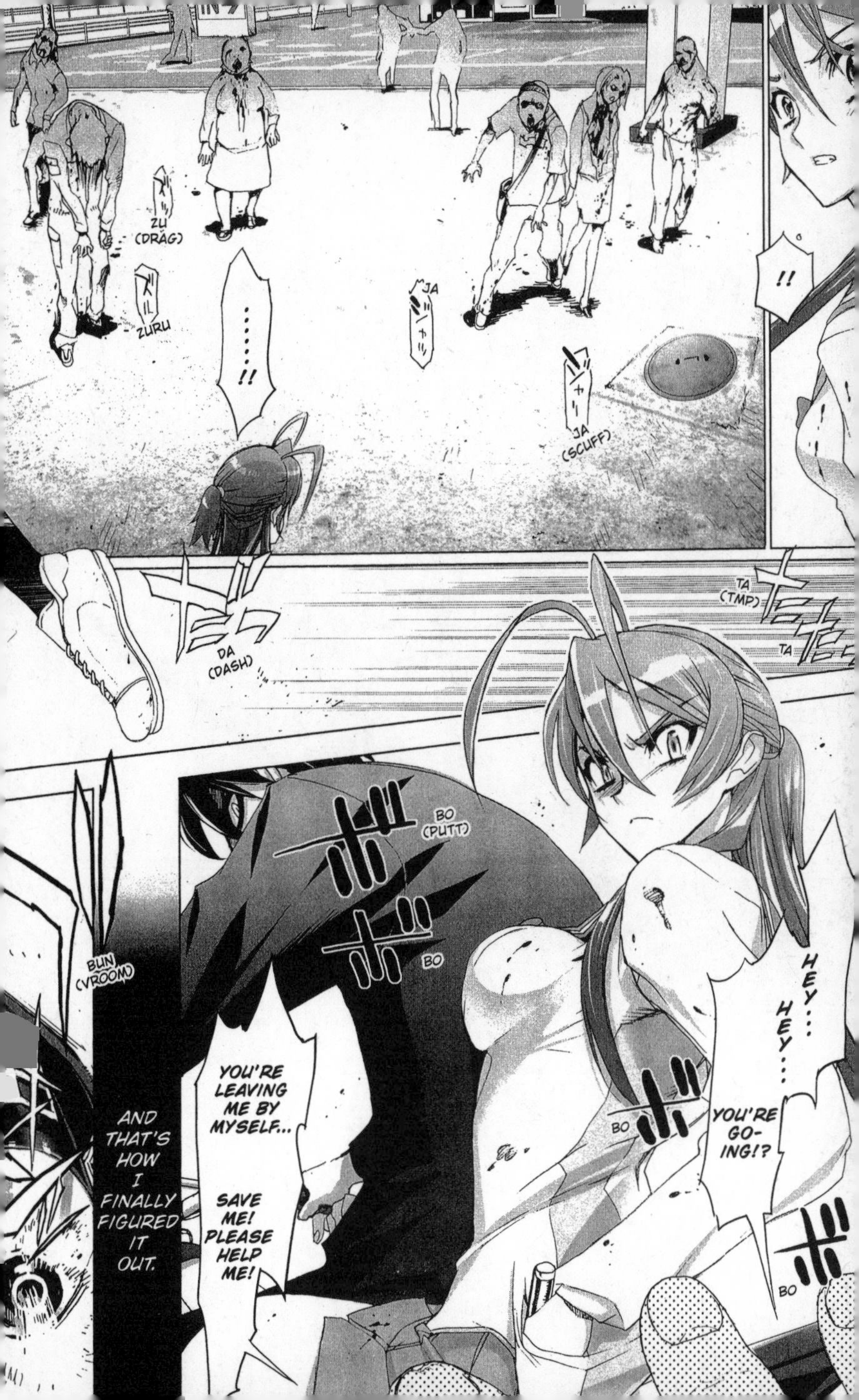
!!
JA (SCUFF)
JA
......!!
ZU (DRAG)
ZURU
TA (TMP)
TA
DA (DASH)
HEY... HEY...
YOU'RE GO-ING!?
BO
BO
BO (PUTT)
BO
YOU'RE LEAVING ME BY MYSELF...
SAVE ME! PLEASE HELP ME!
AND THAT'S HOW I FINALLY FIGURED IT OUT.
BUN (VROOM)
...

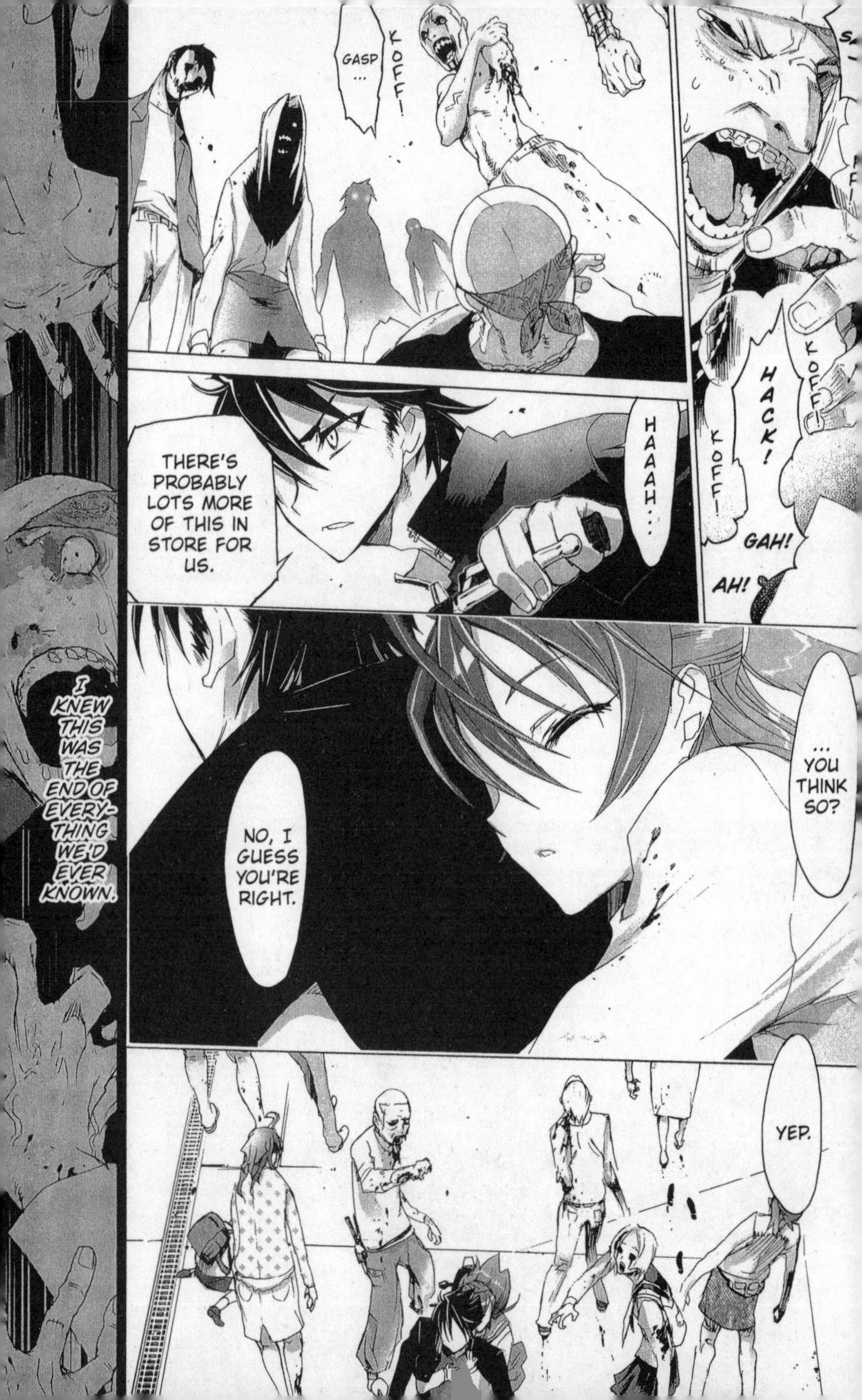
KOFF!
HACK!
KOFF!
GAH!
AH!
GASP ...
KOFF!
HAAAH...
THERE'S PROBABLY LOTS MORE OF THIS IN STORE FOR US.
... YOU THINK SO?
NO, I GUESS YOU'RE RIGHT.
YEP.
I KNEW THIS WAS THE END OF EVERYTHING WE'D EVER KNOWN.

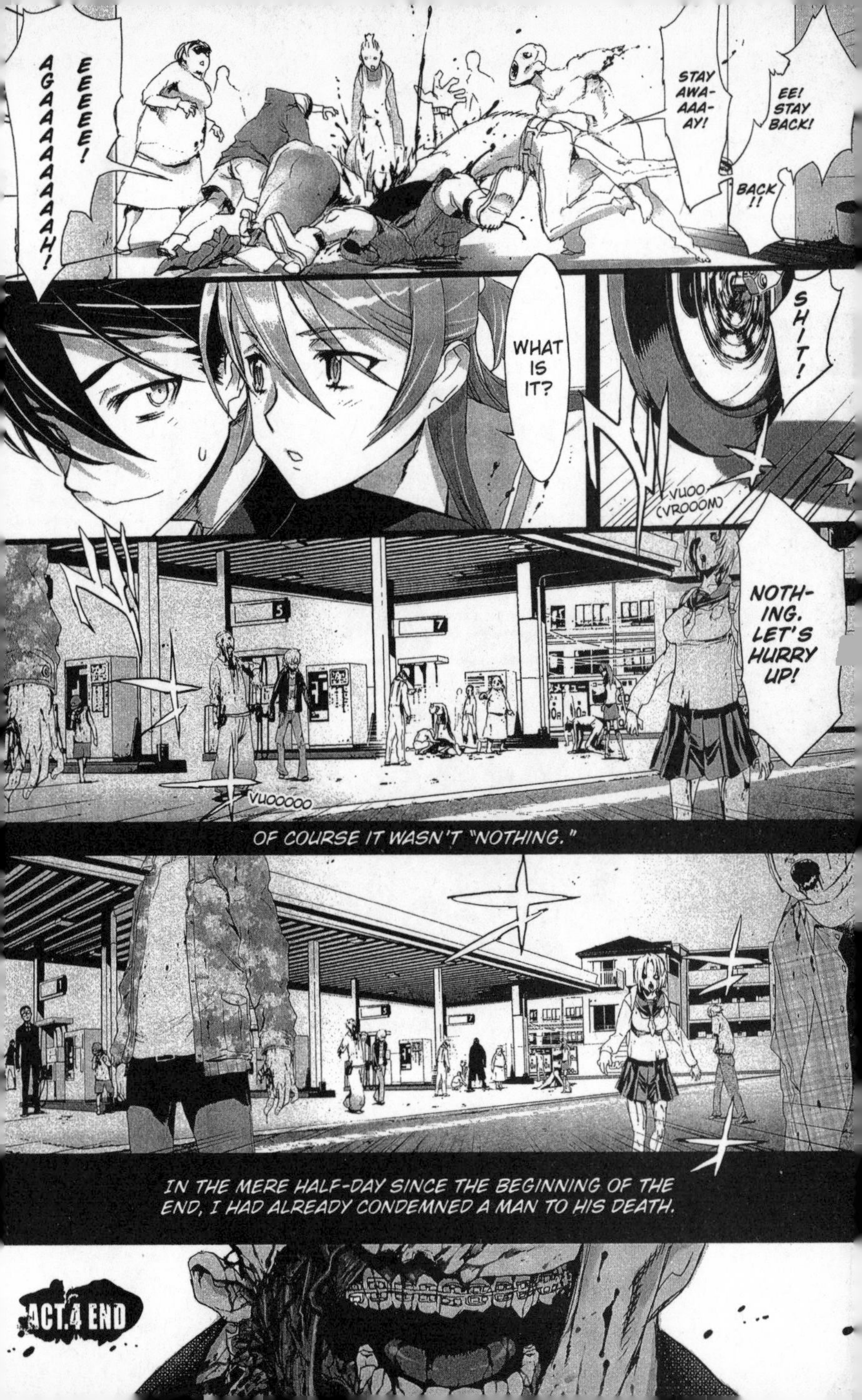
EE! STAY BACK!
STAY AWAAAAAY!
BACK!!
EEEEEE!
AGAAAAAAAAAAAH!
SHIT!
VUOO (VROOOM)
WHAT IS IT?
NOTH-ING. LET'S HURRY UP!
VUOOOOO
OF COURSE IT WASN'T "NOTHING."
IN THE MERE HALF-DAY SINCE THE BEGINNING OF THE END, I HAD ALREADY CONDEMNED A MAN TO HIS DEATH.
ACT.4 END

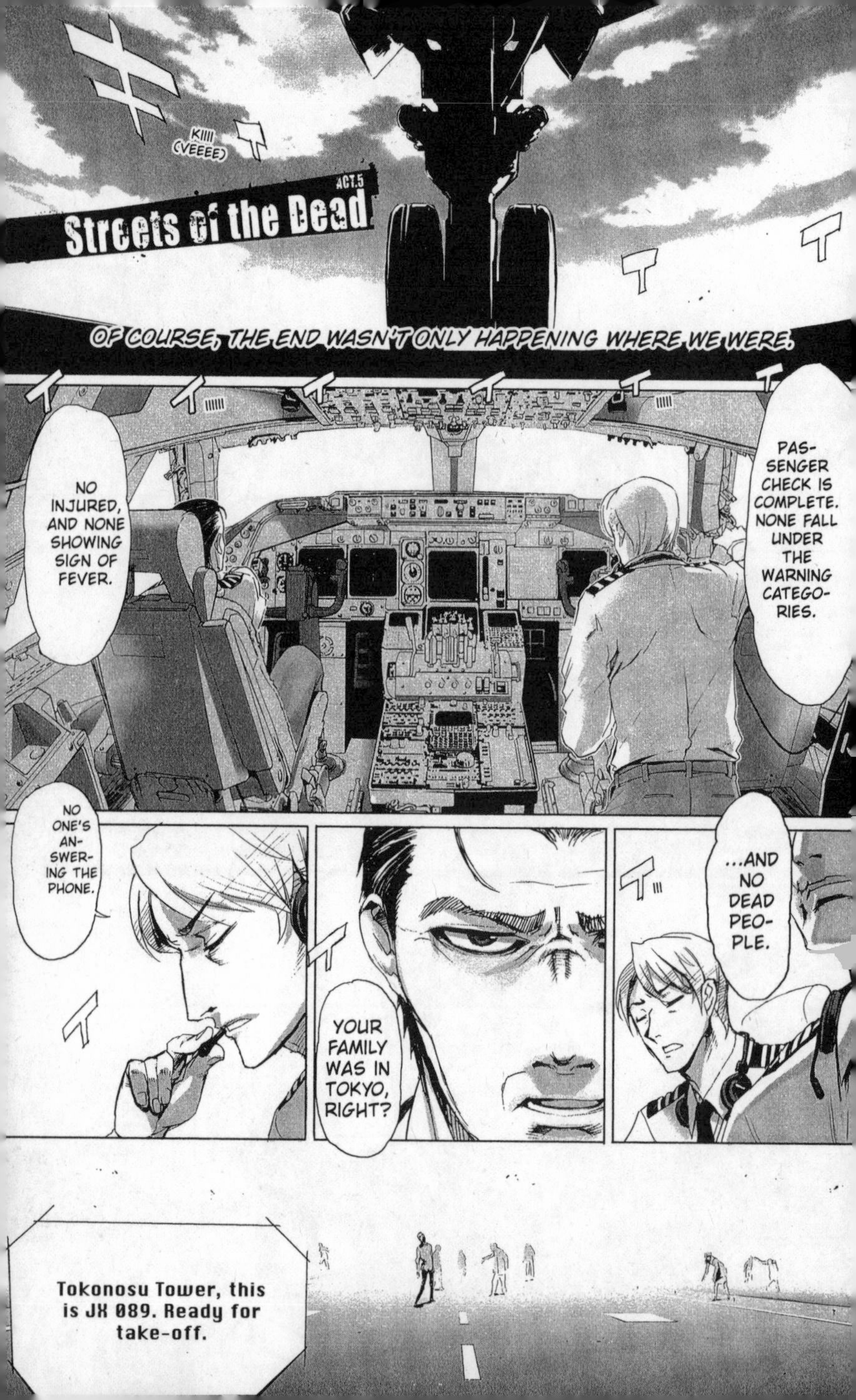
KIIII (VEEEE)
ACT.5
Streets of the Dead
OF COURSE, THE END WASN'T ONLY HAPPENING WHERE WE WERE.
PASSENGER CHECK IS COMPLETE. NONE FALL UNDER THE WARNING CATEGORIES.
NO INJURED, AND NONE SHOWING SIGN OF FEVER.
...AND NO DEAD PEOPLE.
YOUR FAMILY WAS IN TOKYO, RIGHT?
NO ONE'S ANSWERING THE PHONE.
Tokonosu Tower, this is JX 089. Ready for take-off.

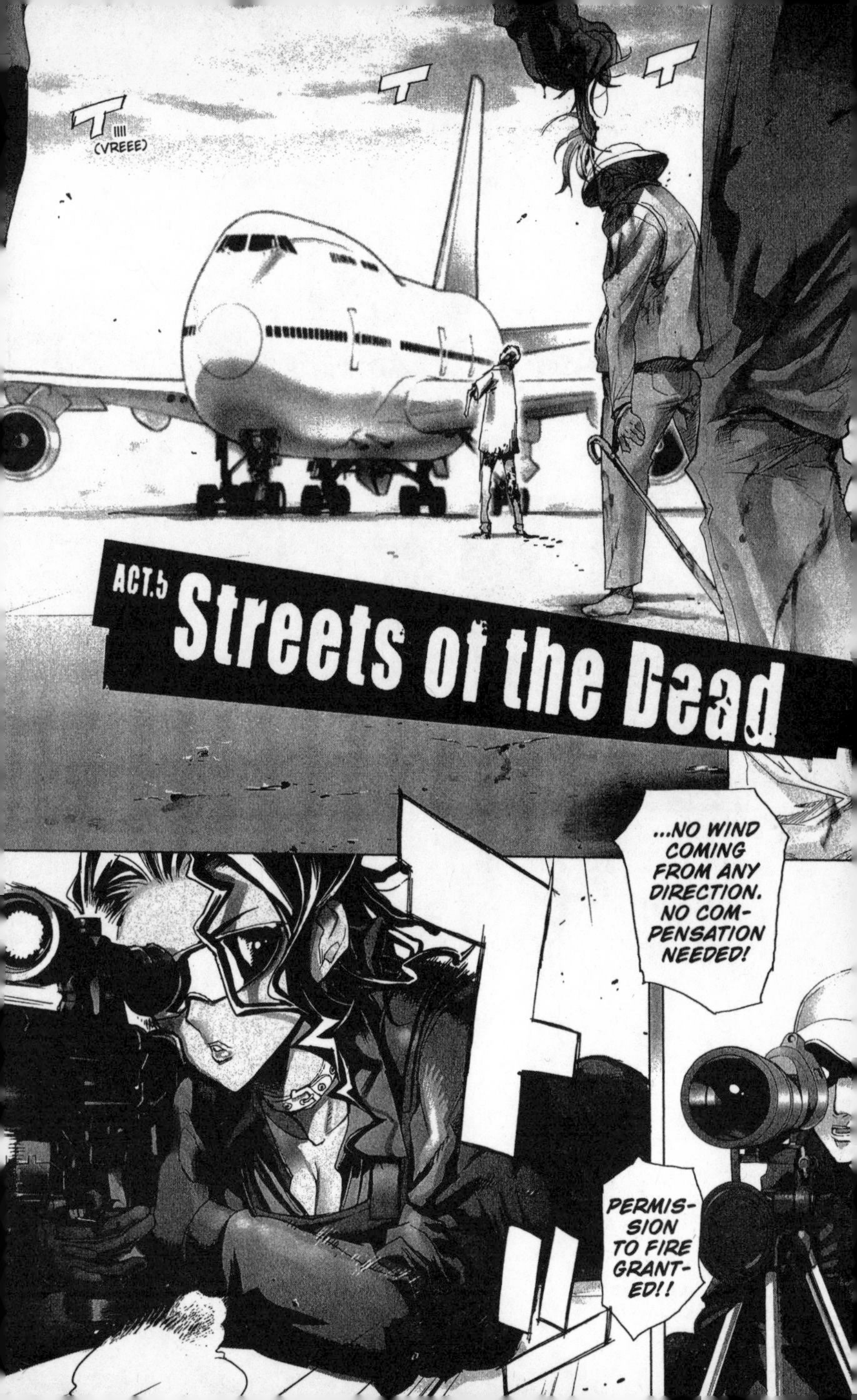
T T T (VREEE)
ACT.5 Streets of the Dead
...NO WIND COMING FROM ANY DIRECTION. NO COMPENSATION NEEDED!
PERMISSION TO FIRE GRANTED!!

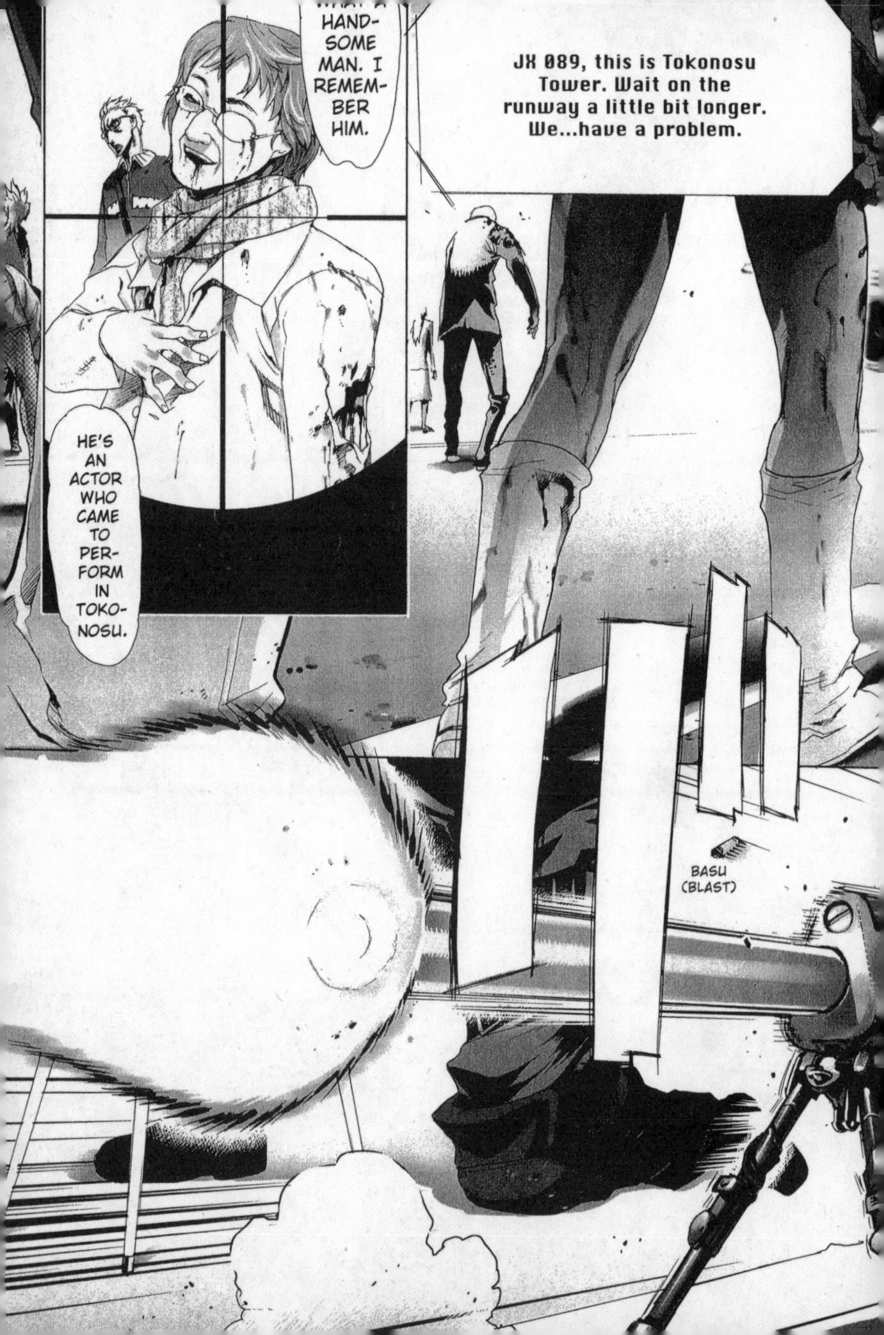
JX 089, this is Tokonosu Tower. Wait on the runway a little bit longer. We...have a problem.
HANDSOME MAN. I REMEMBER HIM.
HE'S AN ACTOR WHO CAME TO PERFORM IN TOKONOSU.
BASU (BLAST)

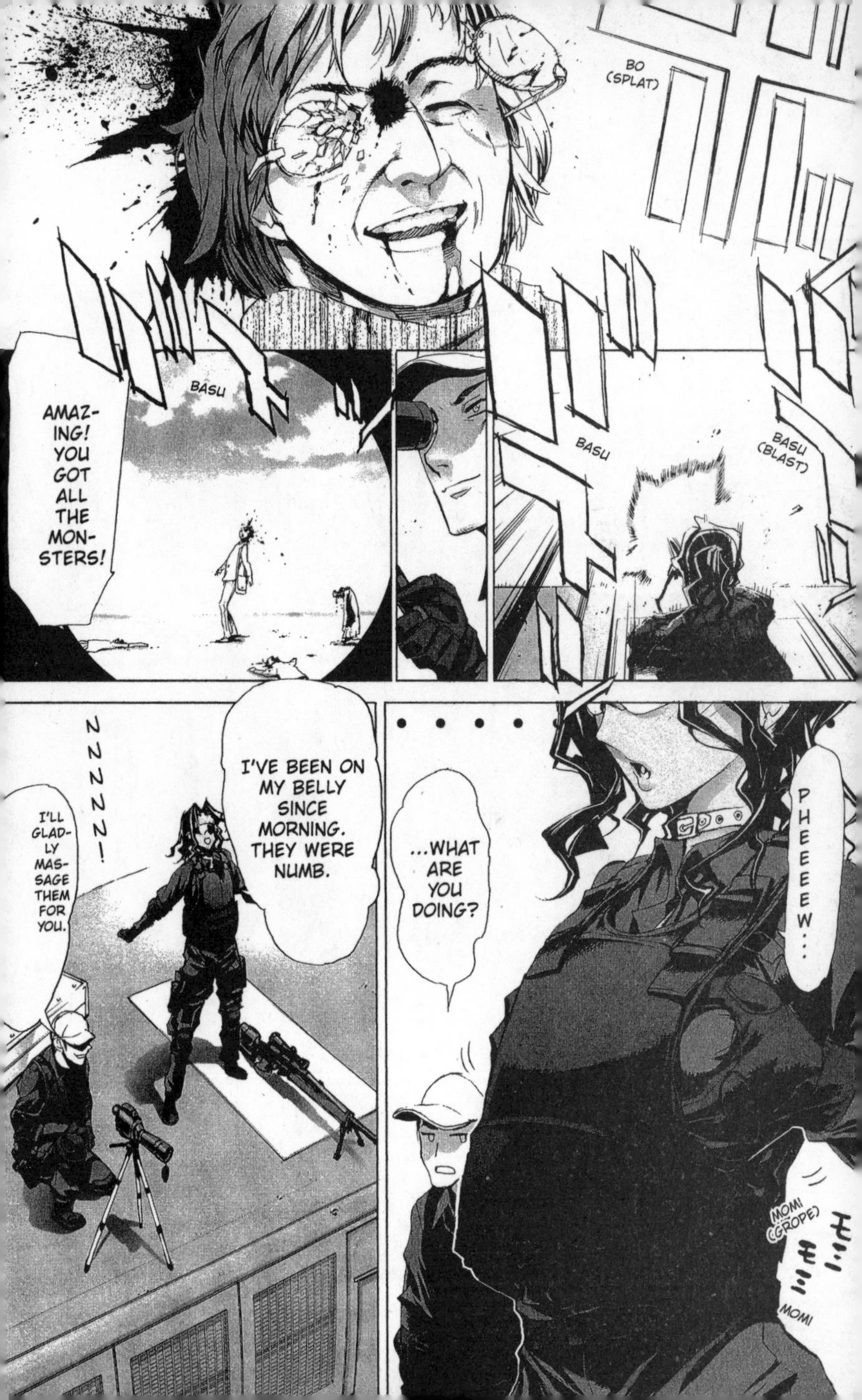
BO (SPLAT)
BASU (BLAST)
BASU
BASU
AMAZ-ING! YOU GOT ALL THE MON-STERS!
PHEEEEW...
...WHAT ARE YOU DOING?
MOMI (GROPE)
MOMI
I'VE BEEN ON MY BELLY SINCE MORNING. THEY WERE NUMB.
NNNNN!
I'LL GLAD-LY MAS-SAGE THEM FOR YOU.

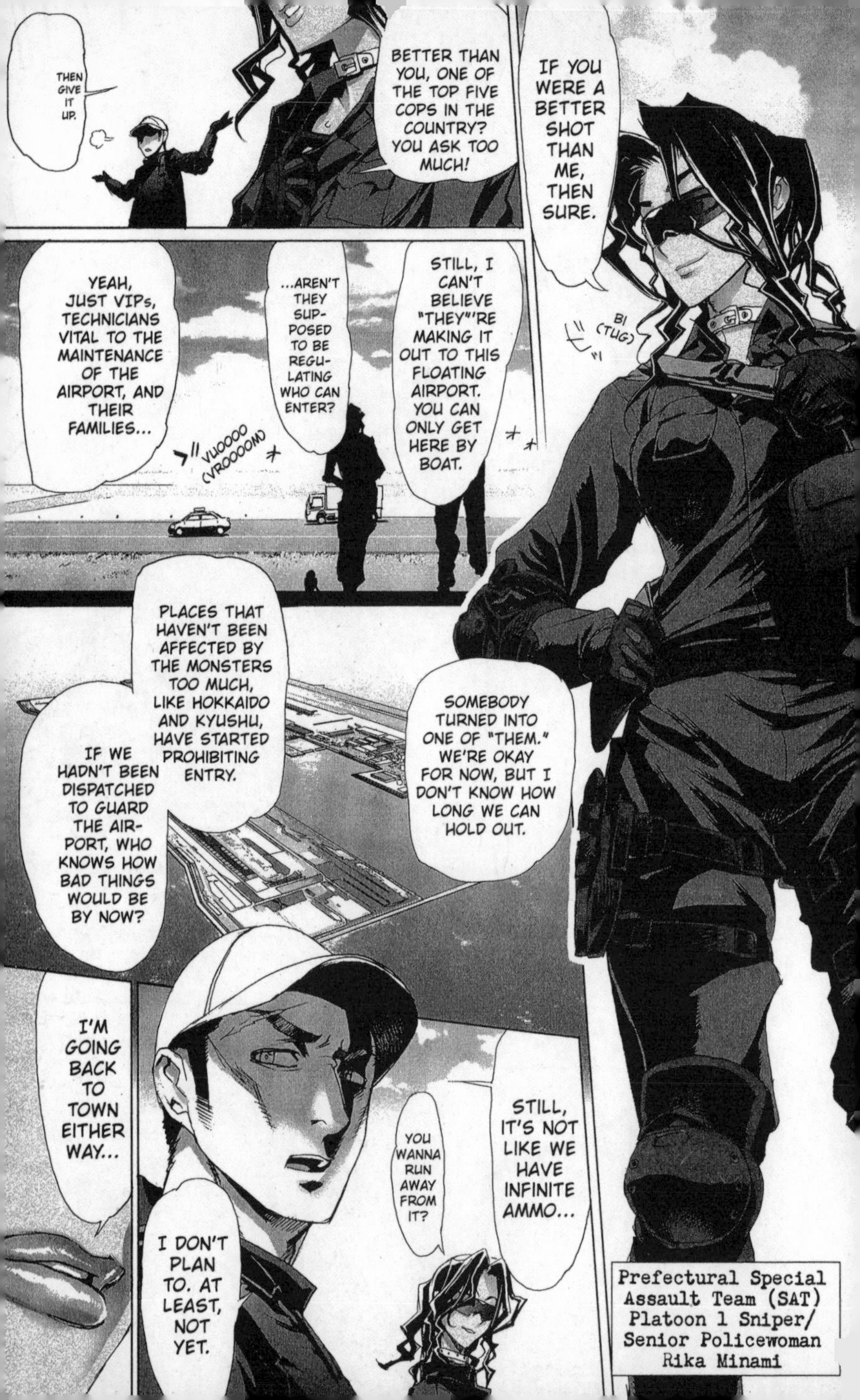
IF YOU WERE A BETTER SHOT THAN ME, THEN SURE.
BETTER THAN YOU, ONE OF THE TOP FIVE COPS IN THE COUNTRY? YOU ASK TOO MUCH!
THEN GIVE IT UP.
BI (TUG)
STILL, I CAN'T BELIEVE "THEY"'RE MAKING IT OUT TO THIS FLOATING AIRPORT. YOU CAN ONLY GET HERE BY BOAT.
...AREN'T THEY SUP-POSED TO BE REGU-LATING WHO CAN ENTER?
YEAH, JUST VIPs, TECHNICIANS VITAL TO THE MAINTENANCE OF THE AIRPORT, AND THEIR FAMILIES...
VUOOOO (VROOOOM)
SOMEBODY TURNED INTO ONE OF "THEM." WE'RE OKAY FOR NOW, BUT I DON'T KNOW HOW LONG WE CAN HOLD OUT.
PLACES THAT HAVEN'T BEEN AFFECTED BY THE MONSTERS TOO MUCH, LIKE HOKKAIDO AND KYUSHU, HAVE STARTED PROHIBITING ENTRY.
IF WE HADN'T BEEN DISPATCHED TO GUARD THE AIR-PORT, WHO KNOWS HOW BAD THINGS WOULD BE BY NOW?
STILL, IT'S NOT LIKE WE HAVE INFINITE AMMO...
YOU WANNA RUN AWAY FROM IT?
I'M GOING BACK TO TOWN EITHER WAY...
I DON'T PLAN TO. AT LEAST, NOT YET.
Prefectural Special Assault Team (SAT) Platoon 1 Sniper/ Senior Policewoman Rika Minami

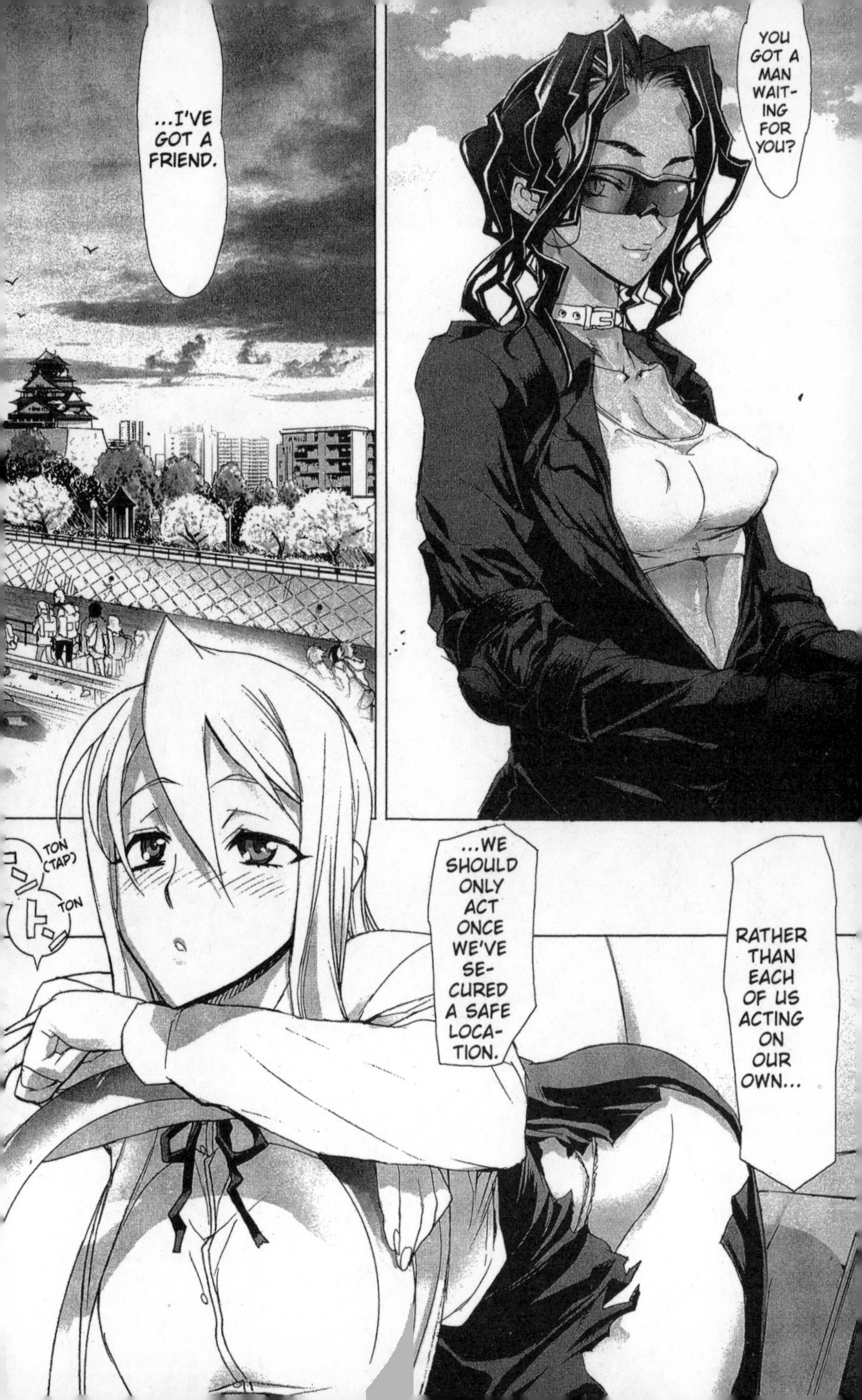
YOU GOT A MAN WAITING FOR YOU?
...I'VE GOT A FRIEND.
RATHER THAN EACH OF US ACTING ON OUR OWN...
...WE SHOULD ONLY ACT ONCE WE'VE SECURED A SAFE LOCATION.
TON (TAP)
TON

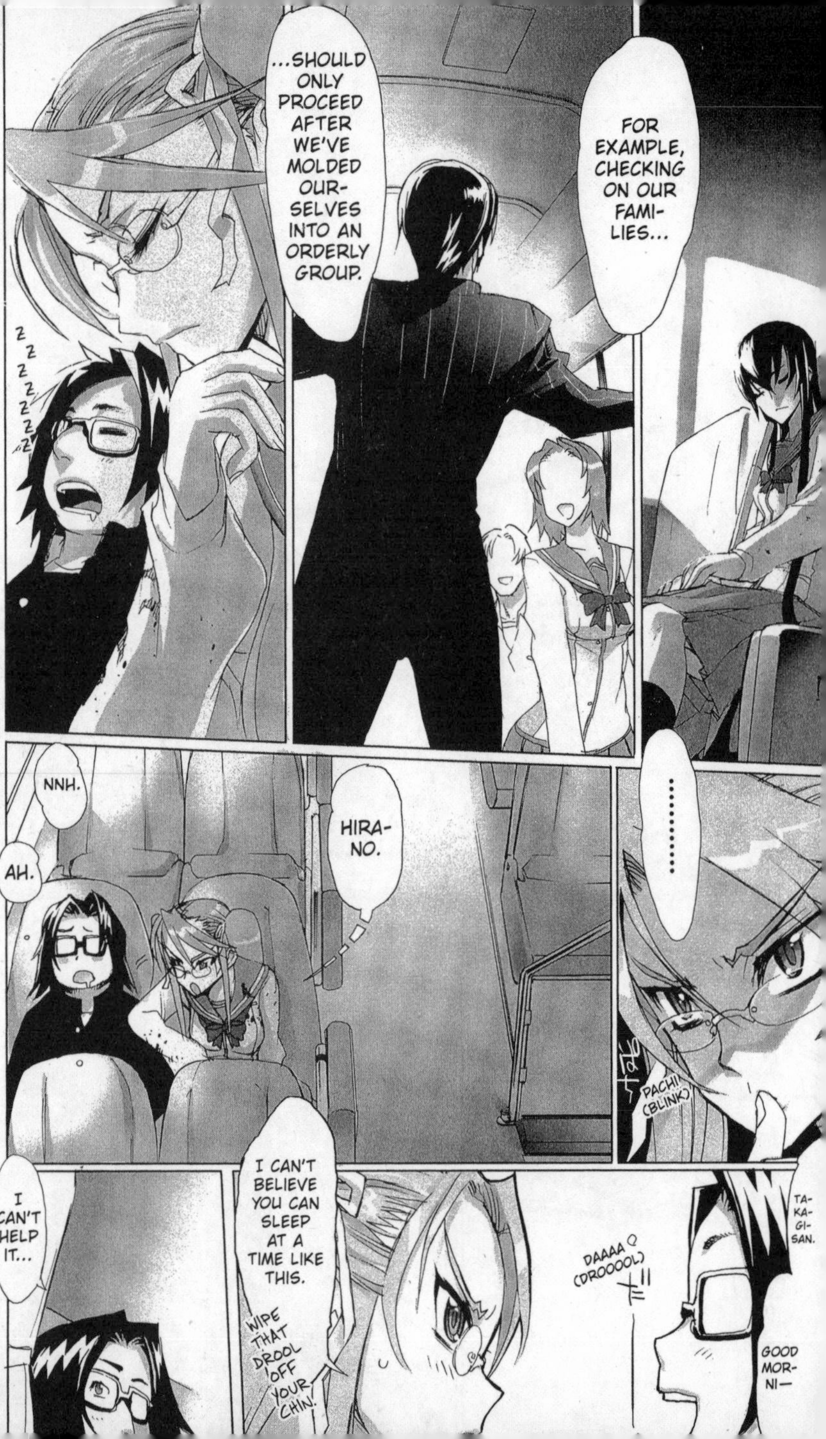
FOR EXAMPLE, CHECKING ON OUR FAMILIES...
...SHOULD ONLY PROCEED AFTER WE'VE MOLDED OURSELVES INTO AN ORDERLY GROUP.
ZZZZZZZ
......
PACHI (BLINK)
HIRANO.
NNH.
AH.
TAKAGI-SAN.
GOOD MORNI—
DAAAA (DROOOOL)
I CAN'T BELIEVE YOU CAN SLEEP AT A TIME LIKE THIS.
WIPE THAT DROOL OFF YOUR CHIN!
I CAN'T HELP IT...

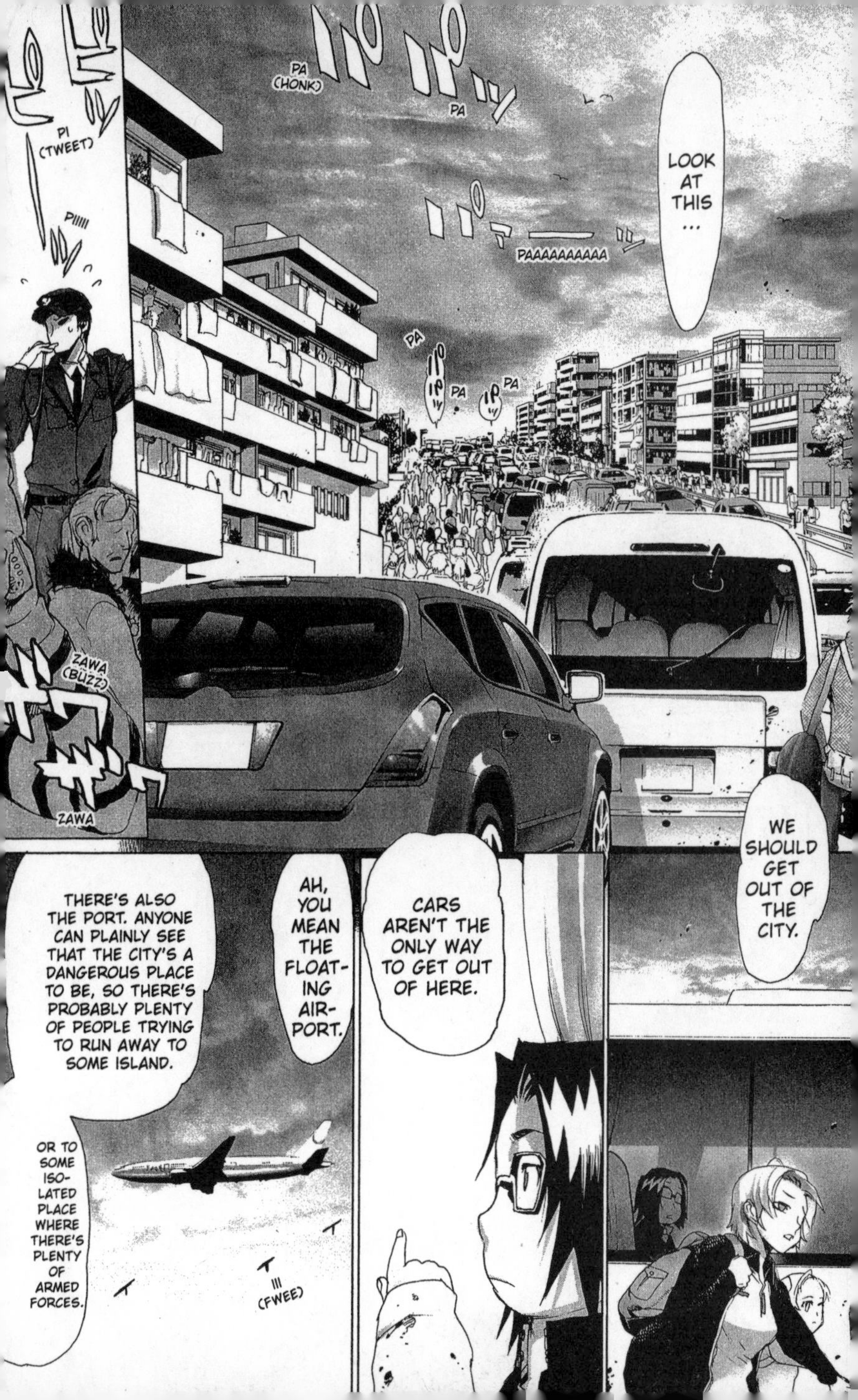
LOOK AT THIS ...
PA (HONK)
PA
PAAAAAAAAAA
PA
PA
PA
PI (TWEET)
PIIII
ZAWA (BUZZ)
ZAWA
WE SHOULD GET OUT OF THE CITY.
CARS AREN'T THE ONLY WAY TO GET OUT OF HERE.
AH, YOU MEAN THE FLOAT-ING AIR-PORT.
THERE'S ALSO THE PORT. ANYONE CAN PLAINLY SEE THAT THE CITY'S A DANGEROUS PLACE TO BE, SO THERE'S PROBABLY PLENTY OF PEOPLE TRYING TO RUN AWAY TO SOME ISLAND.
OR TO SOME ISO-LATED PLACE WHERE THERE'S PLENTY OF ARMED FORCES.
III (FWEE)

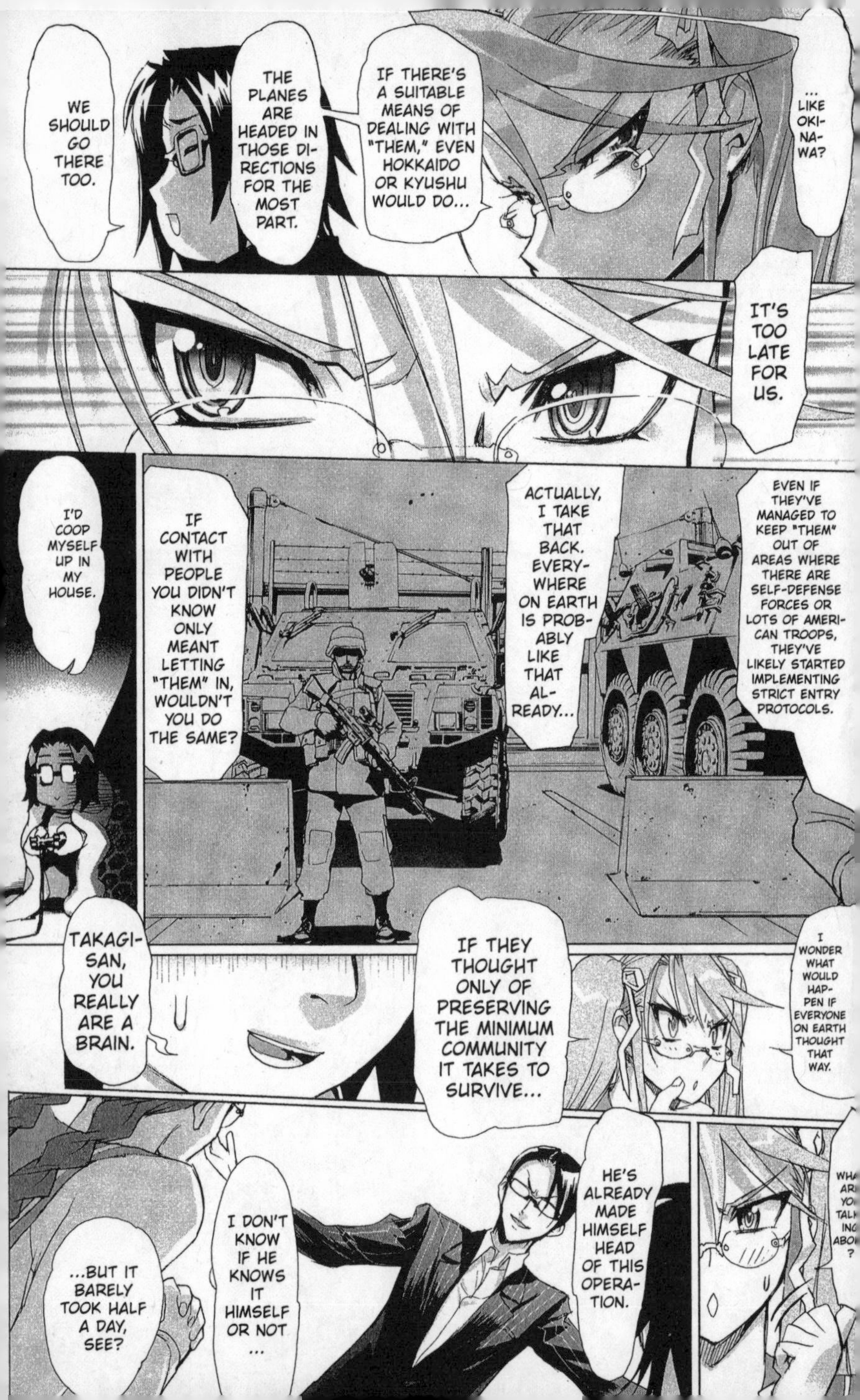
...LIKE OKINAWA?
IF THERE'S A SUITABLE MEANS OF DEALING WITH "THEM," EVEN HOKKAIDO OR KYUSHU WOULD DO...
THE PLANES ARE HEADED IN THOSE DIRECTIONS FOR THE MOST PART.
WE SHOULD GO THERE TOO.
IT'S TOO LATE FOR US.
EVEN IF THEY'VE MANAGED TO KEEP "THEM" OUT OF AREAS WHERE THERE ARE SELF-DEFENSE FORCES OR LOTS OF AMERICAN TROOPS, THEY'VE LIKELY STARTED IMPLEMENTING STRICT ENTRY PROTOCOLS.
ACTUALLY, I TAKE THAT BACK. EVERYWHERE ON EARTH IS PROBABLY LIKE THAT ALREADY...
IF CONTACT WITH PEOPLE YOU DIDN'T KNOW ONLY MEANT LETTING "THEM" IN, WOULDN'T YOU DO THE SAME?
I'D COOP MYSELF UP IN MY HOUSE.
I WONDER WHAT WOULD HAPPEN IF EVERYONE ON EARTH THOUGHT THAT WAY.
IF THEY THOUGHT ONLY OF PRESERVING THE MINIMUM COMMUNITY IT TAKES TO SURVIVE...
TAKAGI-SAN, YOU REALLY ARE A BRAIN.
WHA AR YO TALK ING ABO ?
HE'S ALREADY MADE HIMSELF HEAD OF THIS OPERATION.
I DON'T KNOW IF HE KNOWS IT HIMSELF OR NOT...
...BUT IT BARELY TOOK HALF A DAY, SEE?

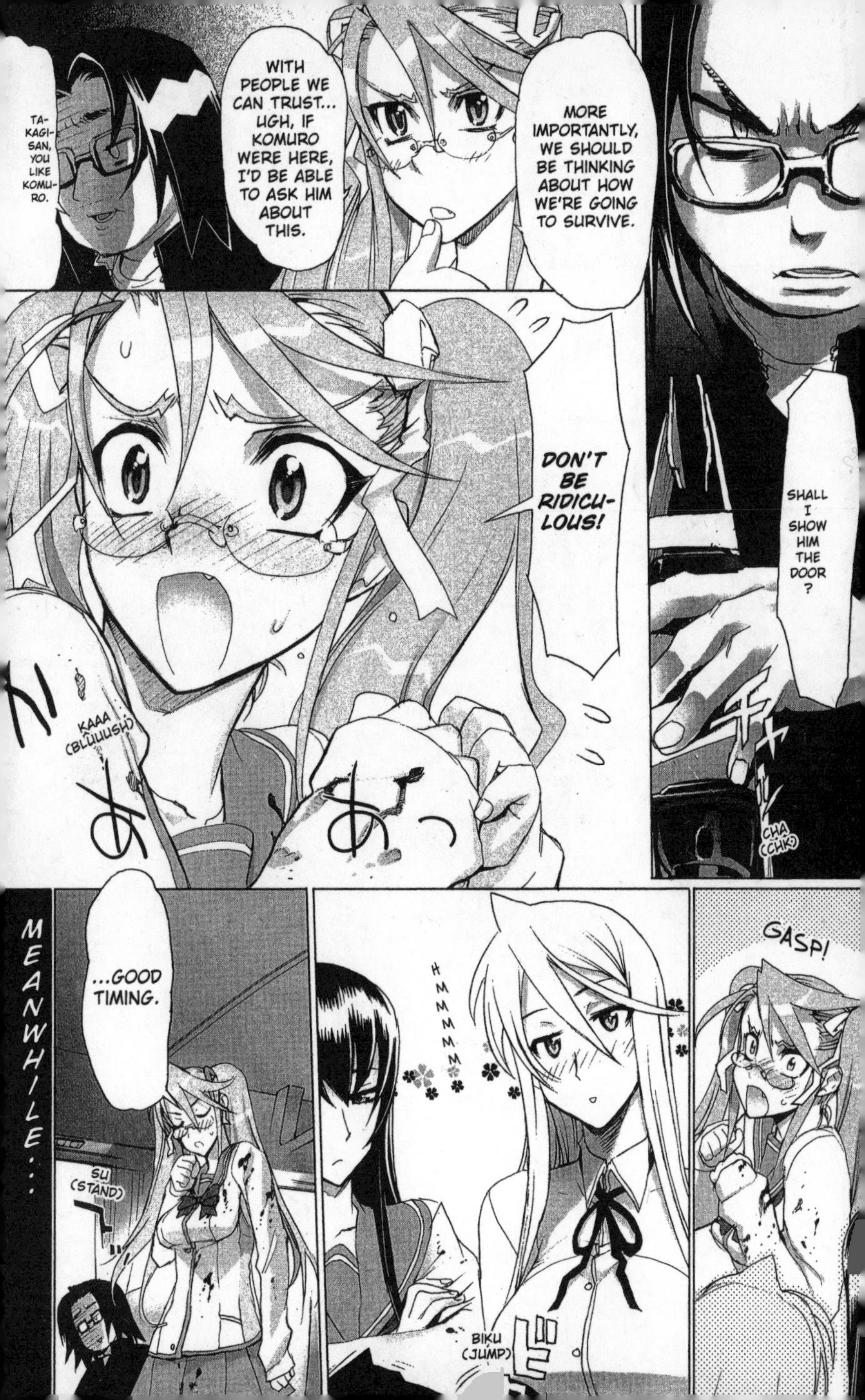
SHALL I SHOW HIM THE DOOR?
CHA (CHK)
WITH PEOPLE WE CAN TRUST... UGH, IF KOMURO WERE HERE, I'D BE ABLE TO ASK HIM ABOUT THIS.
MORE IMPORTANTLY, WE SHOULD BE THINKING ABOUT HOW WE'RE GOING TO SURVIVE.
TA-KAGI-SAN, YOU LIKE KOMU-RO.
DON'T BE RIDICU-LOUS!
KAAA (BLUUUSH)
GASP!
HMMMMM
BIKU (JUMP)
...GOOD TIMING.
SU (STAND)
MEANWHILE...

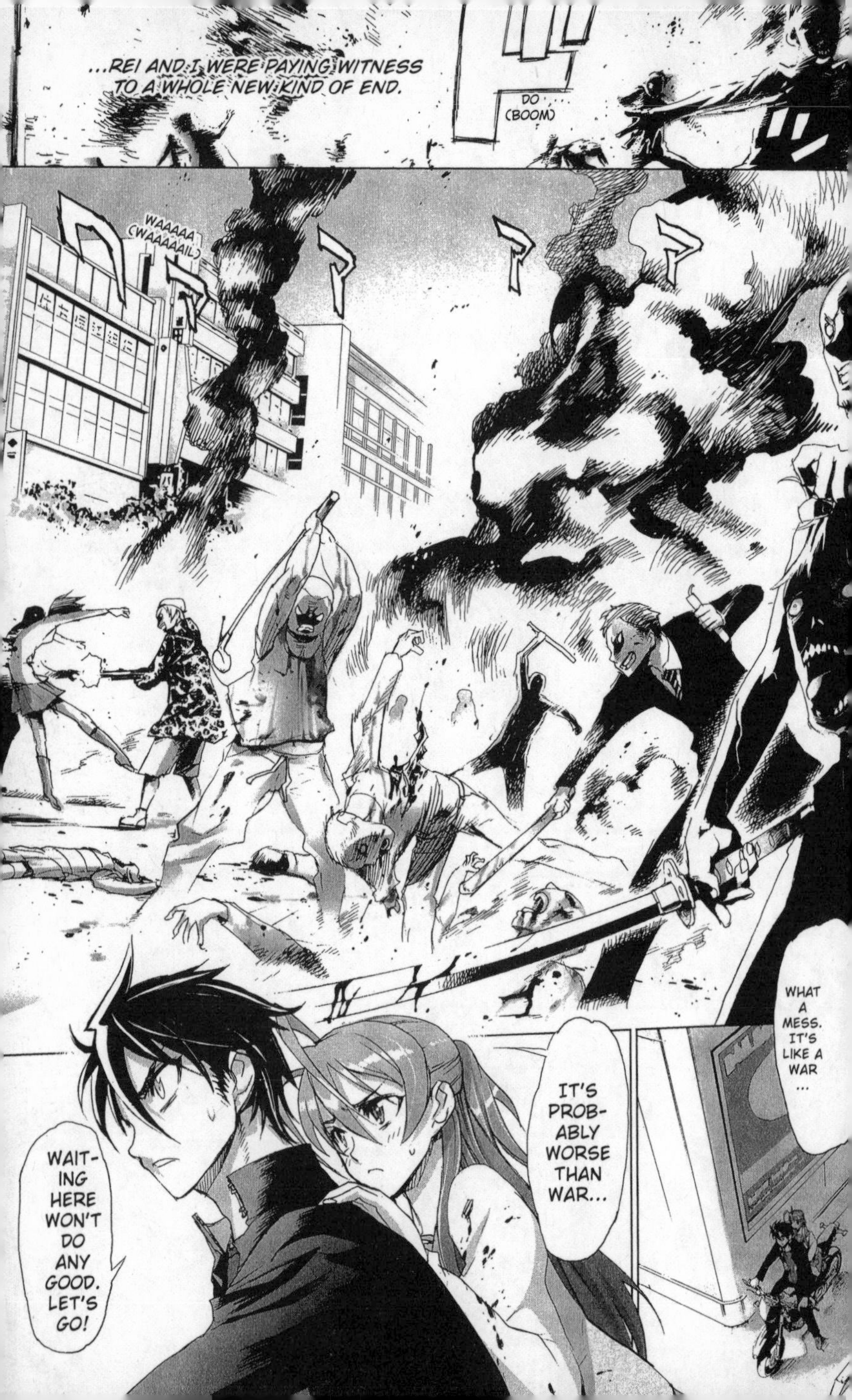
...REI AND I WERE PAYING WITNESS TO A WHOLE NEW KIND OF END.
DO (BOOM)
WAAAAA (WAAAAAIL)
WHAT A MESS. IT'S LIKE A WAR...
IT'S PROBABLY WORSE THAN WAR...
WAITING HERE WON'T DO ANY GOOD. LET'S GO!

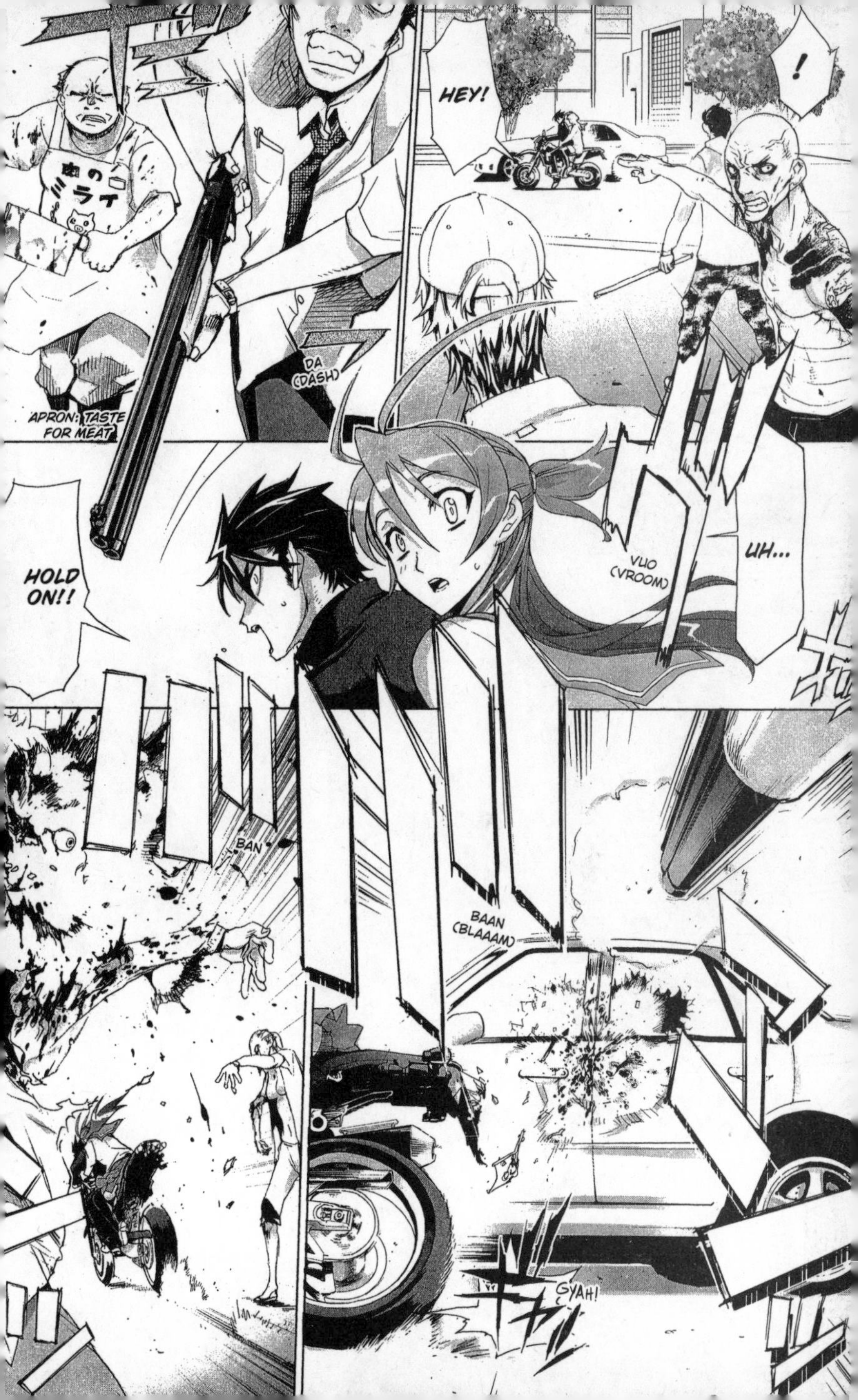
!
HEY!
DA (DASH)
肉のミライ
APRON: TASTE FOR MEAT
UH...
VUO (VROOM)
HOLD ON!!
BAAN (BLAAAM)
GYAH!
BAN

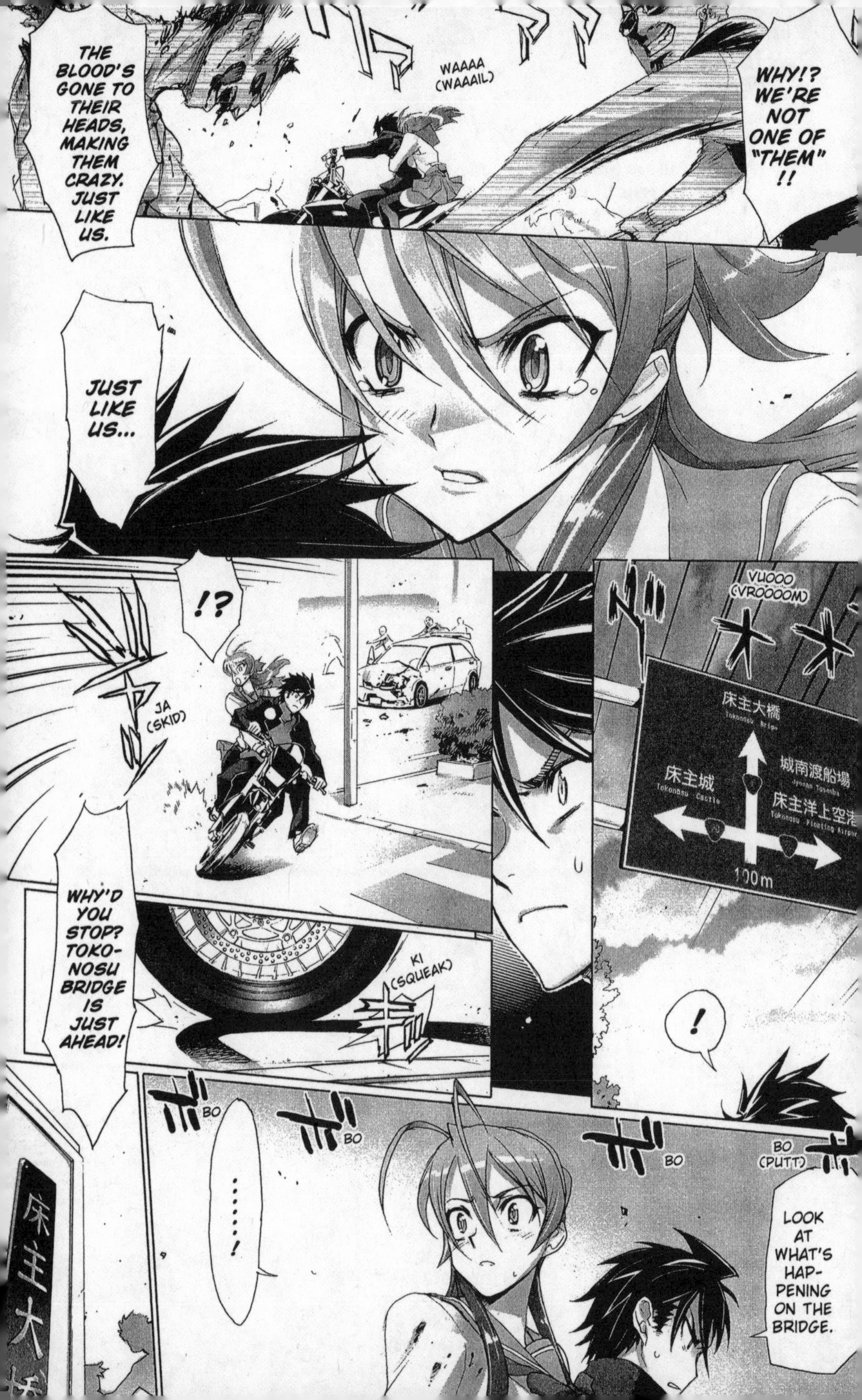
WHY!? WE'RE NOT ONE OF "THEM" !!
WAAAA (WAAAIL)
THE BLOOD'S GONE TO THEIR HEADS, MAKING THEM CRAZY. JUST LIKE US.
JUST LIKE US...
VUOOO (VROOOOM)
床主大橋
城南渡船場
床主城
床主洋上空港
100m
!
!?
JA (SKID)
KI (SQUEAK)
WHY'D YOU STOP? TOKONOSU BRIDGE IS JUST AHEAD!
BO (PUTT)
LOOK AT WHAT'S HAPPENING ON THE BRIDGE.
BO
BO
......!
BO
床主大

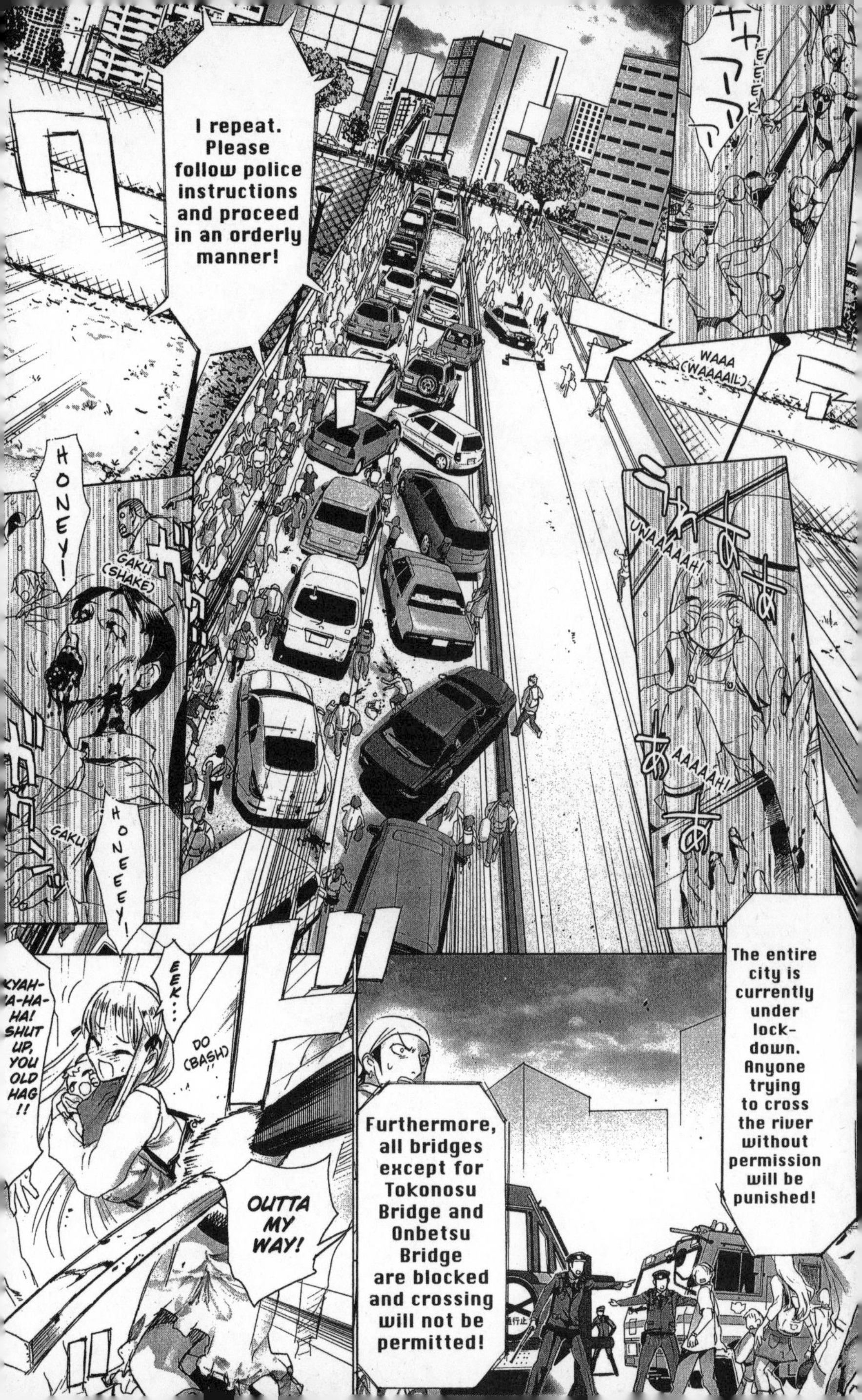
EEEK!
WAAA (WAAAAIL)
UWAAAAAAH!
AAAAAH!
I repeat. Please follow police instructions and proceed in an orderly manner!
HONEY!
GAKU (SHAKE)
HONEEEY!
GAKU
The entire city is currently under lock-down. Anyone trying to cross the river without permission will be punished!
Furthermore, all bridges except for Tokonosu Bridge and Onbetsu Bridge are blocked and crossing will not be permitted!
EEK...
DO (BASH)
KYAH-HA-HA! SHUT UP, YOU OLD HAG!!
OUTTA MY WAY!

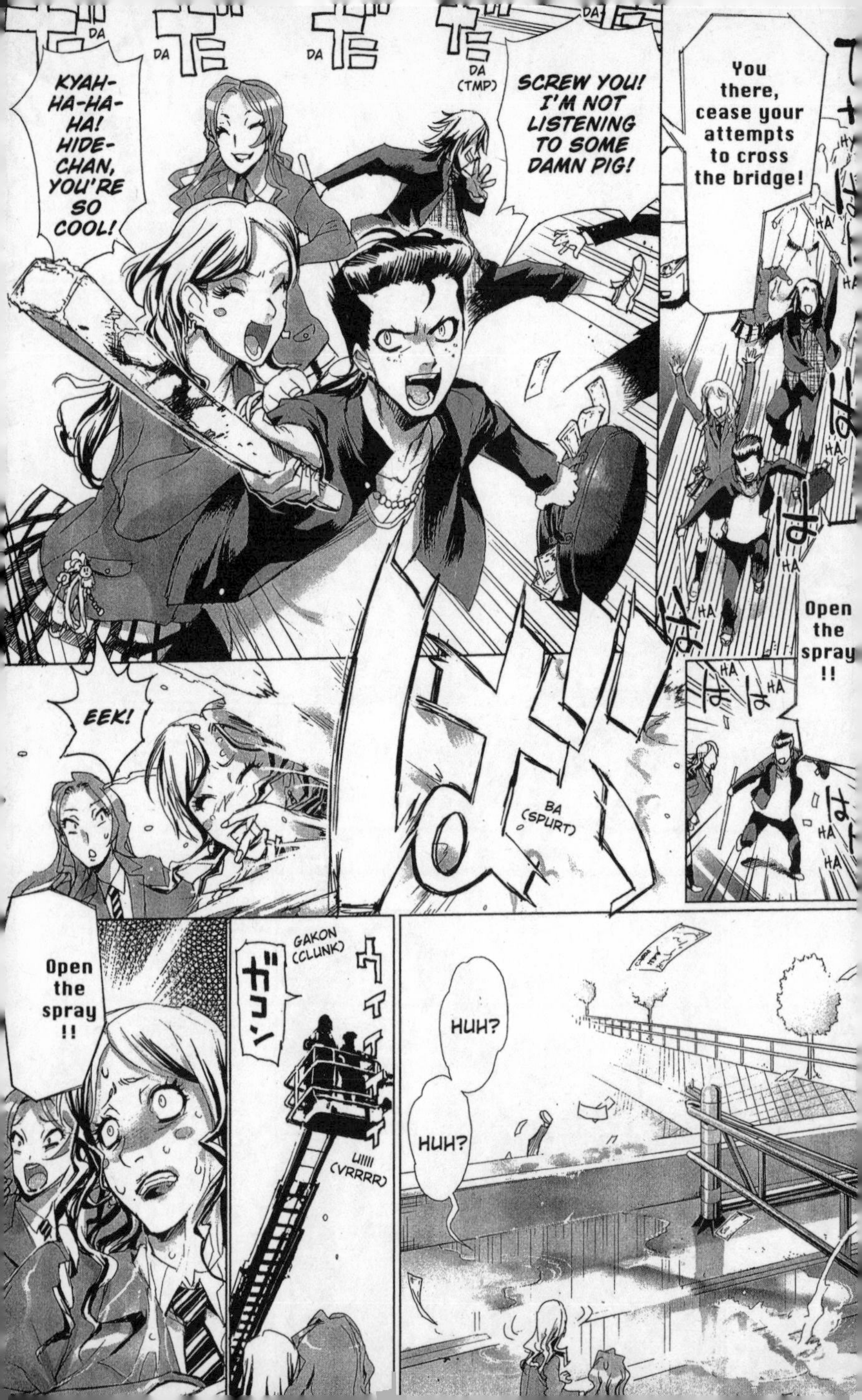
You there, cease your attempts to cross the bridge!
HA HA HA HA
DA DA DA DA DA (TMP)
SCREW YOU! I'M NOT LISTENING TO SOME DAMN PIG!
KYAH-HA-HA-HA! HIDE-CHAN, YOU'RE SO COOL!
HA HA HA HA HA
Open the spray!!
EEK!
BA (SPURT)
HUH?
HUH?
GAKON (CLUNK)
ガコン
UIIII (VRRRR)
Open the spray!!

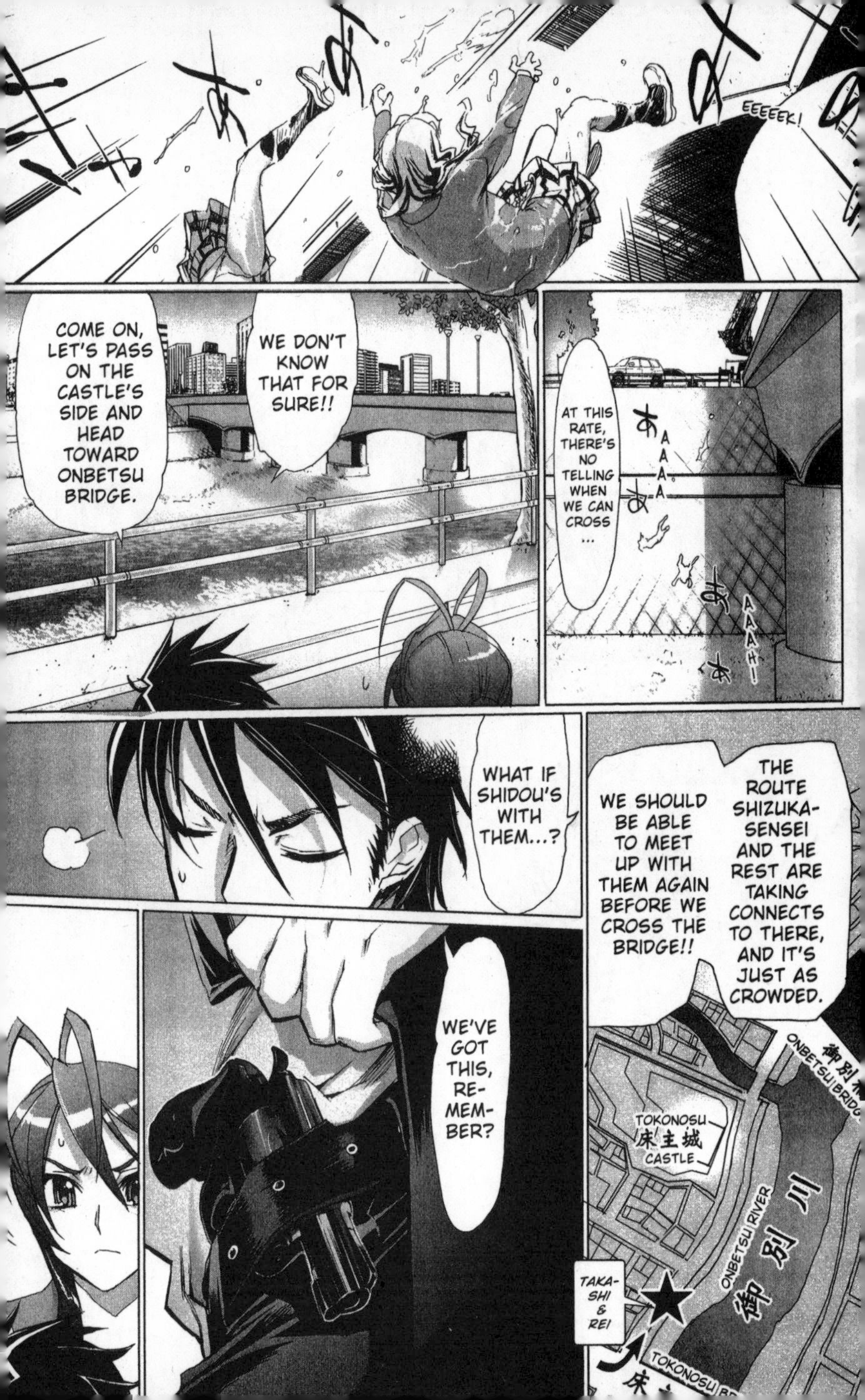

EEEEEK!
AT THIS RATE, THERE'S NO TELLING WHEN WE CAN CROSS...
AAAAA
AAAH!
COME ON, LET'S PASS ON THE CASTLE'S SIDE AND HEAD TOWARD ONBETSU BRIDGE.
WE DON'T KNOW THAT FOR SURE!!
THE ROUTE SHIZUKA-SENSEI AND THE REST ARE TAKING CONNECTS TO THERE, AND IT'S JUST AS CROWDED.
WE SHOULD BE ABLE TO MEET UP WITH THEM AGAIN BEFORE WE CROSS THE BRIDGE!!
ONBETSU BRIDG
TOKONOSU 床主城 CASTLE
ONBETSU RIVER
御別川
TAKA-SHI & REI
TOKONOSU BR
WHAT IF SHIDOU'S WITH THEM...?
WE'VE GOT THIS, RE-MEM-BER?

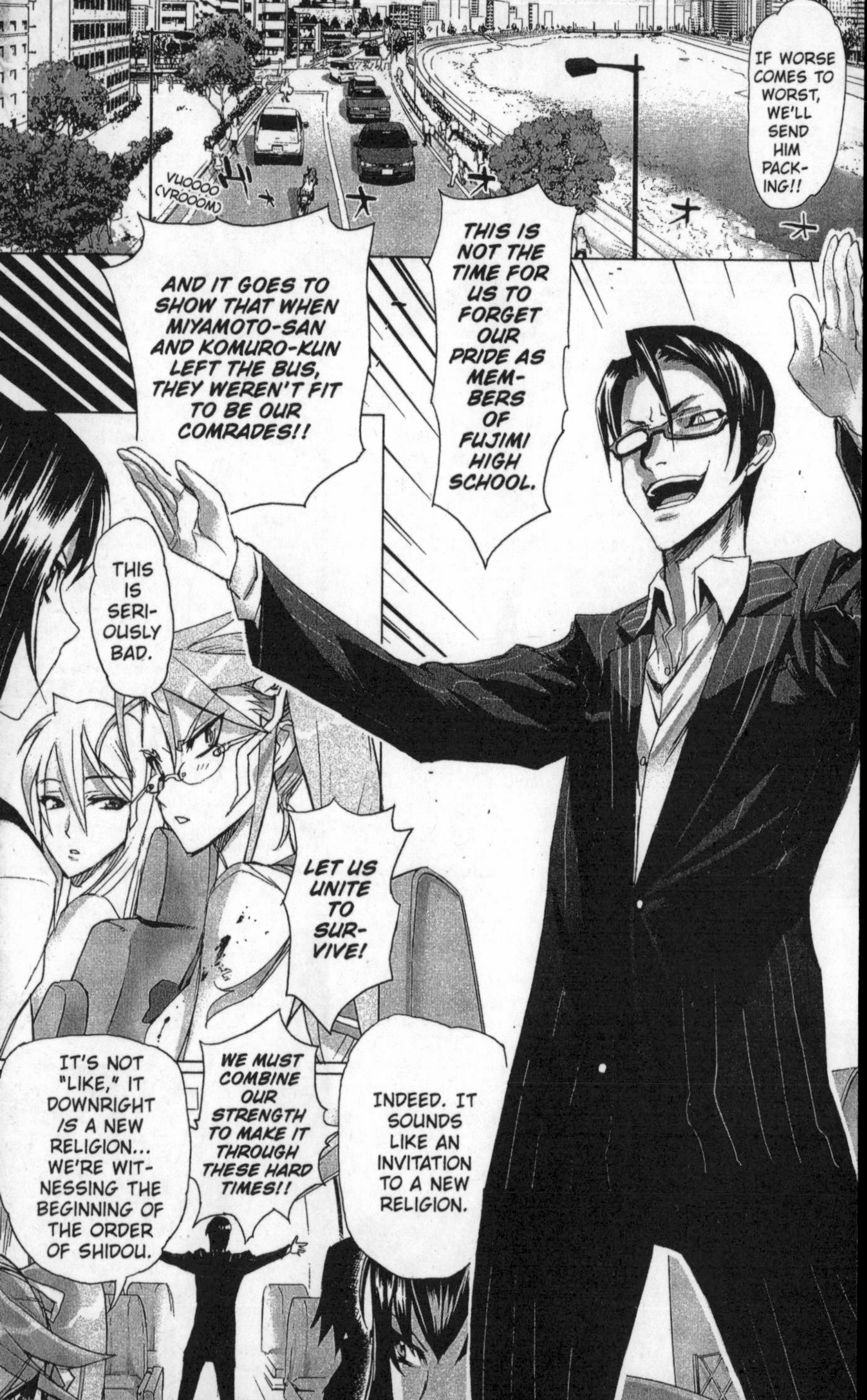
IF WORSE COMES TO WORST, WE'LL SEND HIM PACKING!!
VUOOOO (VROOOM)
THIS IS NOT THE TIME FOR US TO FORGET OUR PRIDE AS MEMBERS OF FUJIMI HIGH SCHOOL.
AND IT GOES TO SHOW THAT WHEN MIYAMOTO-SAN AND KOMURO-KUN LEFT THE BUS, THEY WEREN'T FIT TO BE OUR COMRADES!!
THIS IS SERIOUSLY BAD.
LET US UNITE TO SURVIVE!
INDEED. IT SOUNDS LIKE AN INVITATION TO A NEW RELIGION.
WE MUST COMBINE OUR STRENGTH TO MAKE IT THROUGH THESE HARD TIMES!!
IT'S NOT "LIKE," IT DOWNRIGHT *IS* A NEW RELIGION... WE'RE WITNESSING THE BEGINNING OF THE ORDER OF SHIDOU.

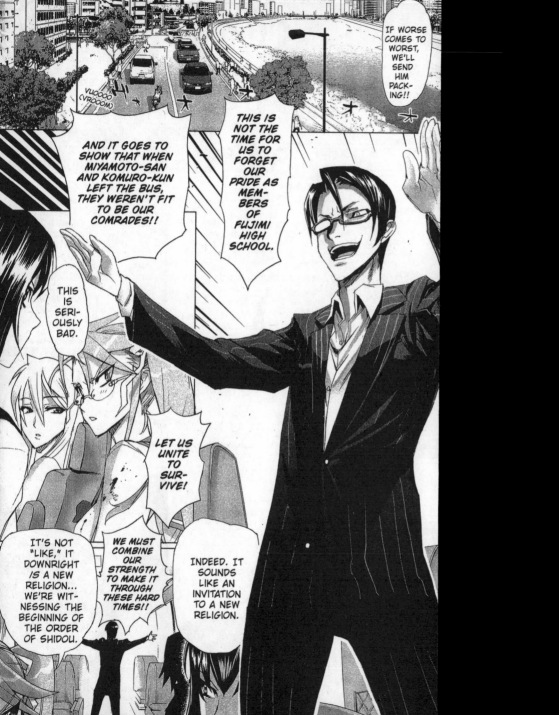

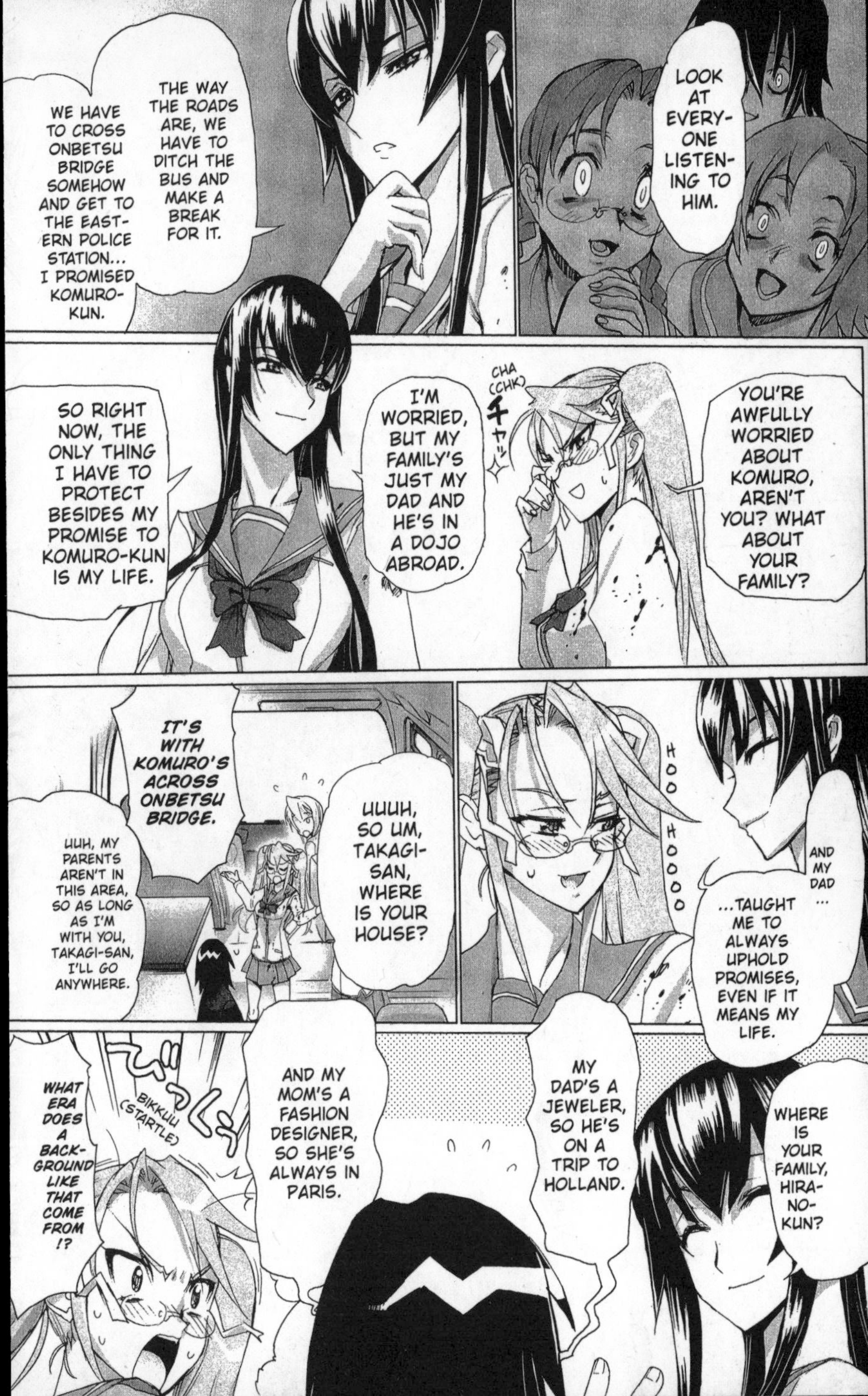
LOOK AT EVERYONE LISTENING TO HIM.
THE WAY THE ROADS ARE, WE HAVE TO DITCH THE BUS AND MAKE A BREAK FOR IT.
WE HAVE TO CROSS ONBETSU BRIDGE SOMEHOW AND GET TO THE EASTERN POLICE STATION... I PROMISED KOMURO-KUN.
YOU'RE AWFULLY WORRIED ABOUT KOMURO, AREN'T YOU? WHAT ABOUT YOUR FAMILY?
CHA (CHK)
I'M WORRIED, BUT MY FAMILY'S JUST MY DAD AND HE'S IN A DOJO ABROAD.
SO RIGHT NOW, THE ONLY THING I HAVE TO PROTECT BESIDES MY PROMISE TO KOMURO-KUN IS MY LIFE.
AND MY DAD...
...TAUGHT ME TO ALWAYS UPHOLD PROMISES, EVEN IF IT MEANS MY LIFE.
HOO HOOOOO
UUUH, SO UM, TAKAGI-SAN, WHERE IS YOUR HOUSE?
IT'S WITH KOMURO'S ACROSS ONBETSU BRIDGE.
UUH, MY PARENTS AREN'T IN THIS AREA, SO AS LONG AS I'M WITH YOU, TAKAGI-SAN, I'LL GO ANYWHERE.
WHERE IS YOUR FAMILY, HIRANO-KUN?
MY DAD'S A JEWELER, SO HE'S ON A TRIP TO HOLLAND.
AND MY MOM'S A FASHION DESIGNER, SO SHE'S ALWAYS IN PARIS.
BIKKUU (STARTLE)
WHAT ERA DOES A BACKGROUND LIKE THAT COME FROM!?

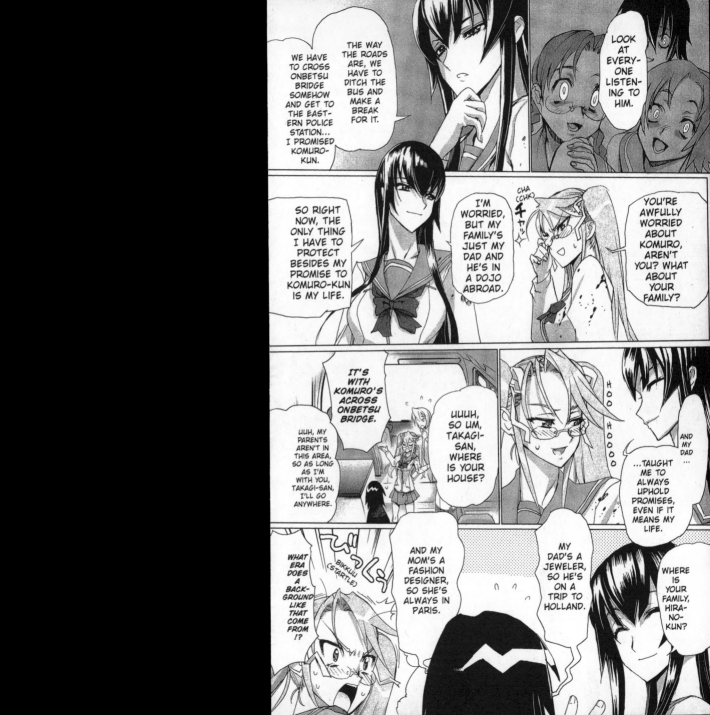

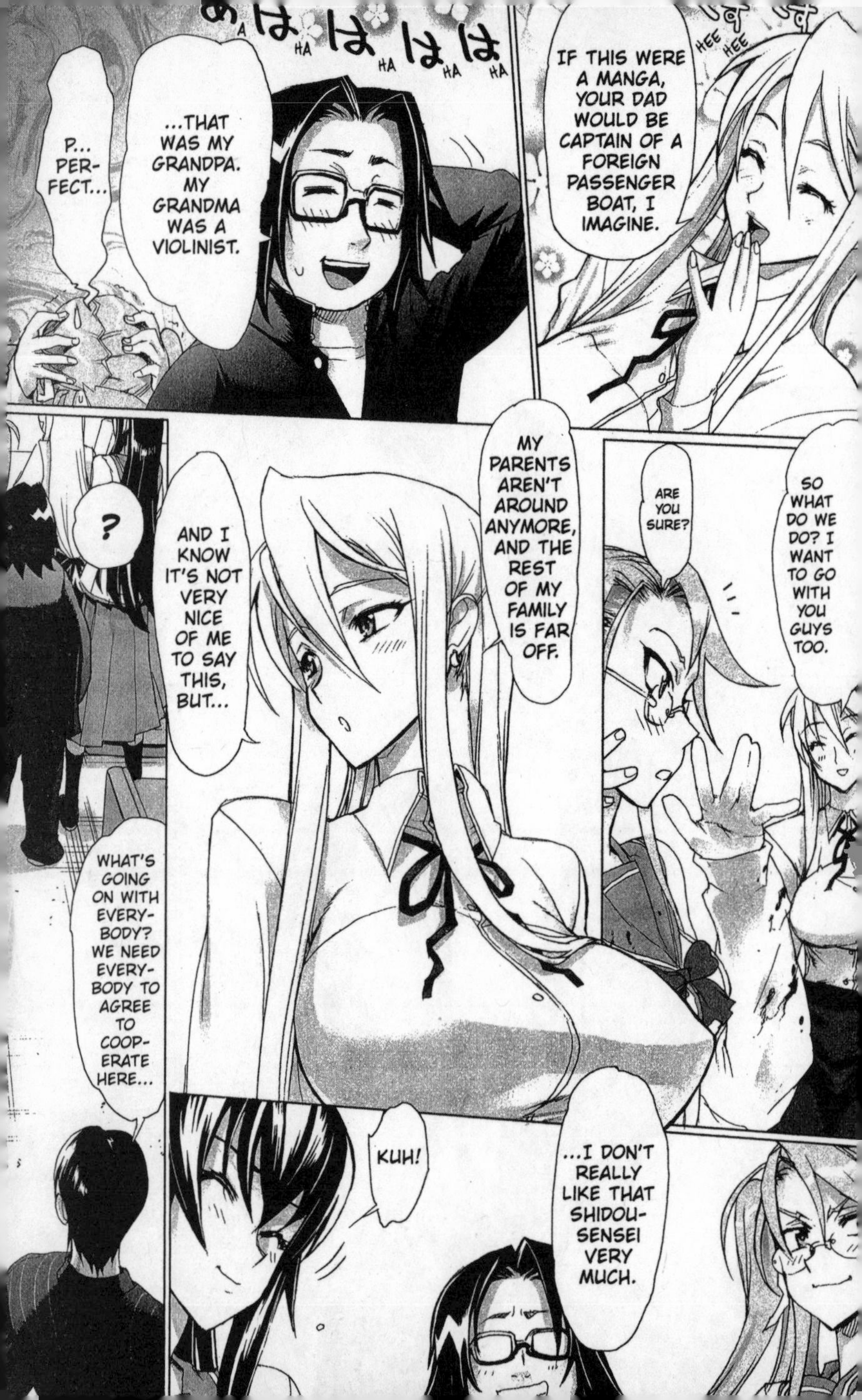
HEE HEE
IF THIS WERE A MANGA, YOUR DAD WOULD BE CAPTAIN OF A FOREIGN PASSENGER BOAT, I IMAGINE.
あはははは A HA HA HA HA
...THAT WAS MY GRANDPA. MY GRANDMA WAS A VIOLINIST.
P... PER-FECT...
SO WHAT DO WE DO? I WANT TO GO WITH YOU GUYS TOO.
ARE YOU SURE?
MY PARENTS AREN'T AROUND ANYMORE, AND THE REST OF MY FAMILY IS FAR OFF.
AND I KNOW IT'S NOT VERY NICE OF ME TO SAY THIS, BUT...
...I DON'T REALLY LIKE THAT SHIDOU-SENSEI VERY MUCH.
KUH!
?
WHAT'S GOING ON WITH EVERY-BODY? WE NEED EVERY-BODY TO AGREE TO COOP-ERATE HERE...

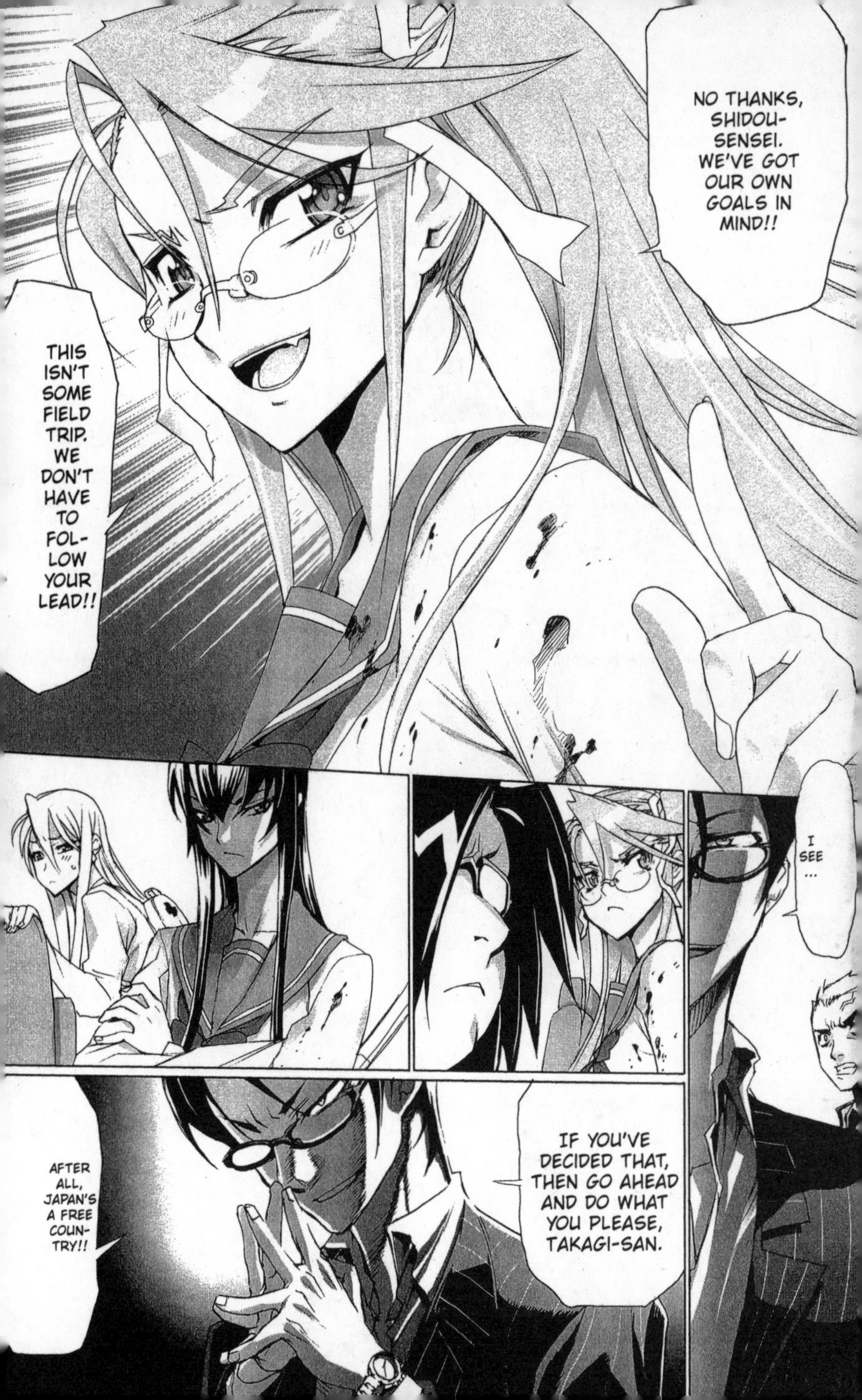
NO THANKS, SHIDOU-SENSEI. WE'VE GOT OUR OWN GOALS IN MIND!!
THIS ISN'T SOME FIELD TRIP. WE DON'T HAVE TO FOL-LOW YOUR LEAD!!
I SEE ...
IF YOU'VE DECIDED THAT, THEN GO AHEAD AND DO WHAT YOU PLEASE, TAKAGI-SAN.
AFTER ALL, JAPAN'S A FREE COUN-TRY!!

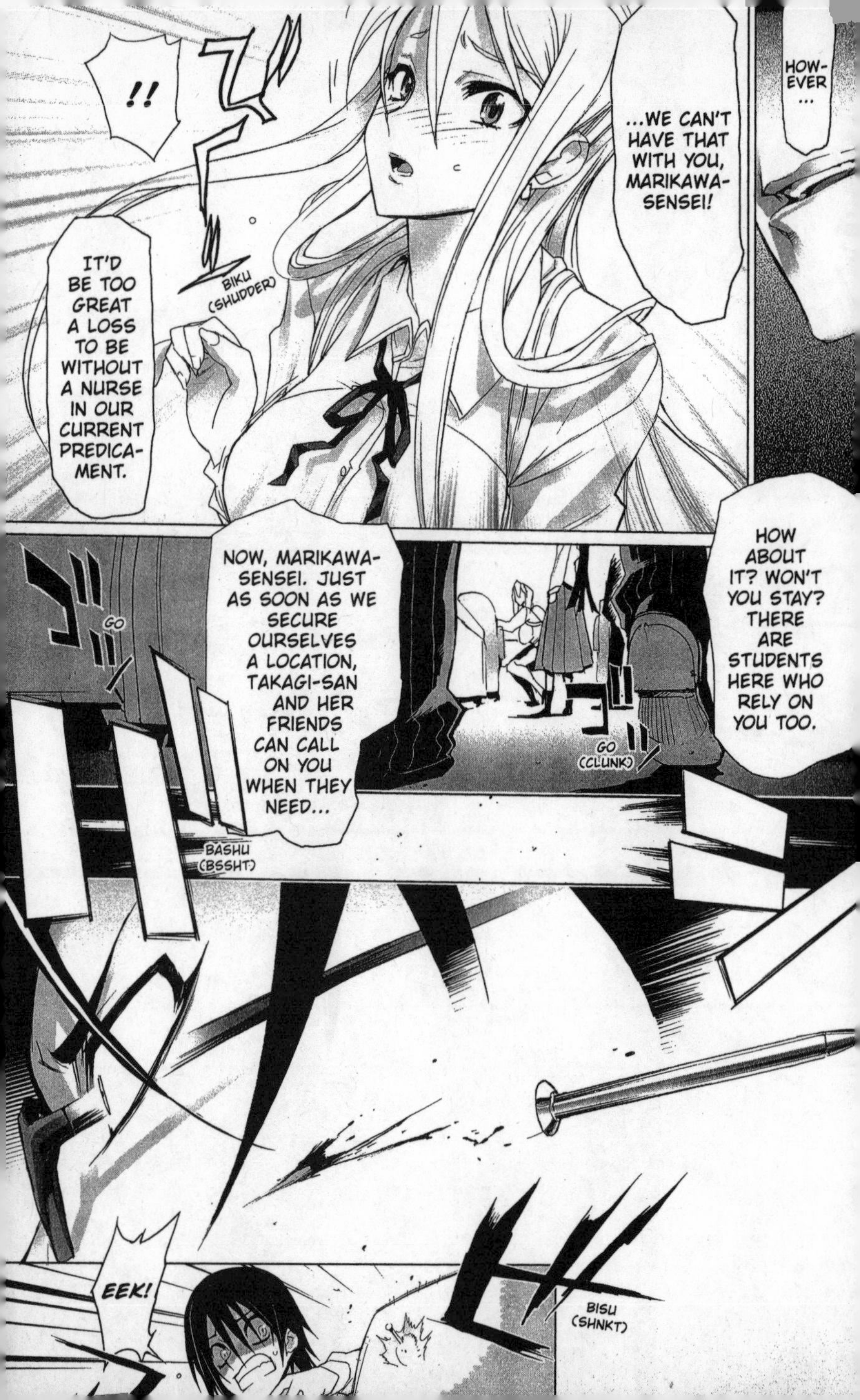
HOW-EVER...
...WE CAN'T HAVE THAT WITH YOU, MARIKAWA-SENSEI!
!!
BIKU (SHUDDER)
IT'D BE TOO GREAT A LOSS TO BE WITHOUT A NURSE IN OUR CURRENT PREDICA-MENT.
HOW ABOUT IT? WON'T YOU STAY? THERE ARE STUDENTS HERE WHO RELY ON YOU TOO.
GO (CLUNK)
NOW, MARIKAWA-SENSEI. JUST AS SOON AS WE SECURE OURSELVES A LOCATION, TAKAGI-SAN AND HER FRIENDS CAN CALL ON YOU WHEN THEY NEED...
GO
BASHU (BSSHT)
BISU (SHNKT)
EEK!

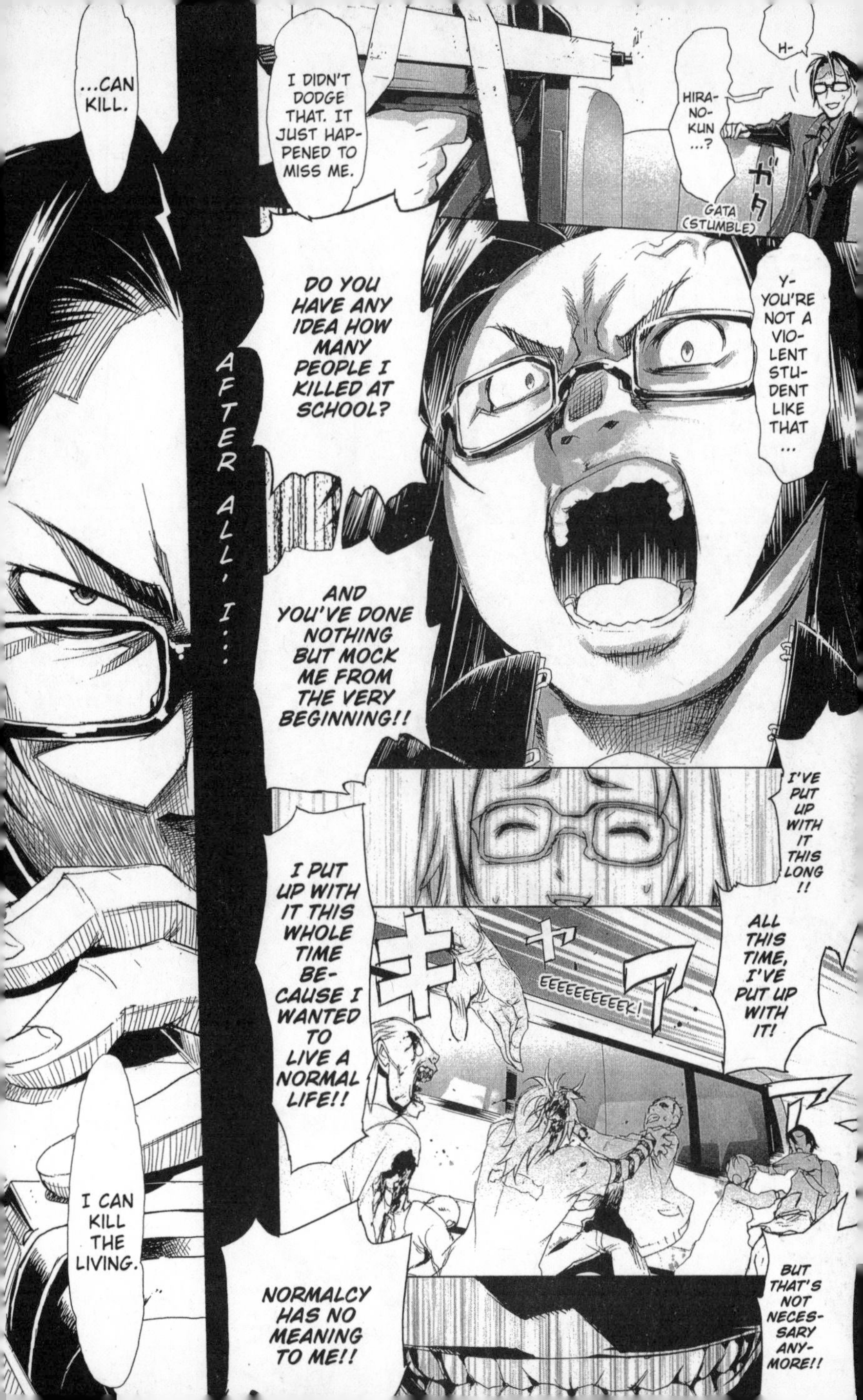
H-
HIRA-NO-KUN ...?
GATA (STUMBLE)
I DIDN'T DODGE THAT. IT JUST HAP-PENED TO MISS ME.
Y-YOU'RE NOT A VIO-LENT STU-DENT LIKE THAT ...
DO YOU HAVE ANY IDEA HOW MANY PEOPLE I KILLED AT SCHOOL?
AND YOU'VE DONE NOTHING BUT MOCK ME FROM THE VERY BEGINNING!!
I'VE PUT UP WITH IT THIS LONG!!
I PUT UP WITH IT THIS WHOLE TIME BE-CAUSE I WANTED TO LIVE A NORMAL LIFE!!
ALL THIS TIME, I'VE PUT UP WITH IT!
EEEEEEEEEEK!
BUT THAT'S NOT NECES-SARY ANY-MORE!!
NORMALCY HAS NO MEANING TO ME!!
AFTER ALL, I...
...CAN KILL.
I CAN KILL THE LIVING.

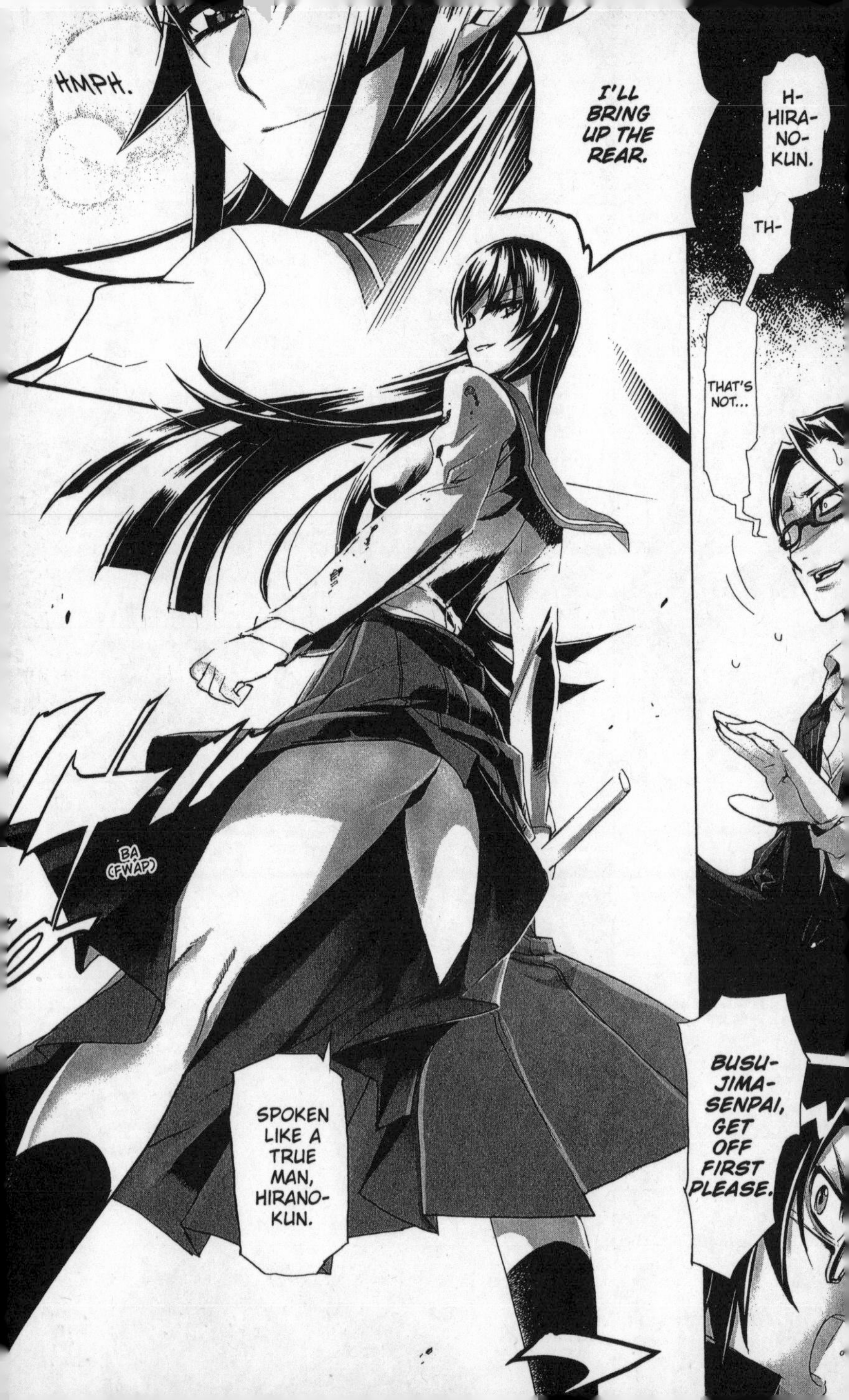
H-HIRA-NO-KUN.
TH-
THAT'S NOT...
BUSU-JIMA-SENPAI, GET OFF FIRST PLEASE.
I'LL BRING UP THE REAR.
HMPH.
BA (FWAP)
SPOKEN LIKE A TRUE MAN, HIRANO-KUN.

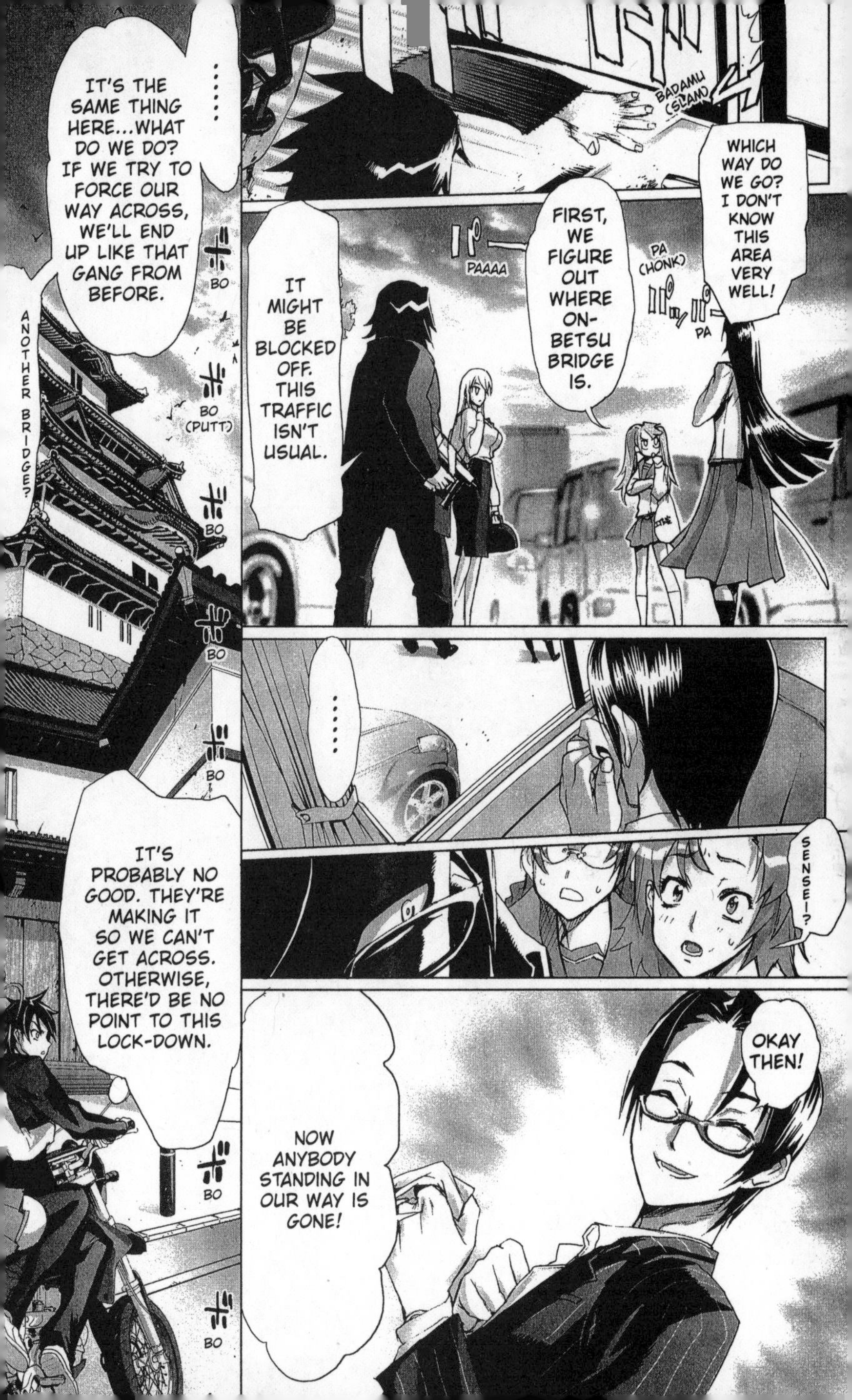
BADAMU (SLAM)
WHICH WAY DO WE GO? I DON'T KNOW THIS AREA VERY WELL!
PA (HONK)
PA
FIRST, WE FIGURE OUT WHERE ON-BETSU BRIDGE IS.
PAAAA
IT MIGHT BE BLOCKED OFF. THIS TRAFFIC ISN'T USUAL.
......
SENSEI?
OKAY THEN!
NOW ANYBODY STANDING IN OUR WAY IS GONE!
......
IT'S THE SAME THING HERE...WHAT DO WE DO? IF WE TRY TO FORCE OUR WAY ACROSS, WE'LL END UP LIKE THAT GANG FROM BEFORE.
BO
ANOTHER BRIDGE?
BO (PUTT)
BO
BO
BO
IT'S PROBABLY NO GOOD. THEY'RE MAKING IT SO WE CAN'T GET ACROSS. OTHERWISE, THERE'D BE NO POINT TO THIS LOCK-DOWN.
BO
BO

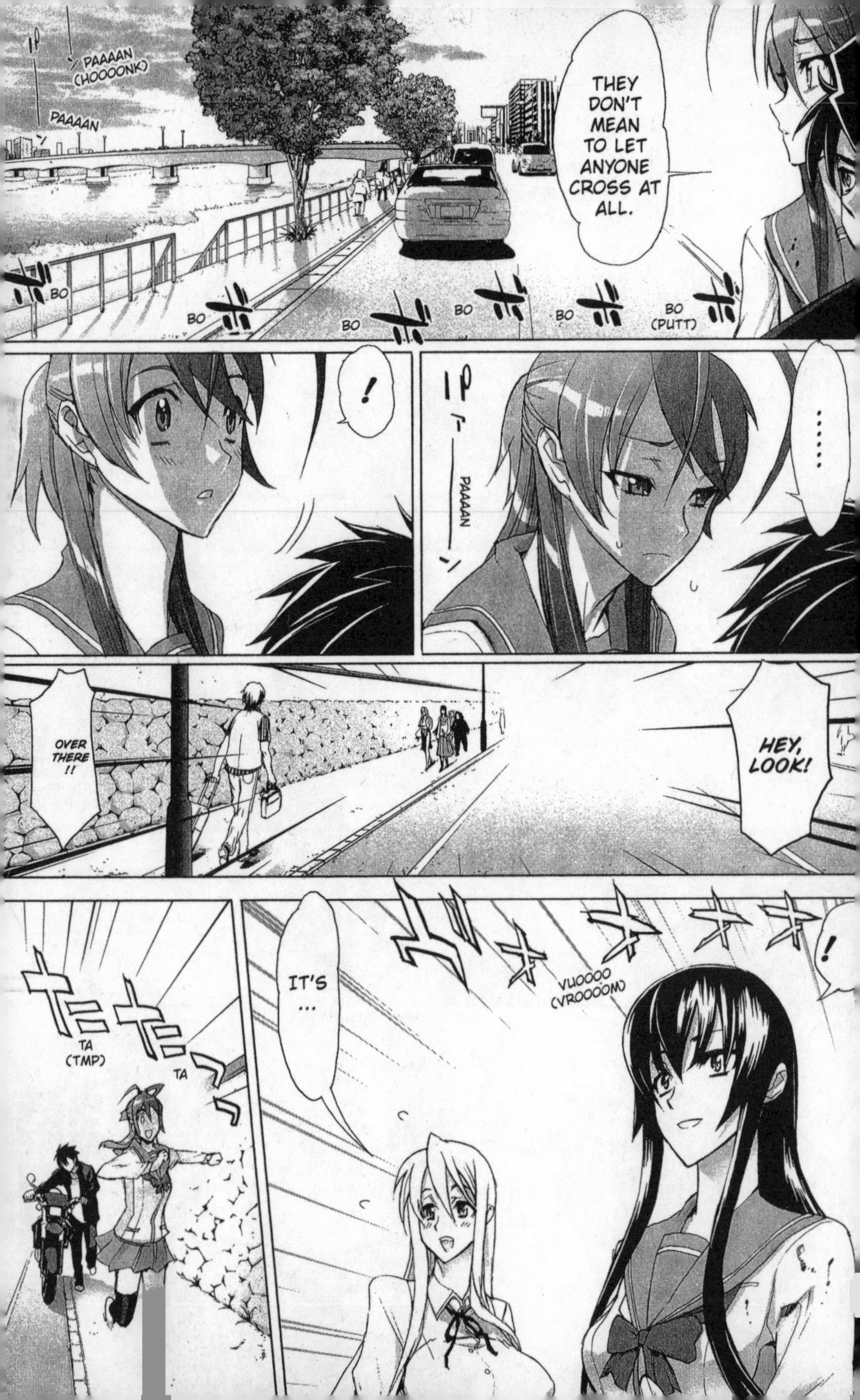
THEY DON'T MEAN TO LET ANYONE CROSS AT ALL.
PAAAAN (HOOOONK)
PAAAAN
BO BO BO BO BO BO (PUTT)
……
PAAAAN
!
HEY, LOOK!
OVER THERE !!
!
VUOOOO (VROOOOM)
IT'S ...
TA (TMP)
TA

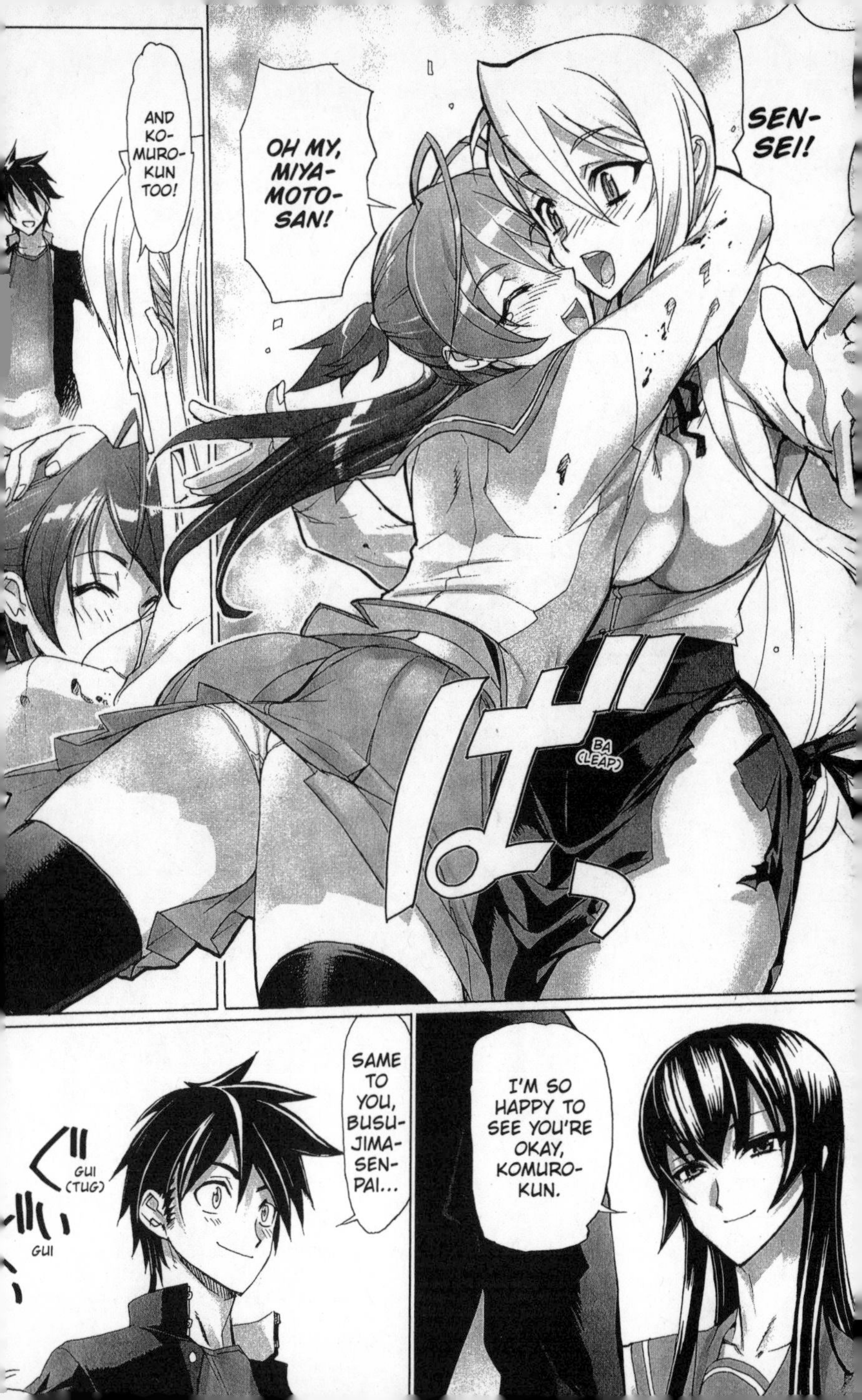
SEN-SEI!
OH MY, MIYA-MOTO-SAN!
AND KO-MURO-KUN TOO!
BA (LEAP)
I'M SO HAPPY TO SEE YOU'RE OKAY, KOMURO-KUN.
SAME TO YOU, BUSU-JIMA-SEN-PAI...
GUI (TUG)
GUI

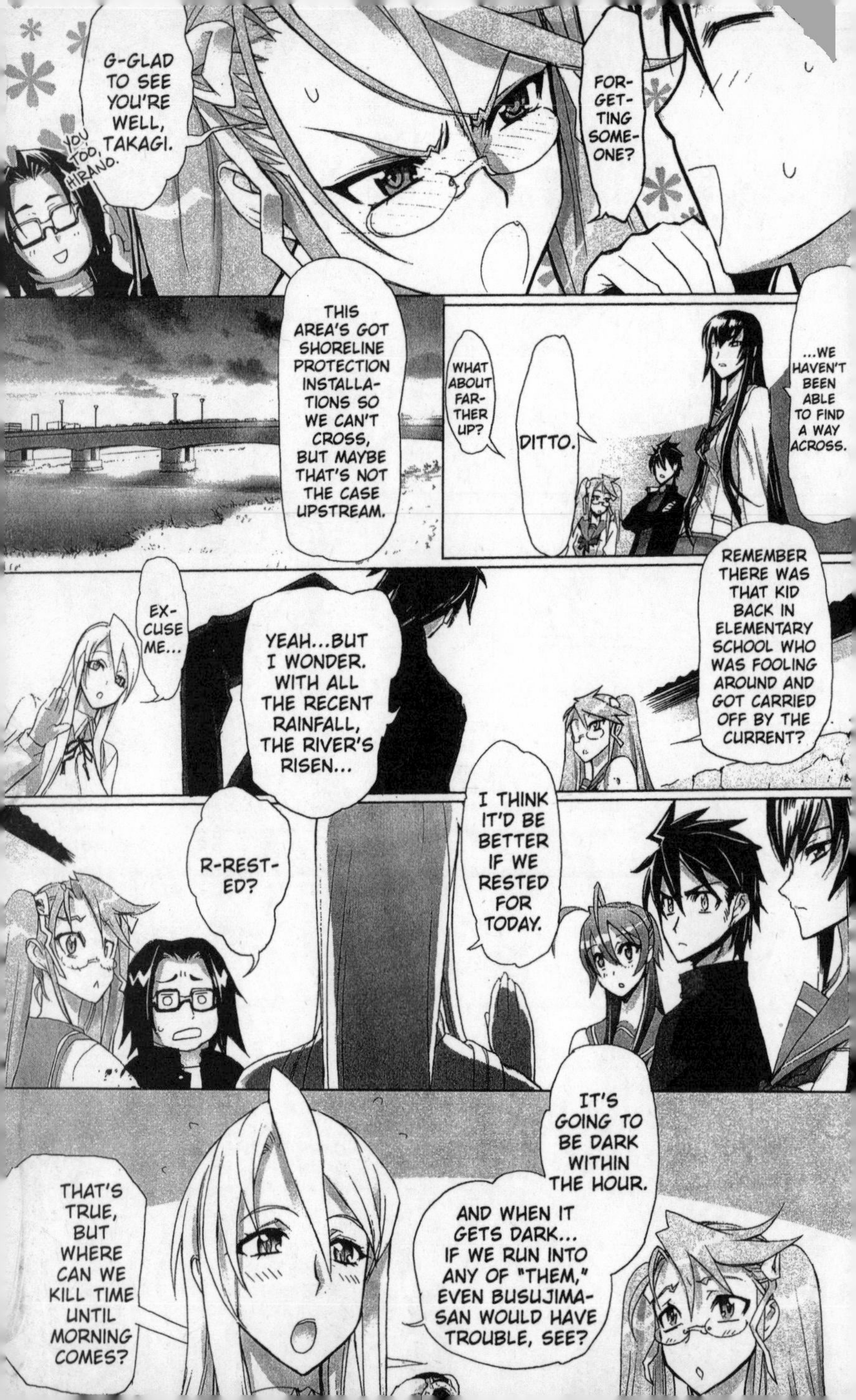
FOR-GET-TING SOME-ONE?
G-GLAD TO SEE YOU'RE WELL, TAKAGI.
YOU TOO, HIRANO.
...WE HAVEN'T BEEN ABLE TO FIND A WAY ACROSS.
WHAT ABOUT FAR-THER UP?
DITTO.
THIS AREA'S GOT SHORELINE PROTECTION INSTALLA-TIONS SO WE CAN'T CROSS, BUT MAYBE THAT'S NOT THE CASE UPSTREAM.
REMEMBER THERE WAS THAT KID BACK IN ELEMENTARY SCHOOL WHO WAS FOOLING AROUND AND GOT CARRIED OFF BY THE CURRENT?
YEAH...BUT I WONDER. WITH ALL THE RECENT RAINFALL, THE RIVER'S RISEN...
EX-CUSE ME...
I THINK IT'D BE BETTER IF WE RESTED FOR TODAY.
R-REST-ED?
IT'S GOING TO BE DARK WITHIN THE HOUR.
AND WHEN IT GETS DARK... IF WE RUN INTO ANY OF "THEM," EVEN BUSUJIMA-SAN WOULD HAVE TROUBLE, SEE?
THAT'S TRUE, BUT WHERE CAN WE KILL TIME UNTIL MORNING COMES?

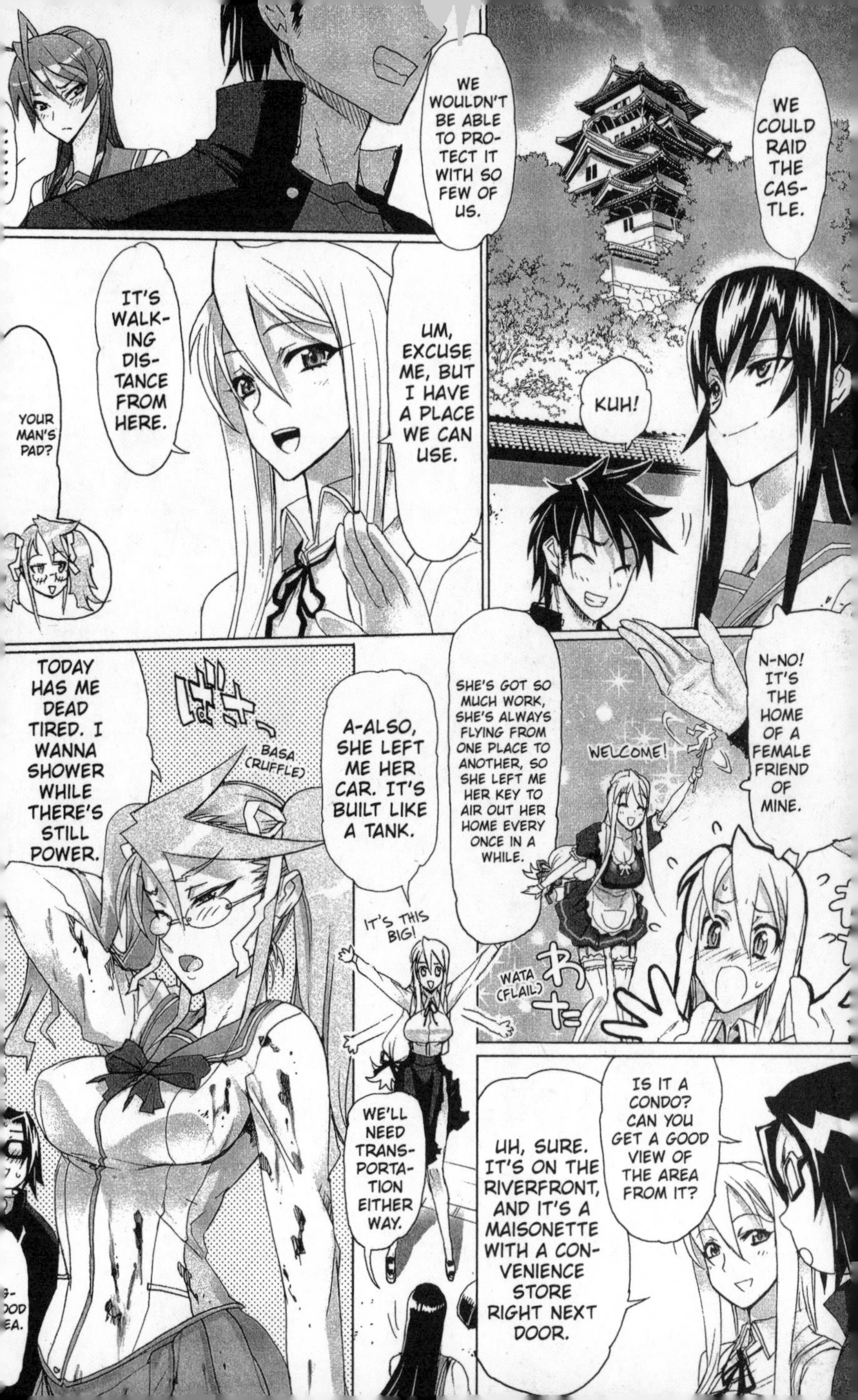
WE COULD RAID THE CAS-TLE.
KUH!
WE WOULDN'T BE ABLE TO PRO-TECT IT WITH SO FEW OF US.
...
UM, EXCUSE ME, BUT I HAVE A PLACE WE CAN USE.
IT'S WALK-ING DIS-TANCE FROM HERE.
YOUR MAN'S PAD?
N-NO! IT'S THE HOME OF A FEMALE FRIEND OF MINE.
WELCOME!
SHE'S GOT SO MUCH WORK, SHE'S ALWAYS FLYING FROM ONE PLACE TO ANOTHER, SO SHE LEFT ME HER KEY TO AIR OUT HER HOME EVERY ONCE IN A WHILE.
WATA (FLAIL)
IS IT A CONDO? CAN YOU GET A GOOD VIEW OF THE AREA FROM IT?
UH, SURE. IT'S ON THE RIVERFRONT, AND IT'S A MAISONETTE WITH A CON-VENIENCE STORE RIGHT NEXT DOOR.
A-ALSO, SHE LEFT ME HER CAR. IT'S BUILT LIKE A TANK.
IT'S THIS BIG!
WE'LL NEED TRANS-PORTA-TION EITHER WAY.
BASA (RUFFLE)
TODAY HAS ME DEAD TIRED. I WANNA SHOWER WHILE THERE'S STILL POWER.

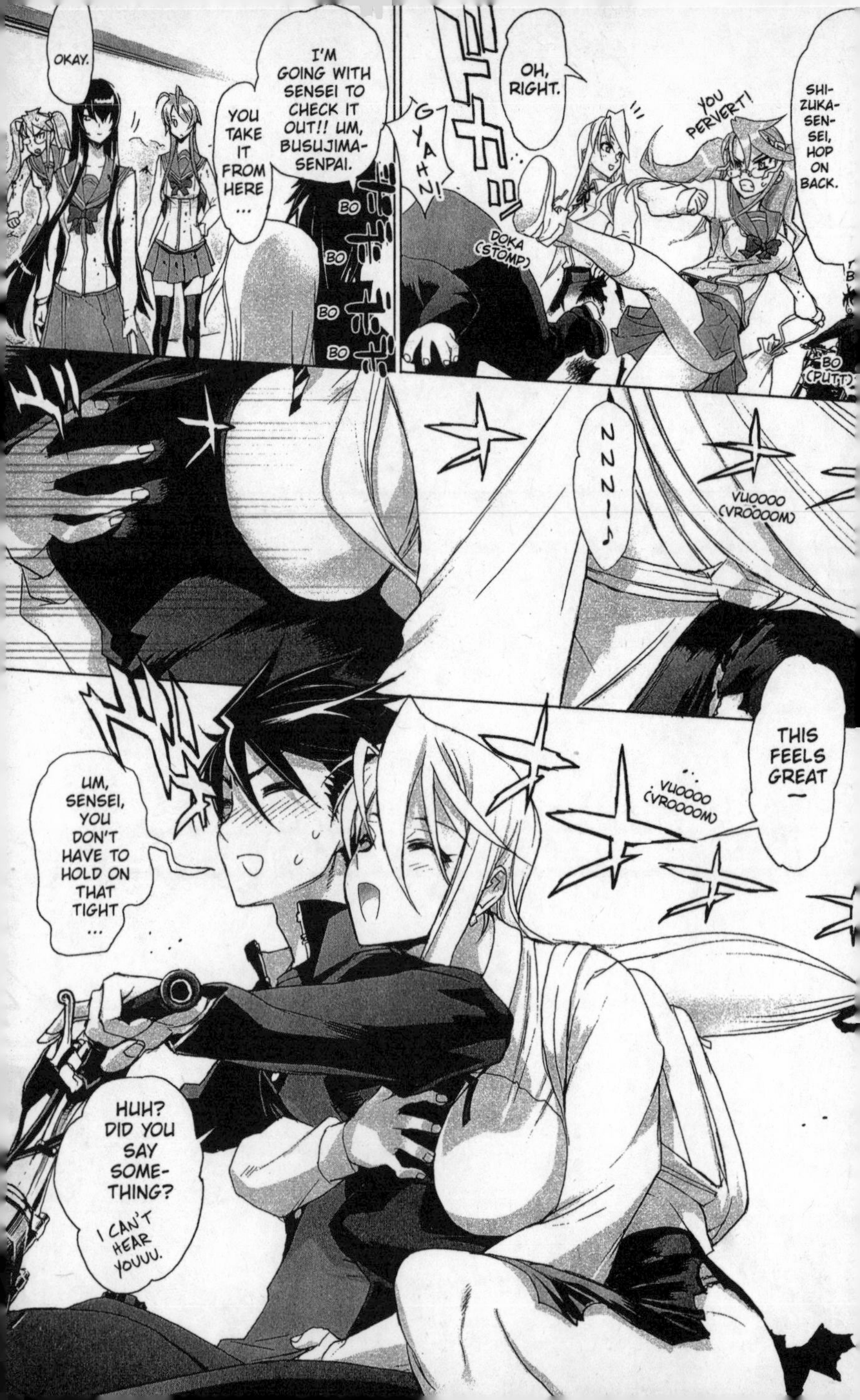
SHI-ZUKA-SEN-SEI, HOP ON BACK.
YOU PERVERT!
OH, RIGHT.
GYAHN!
DOKA (STOMP)
BO (PUTT)
I'M GOING WITH SENSEI TO CHECK IT OUT!! UM, BUSUJIMA-SENPAI.
YOU TAKE IT FROM HERE...
OKAY.
BO
BO
BO
BO
NNN~♪
VUOOOO (VROOOOM)
THIS FEELS GREAT—
VUOOOO (VROOOOM)
UM, SENSEI, YOU DON'T HAVE TO HOLD ON THAT TIGHT...
HUH? DID YOU SAY SOME-THING?
I CAN'T HEAR YOUUU.

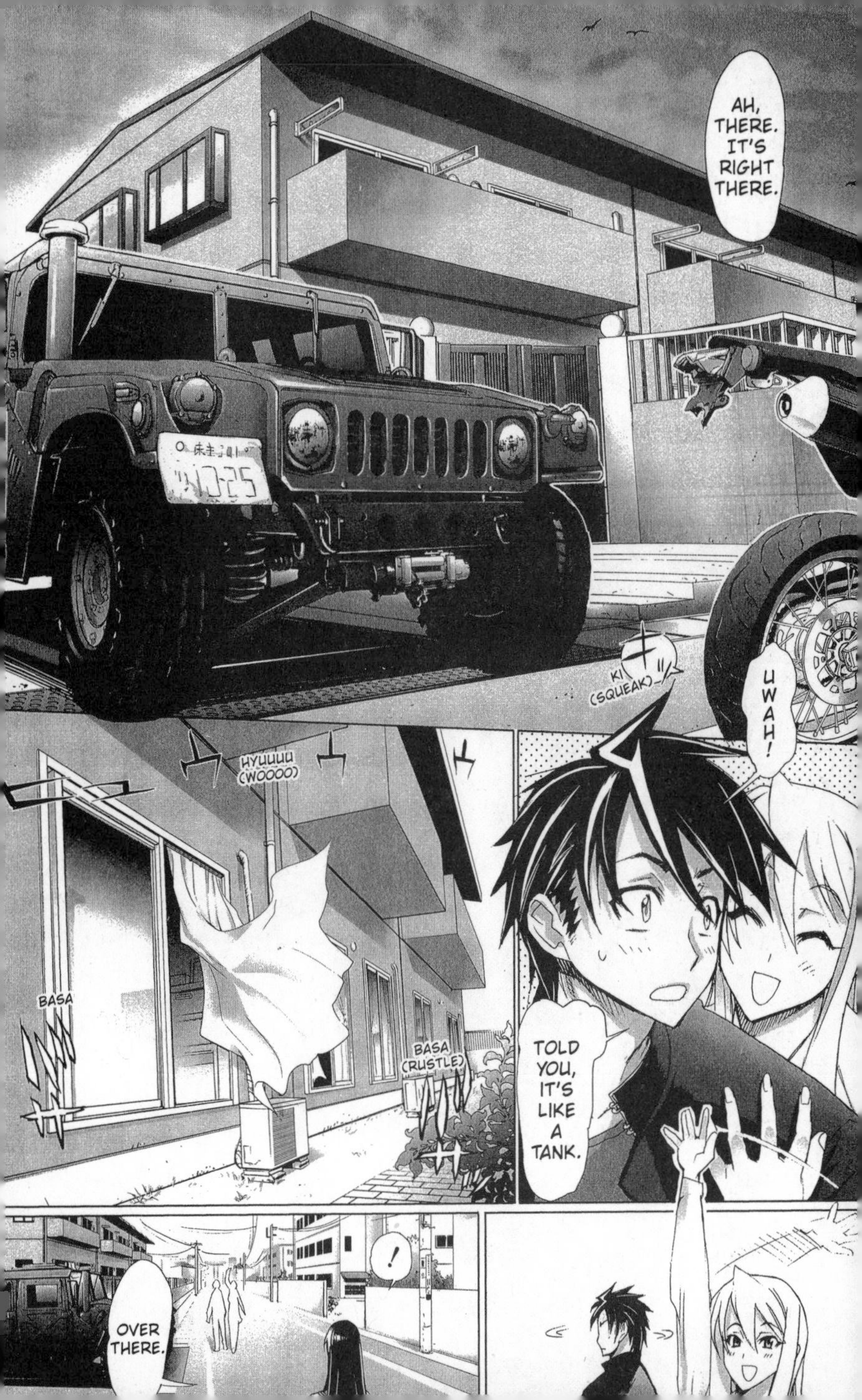
AH, THERE. IT'S RIGHT THERE.
KI (SQUEAK)
UWAH!
TOLD YOU, IT'S LIKE A TANK.
HYUUUU (WOOOO)
BASA (RUSTLE)
BASA
!
OVER THERE.

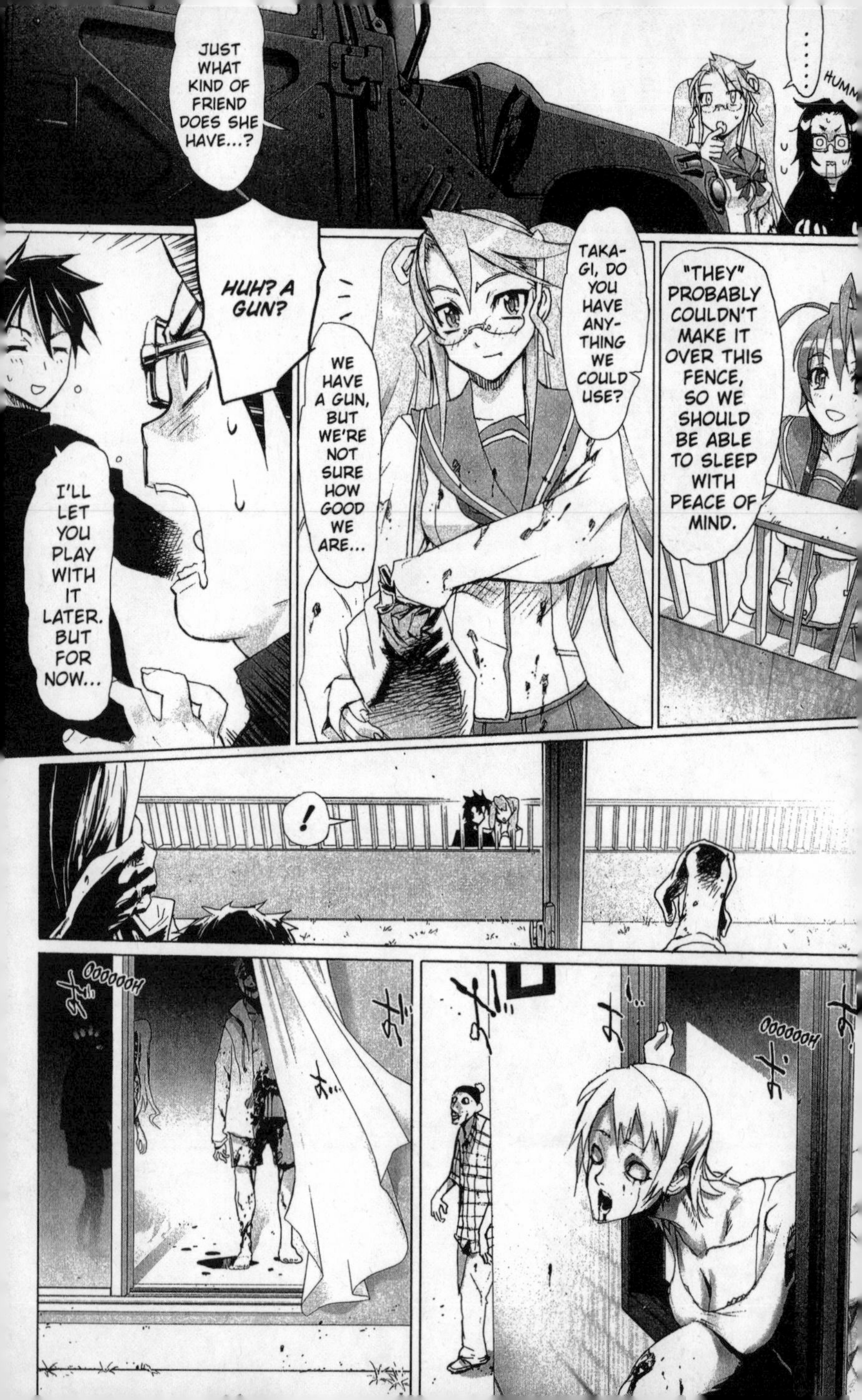

......
HUMM
JUST WHAT KIND OF FRIEND DOES SHE HAVE...?
"THEY" PROBABLY COULDN'T MAKE IT OVER THIS FENCE, SO WE SHOULD BE ABLE TO SLEEP WITH PEACE OF MIND.
TAKA-GI, DO YOU HAVE ANY-THING WE COULD USE?
WE HAVE A GUN, BUT WE'RE NOT SURE HOW GOOD WE ARE...
HUH? A GUN?
I'LL LET YOU PLAY WITH IT LATER. BUT FOR NOW...
!
OOOOOOH
OOOOOOH

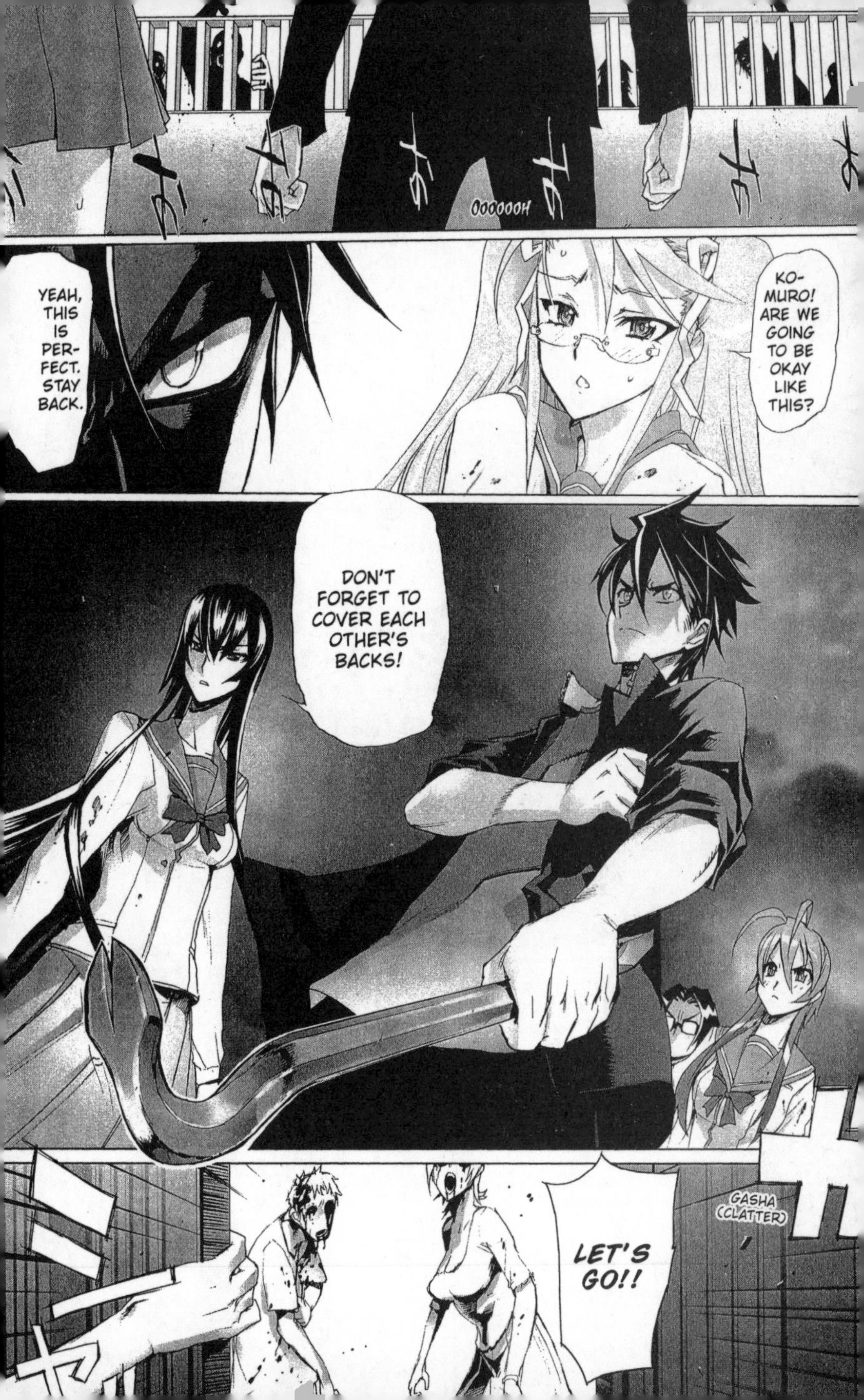
OOOOOOH
KO-MURO! ARE WE GOING TO BE OKAY LIKE THIS?
YEAH, THIS IS PER-FECT. STAY BACK.
DON'T FORGET TO COVER EACH OTHER'S BACKS!
GASHA (CLATTER)
LET'S GO!!

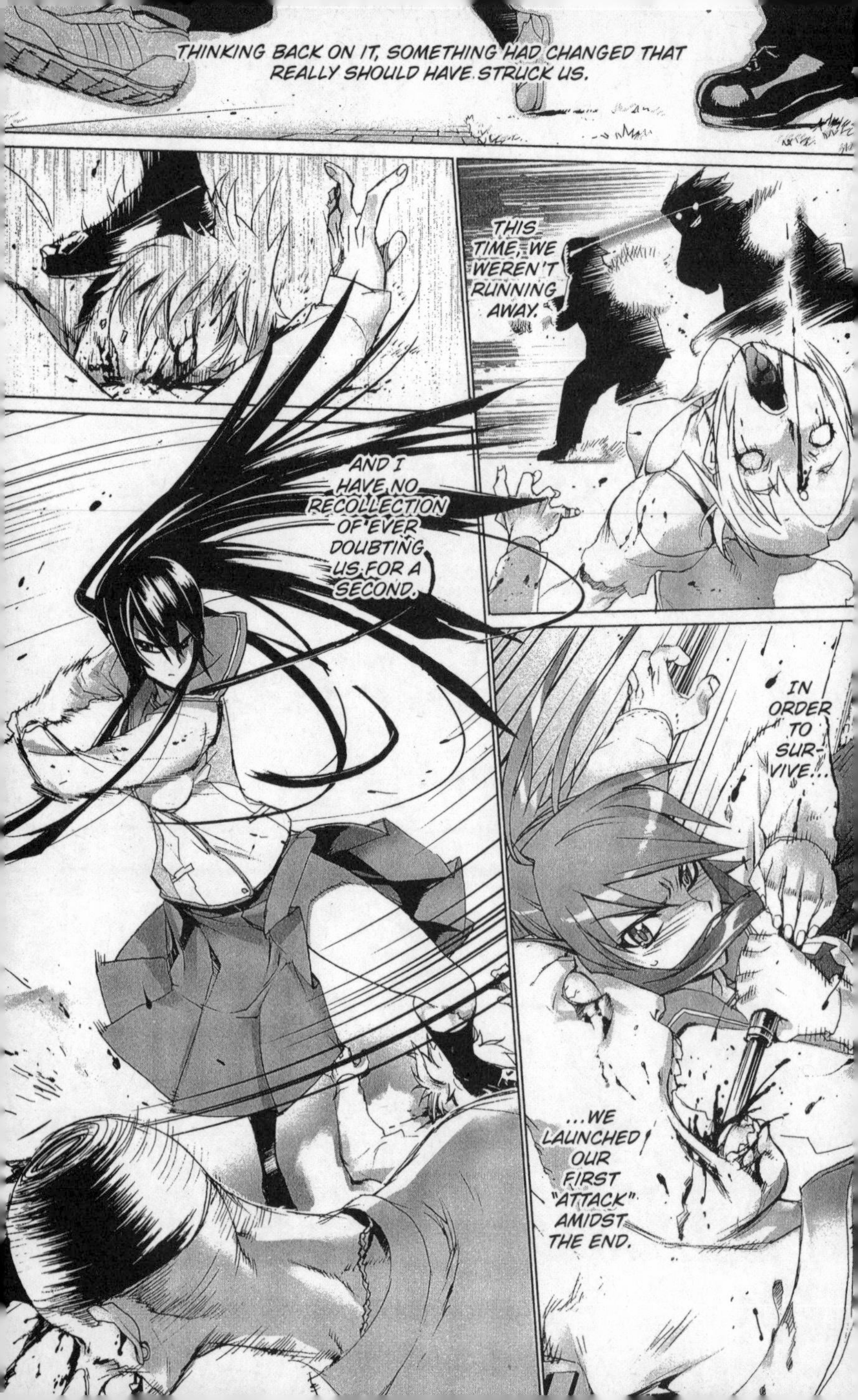
THINKING BACK ON IT, SOMETHING HAD CHANGED THAT REALLY SHOULD HAVE STRUCK US.
THIS TIME, WE WEREN'T RUNNING AWAY.
AND I HAVE NO RECOLLECTION OF EVER DOUBTING US FOR A SECOND.
IN ORDER TO SUR-VIVE...
...WE LAUNCHED OUR FIRST "ATTACK" AMIDST THE END.

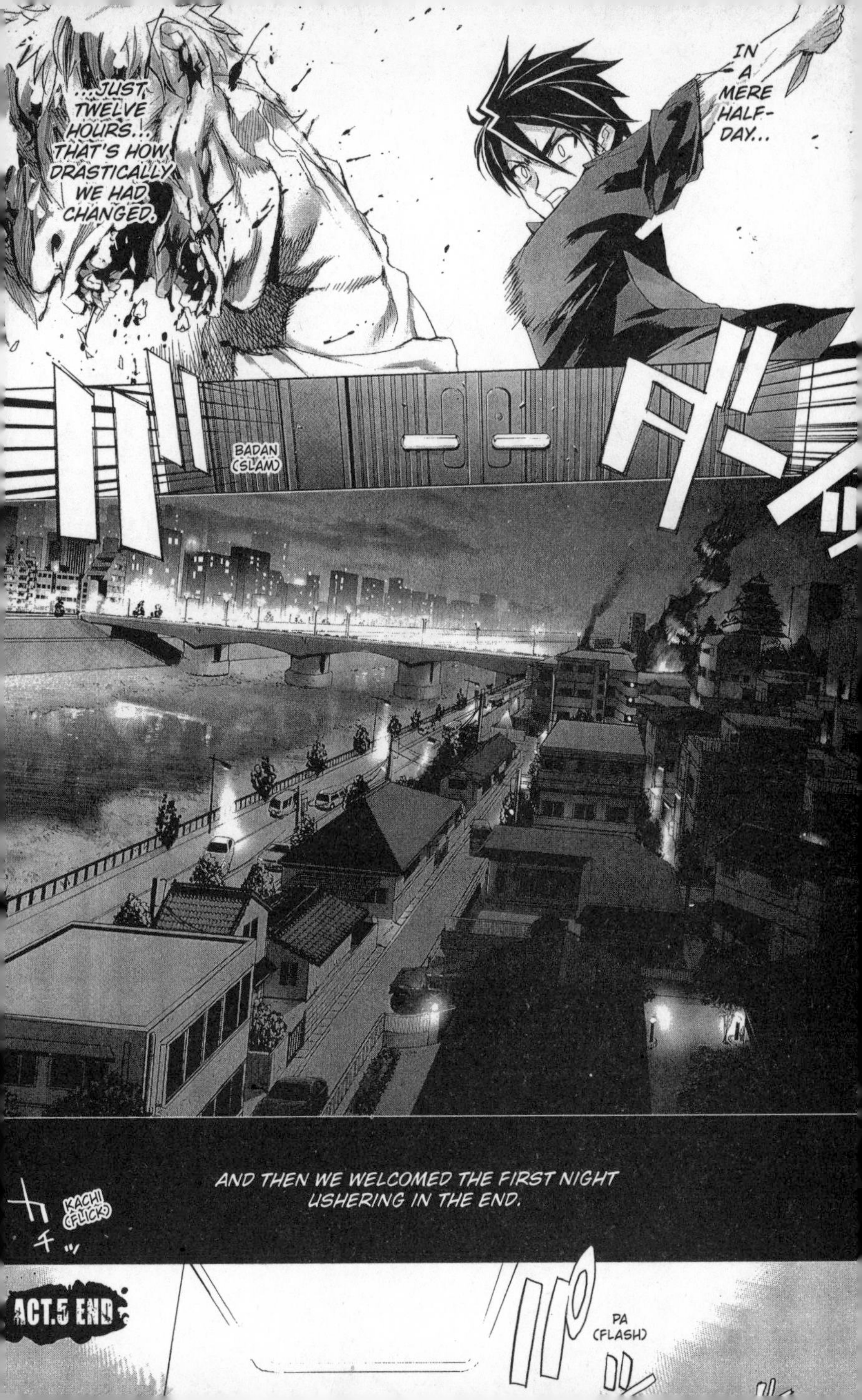
IN A MERE HALF-DAY...
...JUST TWELVE HOURS... THAT'S HOW DRASTICALLY WE HAD CHANGED.
BADAN (SLAM)
AND THEN WE WELCOMED THE FIRST NIGHT USHERING IN THE END.
KACHI (FLICK)
PA (FLASH)
ACT.5 END

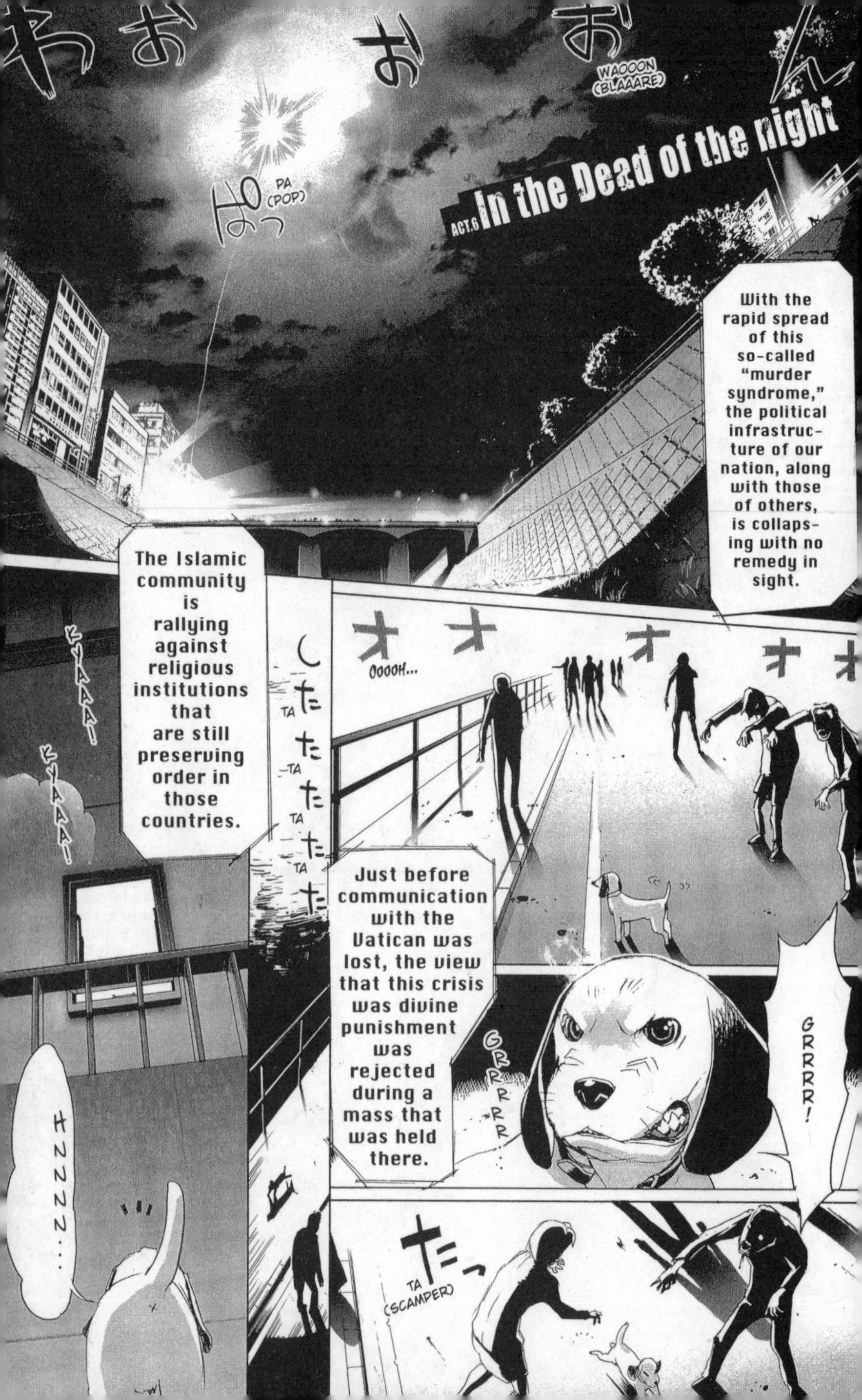

WAOOON (BLAAARE)
PA (POP)
ACT.6 In the Dead of the night
With the rapid spread of this so-called "murder syndrome," the political infrastructure of our nation, along with those of others, is collapsing with no remedy in sight.
OOOOH...
The Islamic community is rallying against religious institutions that are still preserving order in those countries.
TA TA TA TA
GRRRR!
Just before communication with the Vatican was lost, the view that this crisis was divine punishment was rejected during a mass that was held there.
GRRRR
TA (SCAMPER)
KYAAAA!
KYAAAA!
HNNNN...

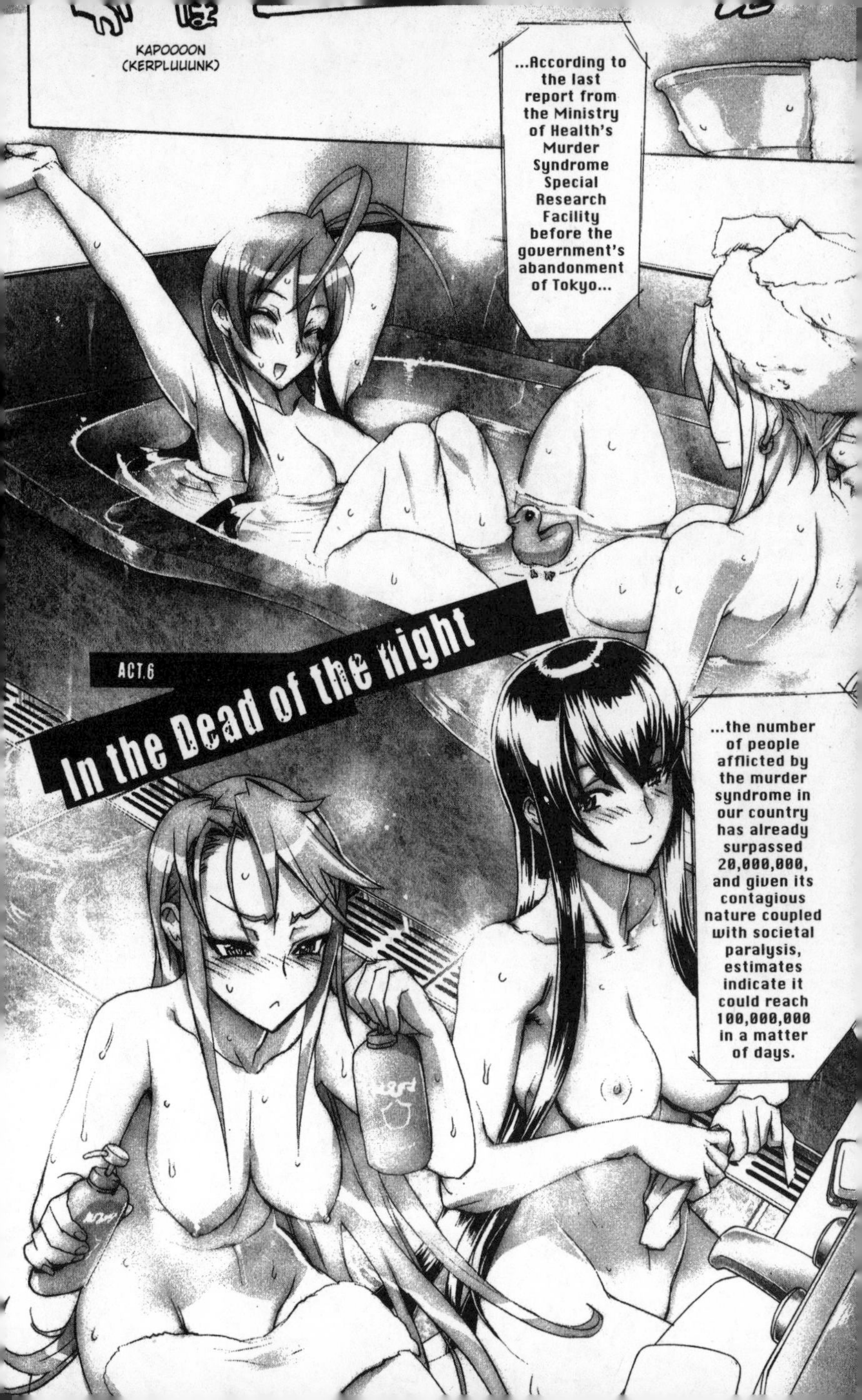
KAPOOOON
(KERPLUUUNK)
...According to the last report from the Ministry of Health's Murder Syndrome Special Research Facility before the government's abandonment of Tokyo...
ACT.6
In the Dead of the Night
...the number of people afflicted by the murder syndrome in our country has already surpassed 20,000,000, and given its contagious nature coupled with societal paralysis, estimates indicate it could reach 100,000,000 in a matter of days.

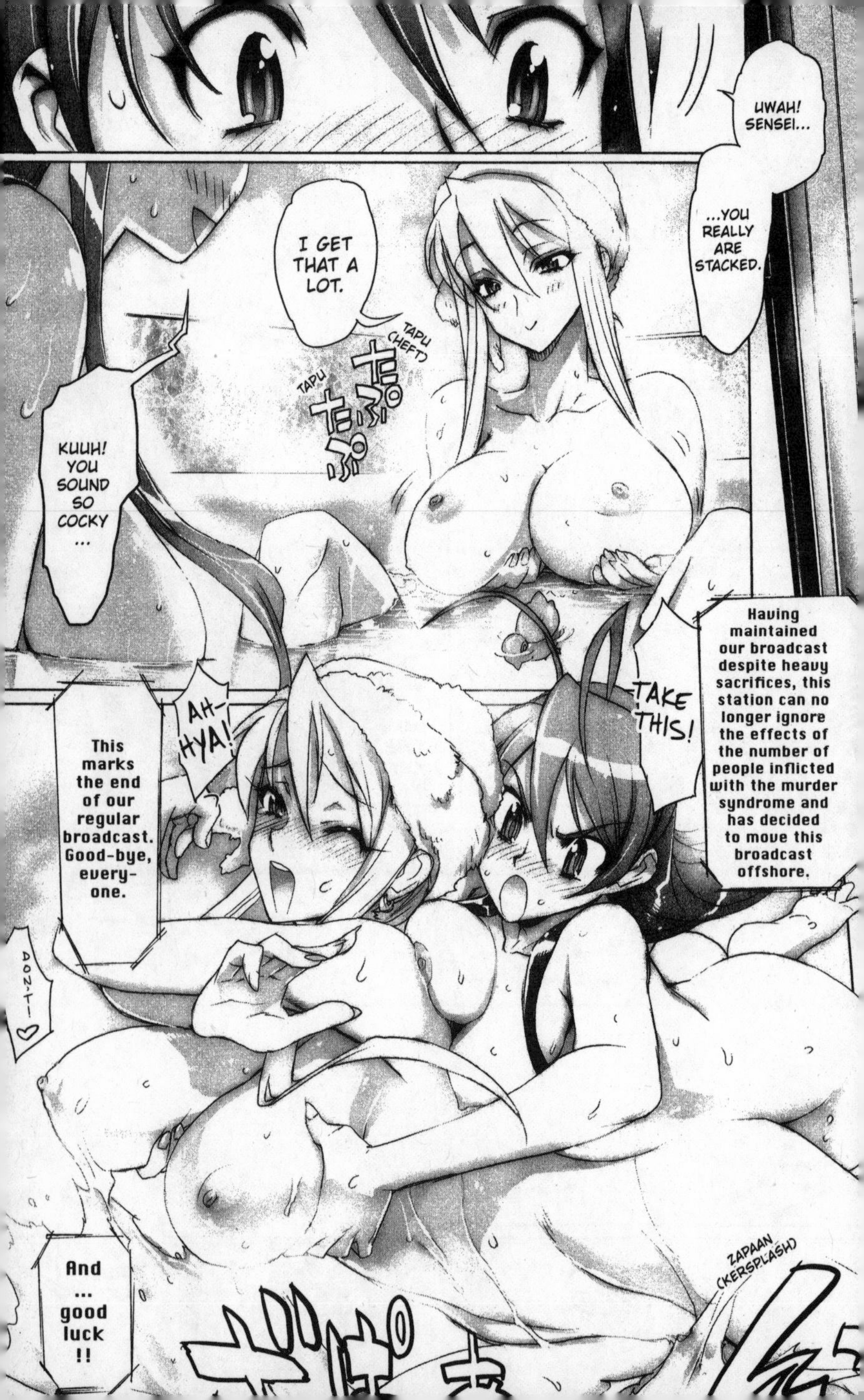
UWAH! SENSEI...
...YOU REALLY ARE STACKED.
I GET THAT A LOT.
TAPU (HEFT)
TAPU
KUUH! YOU SOUND SO COCKY ...
Having maintained our broadcast despite heavy sacrifices, this station can no longer ignore the effects of the number of people inflicted with the murder syndrome and has decided to move this broadcast offshore.
TAKE THIS!
AH-HYA!
This marks the end of our regular broadcast. Good-bye, every-one.
DON'T!♡
ZAPAAN (KERSPLASH)
And ... good luck !!

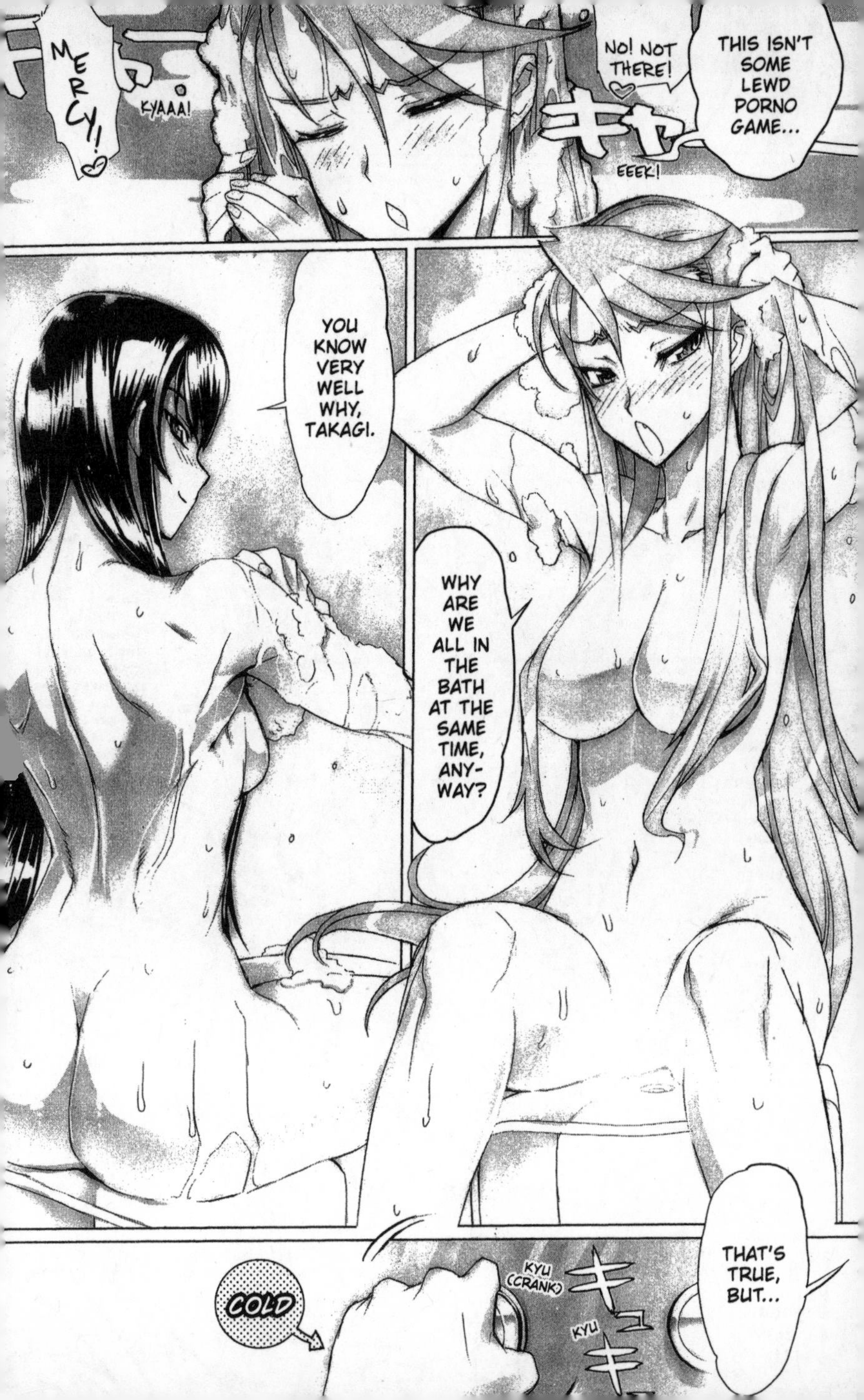
THIS ISN'T SOME LEWD PORNO GAME...
NO! NOT THERE! ♡
EEEK!
KYAAA!
MERCY! ♡
WHY ARE WE ALL IN THE BATH AT THE SAME TIME, ANY-WAY?
YOU KNOW VERY WELL WHY, TAKAGI.
THAT'S TRUE, BUT...
KYU (CRANK)
KYU
COLD

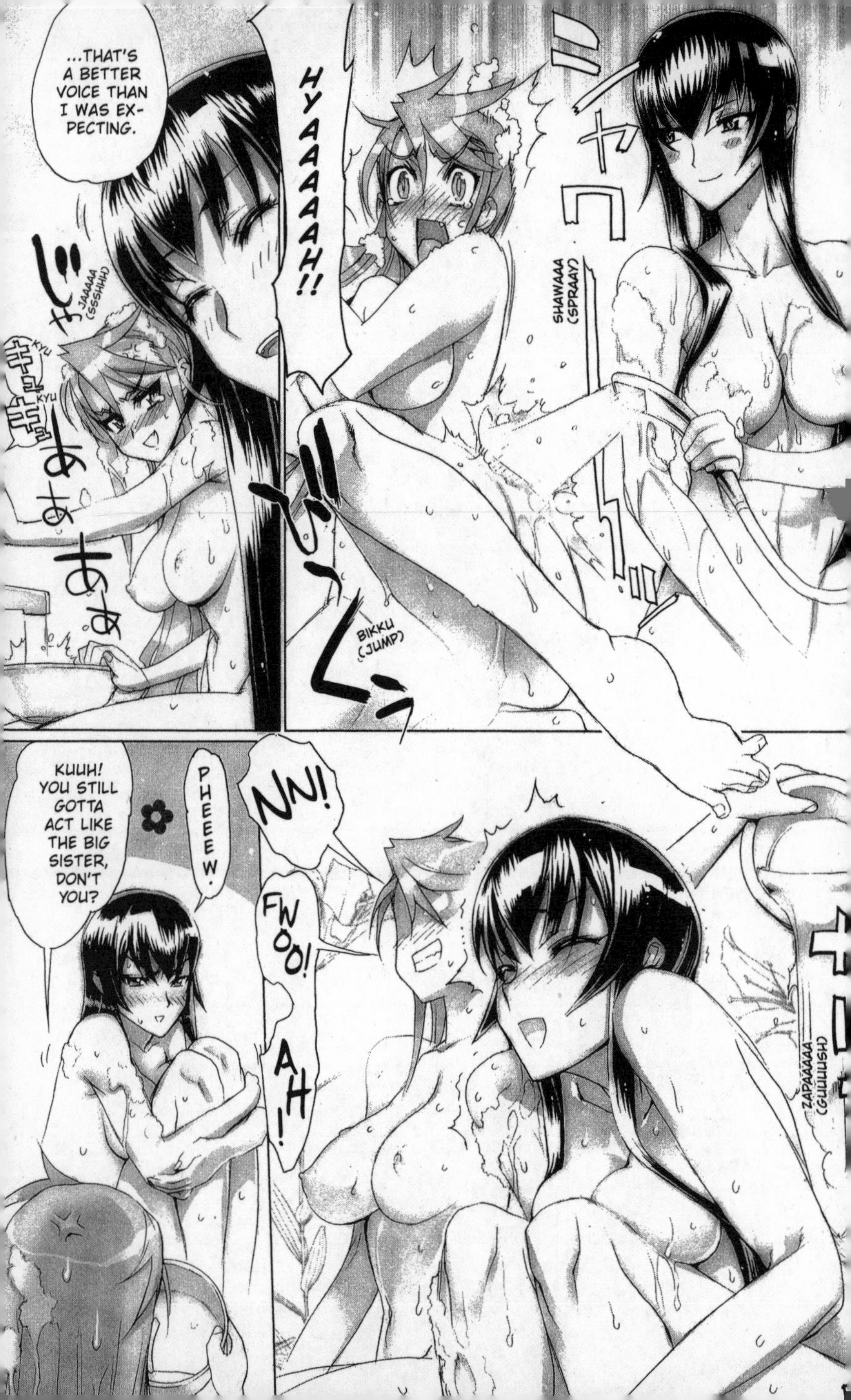
SHAWAAA (SPRAAY)
HYAAAAAAH!!
BIKKU (JUMP)
...THAT'S A BETTER VOICE THAN I WAS EXPECTING.
JAAAAA (SSSHHH)
KYU
KYU
ZAPAAAAA (GUUUUSH)
NN!
FWOO!
AH!
PHEEEEW.
KUUH! YOU STILL GOTTA ACT LIKE THE BIG SISTER, DON'T YOU?

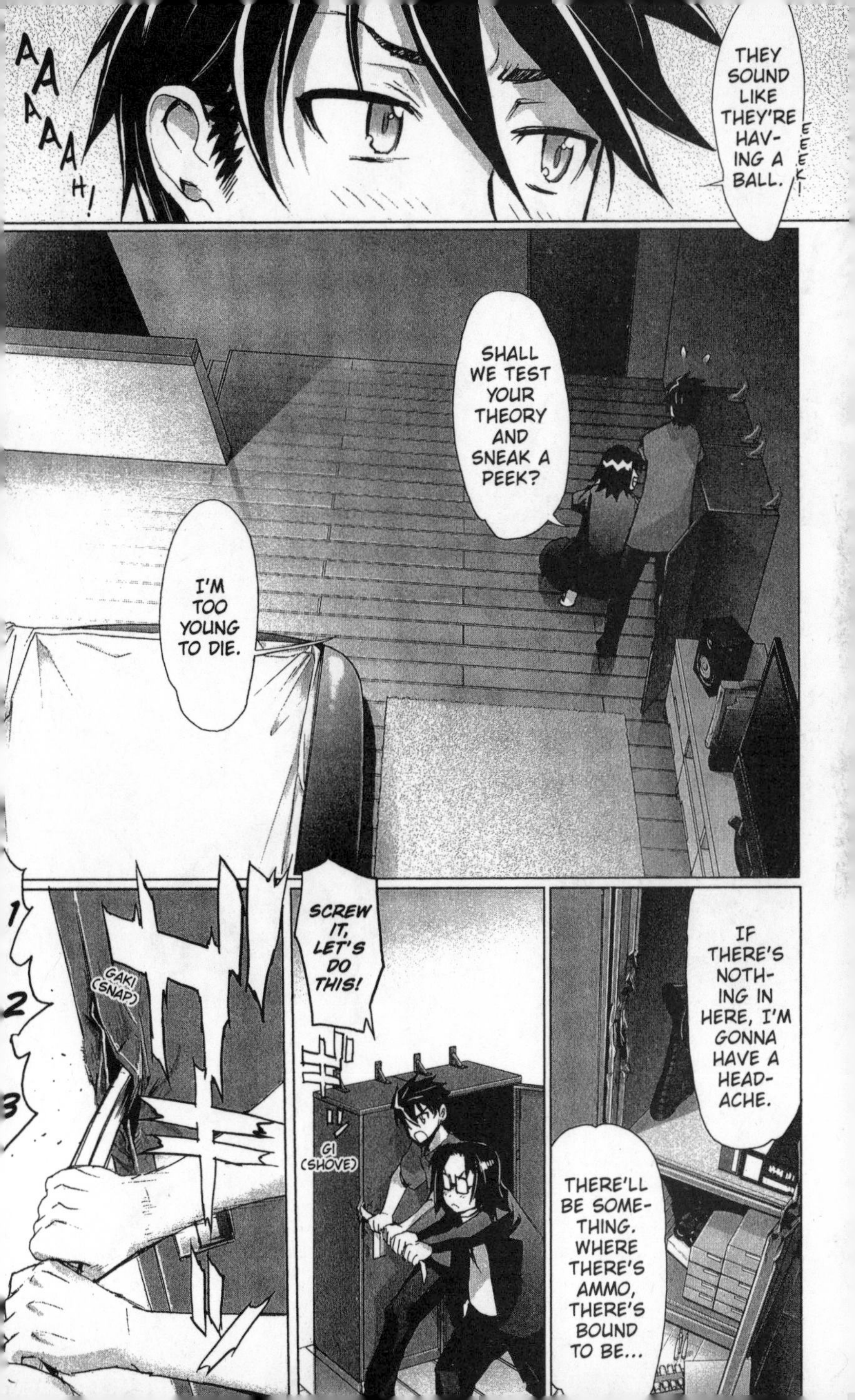
THEY SOUND LIKE THEY'RE HAV-ING A BALL.
EEEK!
AAAAAAH!
SHALL WE TEST YOUR THEORY AND SNEAK A PEEK?
I'M TOO YOUNG TO DIE.
IF THERE'S NOTH-ING IN HERE, I'M GONNA HAVE A HEAD-ACHE.
THERE'LL BE SOME-THING. WHERE THERE'S AMMO, THERE'S BOUND TO BE...
SCREW IT, LET'S DO THIS!
GI (SHOVE)
1
2
3
GAKI (SNAP)

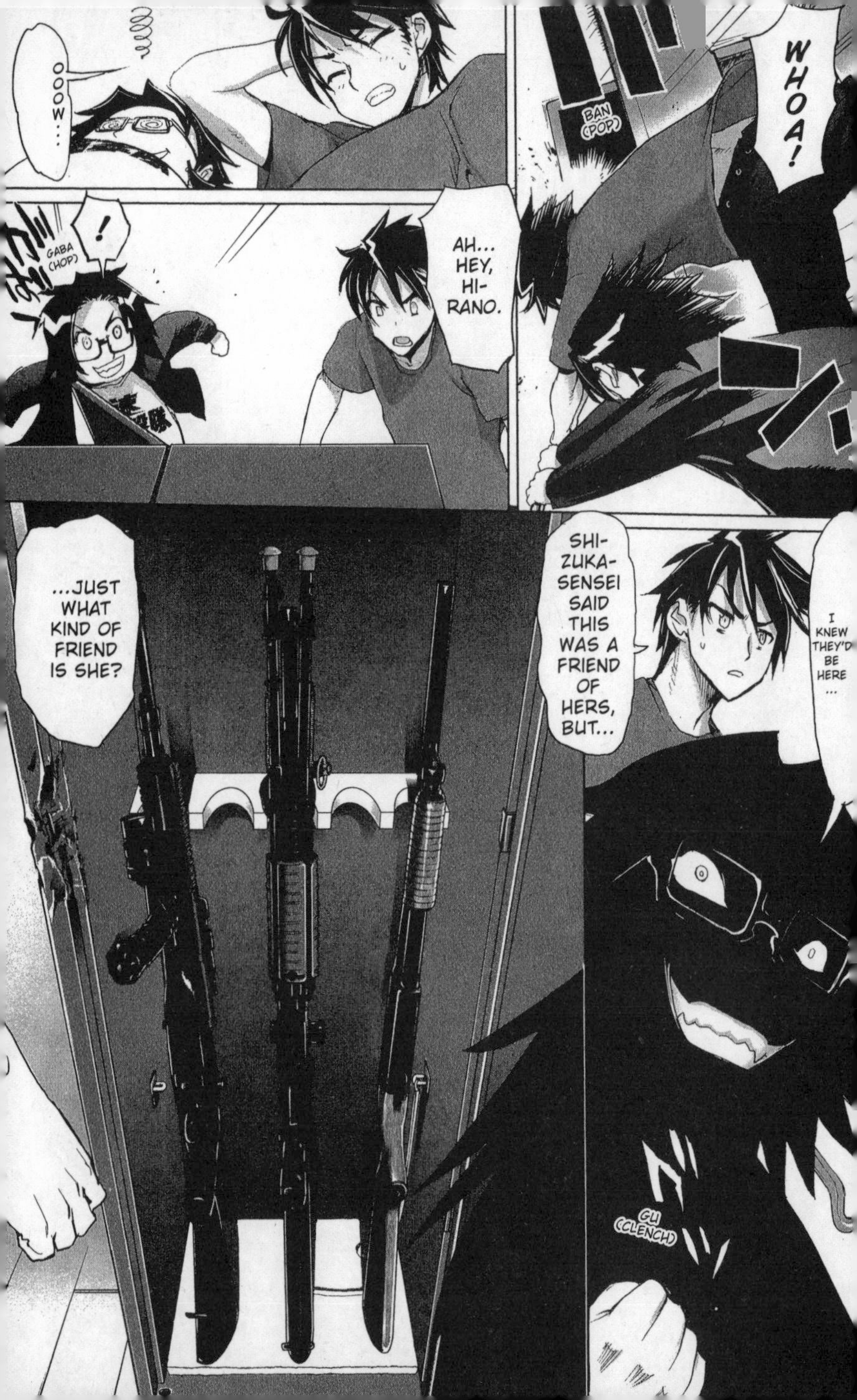
WHOA!
BAN (POP)
OOOW...
AH... HEY, HI-RANO.
!
GABA (HOP)
I KNEW THEY'D BE HERE...
SHI-ZUKA-SENSEI SAID THIS WAS A FRIEND OF HERS, BUT...
GU (CLENCH)
...JUST WHAT KIND OF FRIEND IS SHE?

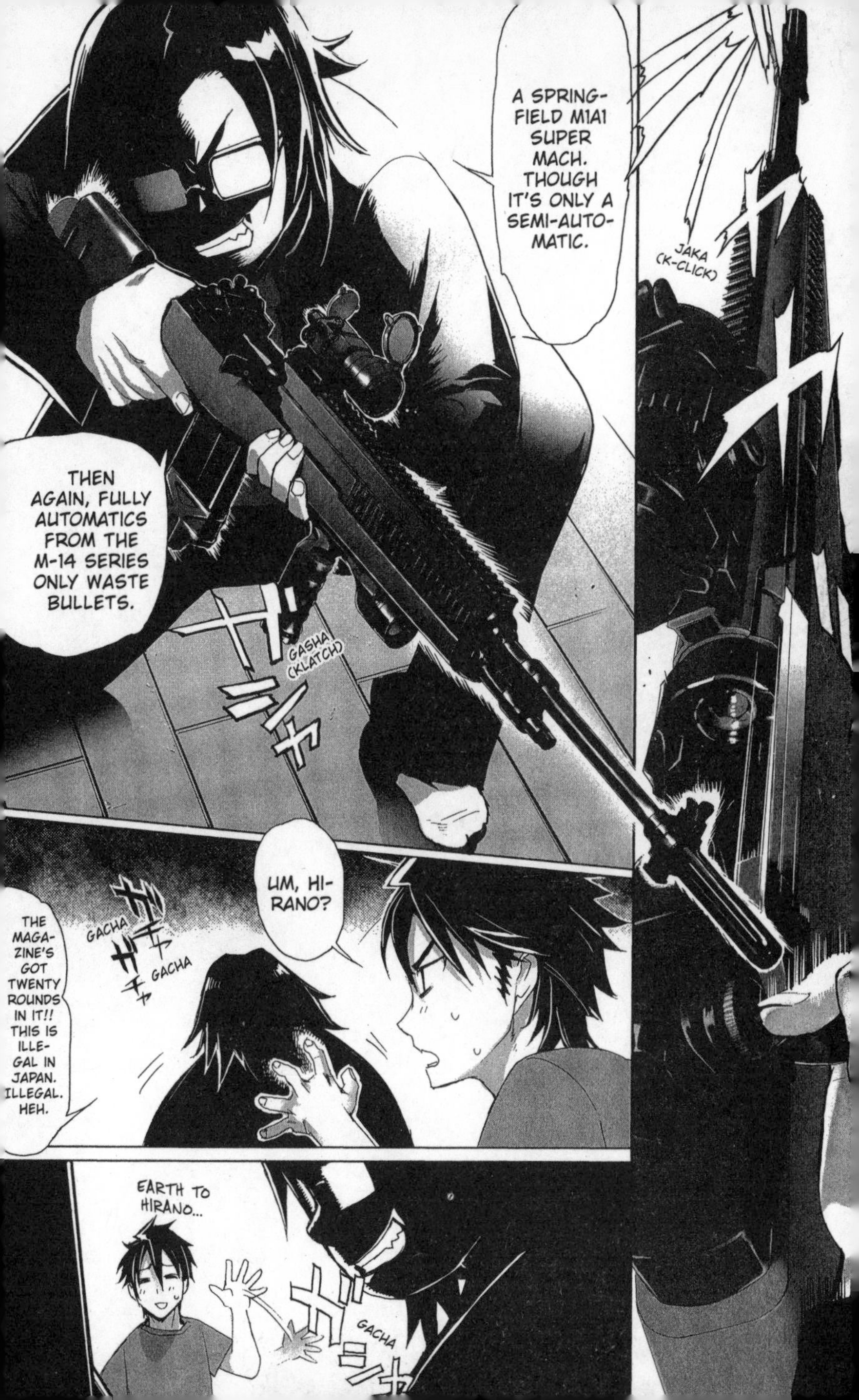
JAKA (K-CLICK)
A SPRING-FIELD M1A1 SUPER MACH. THOUGH IT'S ONLY A SEMI-AUTO-MATIC.
THEN AGAIN, FULLY AUTOMATICS FROM THE M-14 SERIES ONLY WASTE BULLETS.
GASHA (KLATCH)
UM, HI-RANO?
GACHA
GACHA
THE MAGA-ZINE'S GOT TWENTY ROUNDS IN IT!! THIS IS ILLE-GAL IN JAPAN. ILLEGAL. HEH.
GACHA
EARTH TO HIRANO...

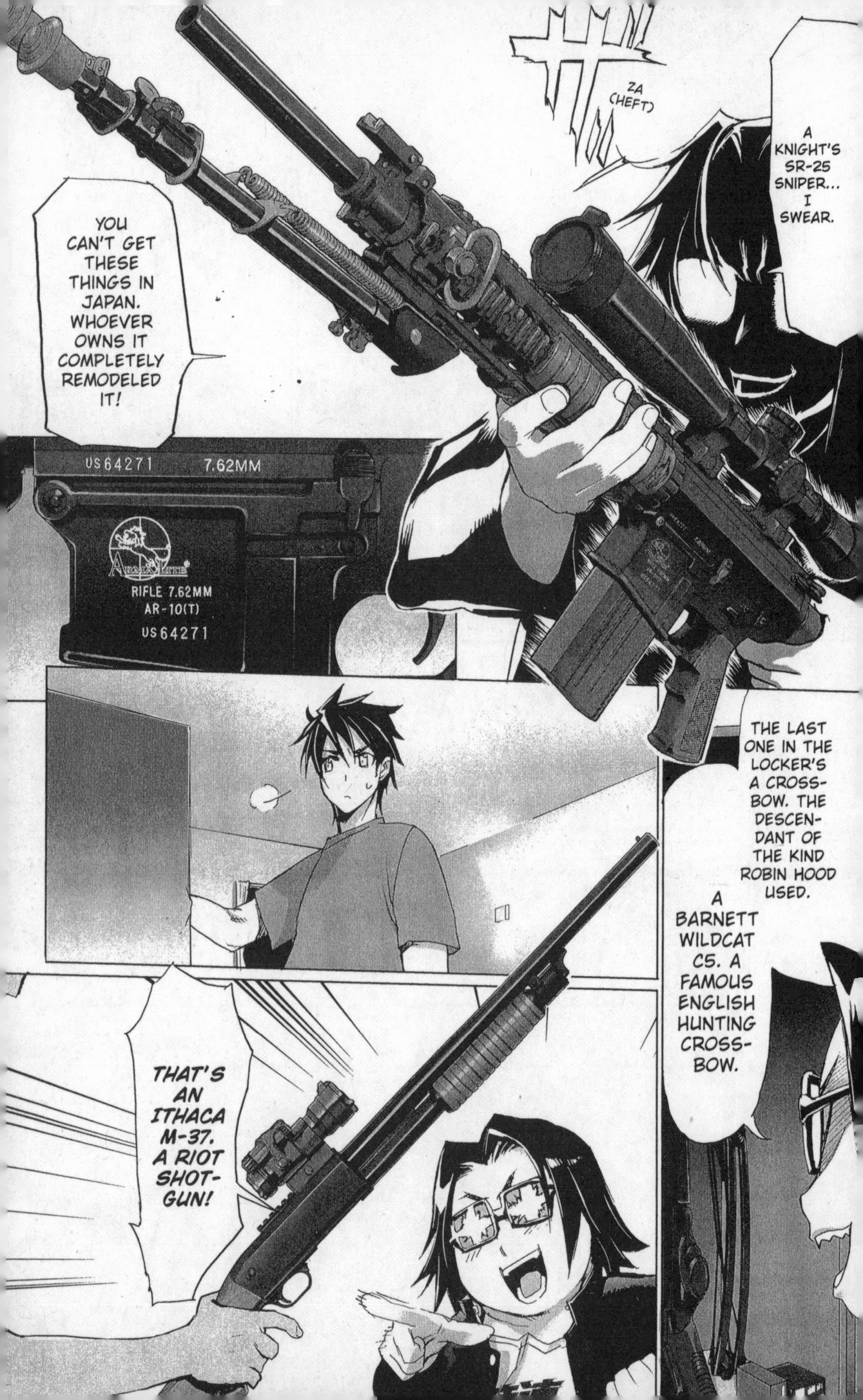
ZA (HEFT)
A KNIGHT'S SR-25 SNIPER... I SWEAR.
YOU CAN'T GET THESE THINGS IN JAPAN. WHOEVER OWNS IT COMPLETELY REMODELED IT!
US64271 7.62MM
RIFLE 7.62MM AR-10(T) US64271
THE LAST ONE IN THE LOCKER'S A CROSSBOW. THE DESCENDANT OF THE KIND ROBIN HOOD USED.
A BARNETT WILDCAT C5. A FAMOUS ENGLISH HUNTING CROSSBOW.
THAT'S AN ITHACA M-37. A RIOT SHOTGUN!

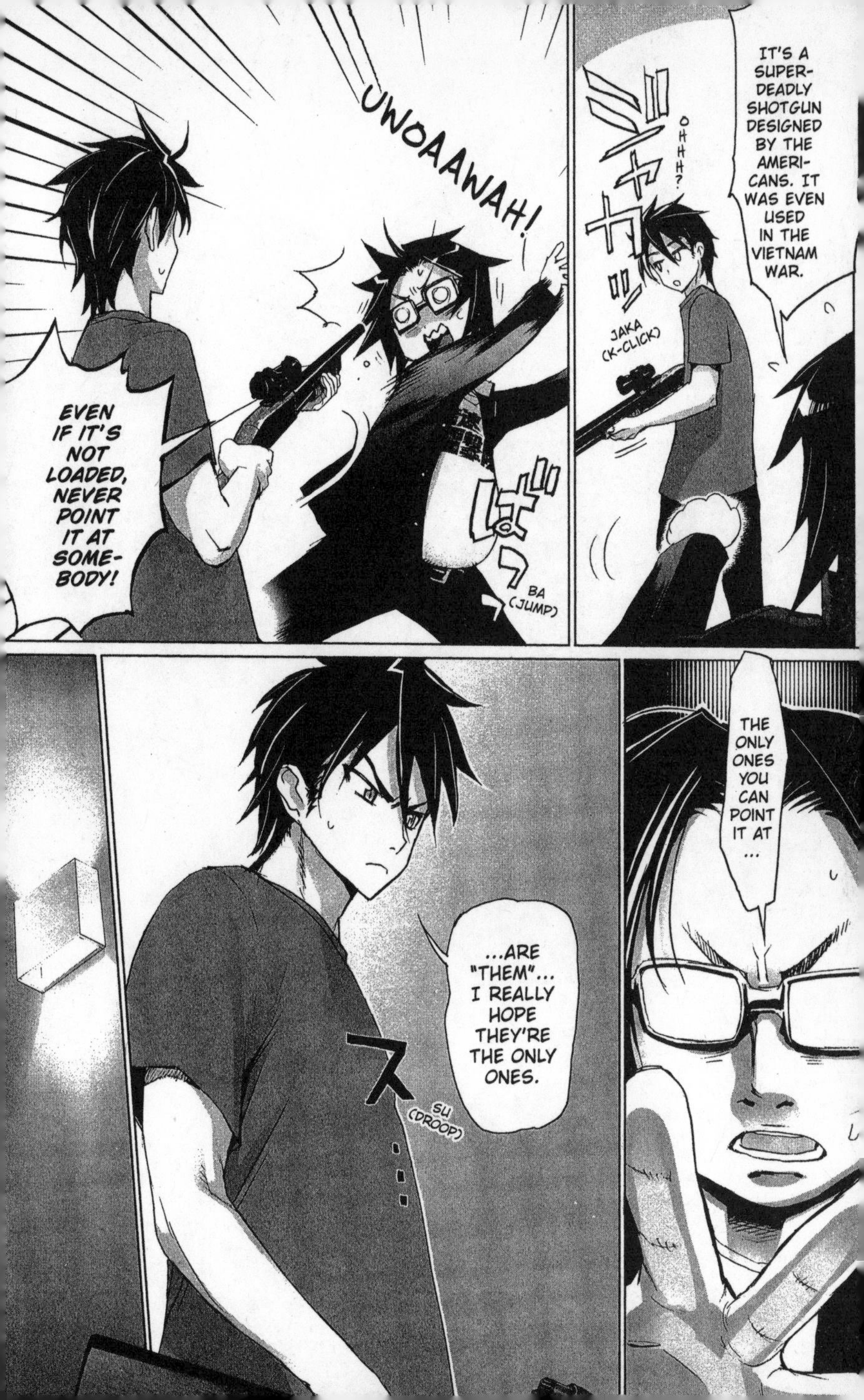
IT'S A SUPER-DEADLY SHOTGUN DESIGNED BY THE AMERICANS. IT WAS EVEN USED IN THE VIETNAM WAR.
OHHH?
JAKA (K-CLICK)
UWOAAAWAH!
EVEN IF IT'S NOT LOADED, NEVER POINT IT AT SOMEBODY!
BA (JUMP)
THE ONLY ONES YOU CAN POINT IT AT ...
...ARE "THEM"... I REALLY HOPE THEY'RE THE ONLY ONES.
SU (DROOP)

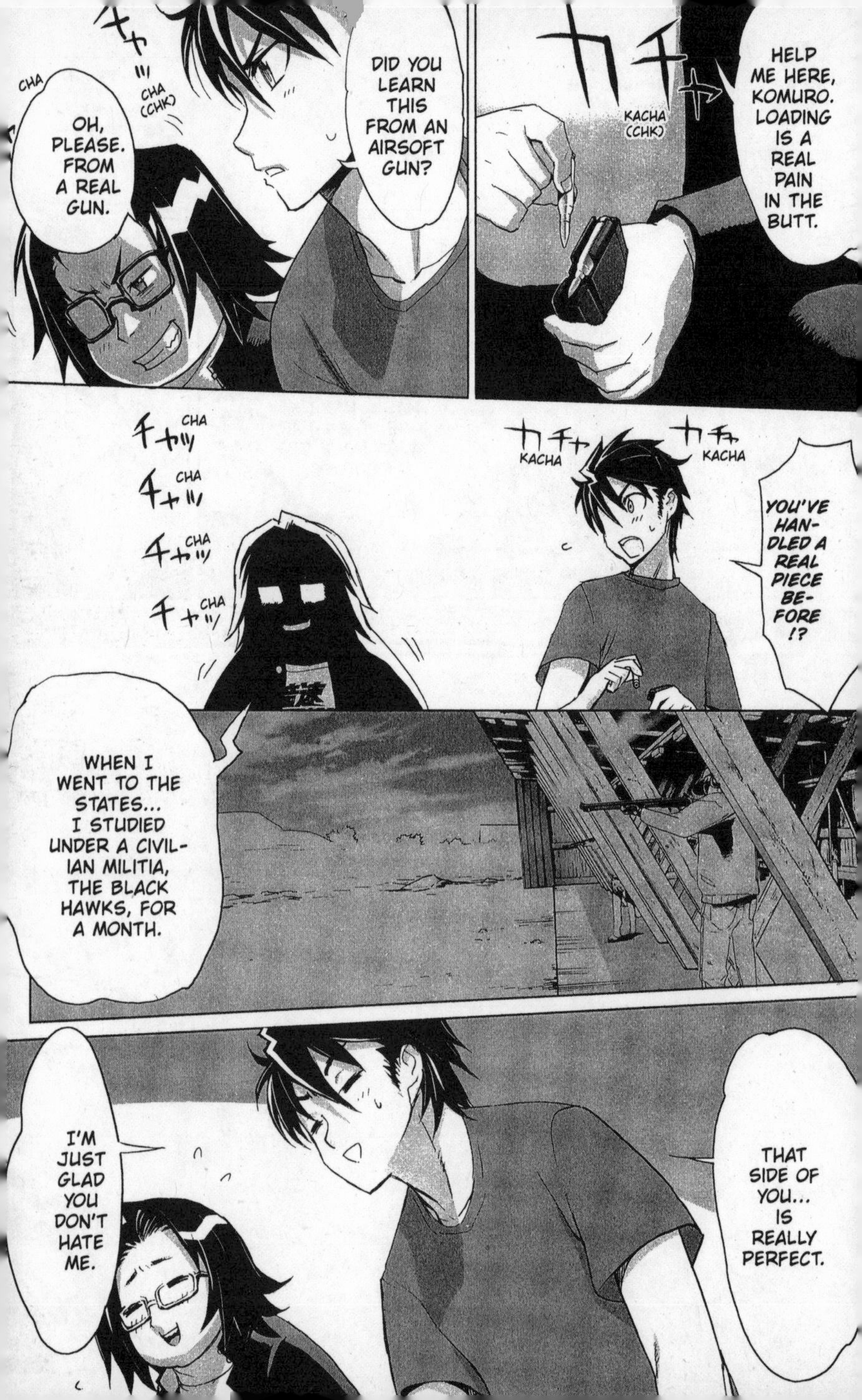
KACHA (CHK)
HELP ME HERE, KOMURO. LOADING IS A REAL PAIN IN THE BUTT.
DID YOU LEARN THIS FROM AN AIRSOFT GUN?
CHA (CHK)
CHA
OH, PLEASE. FROM A REAL GUN.
KACHA
KACHA
YOU'VE HAN-DLED A REAL PIECE BE-FORE!?
CHA
CHA
CHA
CHA
WHEN I WENT TO THE STATES... I STUDIED UNDER A CIVIL-IAN MILITIA, THE BLACK HAWKS, FOR A MONTH.
THAT SIDE OF YOU... IS REALLY PERFECT.
I'M JUST GLAD YOU DON'T HATE ME.

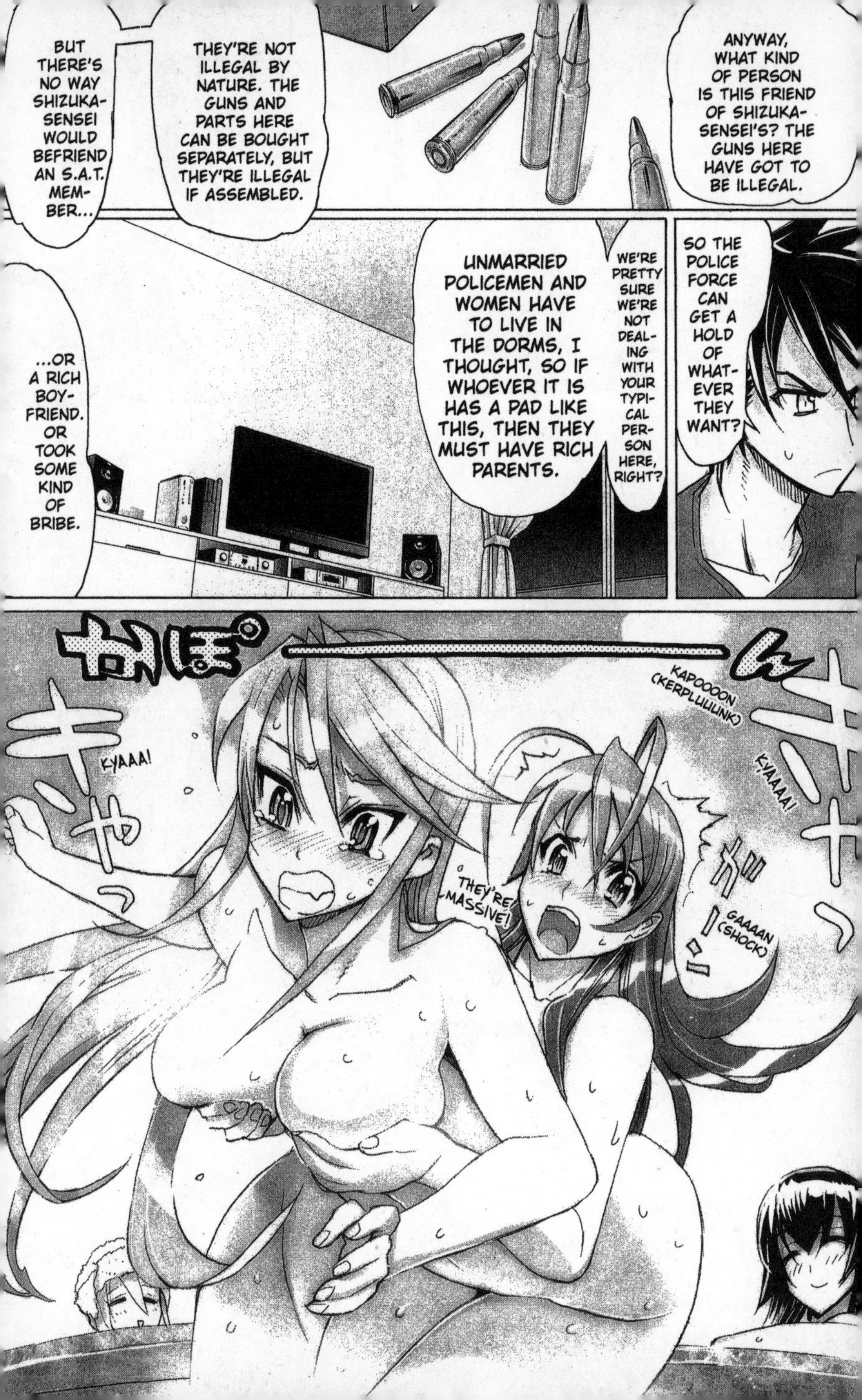
ANYWAY, WHAT KIND OF PERSON IS THIS FRIEND OF SHIZUKA-SENSEI'S? THE GUNS HERE HAVE GOT TO BE ILLEGAL.
THEY'RE NOT ILLEGAL BY NATURE. THE GUNS AND PARTS HERE CAN BE BOUGHT SEPARATELY, BUT THEY'RE ILLEGAL IF ASSEMBLED.
BUT THERE'S NO WAY SHIZUKA-SENSEI WOULD BEFRIEND AN S.A.T. MEMBER...
SO THE POLICE FORCE CAN GET A HOLD OF WHATEVER THEY WANT?
WE'RE PRETTY SURE WE'RE NOT DEALING WITH YOUR TYPICAL PERSON HERE, RIGHT?
UNMARRIED POLICEMEN AND WOMEN HAVE TO LIVE IN THE DORMS, I THOUGHT, SO IF WHOEVER IT IS HAS A PAD LIKE THIS, THEN THEY MUST HAVE RICH PARENTS.
...OR A RICH BOYFRIEND. OR TOOK SOME KIND OF BRIBE.
かぽーーーん
KAPOOOOON (KERPLUUUNK)
キャーッ
KYAAAA!
ガーン
GAAAAN (SHOCK)
THEY'RE MASSIVE!
キャーッ
KYAAA!

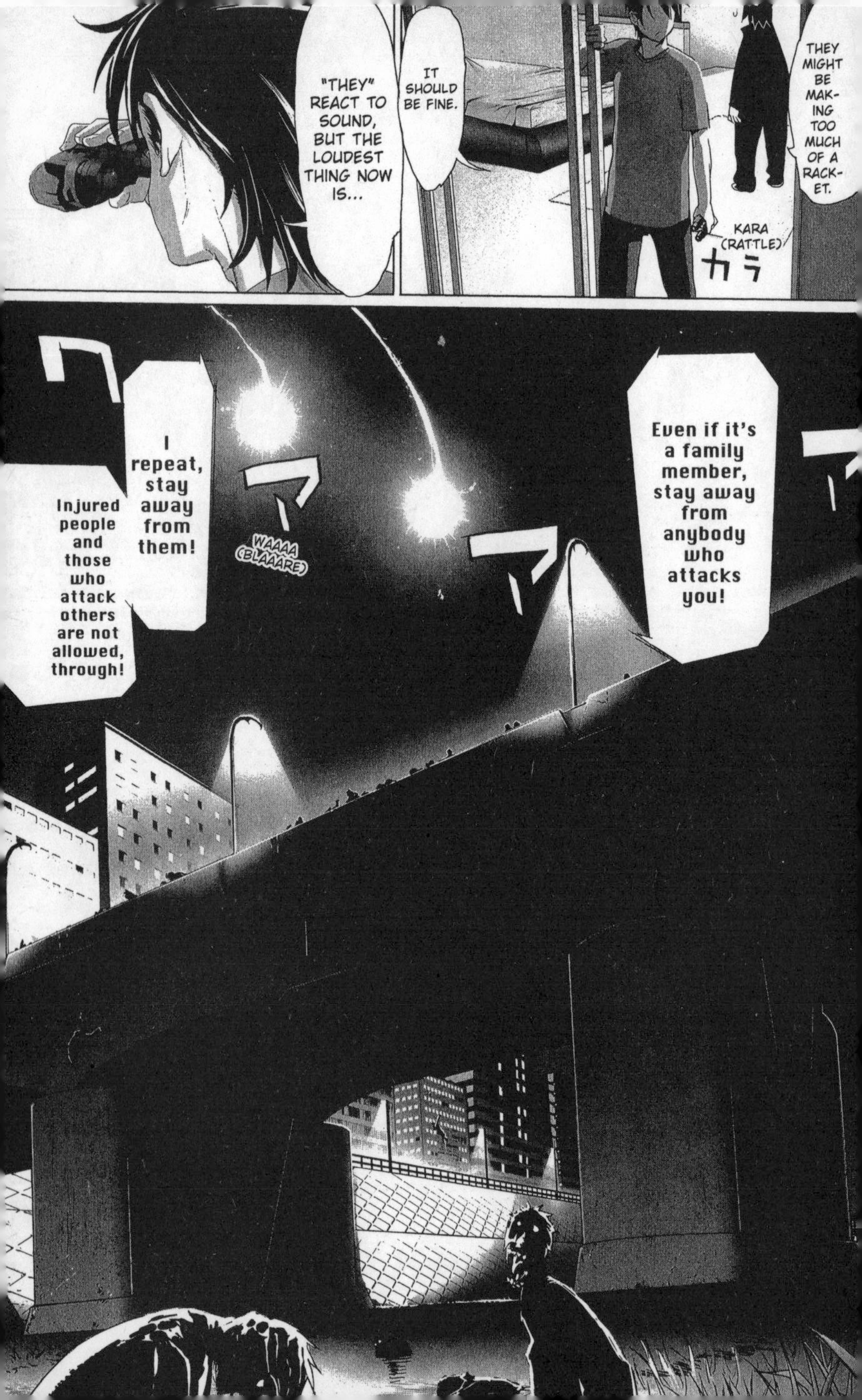
THEY MIGHT BE MAKING TOO MUCH OF A RACKET.
KARA (RATTLE)
カラ
IT SHOULD BE FINE.
"THEY" REACT TO SOUND, BUT THE LOUDEST THING NOW IS...
Even if it's a family member, stay away from anybody who attacks you!
ワァァ
WAAAA (BLAAARE)
I repeat, stay away from them!
Injured people and those who attack others are not allowed, through!

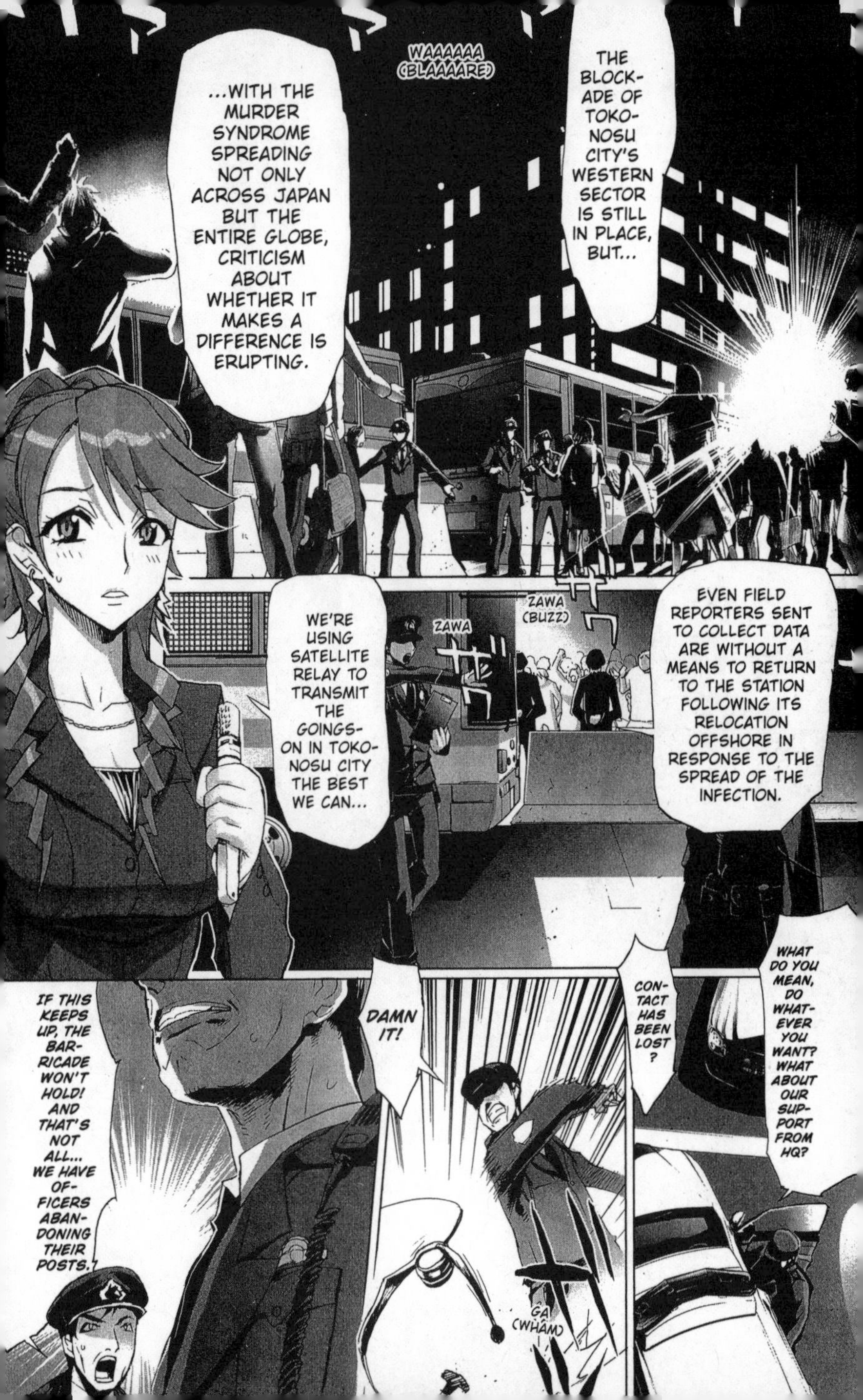
THE BLOCKADE OF TOKONOSU CITY'S WESTERN SECTOR IS STILL IN PLACE, BUT...
WAAAAAA (BLAAAARE)
...WITH THE MURDER SYNDROME SPREADING NOT ONLY ACROSS JAPAN BUT THE ENTIRE GLOBE, CRITICISM ABOUT WHETHER IT MAKES A DIFFERENCE IS ERUPTING.
EVEN FIELD REPORTERS SENT TO COLLECT DATA ARE WITHOUT A MEANS TO RETURN TO THE STATION FOLLOWING ITS RELOCATION OFFSHORE IN RESPONSE TO THE SPREAD OF THE INFECTION.
ZAWA (BUZZ)
ZAWA
WE'RE USING SATELLITE RELAY TO TRANSMIT THE GOINGS-ON IN TOKONOSU CITY THE BEST WE CAN...
WHAT DO YOU MEAN, DO WHATEVER YOU WANT? WHAT ABOUT OUR SUPPORT FROM HQ?
CONTACT HAS BEEN LOST?
DAMN IT!
GA (WHAM)
IF THIS KEEPS UP, THE BARRICADE WON'T HOLD! AND THAT'S NOT ALL... WE HAVE OFFICERS ABANDONING THEIR POSTS.

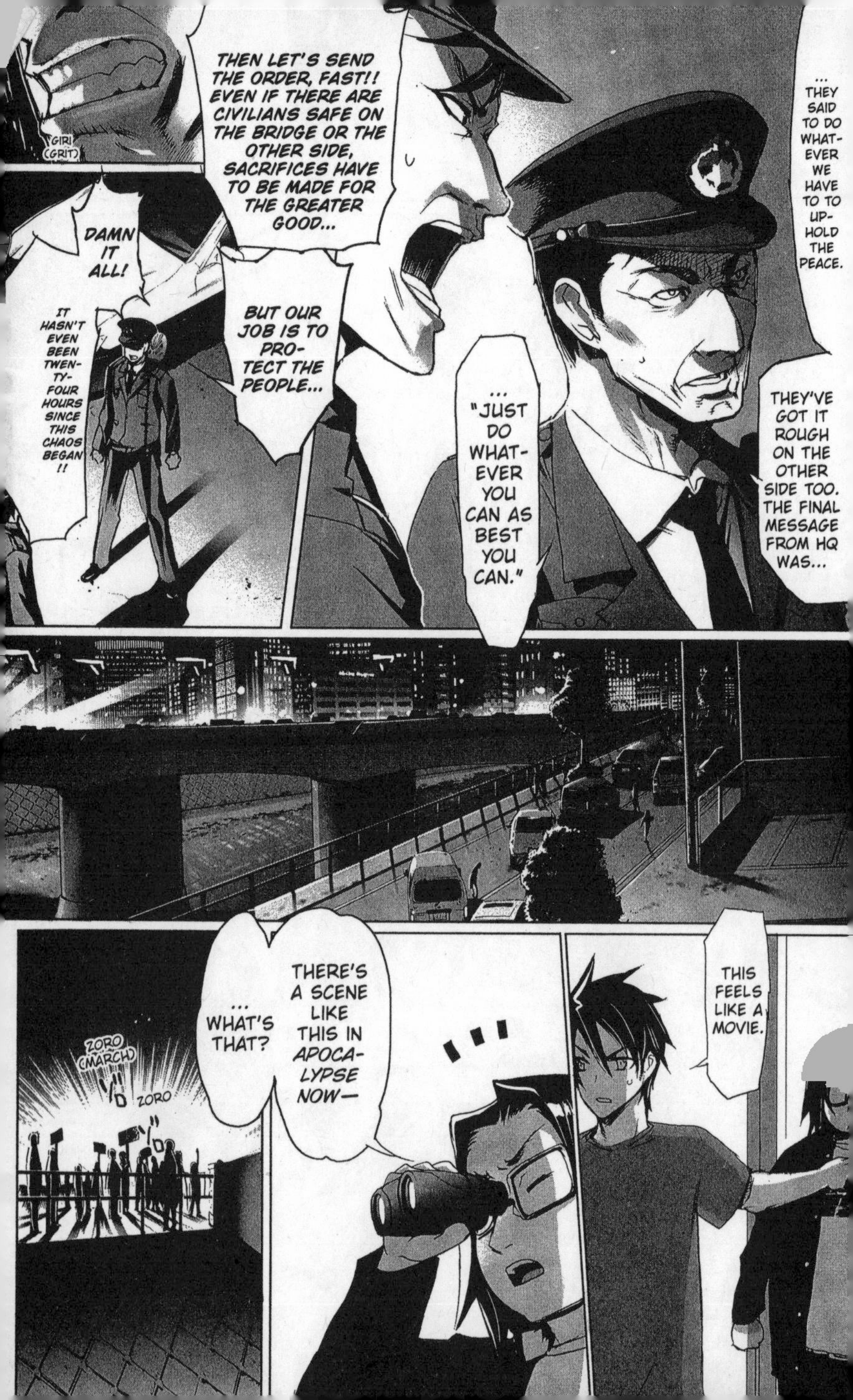

... THEY SAID TO DO WHAT-EVER WE HAVE TO TO UP-HOLD THE PEACE.
THEY'VE GOT IT ROUGH ON THE OTHER SIDE TOO. THE FINAL MESSAGE FROM HQ WAS...
... "JUST DO WHAT-EVER YOU CAN AS BEST YOU CAN."
THEN LET'S SEND THE ORDER, FAST!! EVEN IF THERE ARE CIVILIANS SAFE ON THE BRIDGE OR THE OTHER SIDE, SACRIFICES HAVE TO BE MADE FOR THE GREATER GOOD...
BUT OUR JOB IS TO PRO-TECT THE PEOPLE...
GIRI (GRIT)
DAMN IT ALL!
IT HASN'T EVEN BEEN TWEN-TY-FOUR HOURS SINCE THIS CHAOS BEGAN!!
THIS FEELS LIKE A MOVIE.
...
THERE'S A SCENE LIKE THIS IN APOCA-LYPSE NOW—
... WHAT'S THAT?
ZORO (MARCH)
ZORO

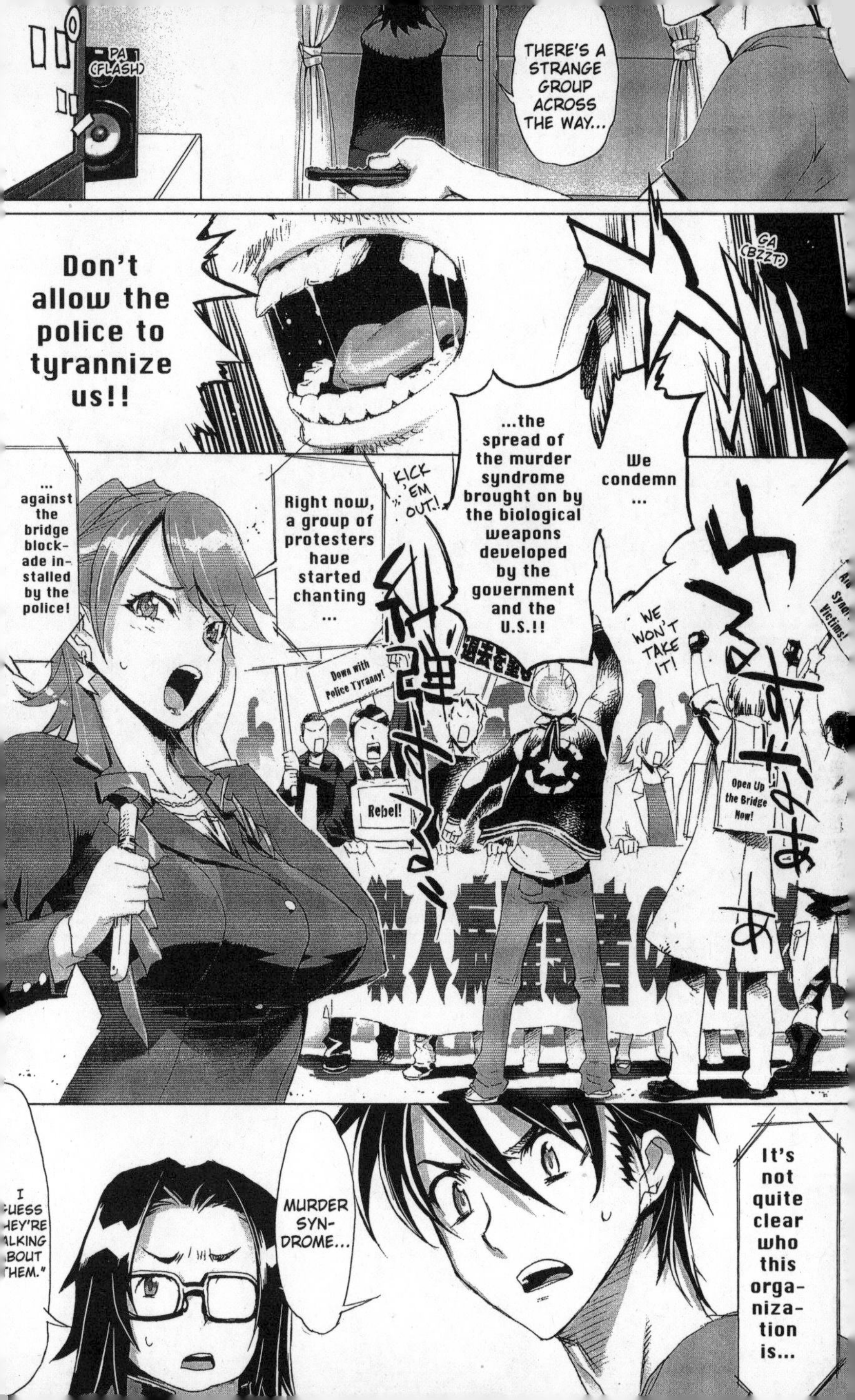
THERE'S A STRANGE GROUP ACROSS THE WAY...
PA (FLASH)
GA (BZZT)
Don't allow the police to tyrannize us!!
We condemn ...
...the spread of the murder syndrome brought on by the biological weapons developed by the government and the U.S.!!
WE WON'T TAKE IT!
KICK 'EM OUT!
Right now, a group of protesters have started chanting ...
... against the bridge blockade installed by the police!
Down with Police Tyranny!
Rebel!
Open Up the Bridge Now!
It's not quite clear who this organization is...
MURDER SYNDROME...
I UESS HEY'RE ALKING BOUT THEM."

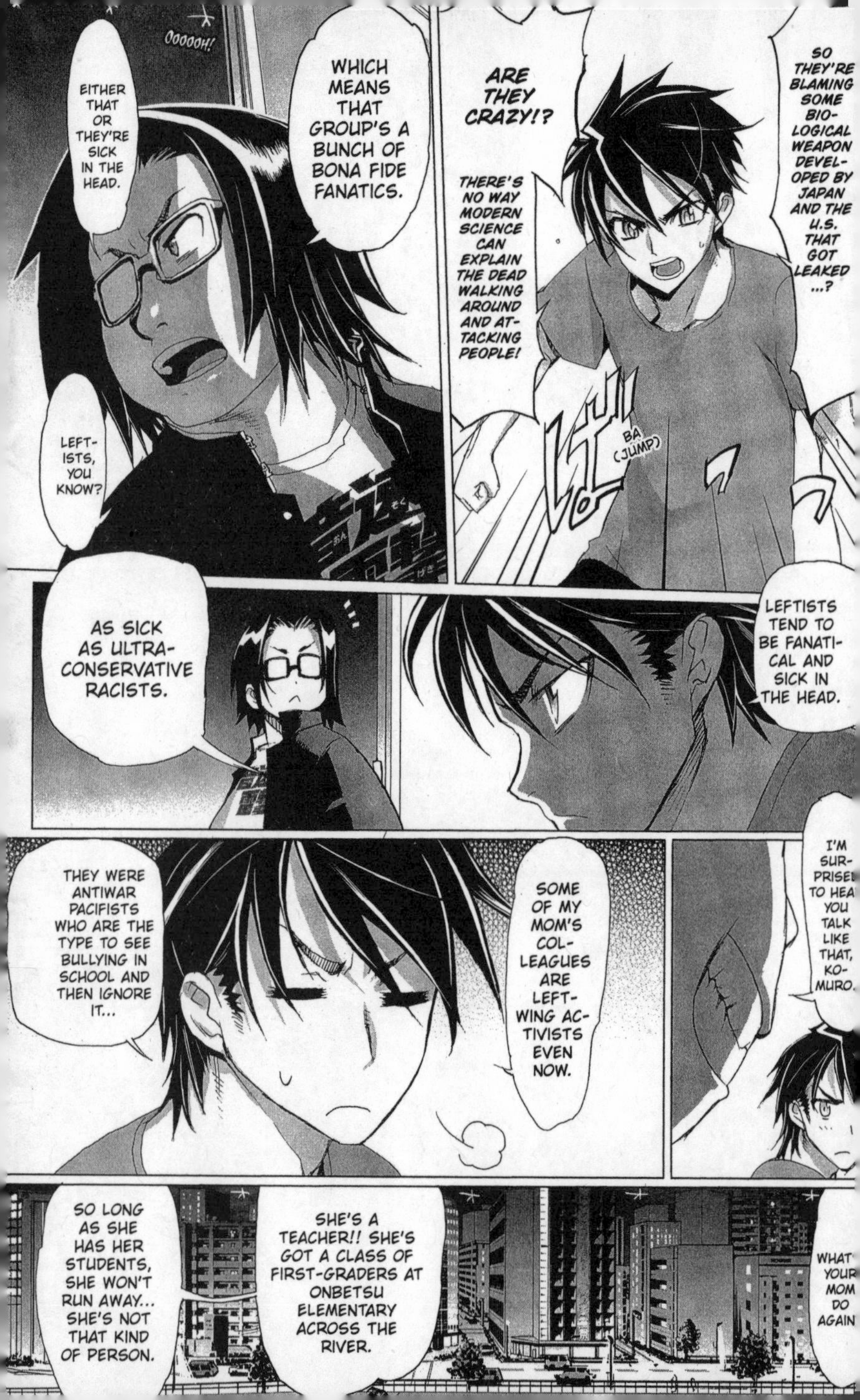
SO THEY'RE BLAMING SOME BIOLOGICAL WEAPON DEVELOPED BY JAPAN AND THE U.S. THAT GOT LEAKED ...?
ARE THEY CRAZY!?
THERE'S NO WAY MODERN SCIENCE CAN EXPLAIN THE DEAD WALKING AROUND AND ATTACKING PEOPLE!
BA (JUMP)
WHICH MEANS THAT GROUP'S A BUNCH OF BONA FIDE FANATICS.
OOOOOH!
EITHER THAT OR THEY'RE SICK IN THE HEAD.
LEFTISTS, YOU KNOW?
LEFTISTS TEND TO BE FANATICAL AND SICK IN THE HEAD.
AS SICK AS ULTRA-CONSERVATIVE RACISTS.
I'M SURPRISE TO HEA YOU TALK LIKE THAT, KOMURO.
SOME OF MY MOM'S COLLEAGUES ARE LEFT-WING ACTIVISTS EVEN NOW.
THEY WERE ANTIWAR PACIFISTS WHO ARE THE TYPE TO SEE BULLYING IN SCHOOL AND THEN IGNORE IT...
WHAT YOUR MOM DO AGAIN
SHE'S A TEACHER!! SHE'S GOT A CLASS OF FIRST-GRADERS AT ONBETSU ELEMENTARY ACROSS THE RIVER.
SO LONG AS SHE HAS HER STUDENTS, SHE WON'T RUN AWAY... SHE'S NOT THAT KIND OF PERSON.

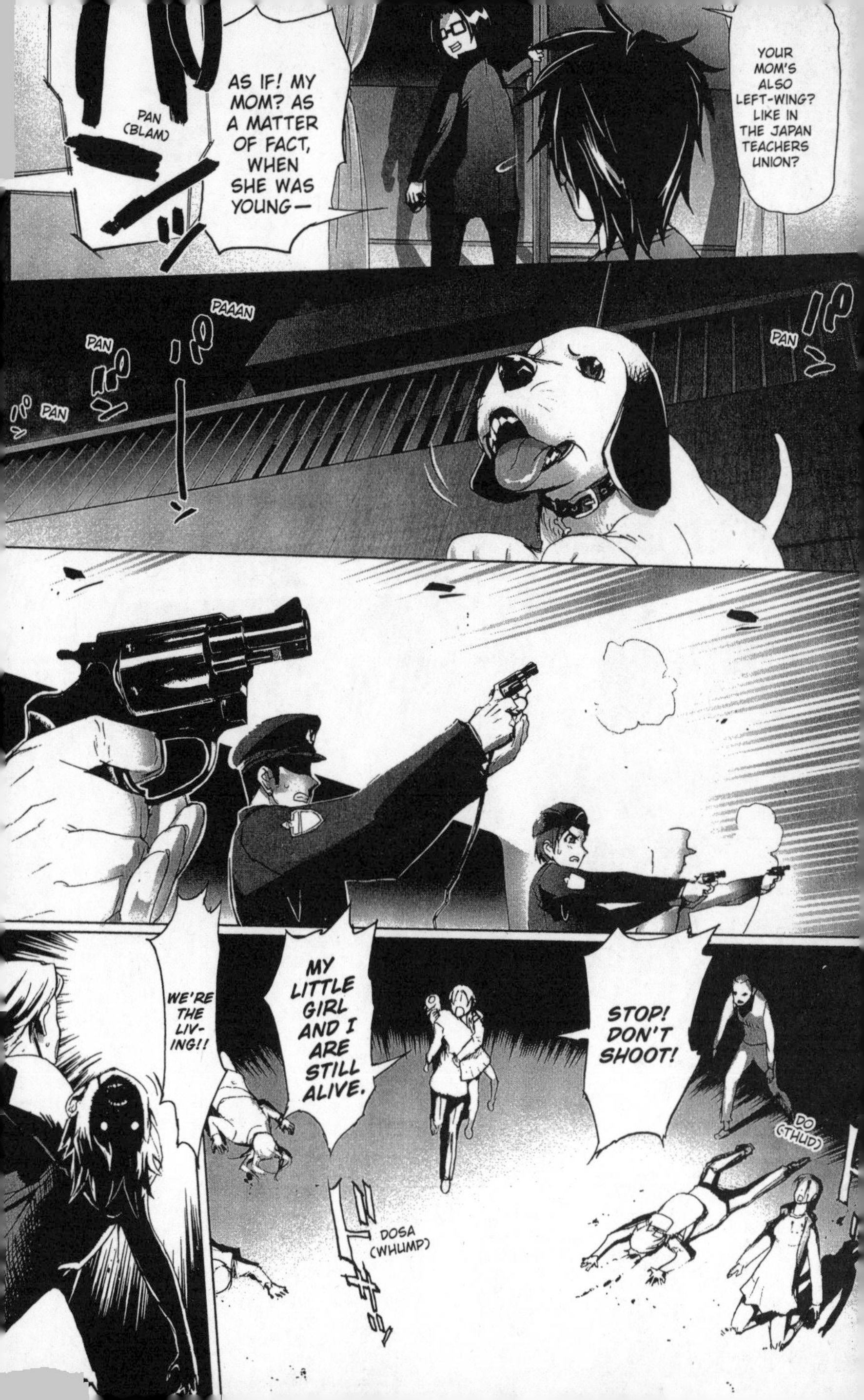
YOUR MOM'S ALSO LEFT-WING? LIKE IN THE JAPAN TEACHERS UNION?
AS IF! MY MOM? AS A MATTER OF FACT, WHEN SHE WAS YOUNG—
PAN (BLAM)
PAN
PAAAN
PAN
PAN
STOP! DON'T SHOOT!
DO (THUD)
MY LITTLE GIRL AND I ARE STILL ALIVE.
DOSA (WHUMP)
WE'RE THE LIV-ING!!

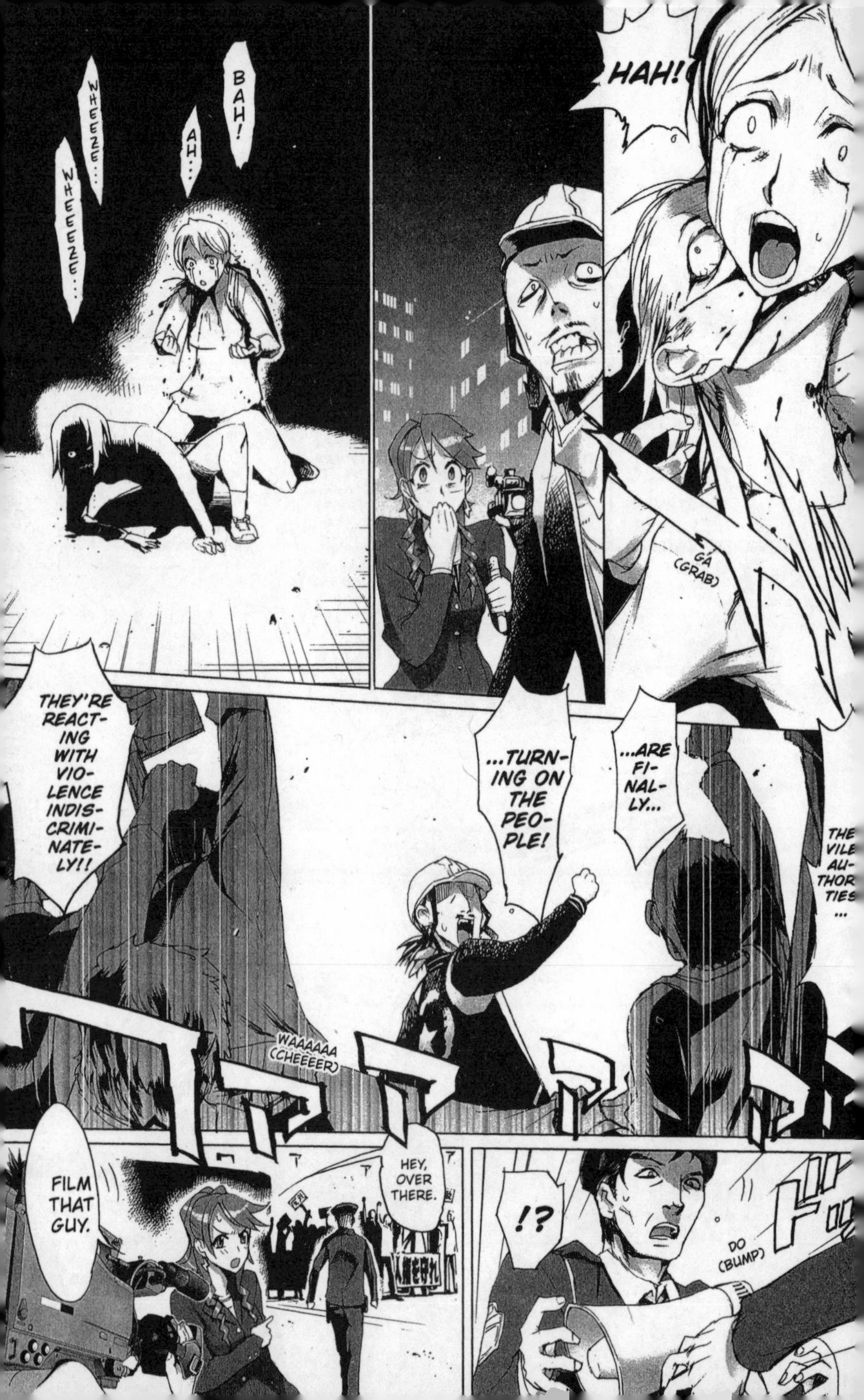
HAH!
GA (GRAB)
BAH!
AH...
WHEEZE...
WHEEEZE...
THE VILE AUTHORITIES...
...ARE FINALLY...
...TURNING ON THE PEOPLE!
WAAAAAA (CHEEEER)
THEY'RE REACTING WITH VIOLENCE INDISCRIMINATELY!!
!?
DO (BUMP)
HEY, OVER THERE.
FILM THAT GUY.

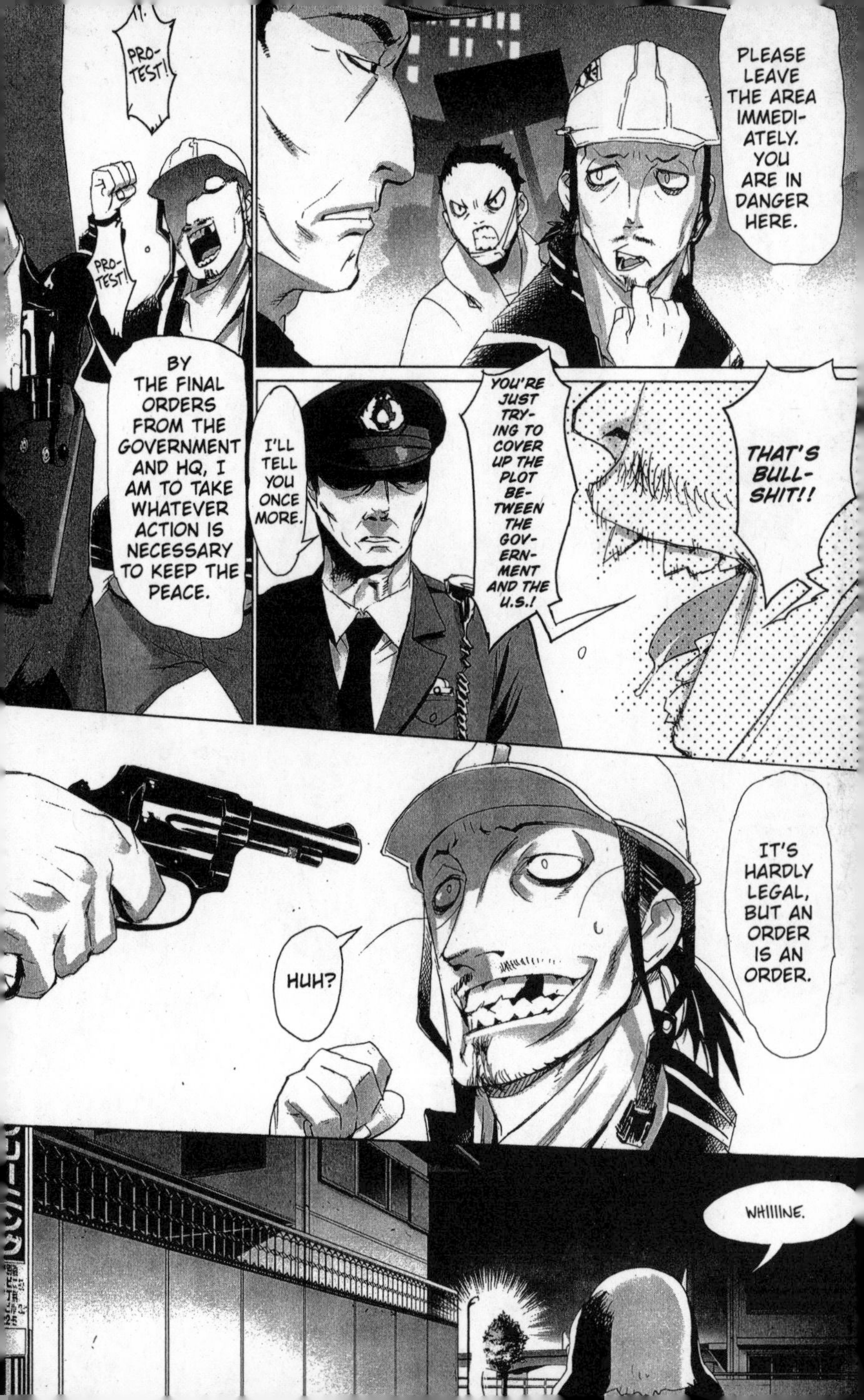
PLEASE LEAVE THE AREA IMMEDIATELY. YOU ARE IN DANGER HERE.
THAT'S BULLSHIT!!
YOU'RE JUST TRYING TO COVER UP THE PLOT BETWEEN THE GOVERNMENT AND THE U.S.!
I'LL TELL YOU ONCE MORE.
PRO-TEST!
PRO-TEST!
BY THE FINAL ORDERS FROM THE GOVERNMENT AND HQ, I AM TO TAKE WHATEVER ACTION IS NECESSARY TO KEEP THE PEACE.
IT'S HARDLY LEGAL, BUT AN ORDER IS AN ORDER.
HUH?
WHIIIINE.

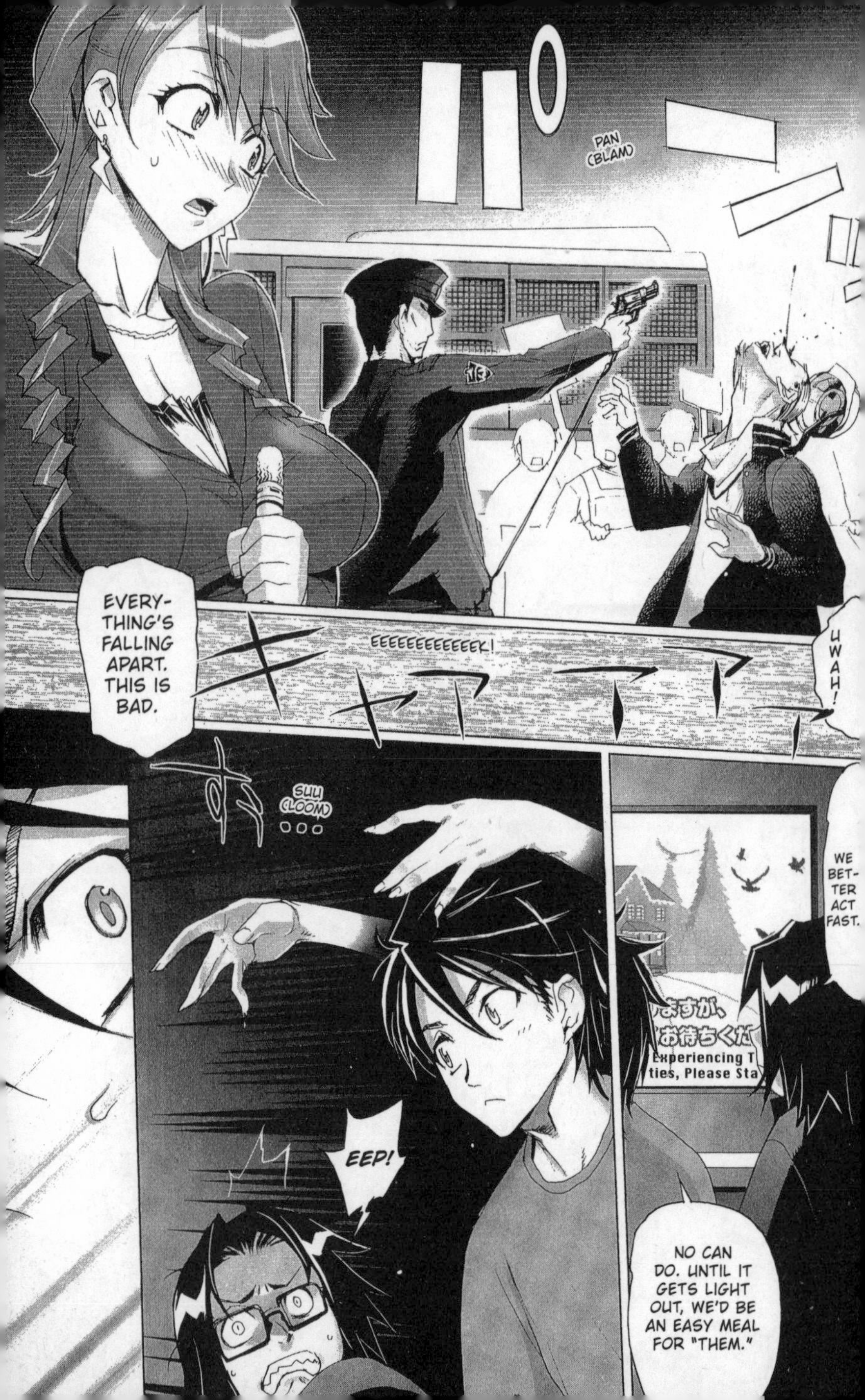
PAN (BLAM)
UWAH!
EEEEEEEEEEEEK!
EVERY-THING'S FALLING APART. THIS IS BAD.
WE BET-TER ACT FAST.
NO CAN DO. UNTIL IT GETS LIGHT OUT, WE'D BE AN EASY MEAL FOR "THEM."
SUU (LOOM)
EEP!

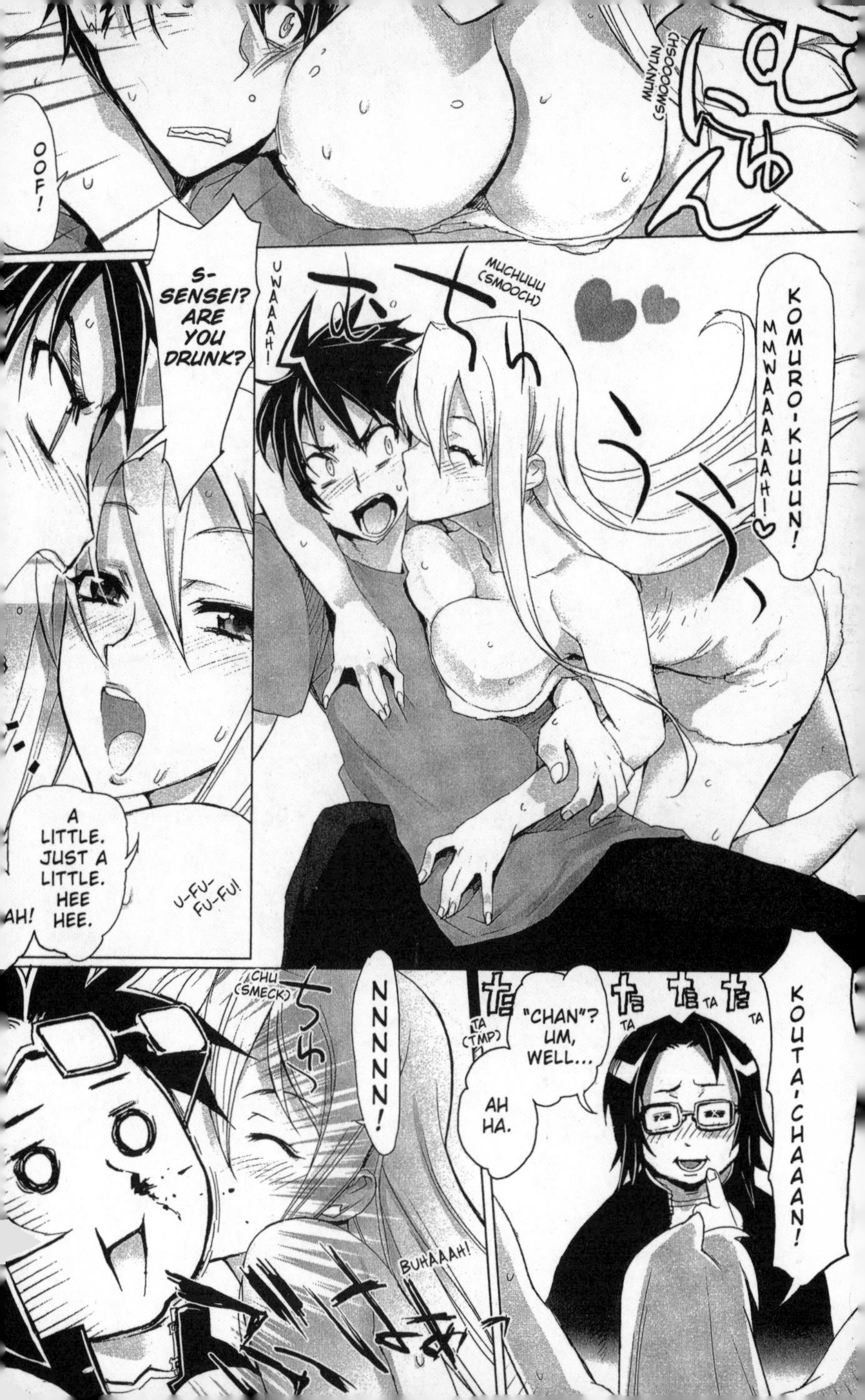
MUNYUN (SMOOOOSH)
OOF!
KOMURO-KUUUUN! MMWAAAAAAAAH!♥
MUCHUUU (SMOOCH)
UWAAAAH!
S-SENSEI? ARE YOU DRUNK?
A LITTLE. JUST A LITTLE. HEE HEE.
U-FU-FU-FU!
AH!
KOUTA-CHAAAAN!
TA TA TA TA
TA (TMP)
"CHAN"? UM, WELL...
AH HA.
NNNNNN!
CHU (SMECK)
BUHAAAH!

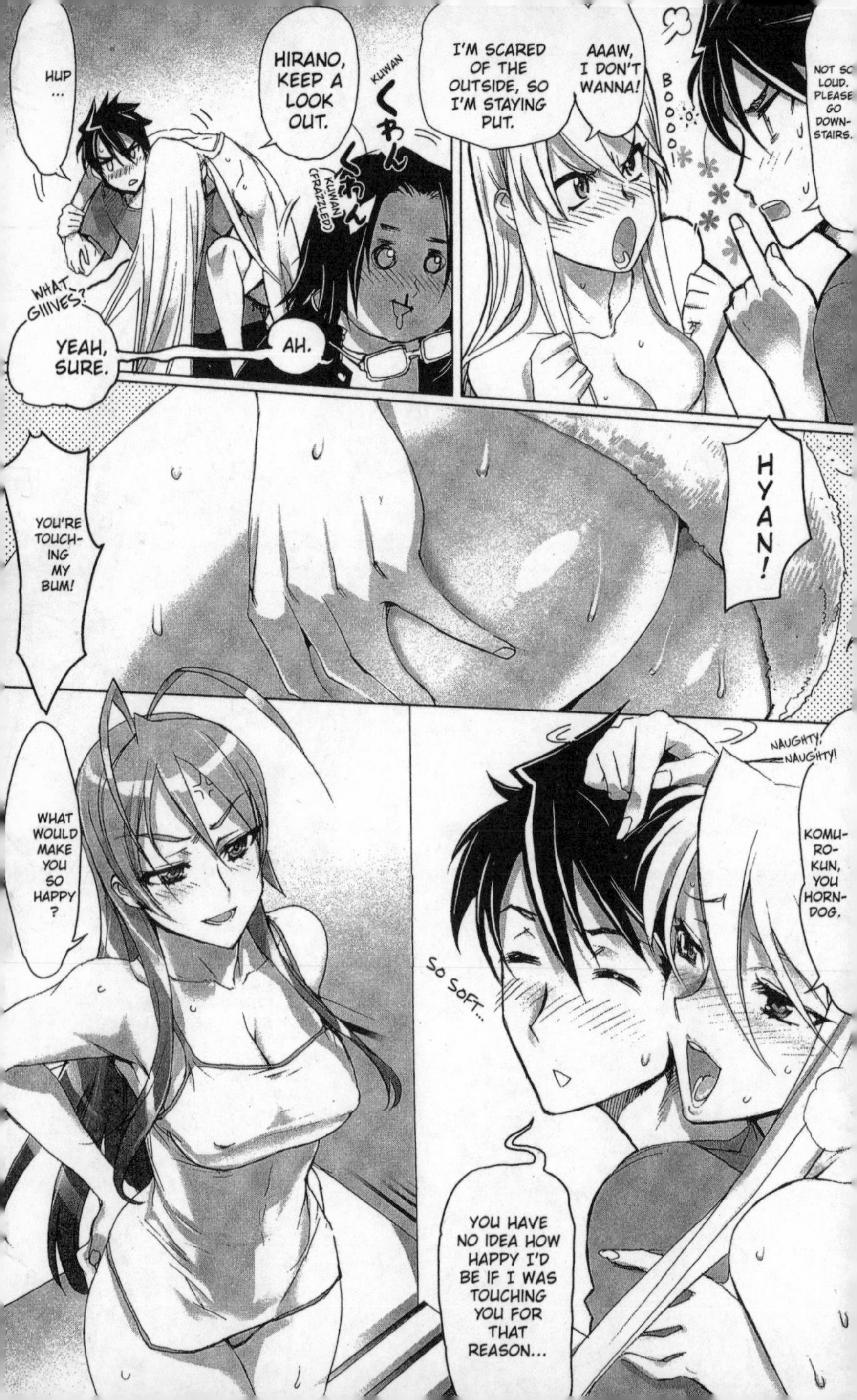
NOT SO LOUD. PLEASE GO DOWNSTAIRS.
BOOOOO!
AAAW, I DON'T WANNA!
I'M SCARED OF THE OUTSIDE, SO I'M STAYING PUT.
HIRANO, KEEP A LOOK OUT.
くわん KUWAN
くわん KUWAN (FRAZZLED)
HUP...
AH.
YEAH, SURE.
WHAT GIIVES?
HYAN!
YOU'RE TOUCHING MY BUM!
NAUGHTY, NAUGHTY!
KOMURO-KUN, YOU HORNDOG.
SO SOFT...
YOU HAVE NO IDEA HOW HAPPY I'D BE IF I WAS TOUCHING YOU FOR THAT REASON...
WHAT WOULD MAKE YOU SO HAPPY?

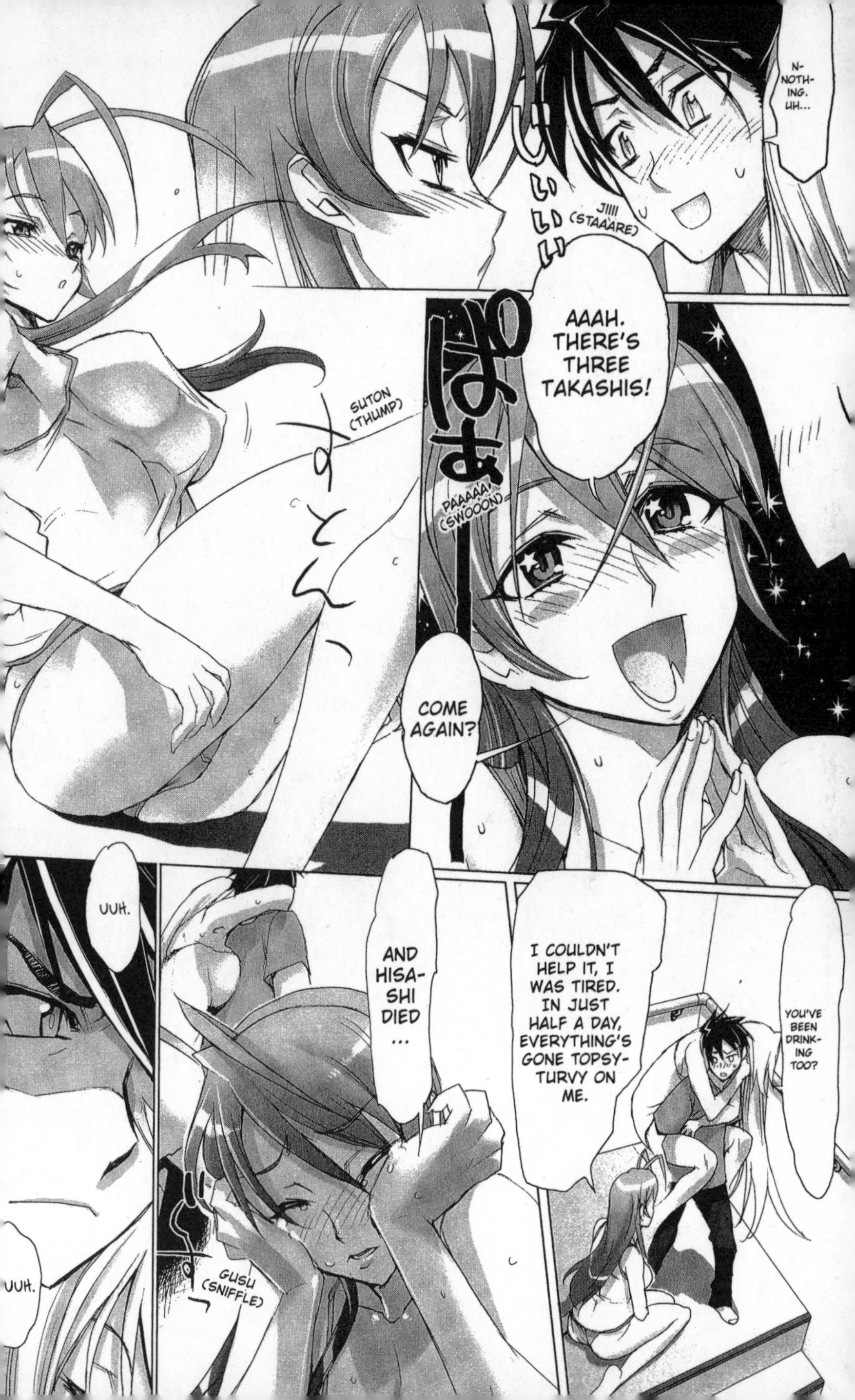
N-NOTHING. UH...
JIIII (STAAARE)
AAAH. THERE'S THREE TAKASHIS!
PAAAAA (SWOOON)
COME AGAIN?
SUTON (THUMP)
YOU'VE BEEN DRINKING TOO?
I COULDN'T HELP IT, I WAS TIRED. IN JUST HALF A DAY, EVERYTHING'S GONE TOPSY-TURVY ON ME.
AND HISASHI DIED ...
GUSU (SNIFFLE)
UUH.
UUH.

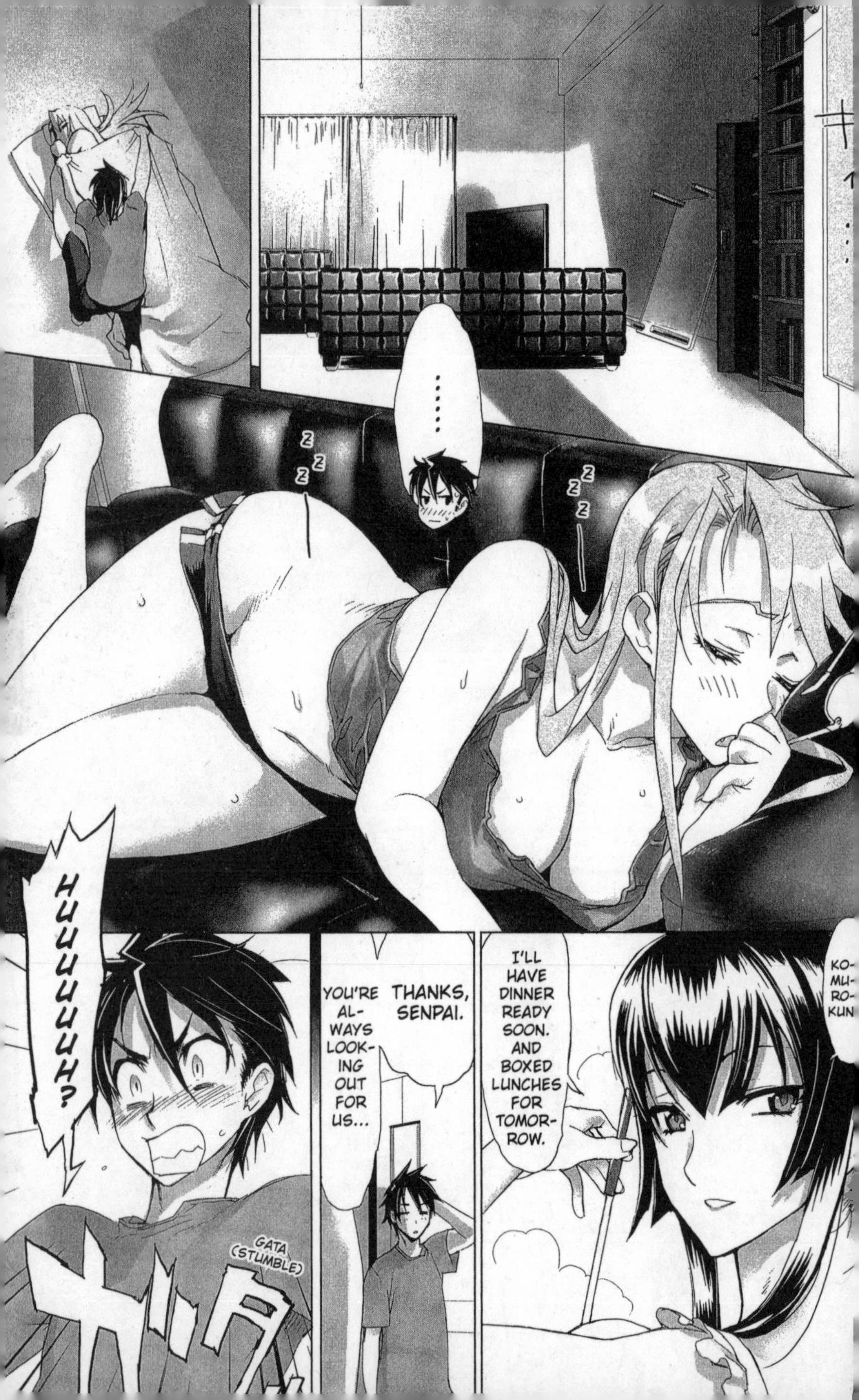
......
Z Z Z
Z Z Z
KO-MU-RO-KUN
I'LL HAVE DINNER READY SOON. AND BOXED LUNCHES FOR TOMORROW.
THANKS, SENPAI.
YOU'RE AL-WAYS LOOK-ING OUT FOR US...
HUUUUUUH?
GATA (STUMBLE)

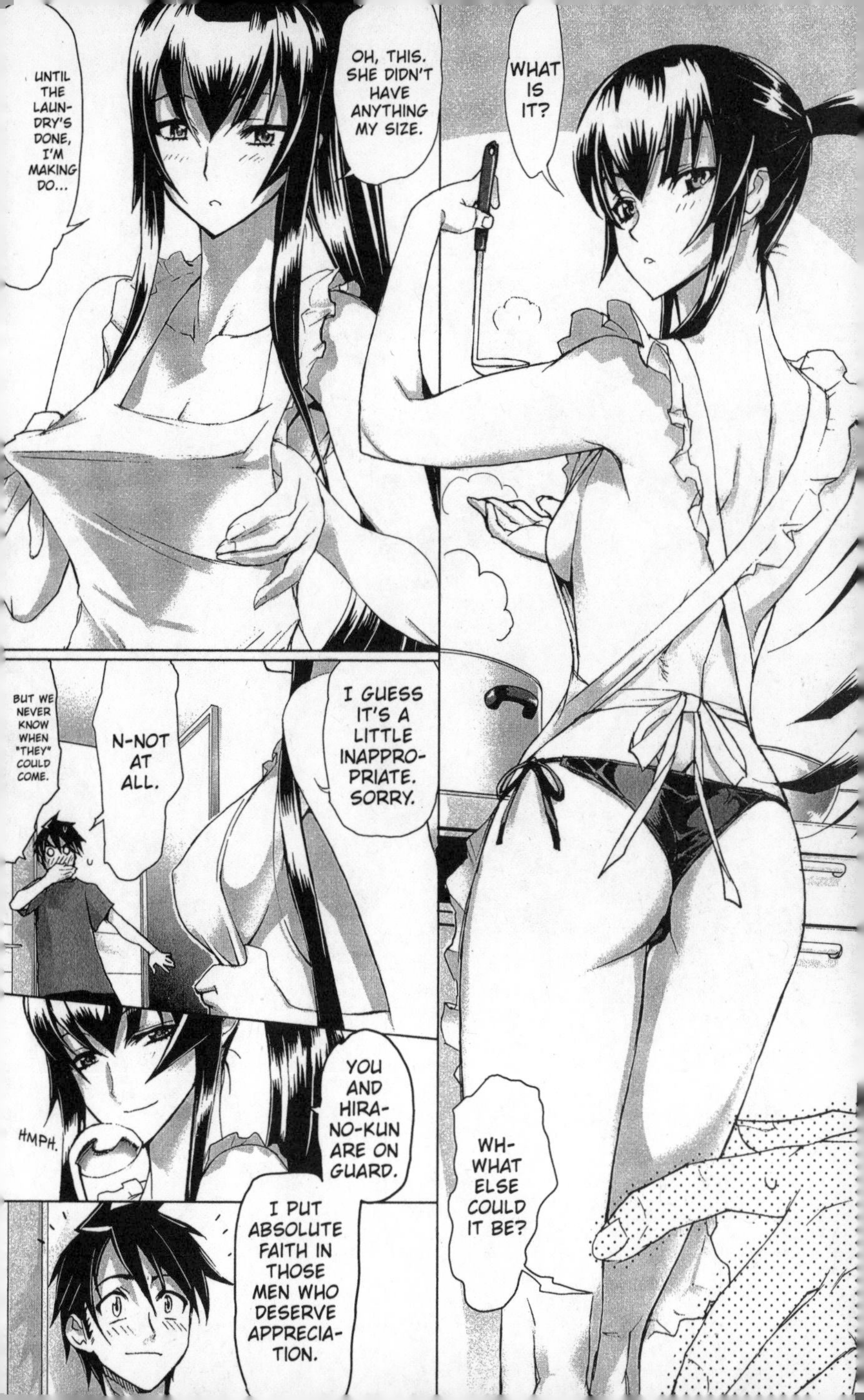
WHAT IS IT?
WH-WHAT ELSE COULD IT BE?
OH, THIS. SHE DIDN'T HAVE ANYTHING MY SIZE.
UNTIL THE LAUNDRY'S DONE, I'M MAKING DO...
I GUESS IT'S A LITTLE INAPPROPRIATE. SORRY.
N-NOT AT ALL.
BUT WE NEVER KNOW WHEN "THEY" COULD COME.
YOU AND HIRANO-KUN ARE ON GUARD.
HMPH.
I PUT ABSOLUTE FAITH IN THOSE MEN WHO DESERVE APPRECIATION.

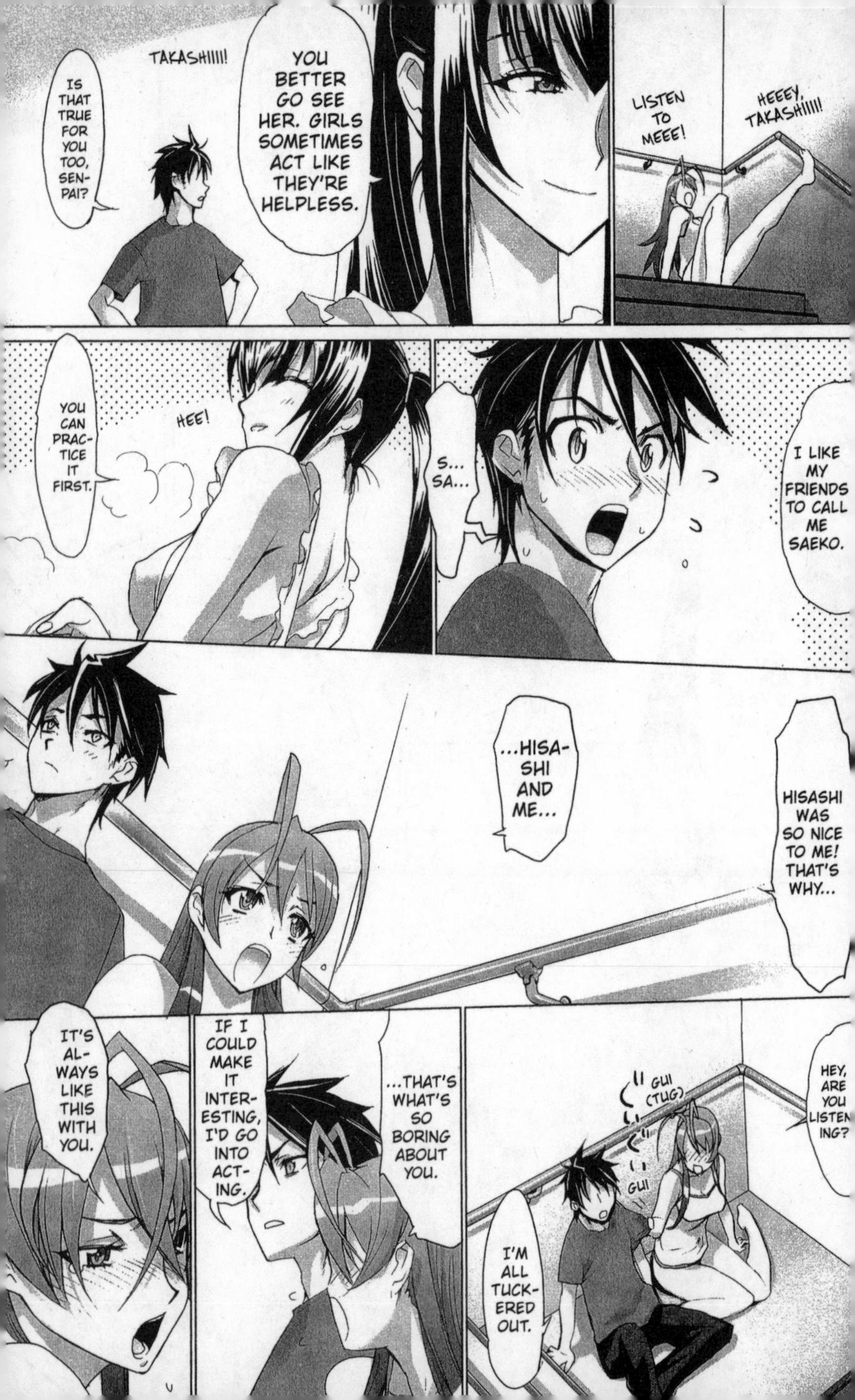
HEEEY, TAKASHIIIII!
LISTEN TO MEEE!
YOU BETTER GO SEE HER. GIRLS SOMETIMES ACT LIKE THEY'RE HELPLESS.
TAKASHIIIII!
IS THAT TRUE FOR YOU TOO, SENPAI?
I LIKE MY FRIENDS TO CALL ME SAEKO.
S... SA...
HEE!
YOU CAN PRACTICE IT FIRST.
HISASHI WAS SO NICE TO ME! THAT'S WHY...
...HISASHI AND ME...
HEY, ARE YOU LISTENING?
GUI (TUG)
GUI
I'M ALL TUCKERED OUT.
...THAT'S WHAT'S SO BORING ABOUT YOU.
IF I COULD MAKE IT INTERESTING, I'D GO INTO ACTING.
IT'S ALWAYS LIKE THIS WITH YOU.

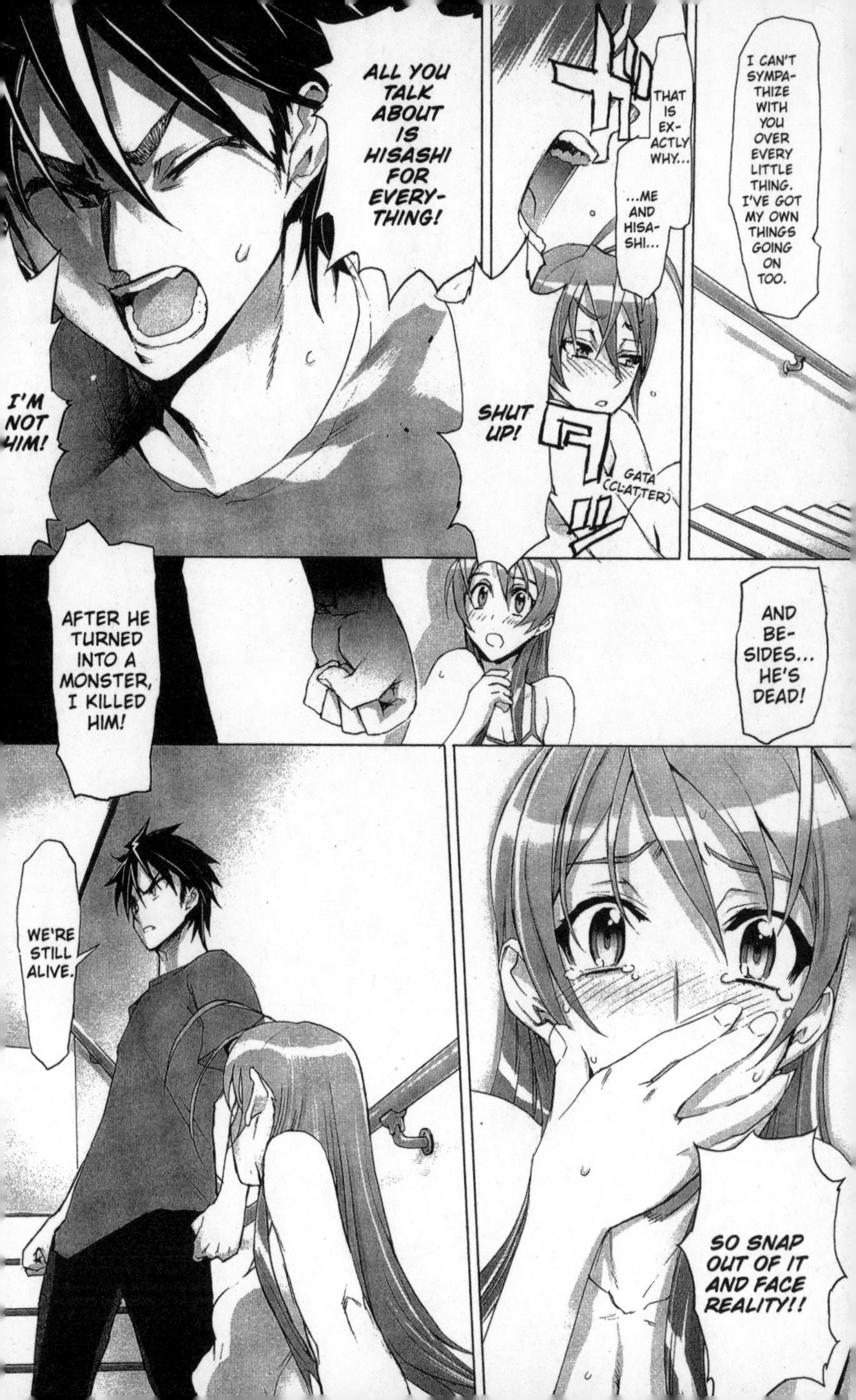
I CAN'T SYMPATHIZE WITH YOU OVER EVERY LITTLE THING. I'VE GOT MY OWN THINGS GOING ON TOO.
THAT IS EXACTLY WHY...
...ME AND HISASHI...
SHUT UP!
GATA (CLATTER)
ALL YOU TALK ABOUT IS HISASHI FOR EVERYTHING!
I'M NOT HIM!
AND BESIDES... HE'S DEAD!
AFTER HE TURNED INTO A MONSTER, I KILLED HIM!
SO SNAP OUT OF IT AND FACE REALITY!!
WE'RE STILL ALIVE.

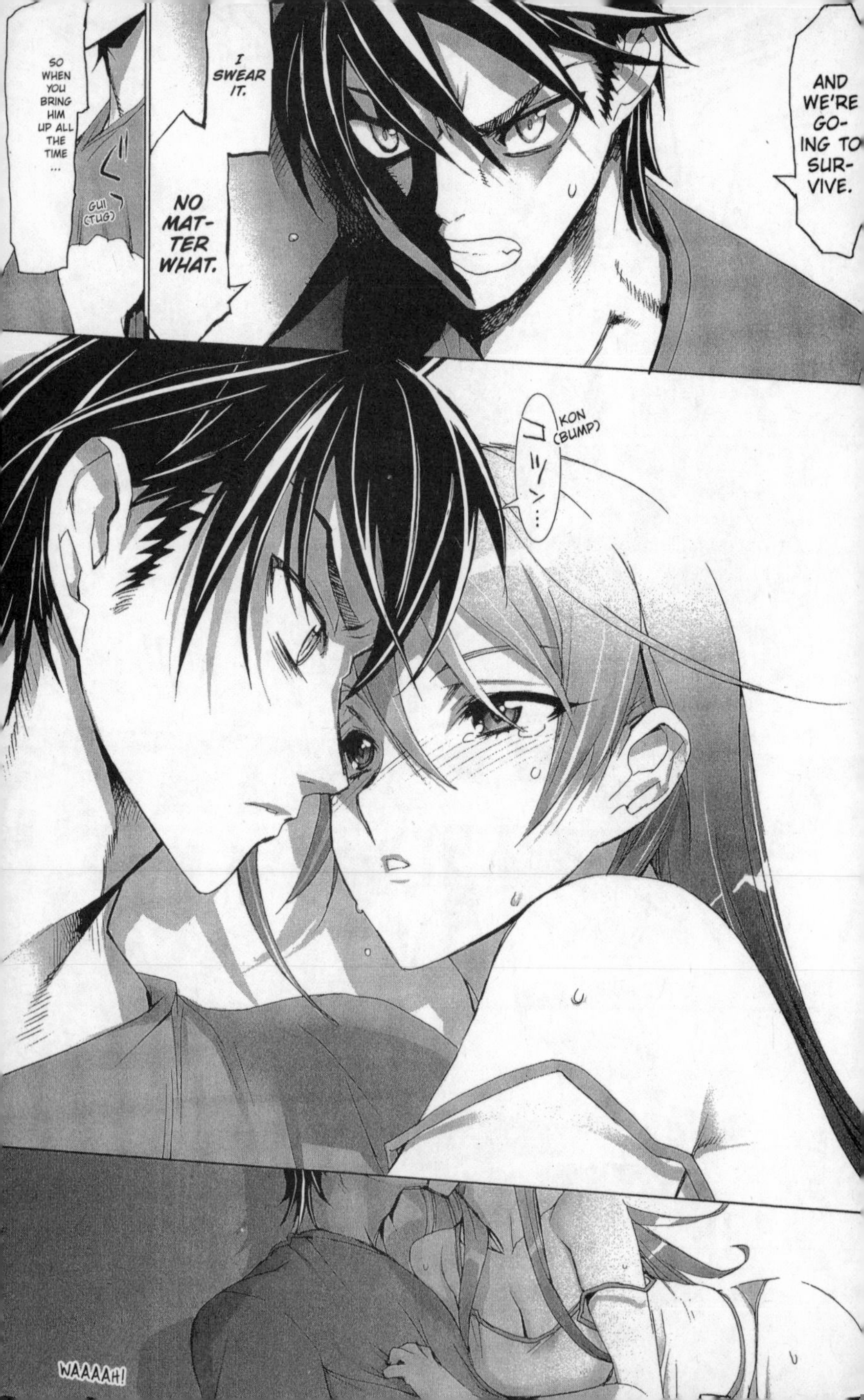
AND WE'RE GO-ING TO SUR-VIVE.
I SWEAR IT.
NO MAT-TER WHAT.
SO WHEN YOU BRING HIM UP ALL THE TIME ...
GUI (TUG)
KON (BUMP)
WAAAAH!

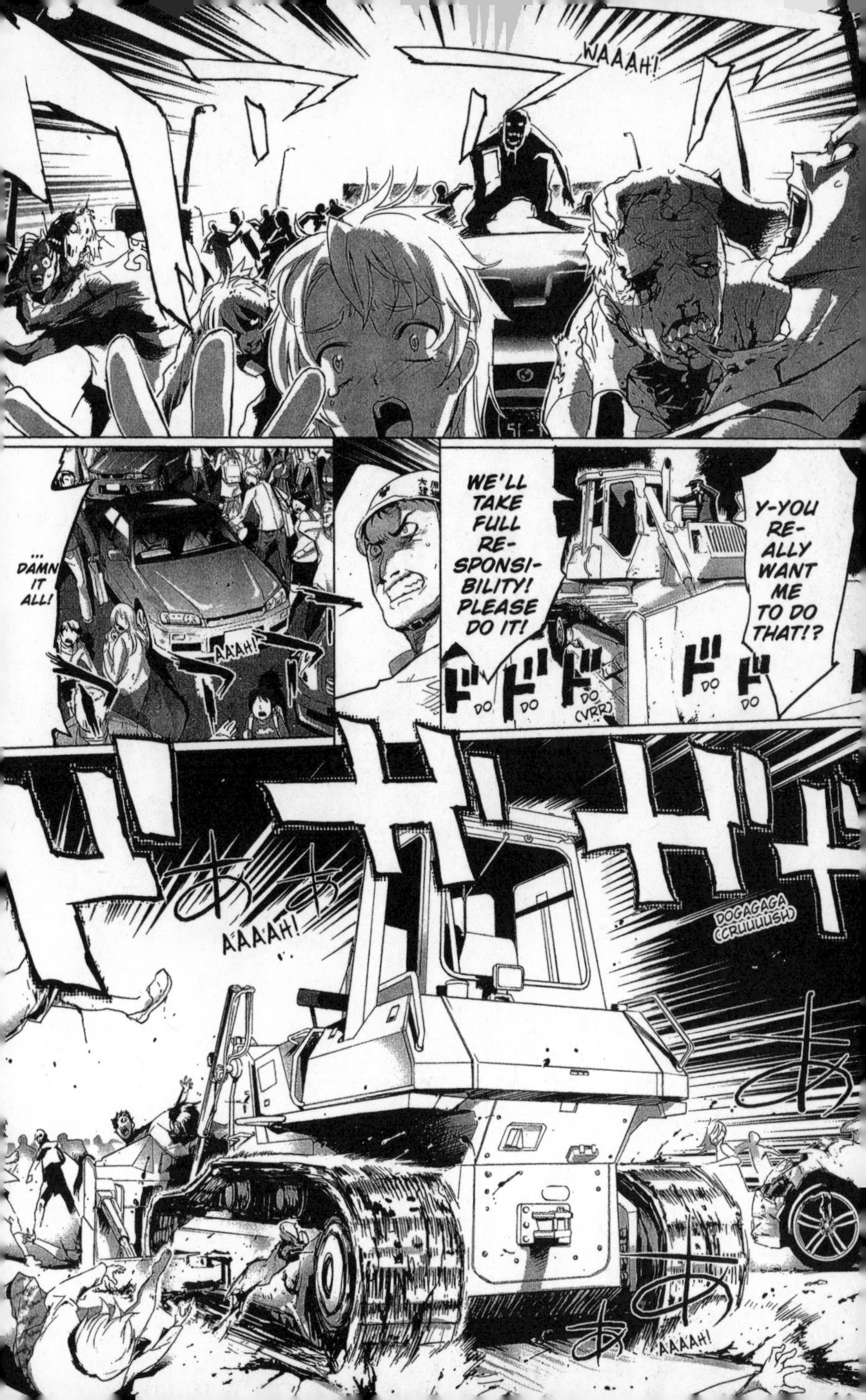
WAAAH!
WE'LL TAKE FULL RE-SPONSIBILITY! PLEASE DO IT!
Y-YOU RE-ALLY WANT ME TO DO THAT!?
DO DO DO DO DO (VRR)
... DAMN IT ALL!
AAAH!
DOGAGAGA (CRUUUUSH)
AAAAH!
AAAAH!

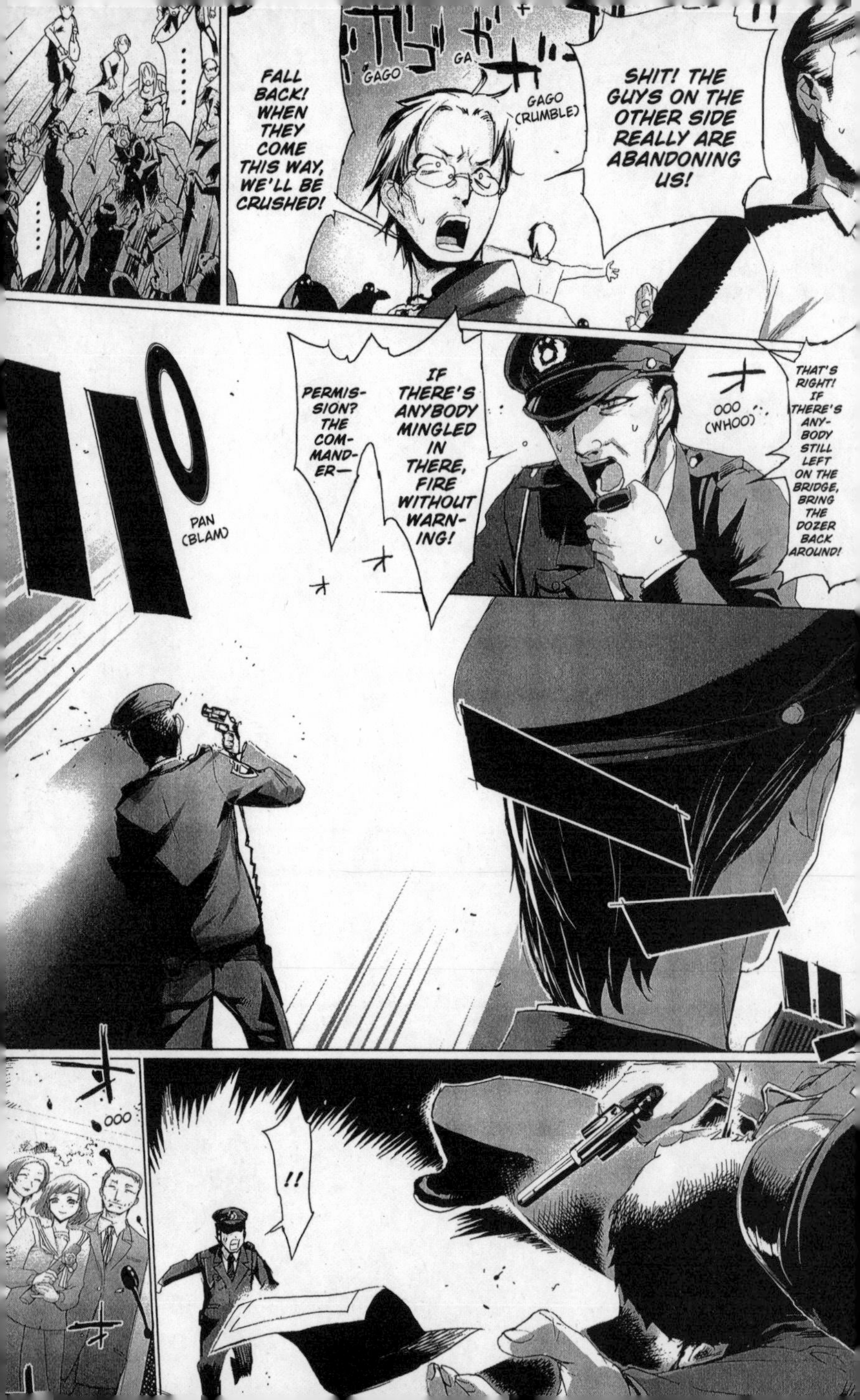
SHIT! THE GUYS ON THE OTHER SIDE REALLY ARE ABANDONING US!
GAGO
GA
GAGO (RUMBLE)
FALL BACK! WHEN THEY COME THIS WAY, WE'LL BE CRUSHED!
THAT'S RIGHT! IF THERE'S ANYBODY STILL LEFT ON THE BRIDGE, BRING THE DOZER BACK AROUND!
OOO (WHOO)
IF THERE'S ANYBODY MINGLED IN THERE, FIRE WITHOUT WARNING!
PERMISSION? THE COMMANDER—
PAN (BLAM)
!!
OOO

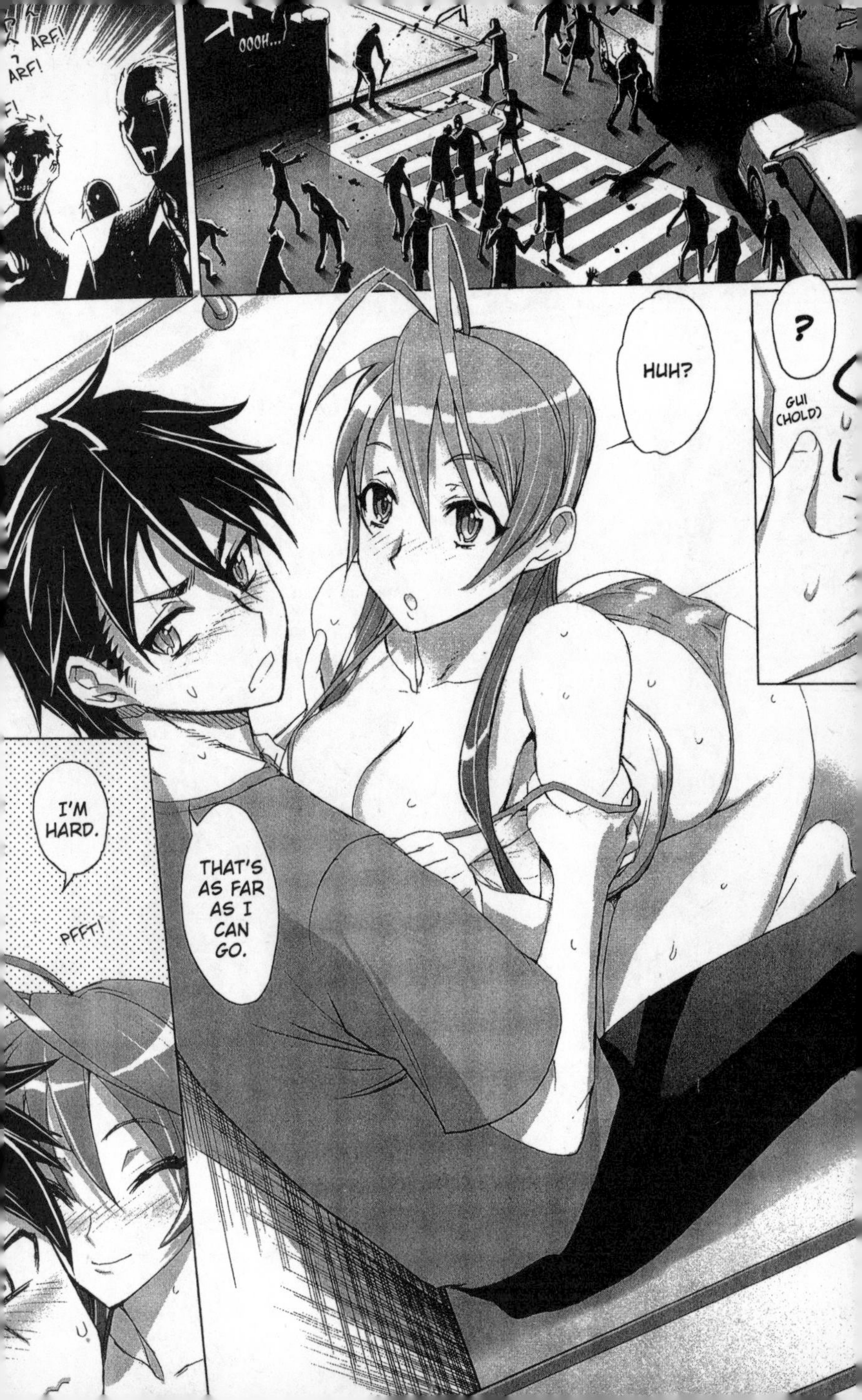
OOOH...
ARF!
ARF!
?
GUI (HOLD)
HUH?
THAT'S AS FAR AS I CAN GO.
I'M HARD.
PFFT!

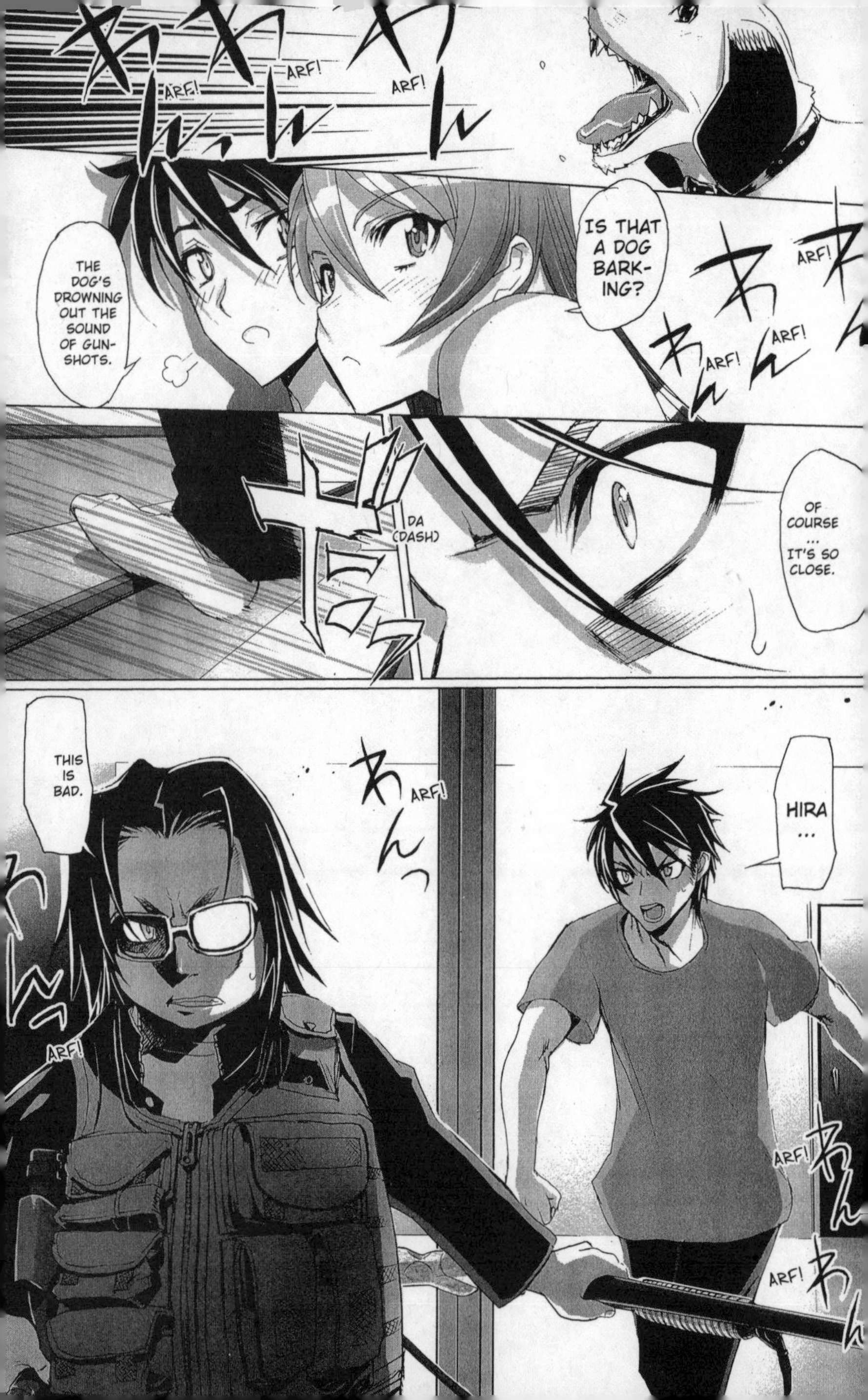
ARF!
ARF!
ARF!
IS THAT A DOG BARKING?
ARF!
ARF!
ARF!
THE DOG'S DROWNING OUT THE SOUND OF GUN-SHOTS.
OF COURSE ... IT'S SO CLOSE.
DA (DASH)
HIRA ...
ARF!
ARF!
THIS IS BAD.
ARF!
ARF!

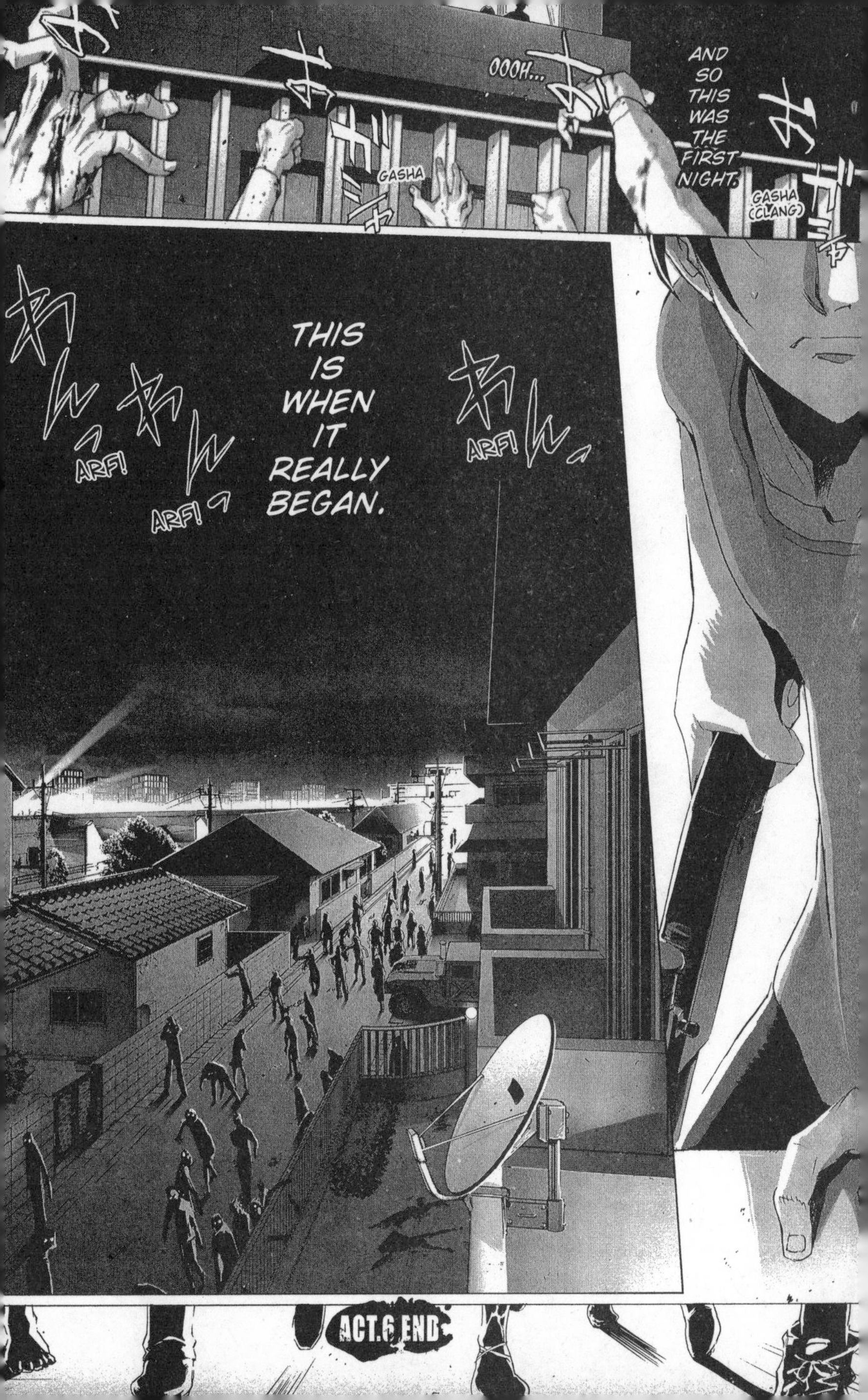
AND SO THIS WAS THE FIRST NIGHT.
GASHA (CLANG)
OOOH...
GASHA
ARF!
THIS IS WHEN IT REALLY BEGAN.
ARF!
ARF!
ACT.6 END

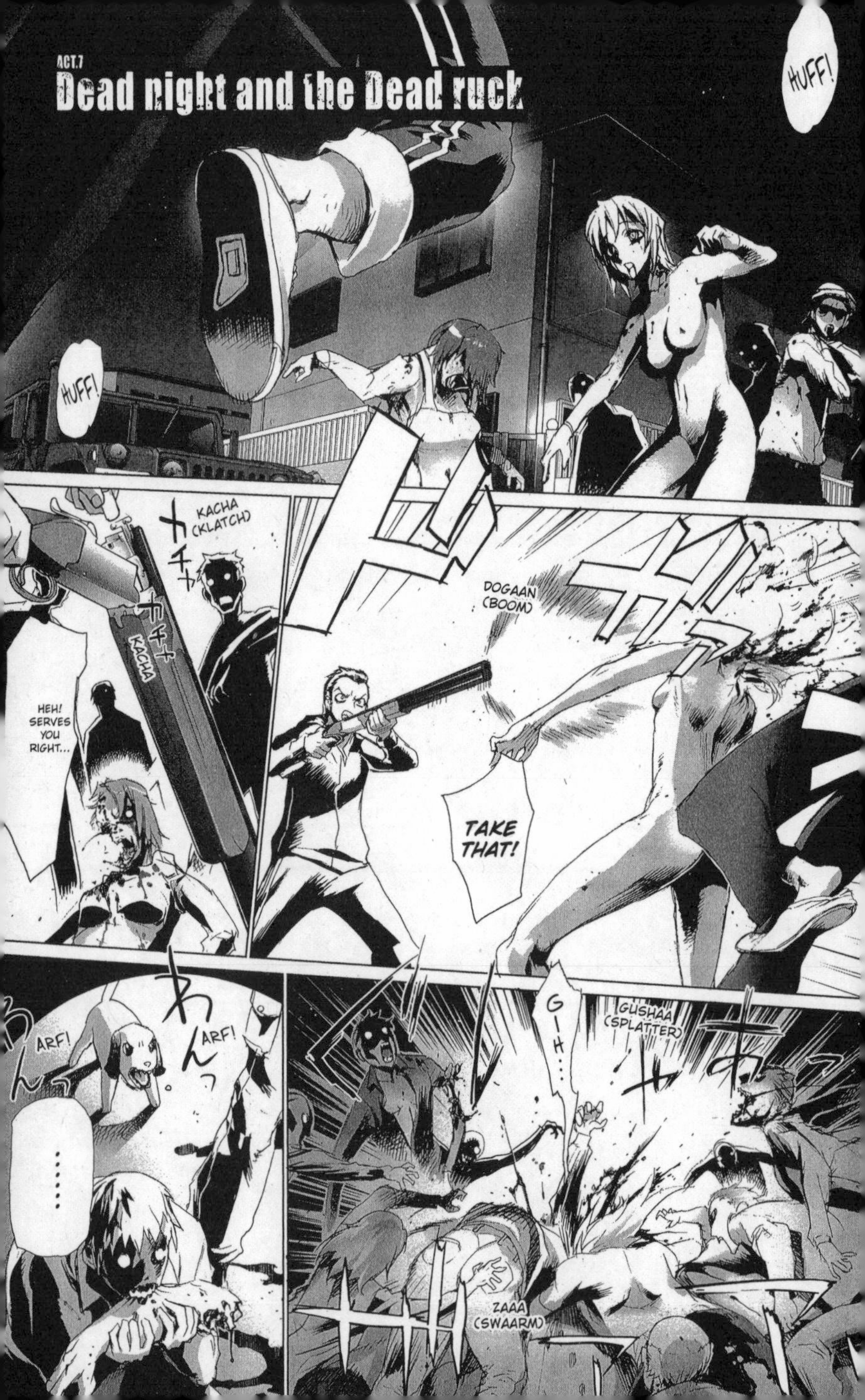
ACT.7
Dead night and the Dead ruck
HUFF!
HUFF!
DOGAAN (BOOM)
TAKE THAT!
KACHA (KLATCH)
KACHA
HEH! SERVES YOU RIGHT...
GUSHAA (SPLATTER)
GIH...
ZAAA (SWAARM)
ARF!
ARF!
......

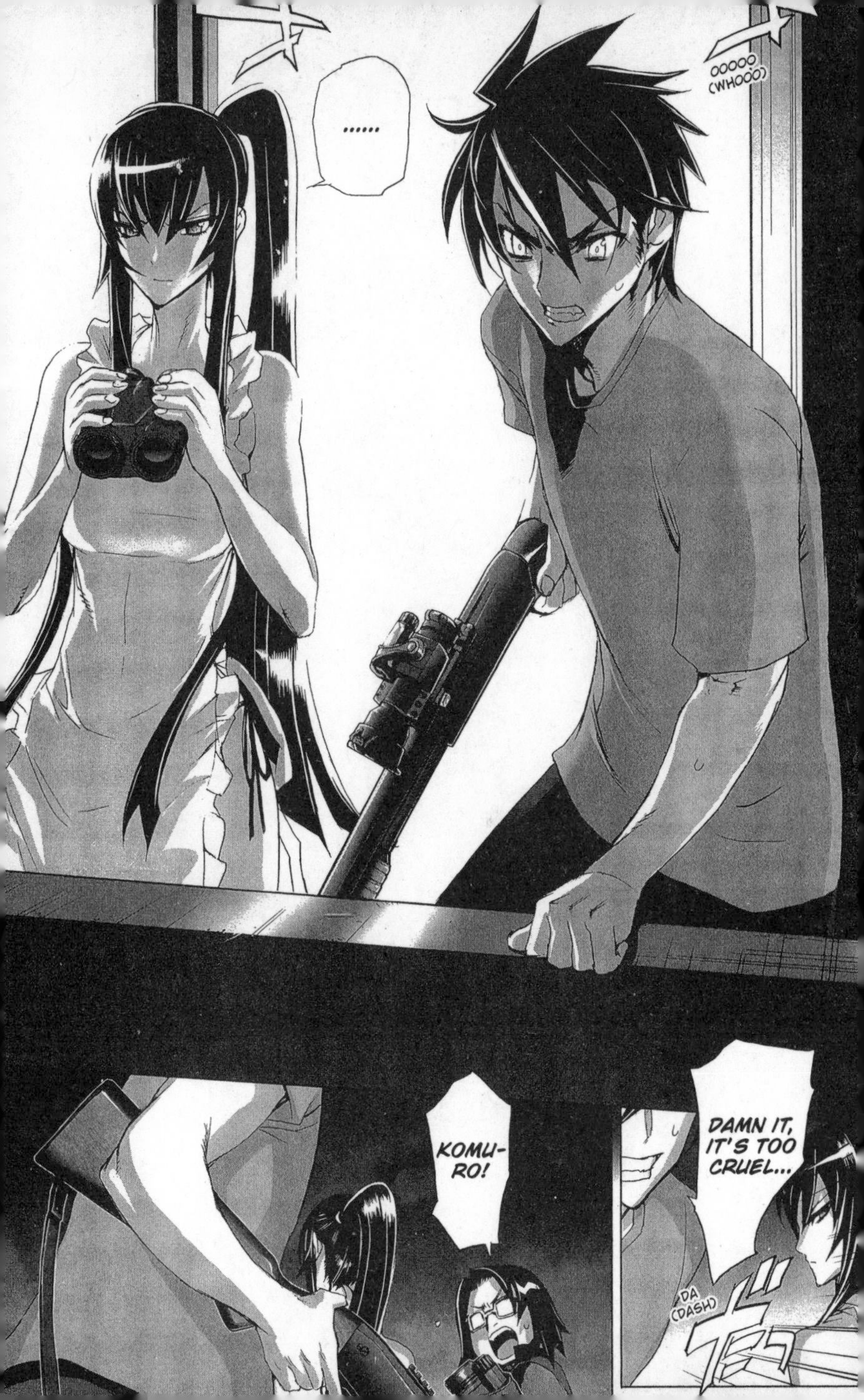
OOOOO (WHOOO)
......
DAMN IT, IT'S TOO CRUEL...
DA (DASH)
KOMU-RO!

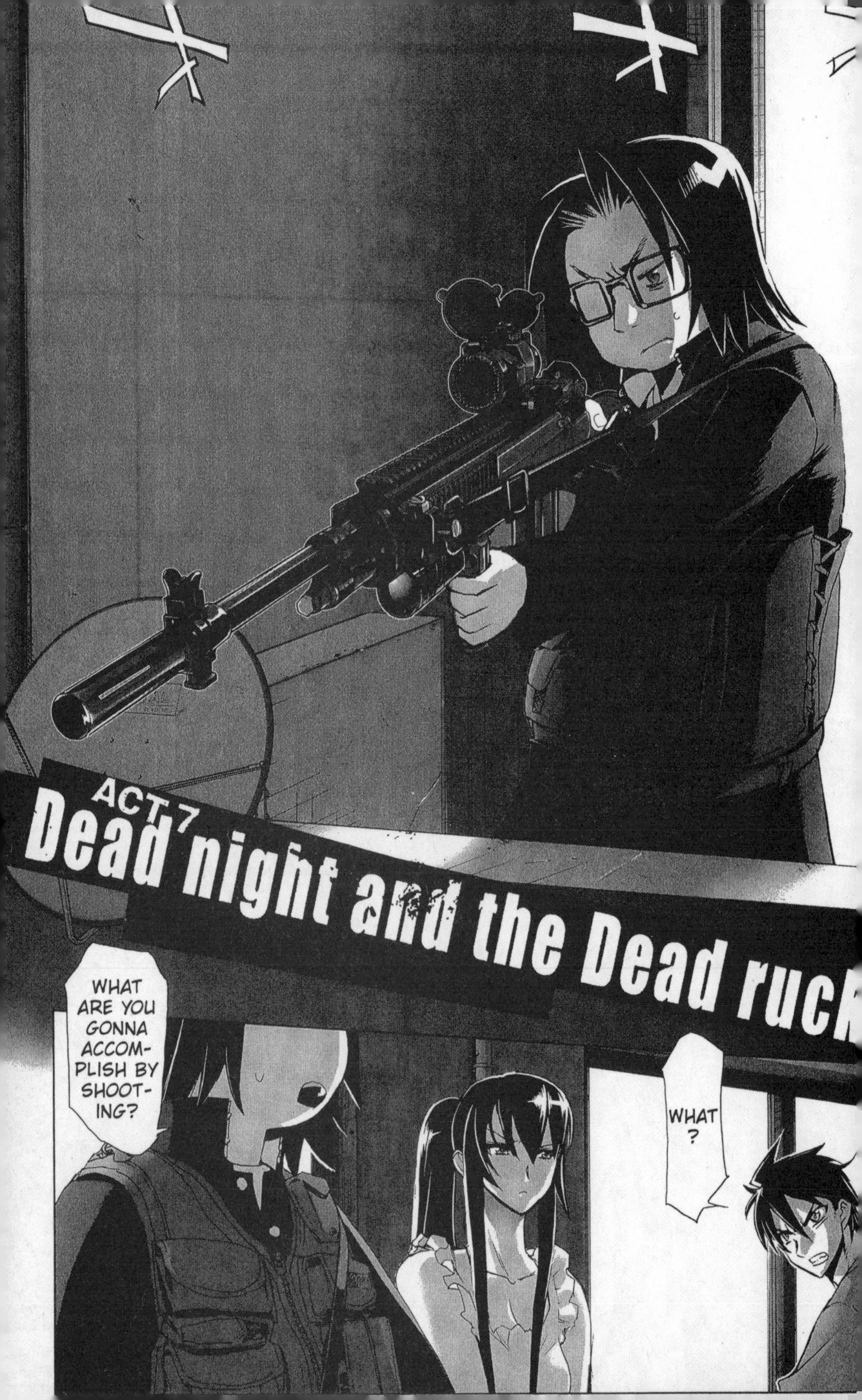
ACT 7
Dead night and the Dead ruck
WHAT ARE YOU GONNA ACCOMPLISH BY SHOOTING?
WHAT?

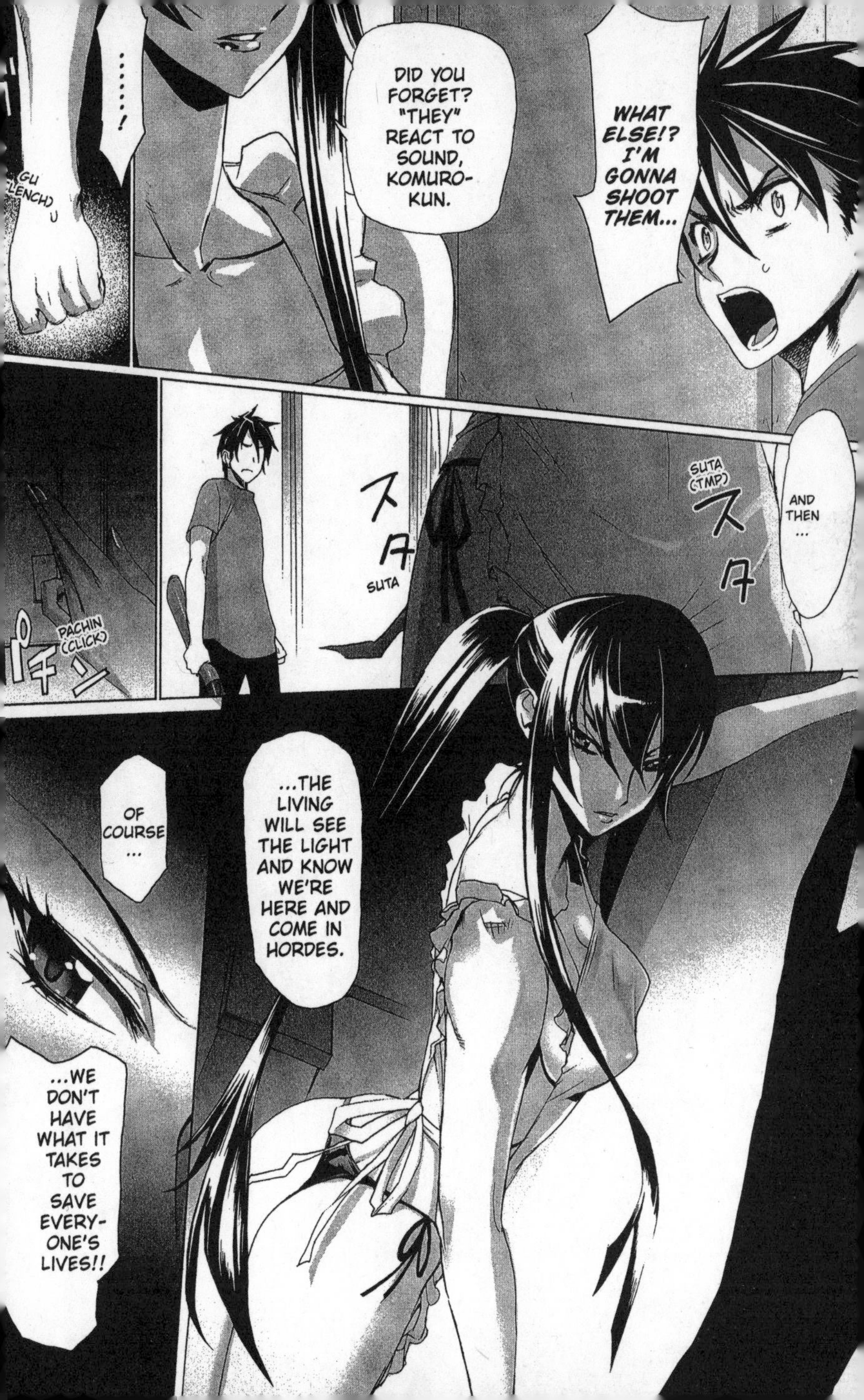
WHAT ELSE!? I'M GONNA SHOOT THEM...
DID YOU FORGET? "THEY" REACT TO SOUND, KOMURO-KUN.
......!
GU (CLENCH)
AND THEN ...
SUTA (TMP)
スタ
スタ
SUTA
パチン
PACHIN (CLICK)
...THE LIVING WILL SEE THE LIGHT AND KNOW WE'RE HERE AND COME IN HORDES.
OF COURSE ...
...WE DON'T HAVE WHAT IT TAKES TO SAVE EVERY-ONE'S LIVES!!

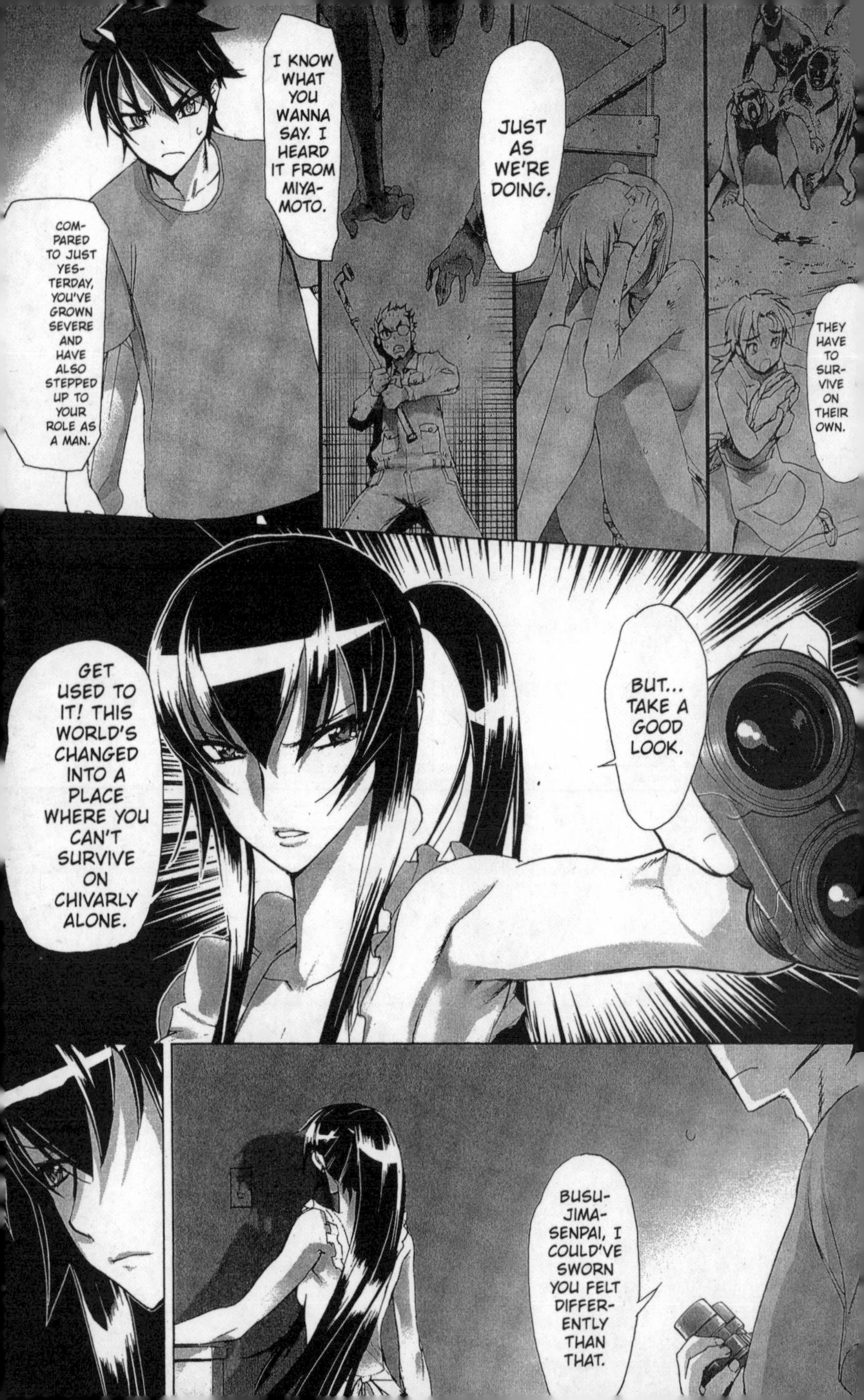
THEY HAVE TO SURVIVE ON THEIR OWN.
JUST AS WE'RE DOING.
I KNOW WHAT YOU WANNA SAY. I HEARD IT FROM MIYAMOTO.
COMPARED TO JUST YESTERDAY, YOU'VE GROWN SEVERE AND HAVE ALSO STEPPED UP TO YOUR ROLE AS A MAN.
BUT... TAKE A GOOD LOOK.
GET USED TO IT! THIS WORLD'S CHANGED INTO A PLACE WHERE YOU CAN'T SURVIVE ON CHIVALRY ALONE.
BUSUJIMA-SENPAI, I COULD'VE SWORN YOU FELT DIFFERENTLY THAN THAT.

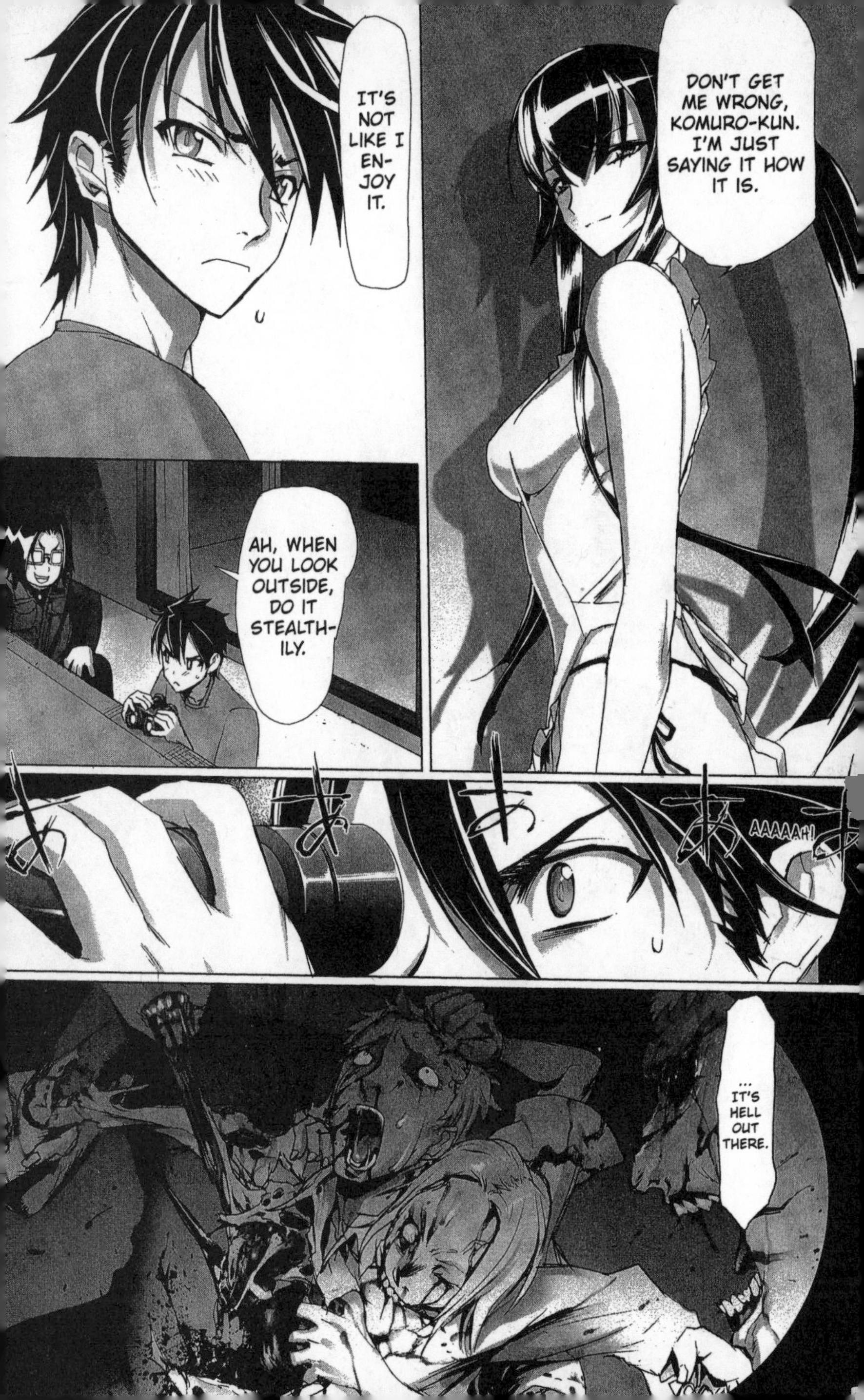
DON'T GET ME WRONG, KOMURO-KUN. I'M JUST SAYING IT HOW IT IS.
IT'S NOT LIKE I EN-JOY IT.
AH, WHEN YOU LOOK OUTSIDE, DO IT STEALTH-ILY.
AAAAAH!
... IT'S HELL OUT THERE.

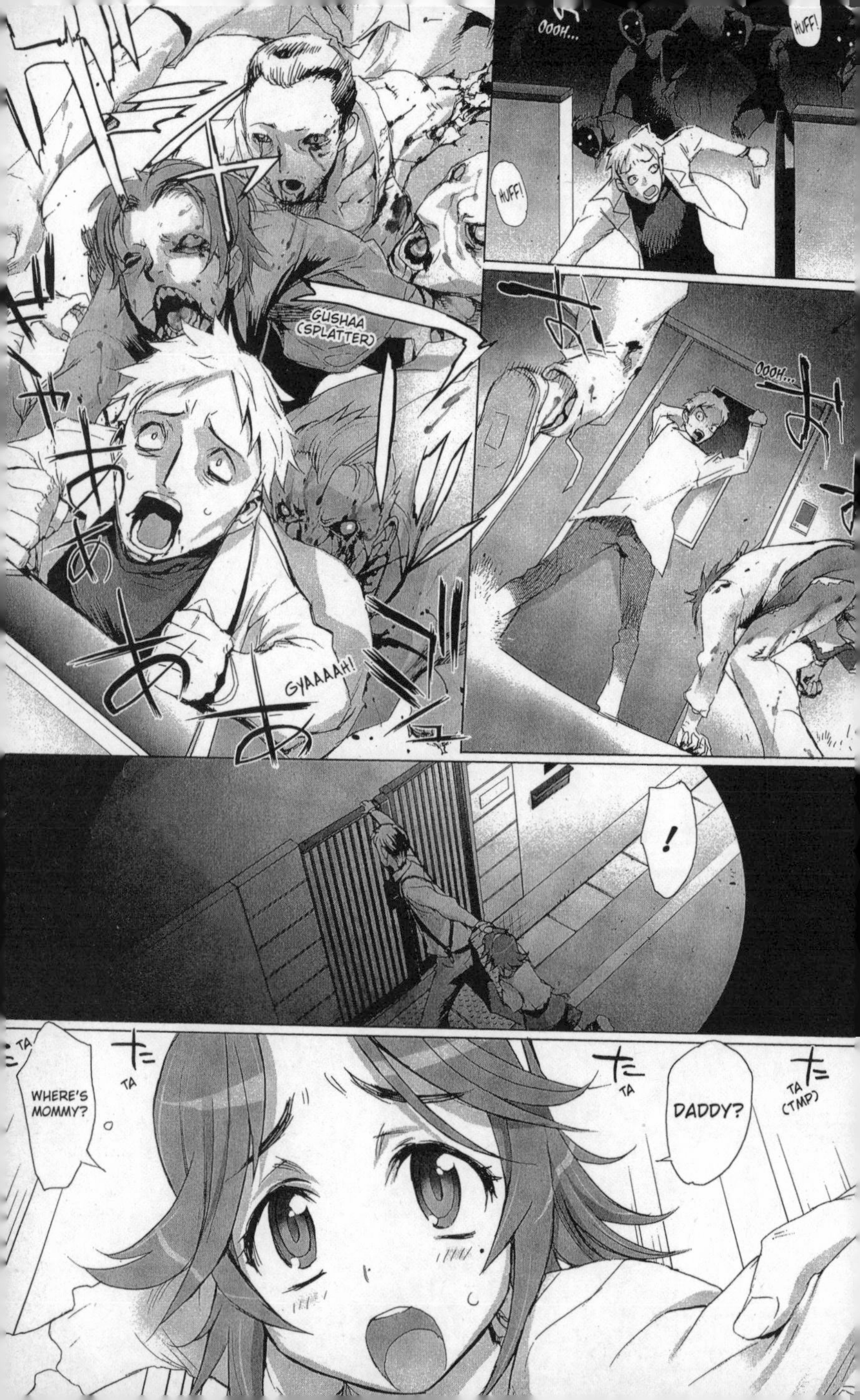
HUFF!
OOOH...
HUFF!
OOOH...
GUSHAA (SPLATTER)
GYAAAAH!
!
TA (TMP)
DADDY?
TA
TA
WHERE'S MOMMY?
TA

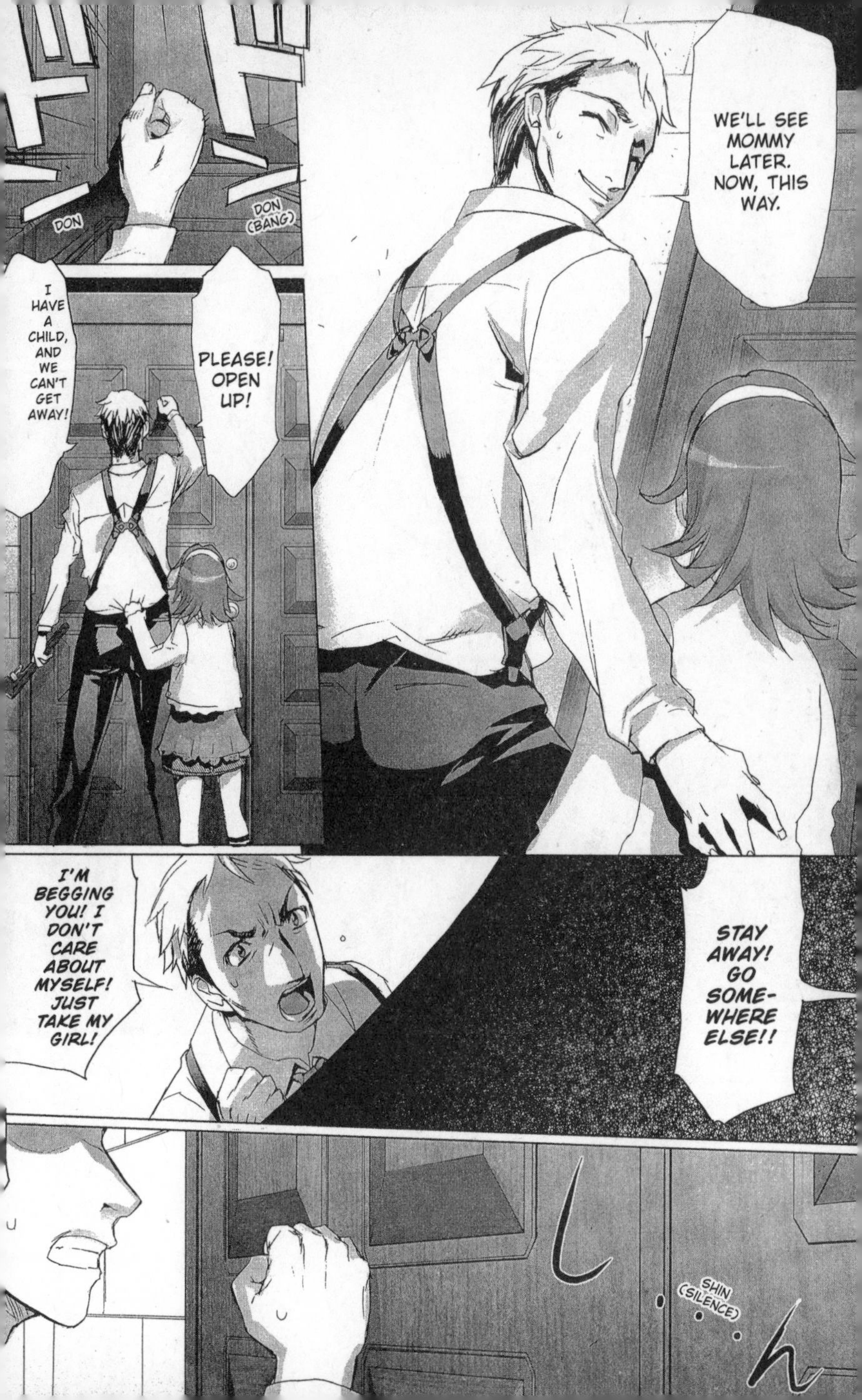
WE'LL SEE MOMMY LATER. NOW, THIS WAY.
DON (BANG)
DON
PLEASE! OPEN UP!
I HAVE A CHILD, AND WE CAN'T GET AWAY!
STAY AWAY! GO SOME-WHERE ELSE!!
I'M BEGGING YOU! I DON'T CARE ABOUT MYSELF! JUST TAKE MY GIRL!
SHIN (SILENCE)

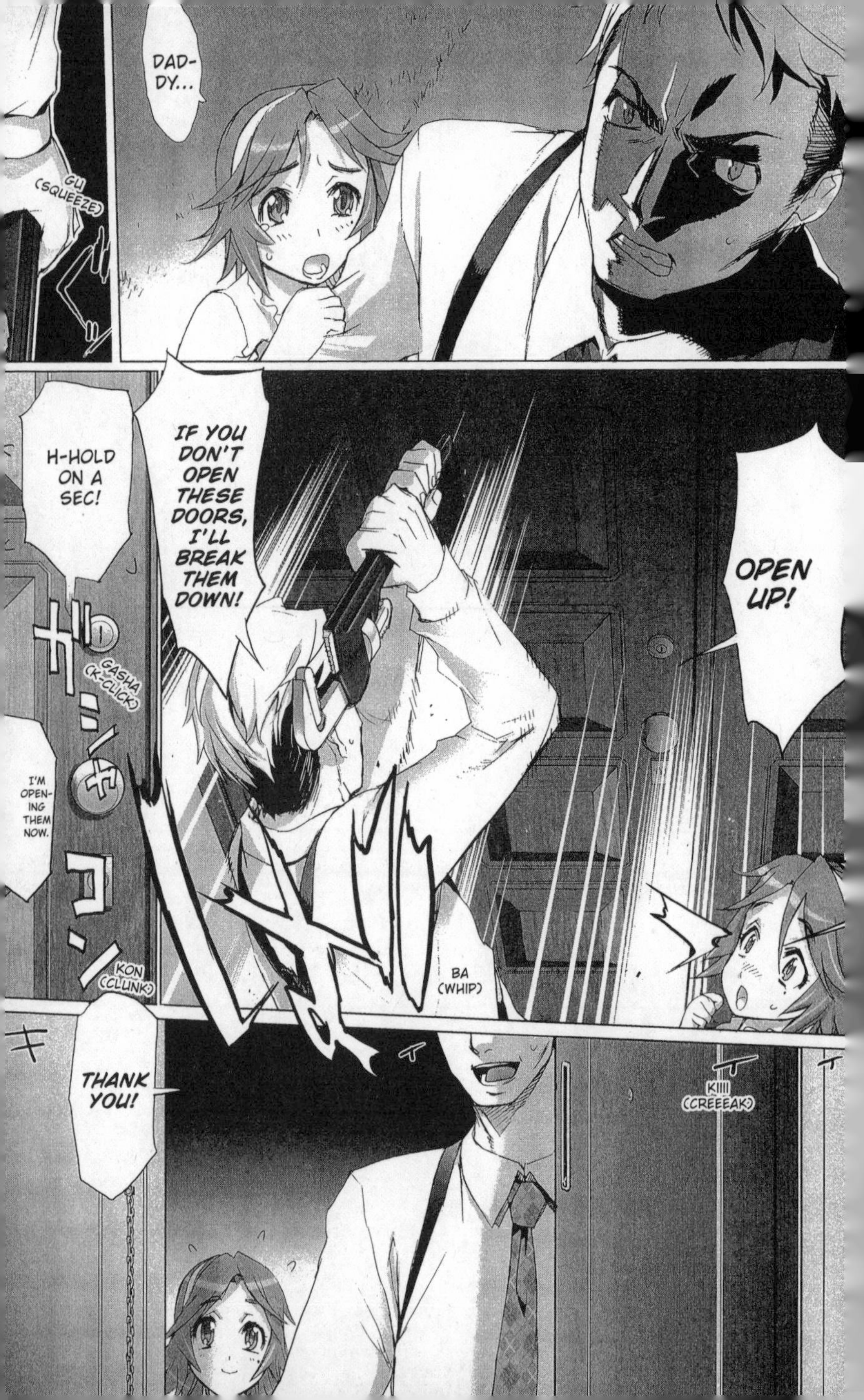
DADDY...
GU (SQUEEZE)
OPEN UP!
IF YOU DON'T OPEN THESE DOORS, I'LL BREAK THEM DOWN!
BA (WHIP)
H-HOLD ON A SEC!
GASHA (K-CLICK)
I'M OPENING THEM NOW.
KON (CLUNK)
KIIII (CREEEAK)
THANK YOU!

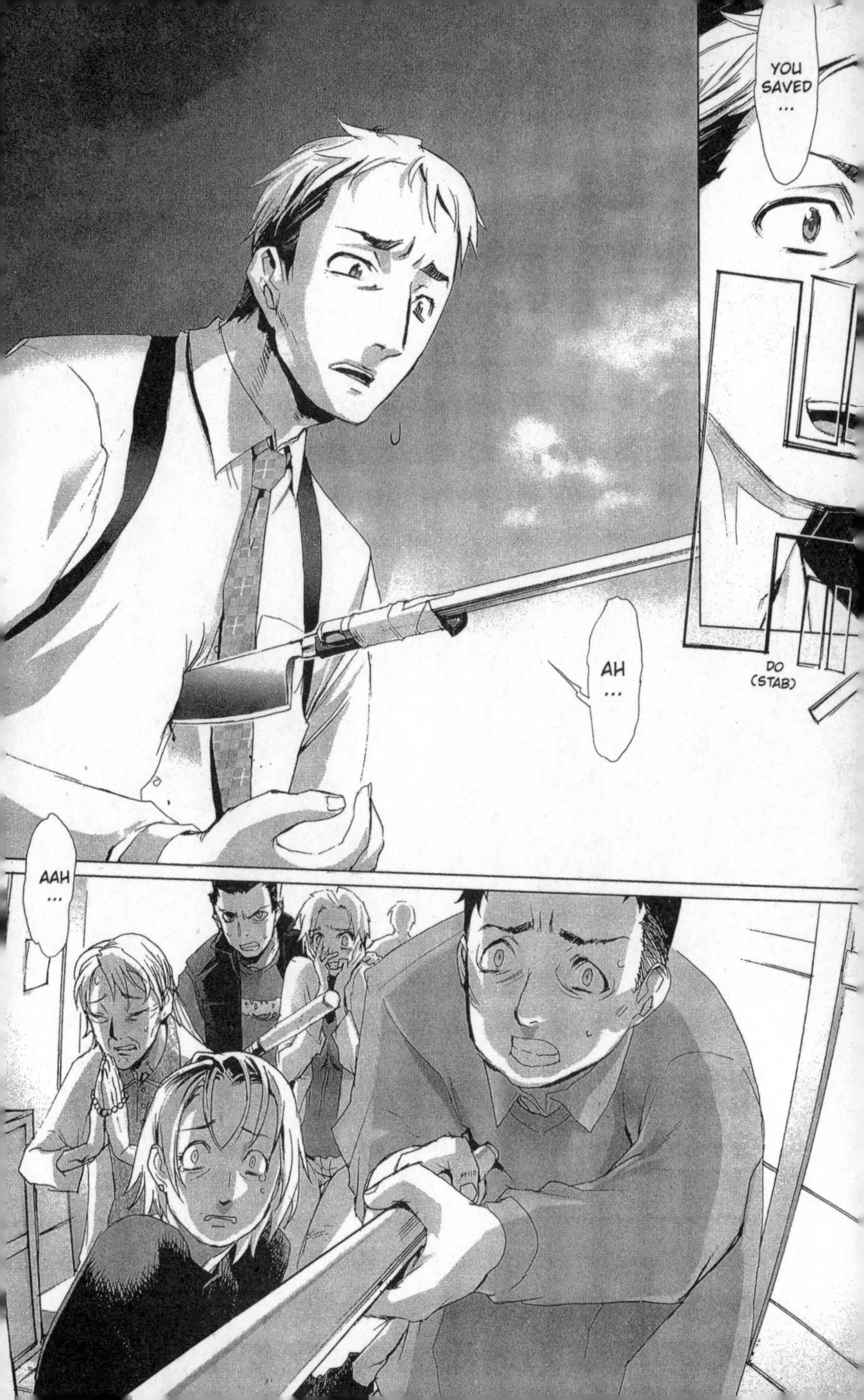
YOU SAVED ...
DO (STAB)
AH ...
AAH ...

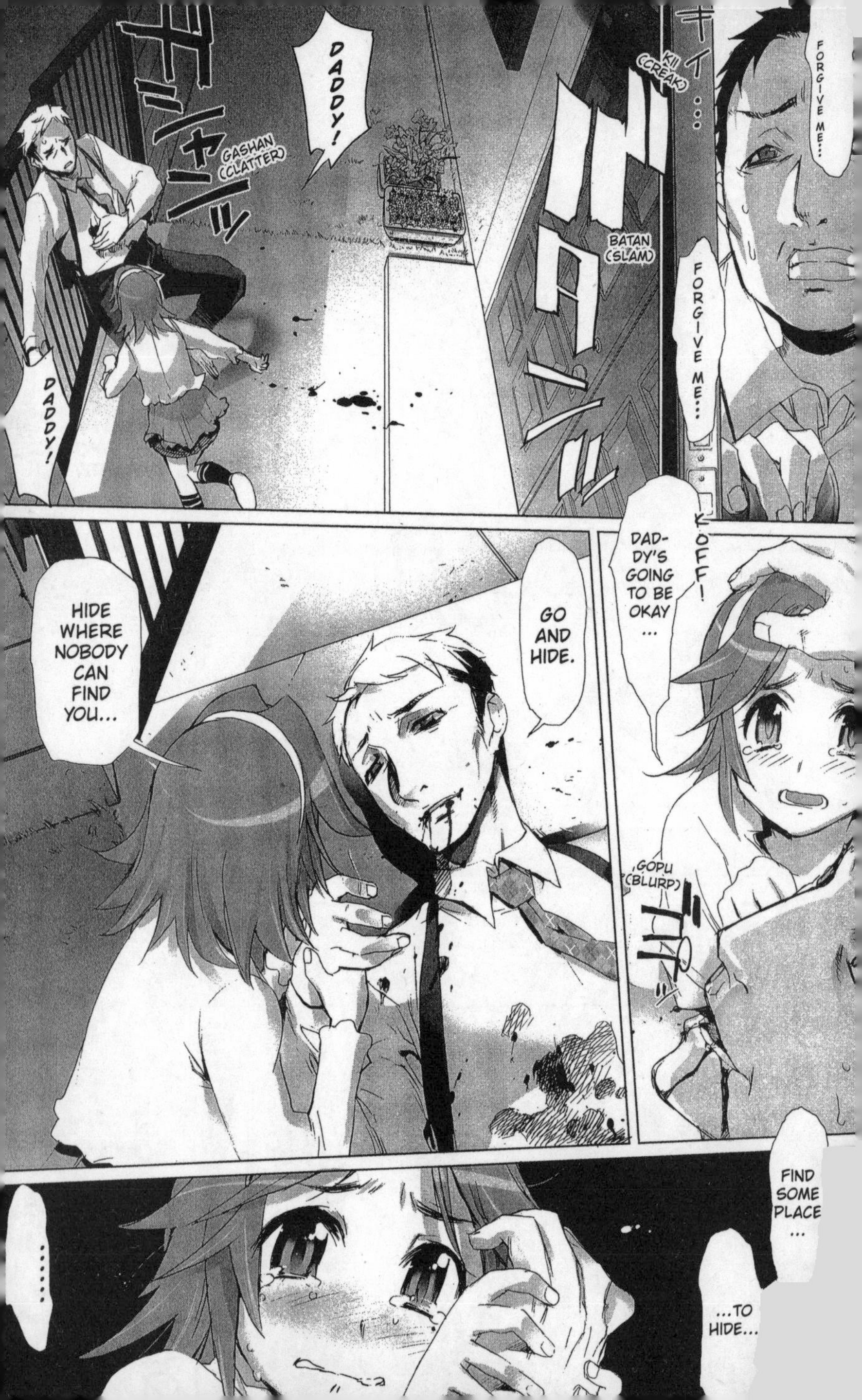
FORGIVE ME...
KII (CREAK) ...
FORGIVE ME...
BATAN (SLAM)
DADDY!
GASHAN (CLATTER)
DADDY!
KOFF!
DAD-DY'S GOING TO BE OKAY...
GOPU (BLURP)
GO AND HIDE.
HIDE WHERE NOBODY CAN FIND YOU...
FIND SOME PLACE...
...TO HIDE...
......

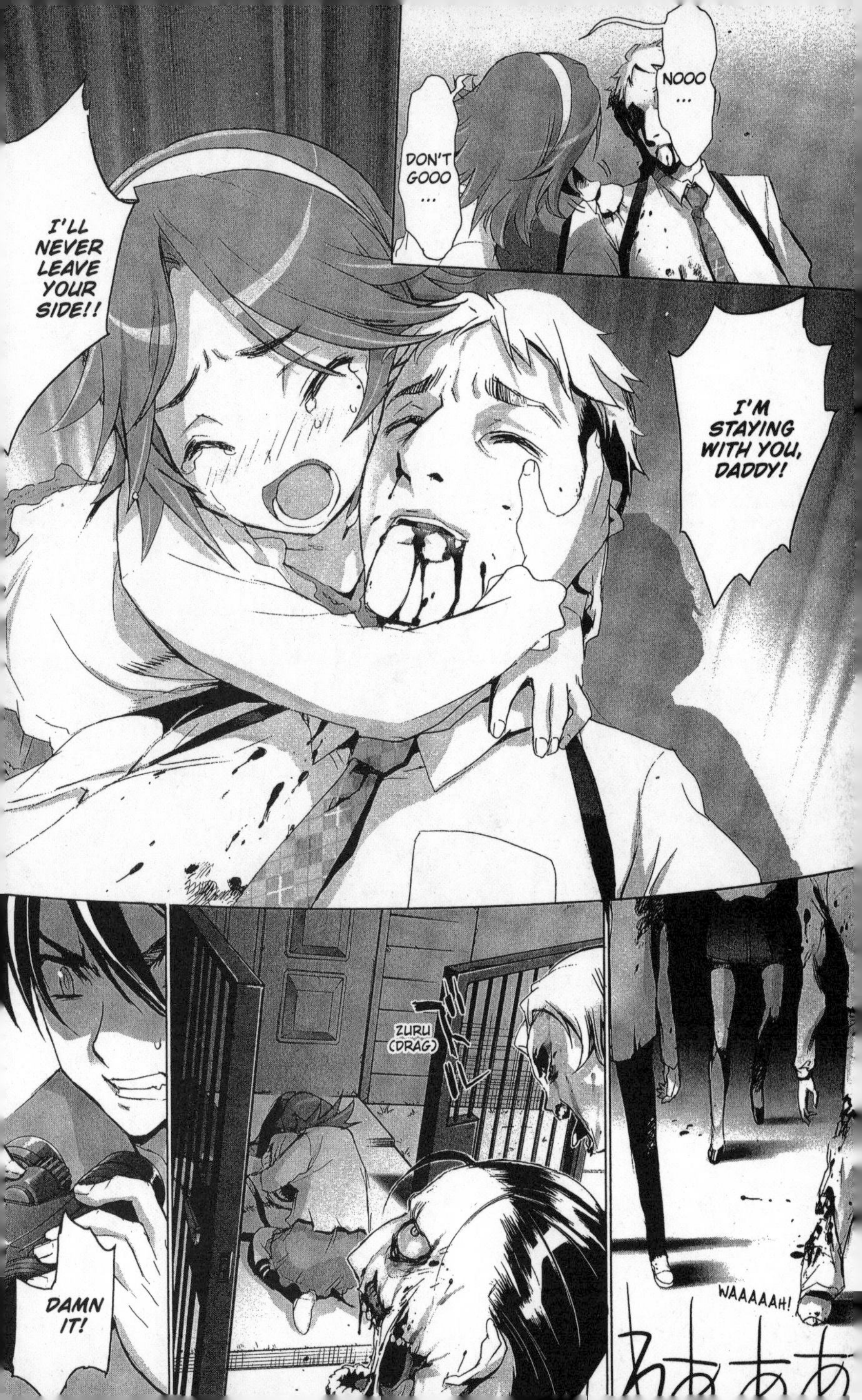

NOOO ...
DON'T GOOO ...
I'M STAYING WITH YOU, DADDY!
I'LL NEVER LEAVE YOUR SIDE!!
WAAAAAH!
あああ
ZURU (DRAG)
DAMN IT!

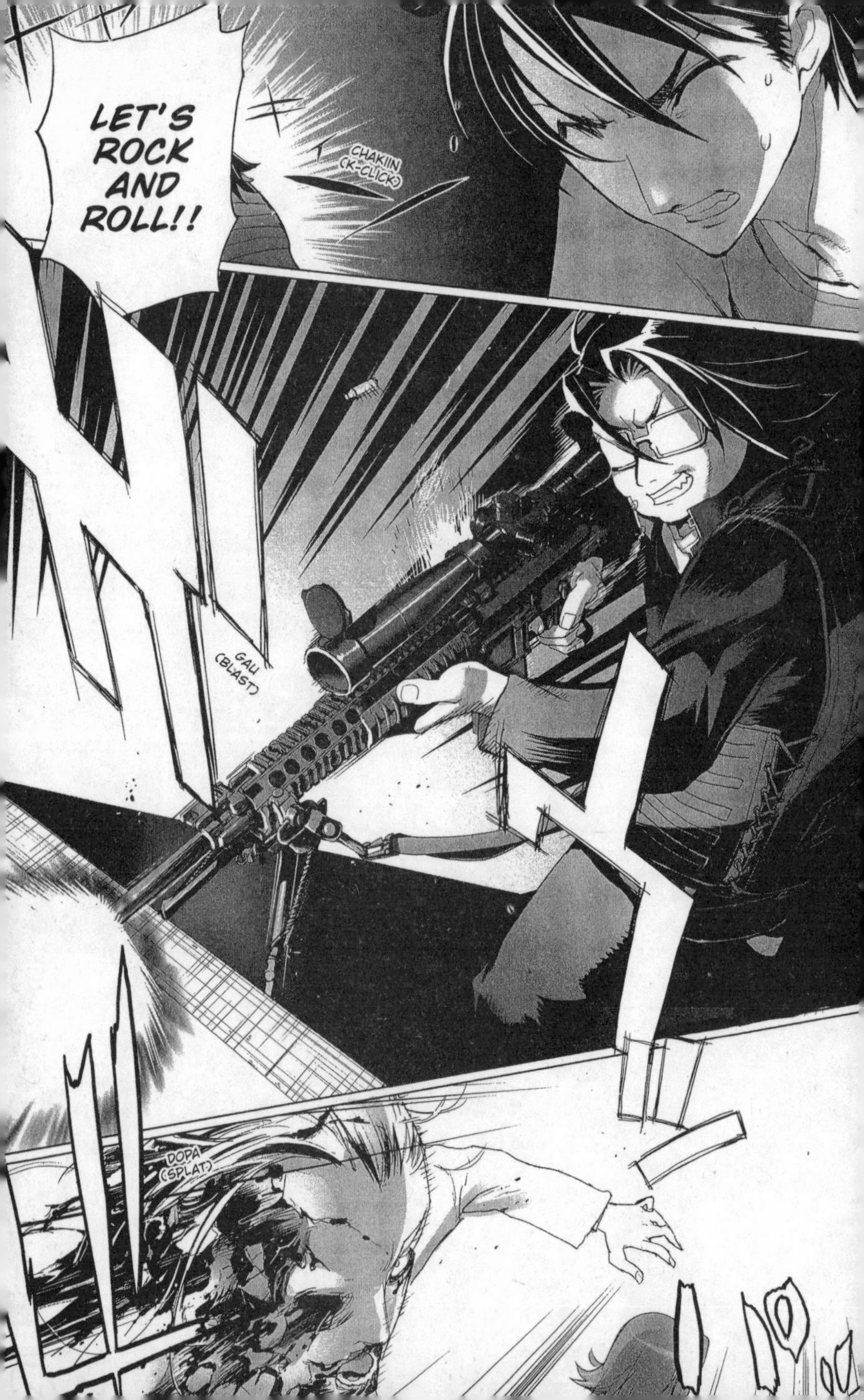
CHAKIIN (K-CLICK)
LET'S ROCK AND ROLL!!
GAU (BLAST)
DOPA (SPLAT)

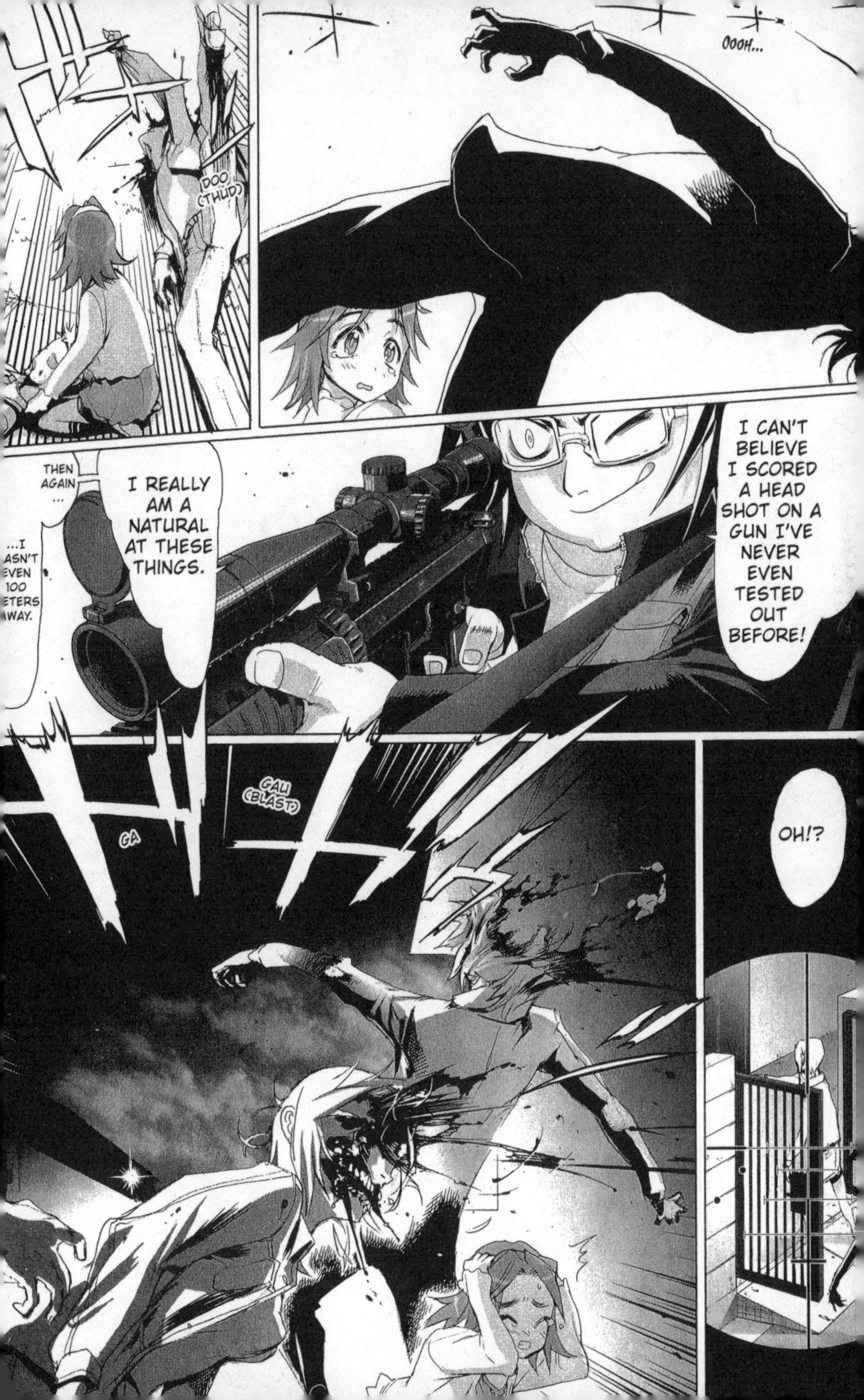
OOOH...
DOO (THUD)
I CAN'T BELIEVE I SCORED A HEAD SHOT ON A GUN I'VE NEVER EVEN TESTED OUT BEFORE!
I REALLY AM A NATURAL AT THESE THINGS.
THEN AGAIN ...
...I ASN'T EVEN 100 ETERS AWAY.
OH!?
GAU (BLAST)
GA

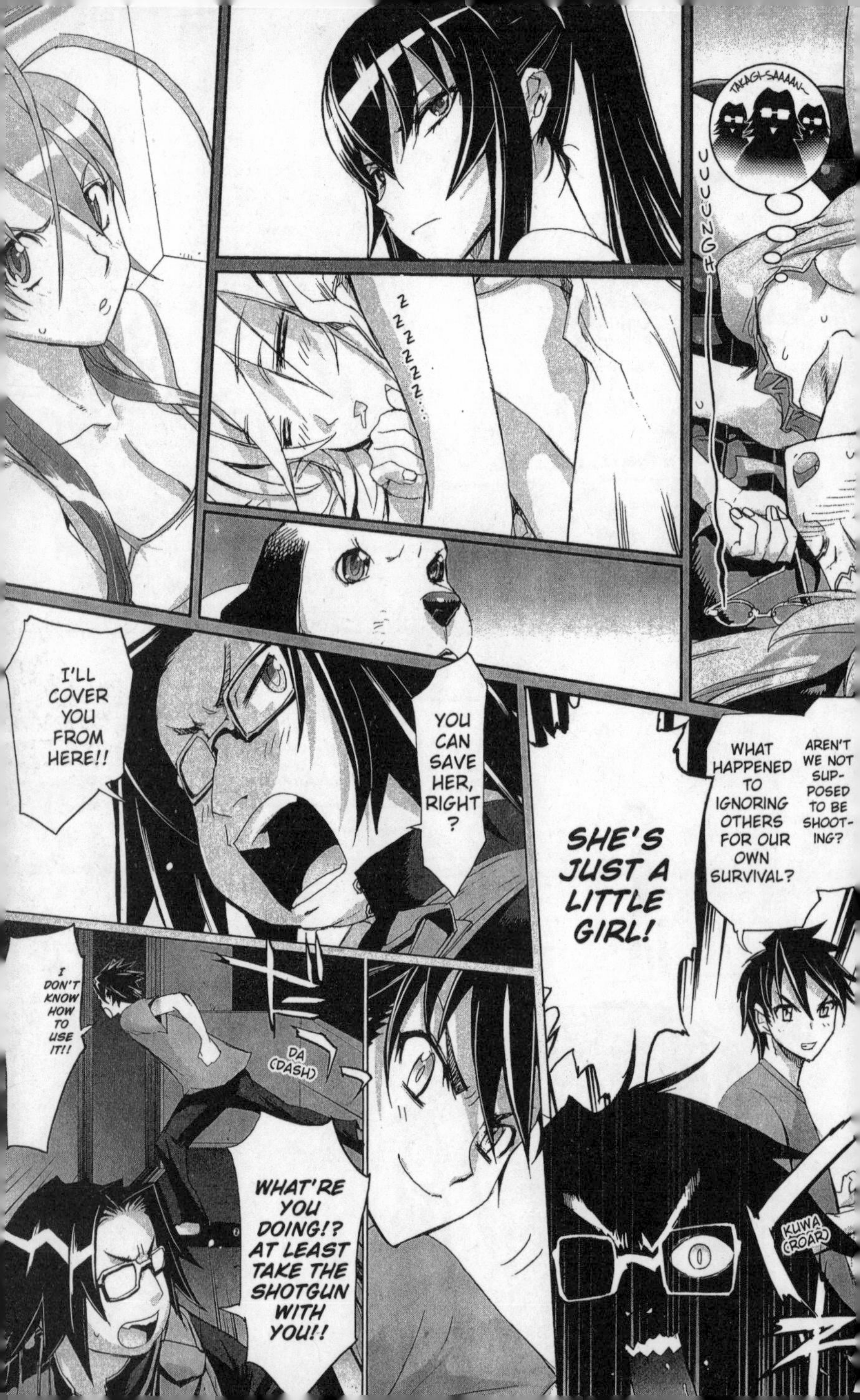
TAKAGI-SAAAAN~
UUUUNGH
Z Z Z Z Z Z...
AREN'T WE NOT SUPPOSED TO BE SHOOTING?
WHAT HAPPENED TO IGNORING OTHERS FOR OUR OWN SURVIVAL?
SHE'S JUST A LITTLE GIRL!
YOU CAN SAVE HER, RIGHT?
I'LL COVER YOU FROM HERE!!
KUWA (ROAR)
WHAT'RE YOU DOING!? AT LEAST TAKE THE SHOTGUN WITH YOU!!
DA (DASH)
I DON'T KNOW HOW TO USE IT!!

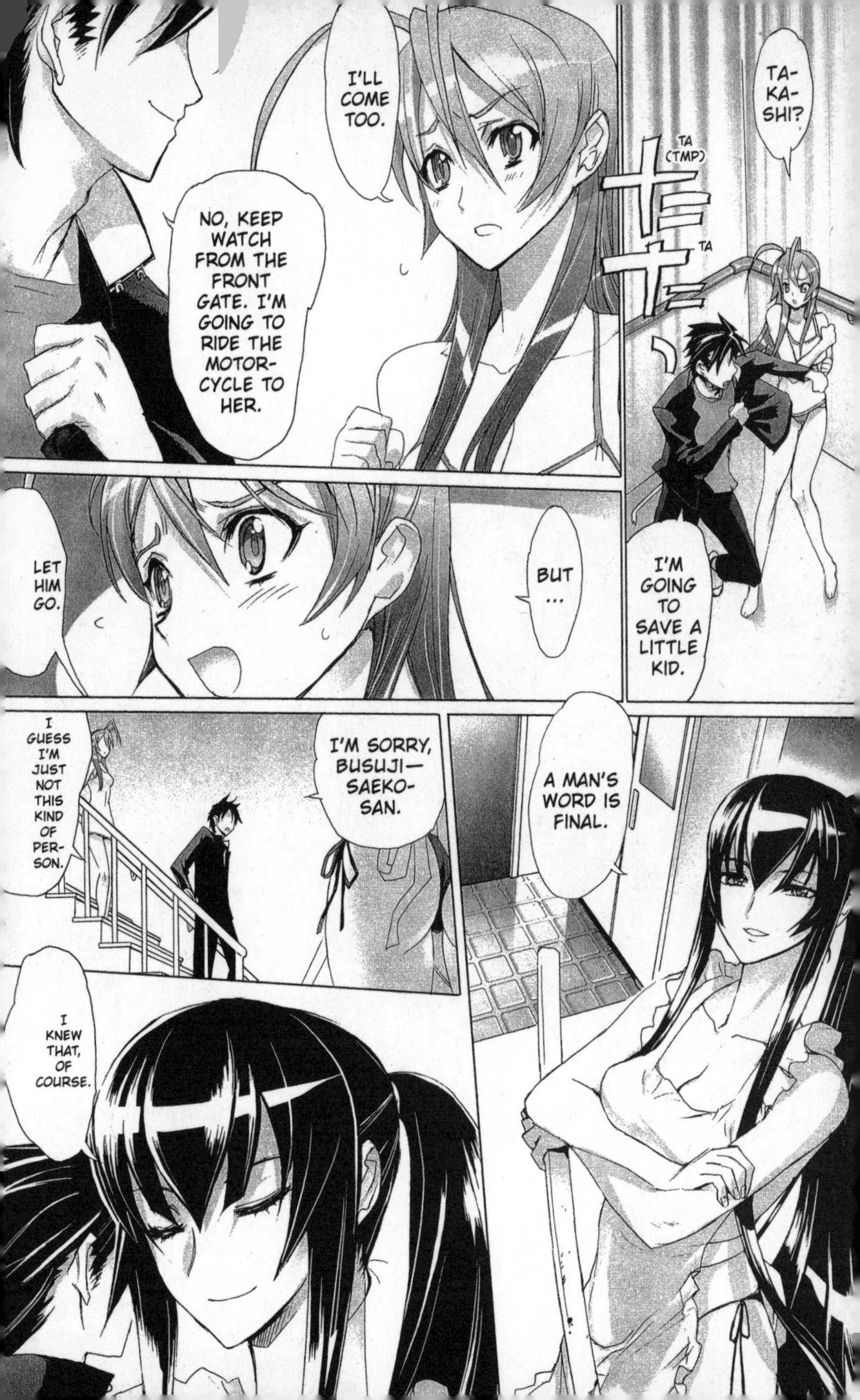
TA-KA-SHI?
TA (TMP)
TA
I'M GOING TO SAVE A LITTLE KID.
I'LL COME TOO.
NO, KEEP WATCH FROM THE FRONT GATE. I'M GOING TO RIDE THE MOTOR-CYCLE TO HER.
BUT...
LET HIM GO.
A MAN'S WORD IS FINAL.
I'M SORRY, BUSUJI— SAEKO-SAN.
I GUESS I'M JUST NOT THIS KIND OF PERSON.
I KNEW THAT, OF COURSE.

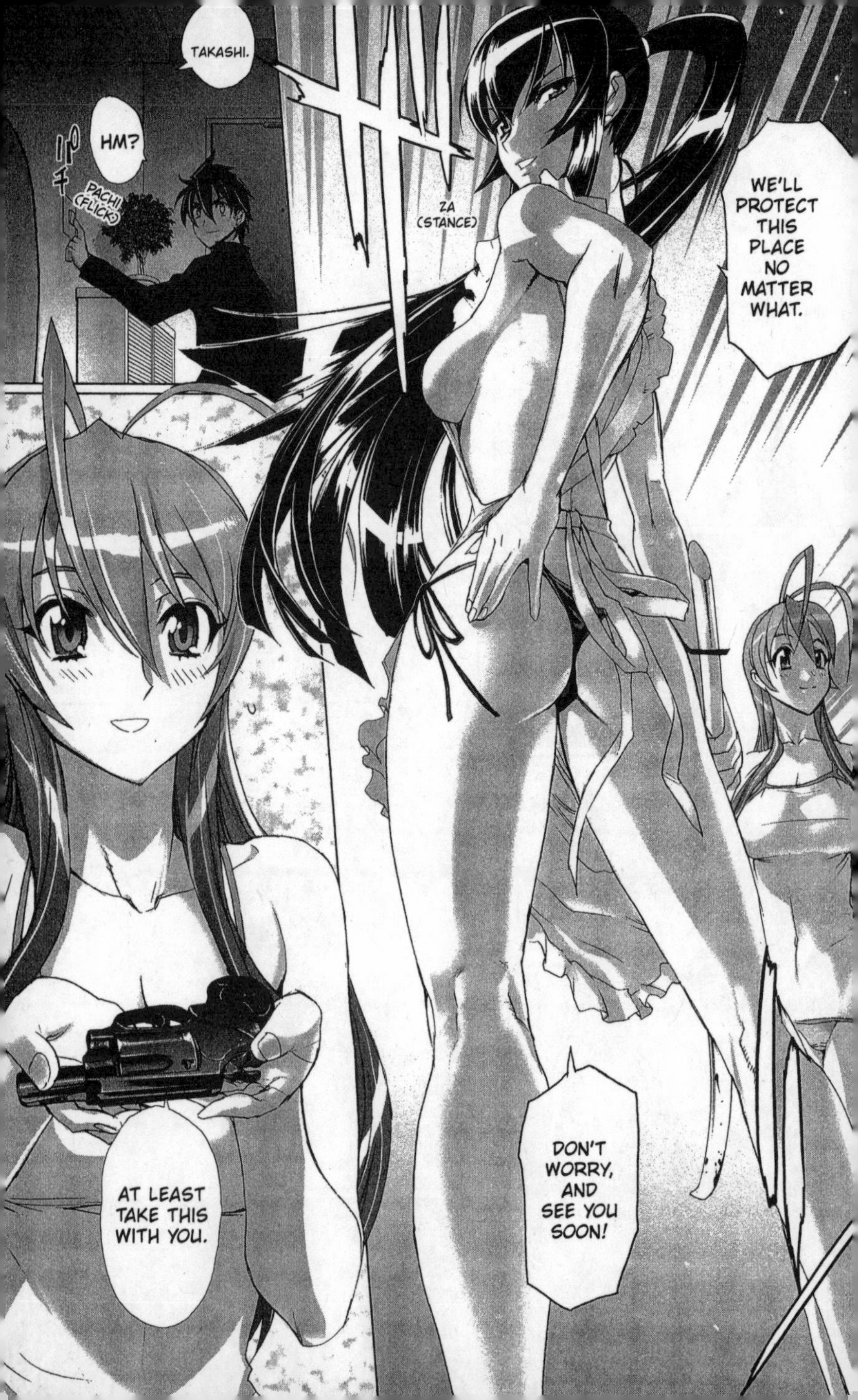

WE'LL PROTECT THIS PLACE NO MATTER WHAT.
ZA (STANCE)
TAKASHI.
HM?
パチ
PACHI (FLICK)
DON'T WORRY, AND SEE YOU SOON!
AT LEAST TAKE THIS WITH YOU.

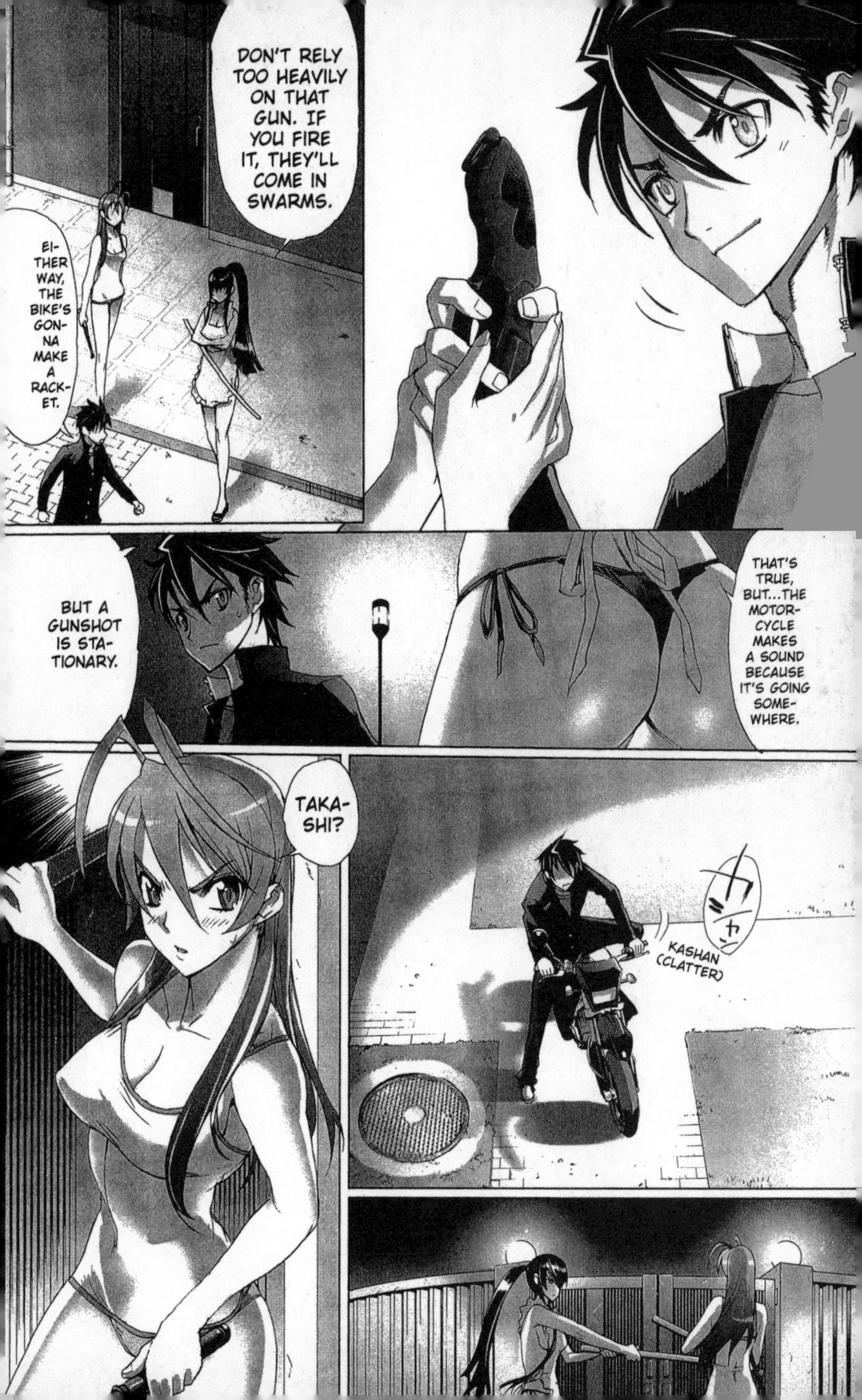
DON'T RELY TOO HEAVILY ON THAT GUN. IF YOU FIRE IT, THEY'LL COME IN SWARMS.
EI-THER WAY, THE BIKE'S GON-NA MAKE A RACK-ET.
THAT'S TRUE, BUT...THE MOTOR-CYCLE MAKES A SOUND BECAUSE IT'S GOING SOME-WHERE.
BUT A GUNSHOT IS STA-TIONARY.
カシャン
KASHAN (CLATTER)
TAKA-SHI?

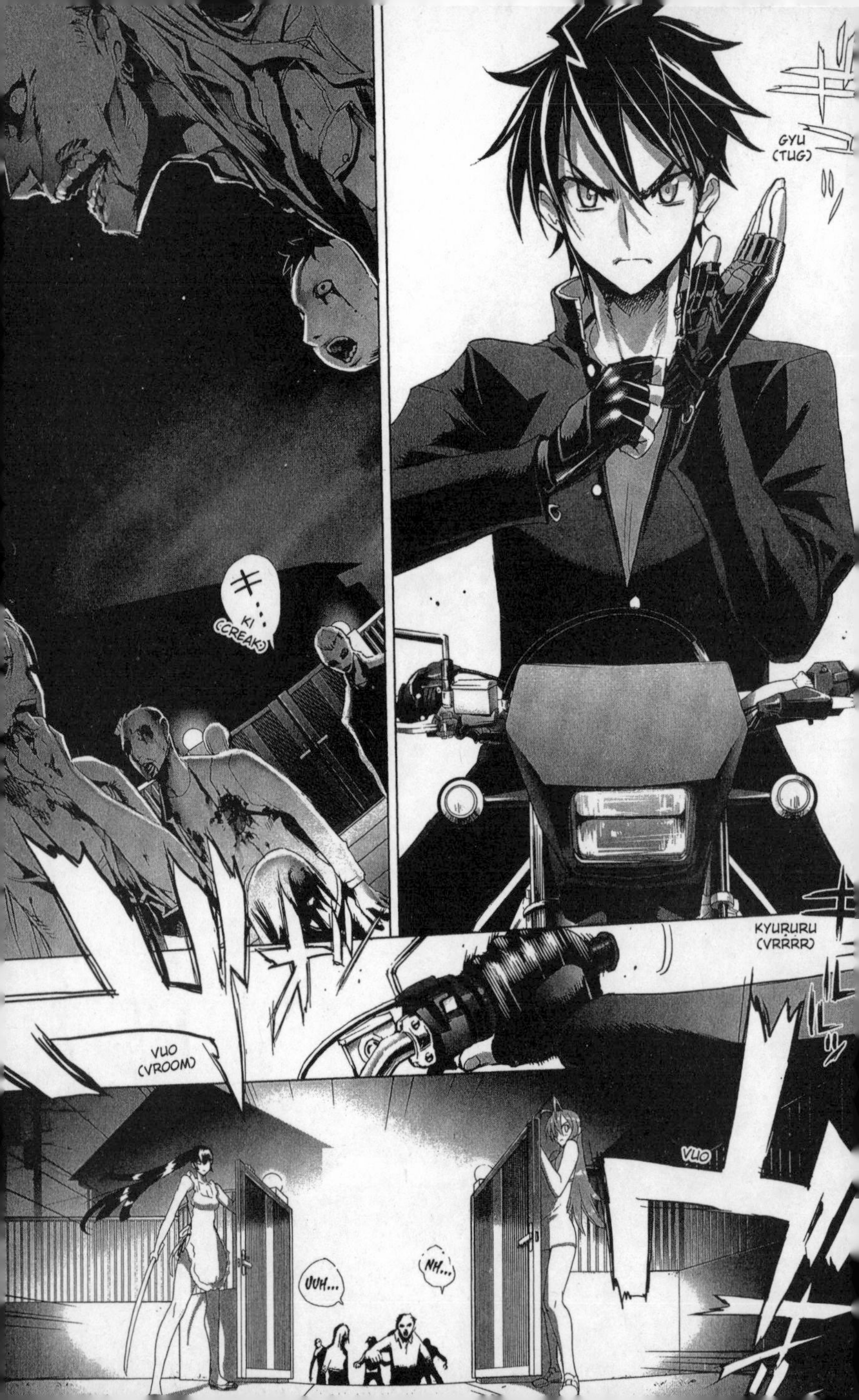
GYU (TUG)
KI (CREAK)
KYURURU (VRRRR)
VUO (VROOM)
VUO
NH...
UUH...

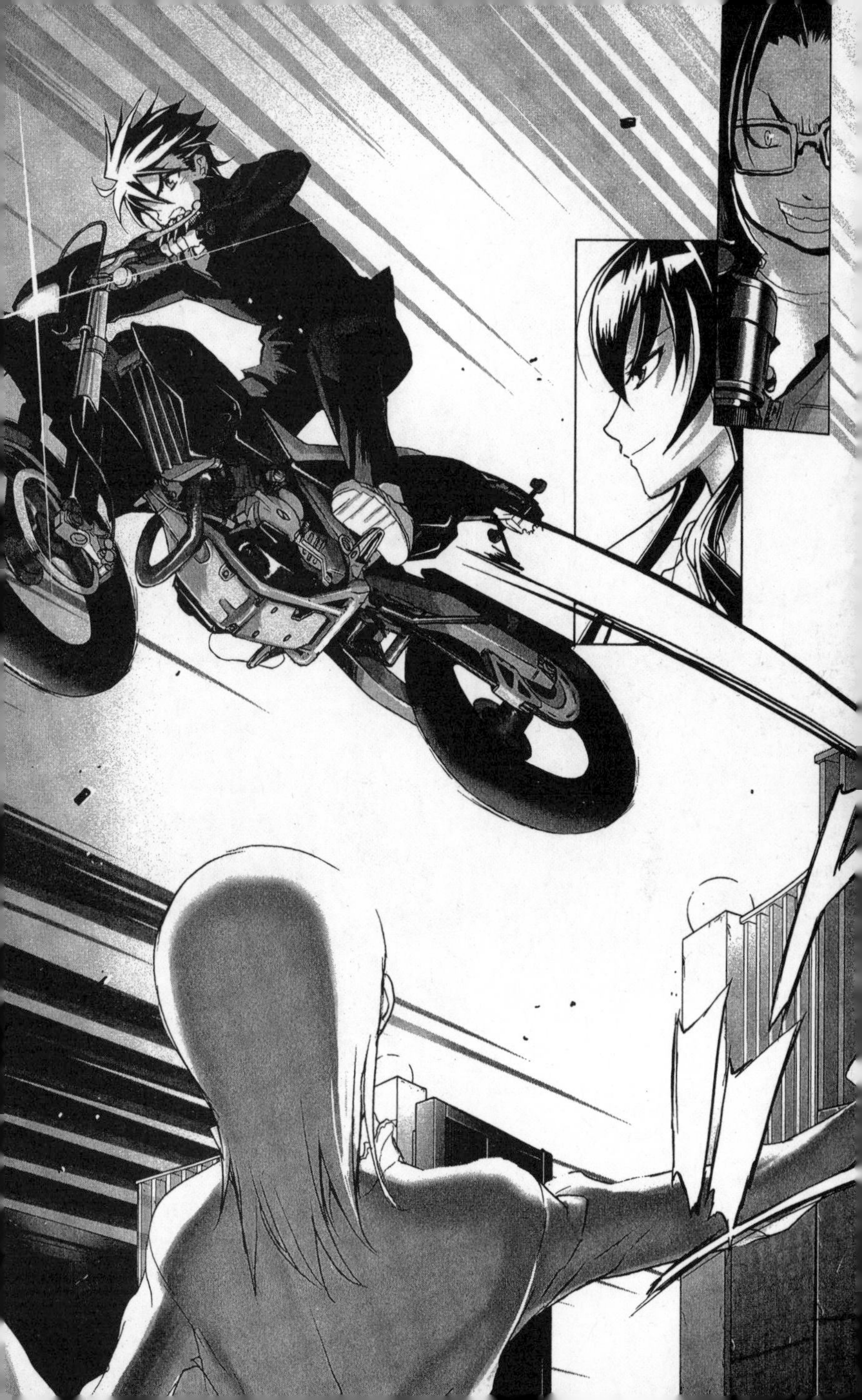

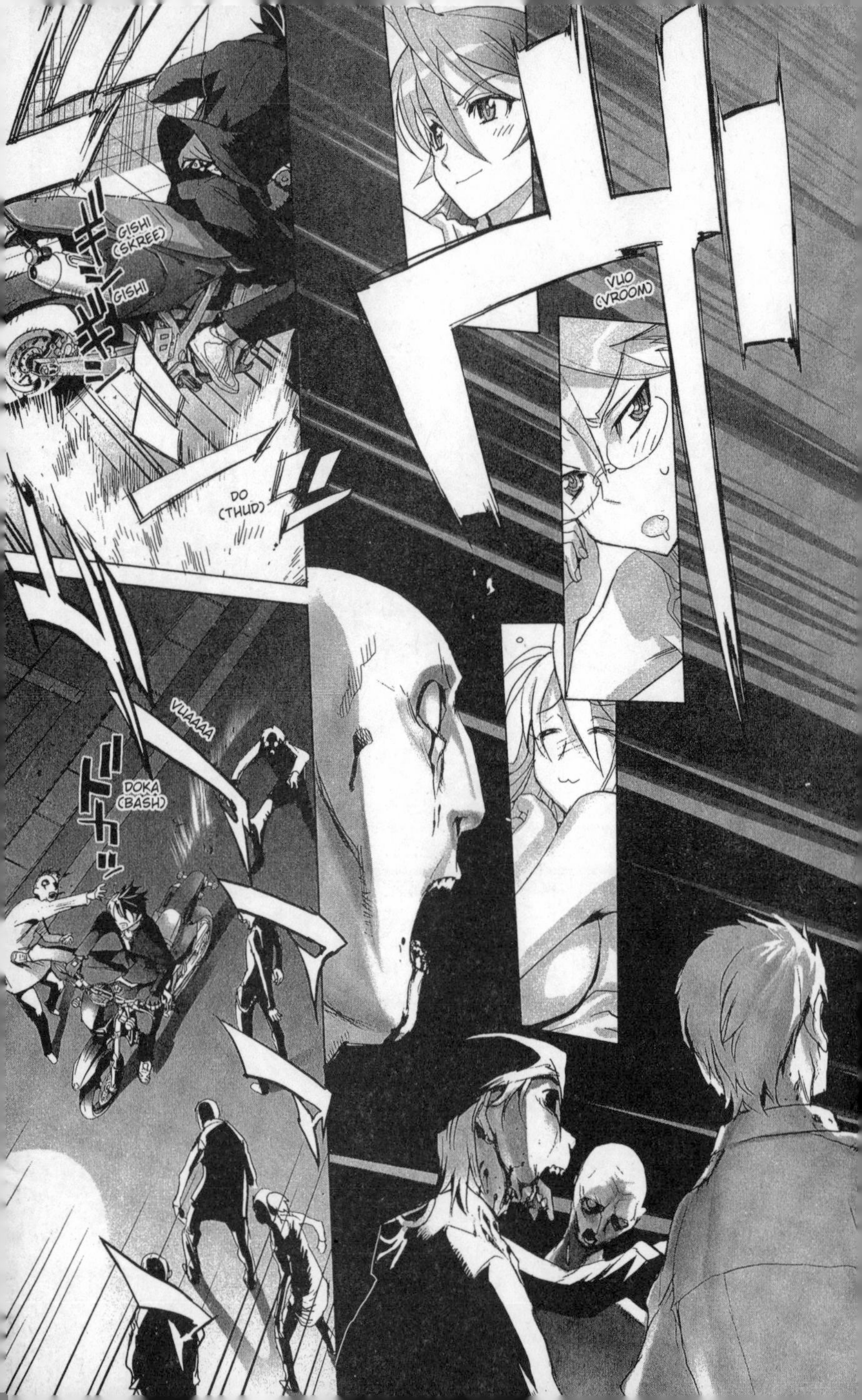
VUO (VROOM)
GISHI (SKREE)
GISHI
DO (THUD)
VUAAAA
DOKA (BASH)

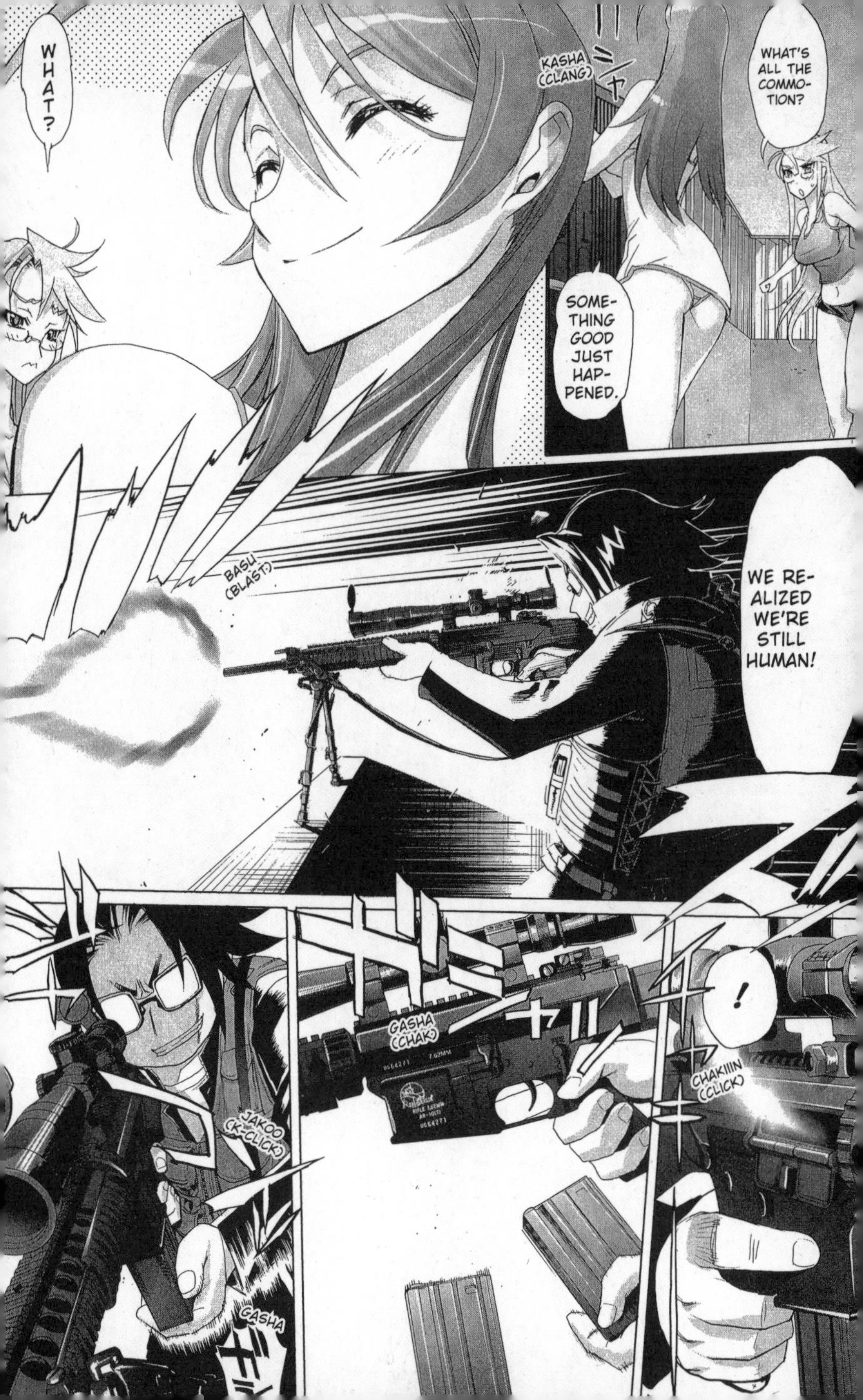
KASHA (CLANG)
WHAT'S ALL THE COMMOTION?
SOMETHING GOOD JUST HAPPENED.
WHAT?
WE REALIZED WE'RE STILL HUMAN!
BASU (BLAST)
!
CHAKIIIN (CLICK)
GASHA (CHAK)
JAKOO (K-CLICK)
GASHA

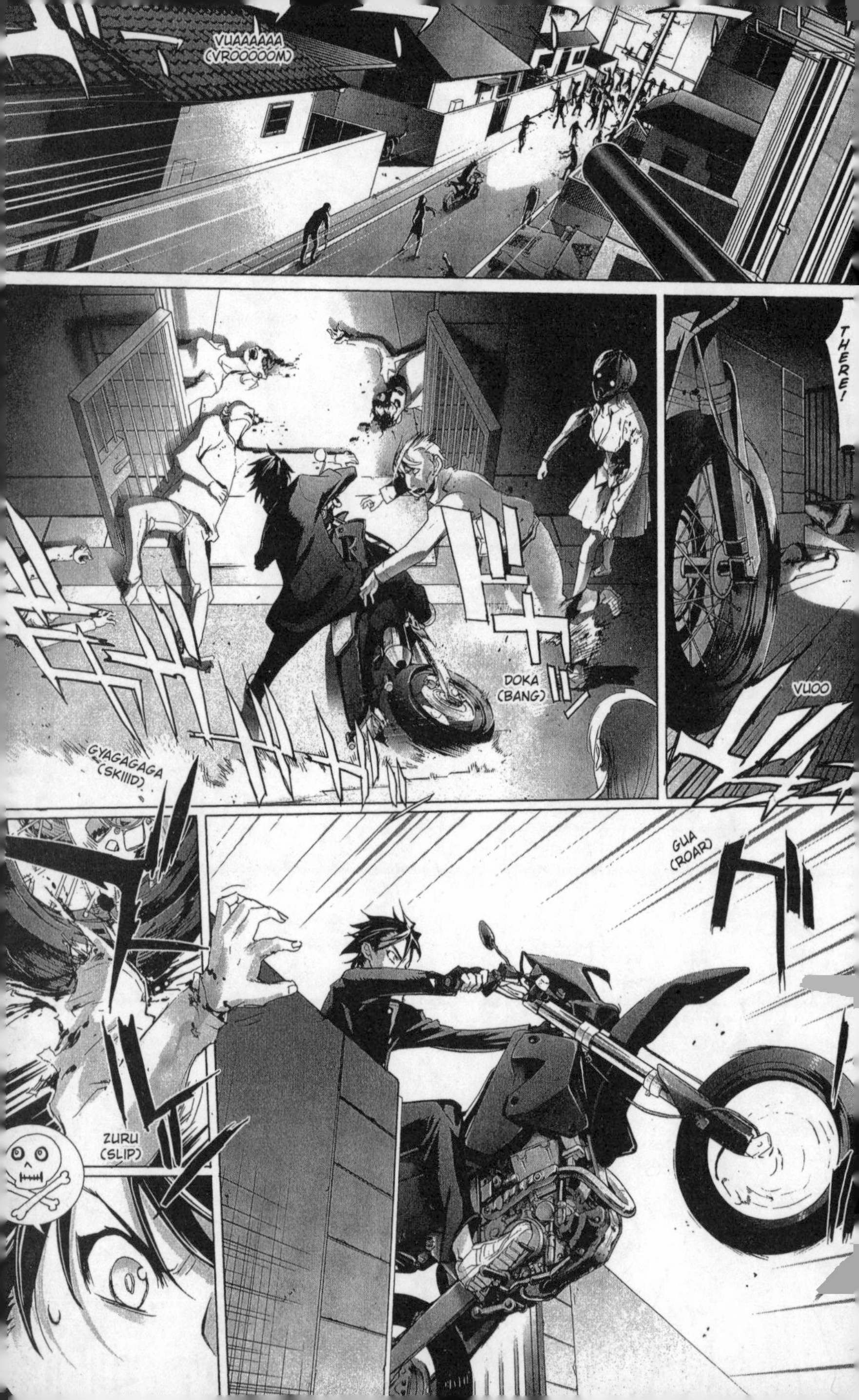

VUAAAAAA (VROOOOOM)
THERE!
VUOO
DOKA (BANG)
GYAGAGAGA (SKIIID)
GUA (ROAR)
ZURU (SLIP)

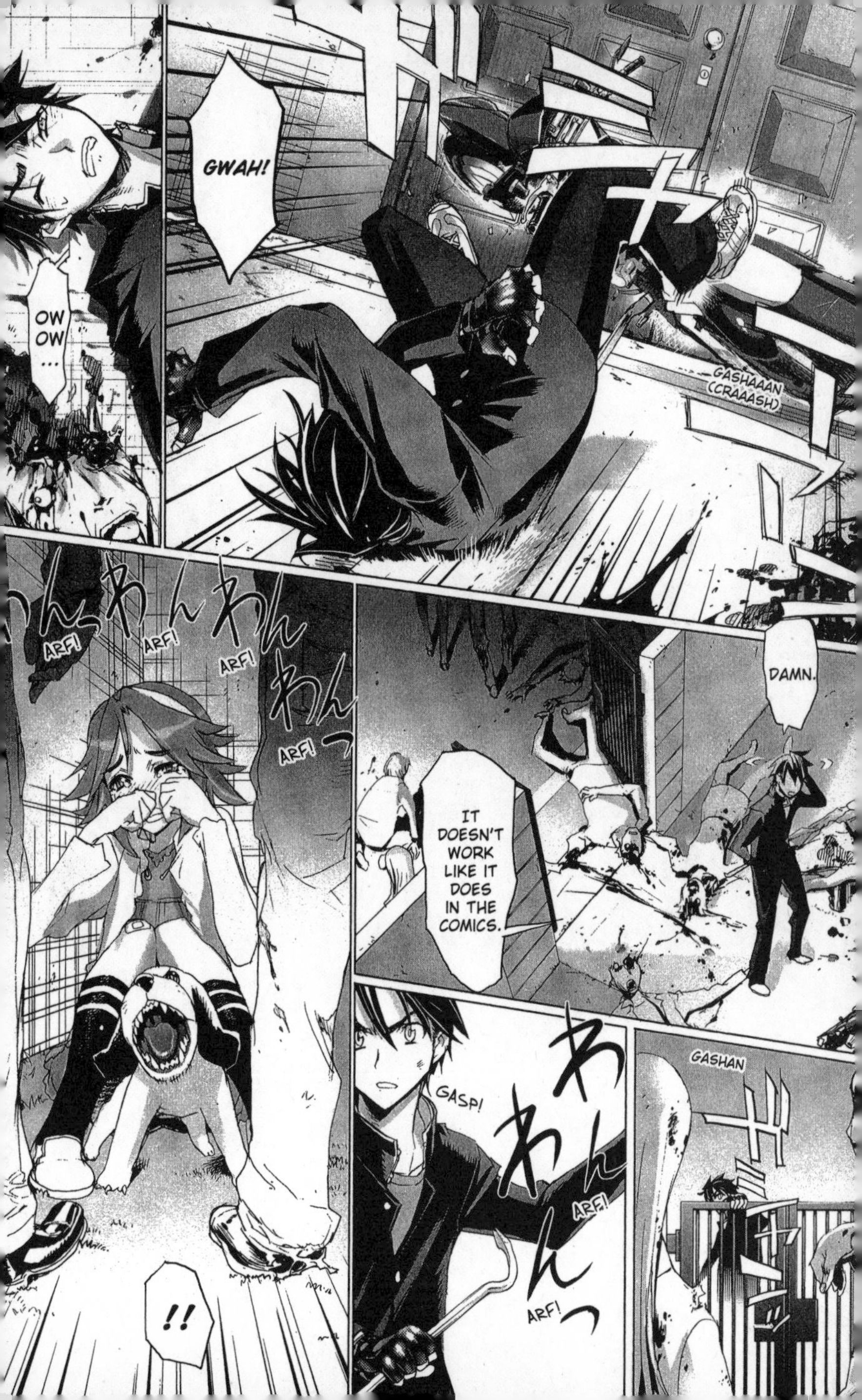
GWAH!
GASHAAAN (CRAAASH)
OW OW ...
DAMN.
IT DOESN'T WORK LIKE IT DOES IN THE COMICS.
GASHAN
わん
ARF!
わん
ARF!
GASP!
わん
ARF!
わん
ARF!
わん
ARF!
わん
ARF!
!!

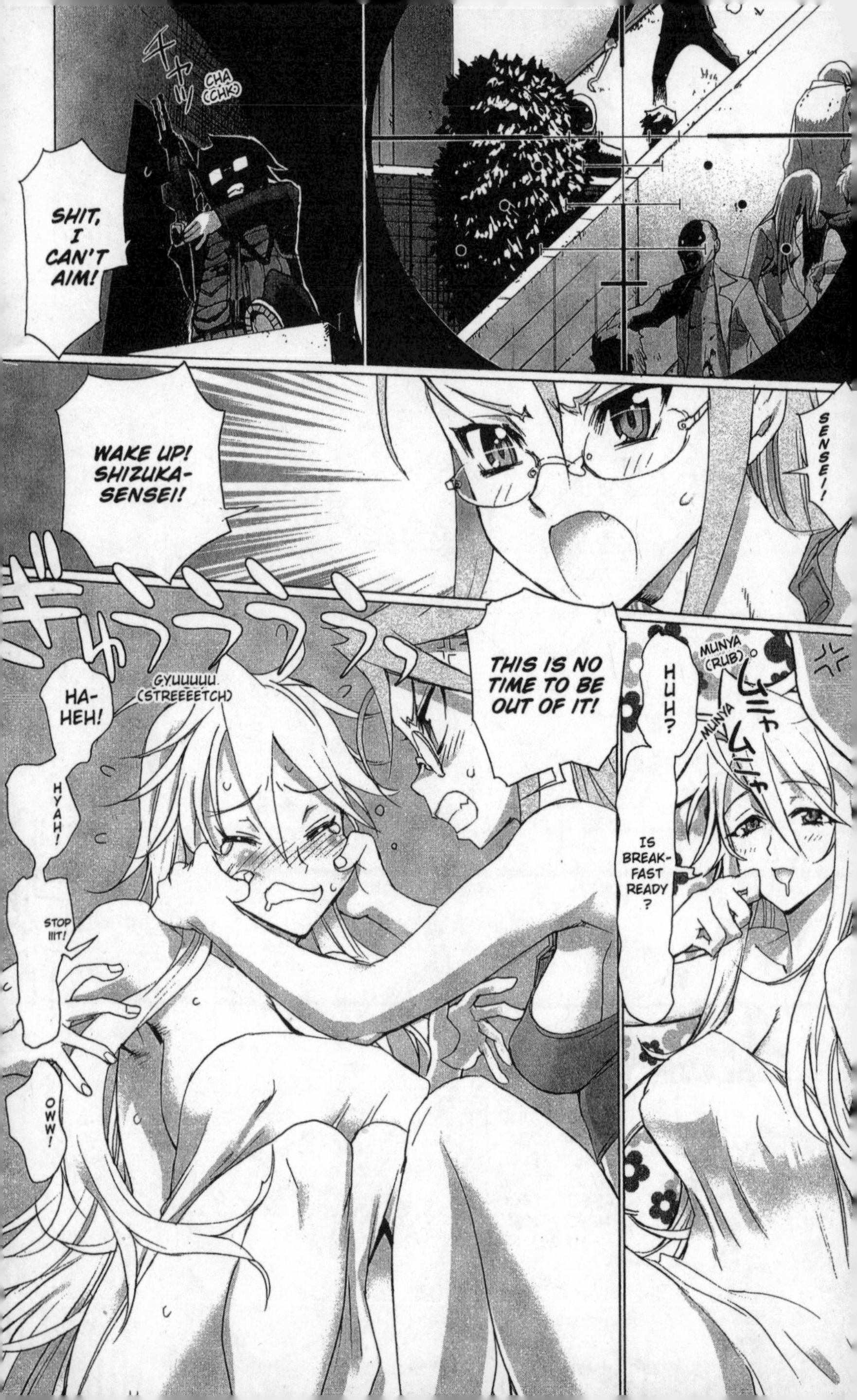
CHA (CHK)
SHIT, I CAN'T AIM!
SENSEI!
WAKE UP! SHIZUKA-SENSEI!
HUH?
MUNYA (RUB)
MUNYA
IS BREAKFAST READY?
THIS IS NO TIME TO BE OUT OF IT!
GYUUUUU (STREEEETCH)
HA-HEH!
HYAH!
STOP IIIT!
OWW!

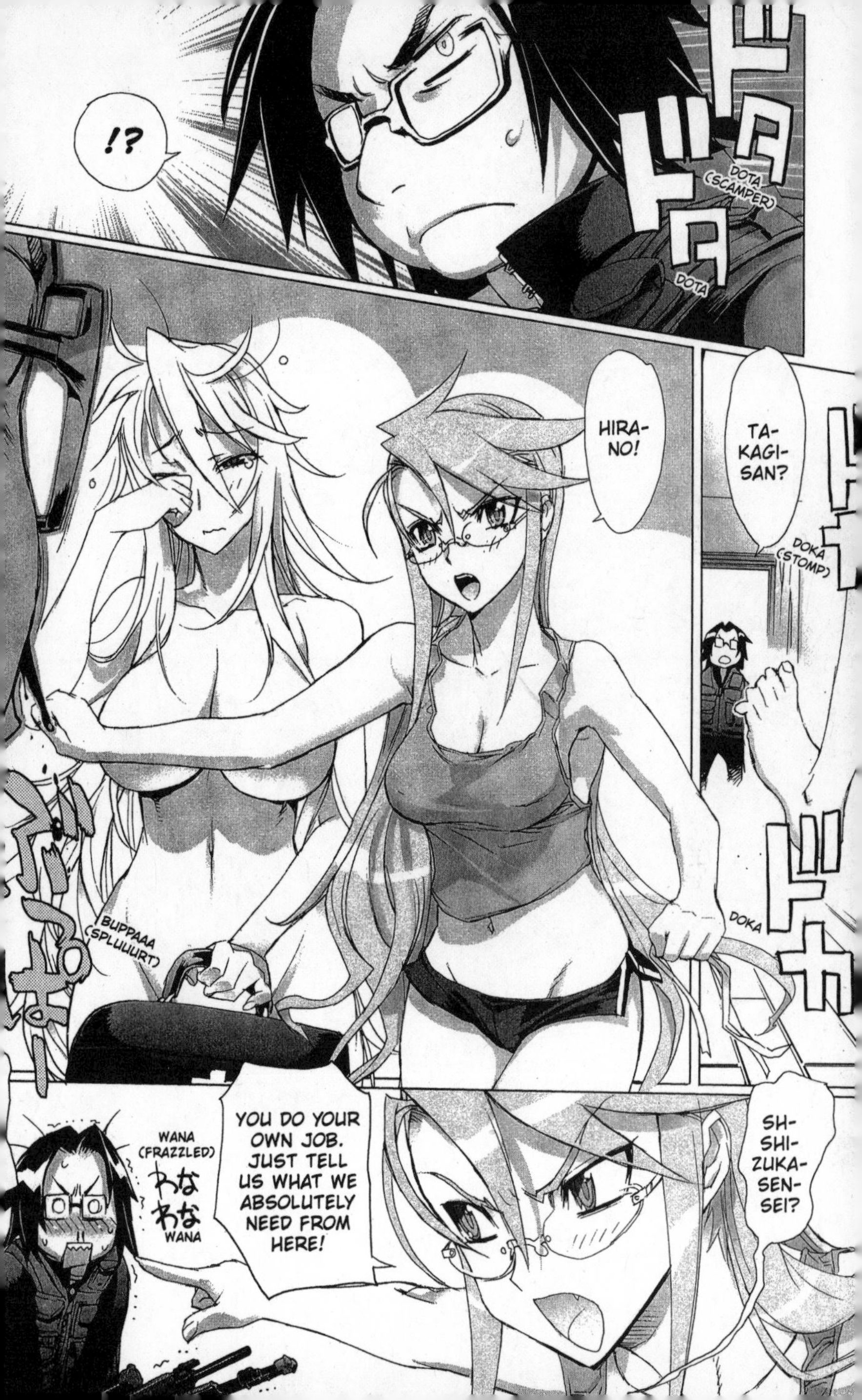
DOTA (SCAMPER)
DOTA
!?
TA-KAGI-SAN?
DOKA (STOMP)
DOKA
HIRA-NO!
BUPPAAA (SPLUUURT)
SH-SHI-ZUKA-SEN-SEI?
YOU DO YOUR OWN JOB. JUST TELL US WHAT WE ABSOLUTELY NEED FROM HERE!
WANA (FRAZZLED)
わなわな
WANA

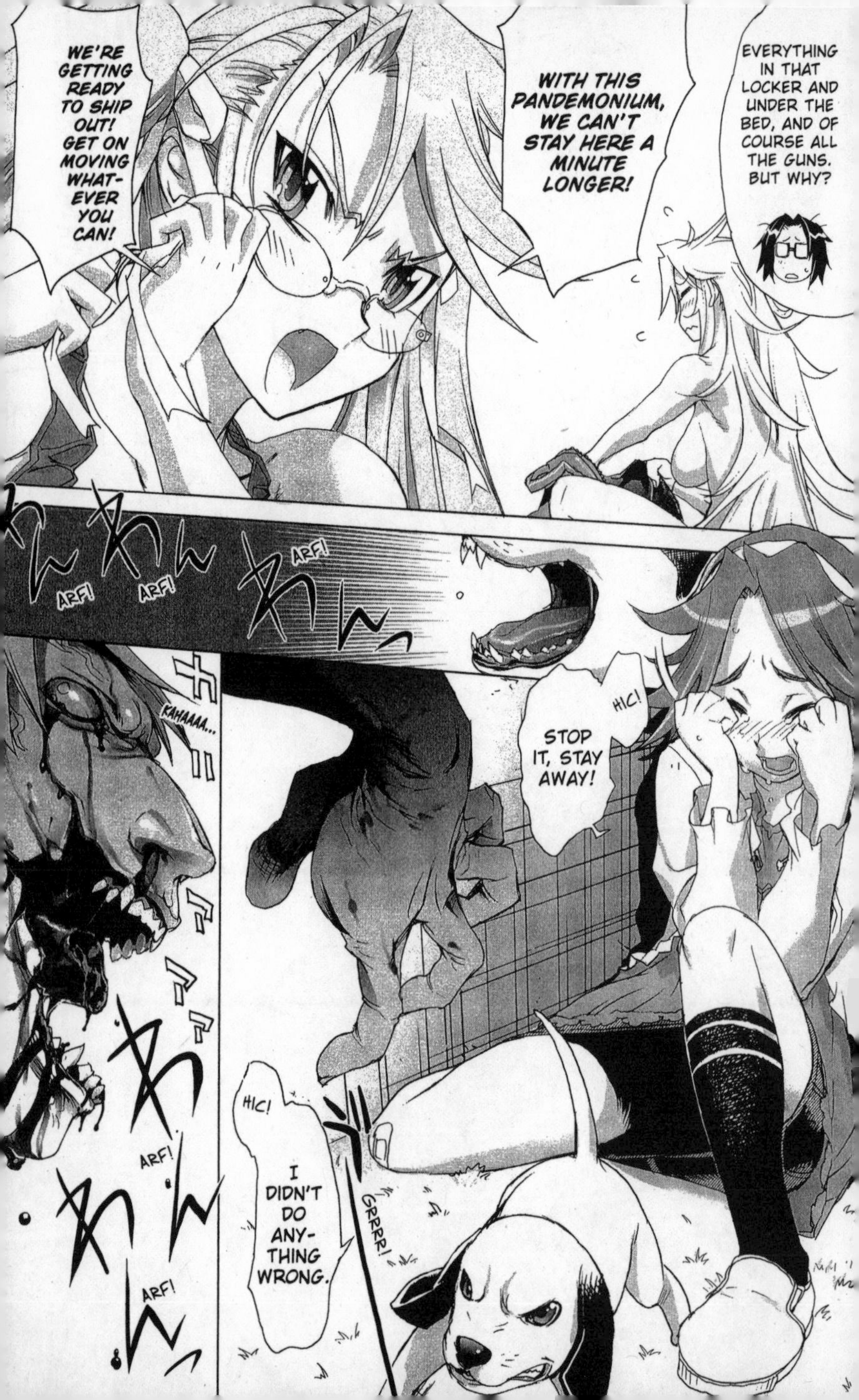
EVERYTHING IN THAT LOCKER AND UNDER THE BED, AND OF COURSE ALL THE GUNS. BUT WHY?
WITH THIS PANDEMONIUM, WE CAN'T STAY HERE A MINUTE LONGER!
WE'RE GETTING READY TO SHIP OUT! GET ON MOVING WHAT-EVER YOU CAN!
ARF!
ARF!
ARF!
HIC!
STOP IT, STAY AWAY!
HIC!
I DIDN'T DO ANY-THING WRONG.
GRRRR!
KAHAAAA...
ARF!
ARF!

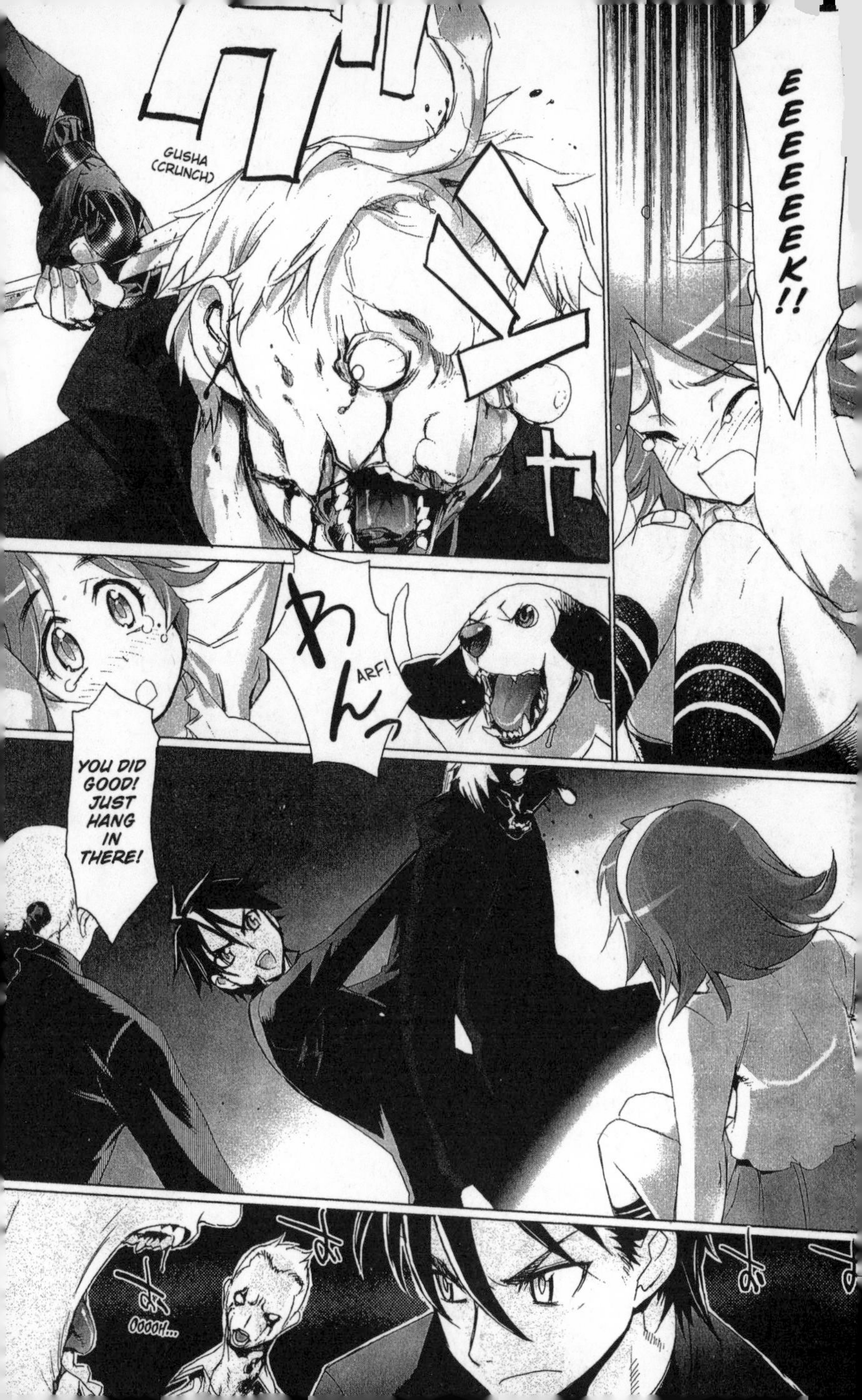
EEEEEEEK!!
GUSHA (CRUNCH)
わんっ
ARF!
YOU DID GOOD! JUST HANG IN THERE!
OOOOH...

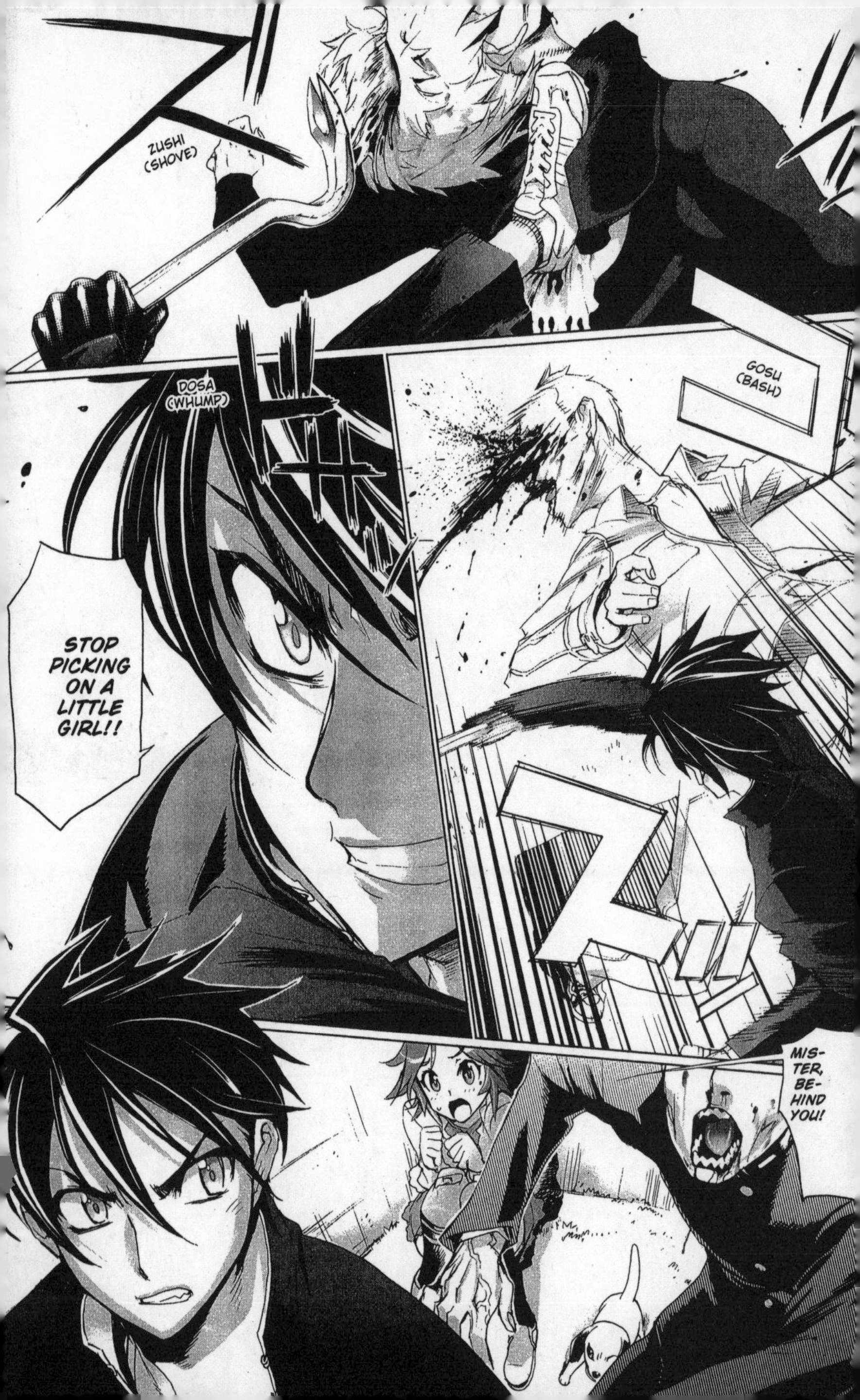
ZUSHI (SHOVE)
GOSU (BASH)
DOSA (WHUMP)
STOP PICKING ON A LITTLE GIRL!!
MIS-TER, BE-HIND YOU!

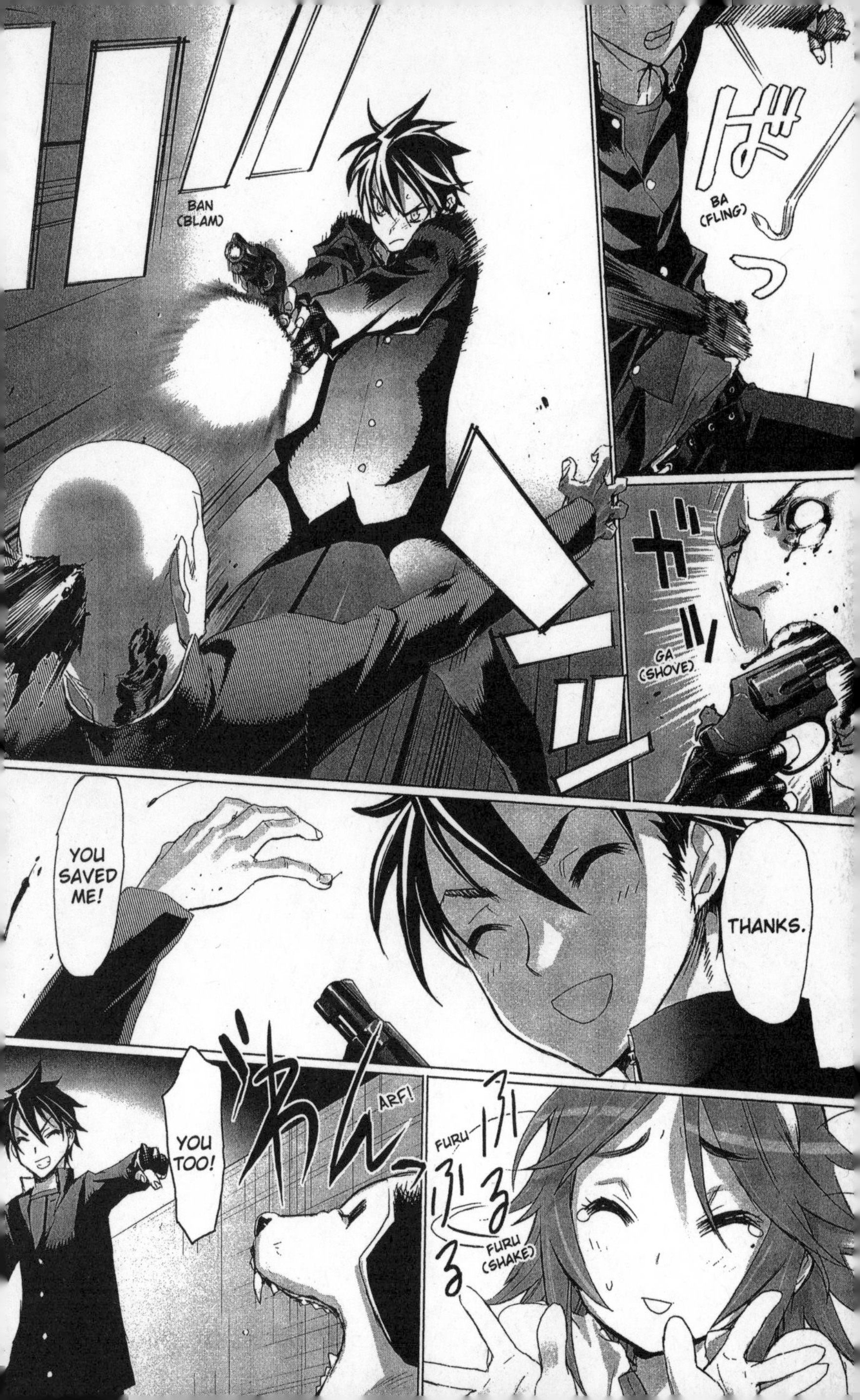
BA (FLING)
GA (SHOVE)
BAN (BLAM)
THANKS.
YOU SAVED ME!
FURU
FURU (SHAKE)
ARF!
YOU TOO!

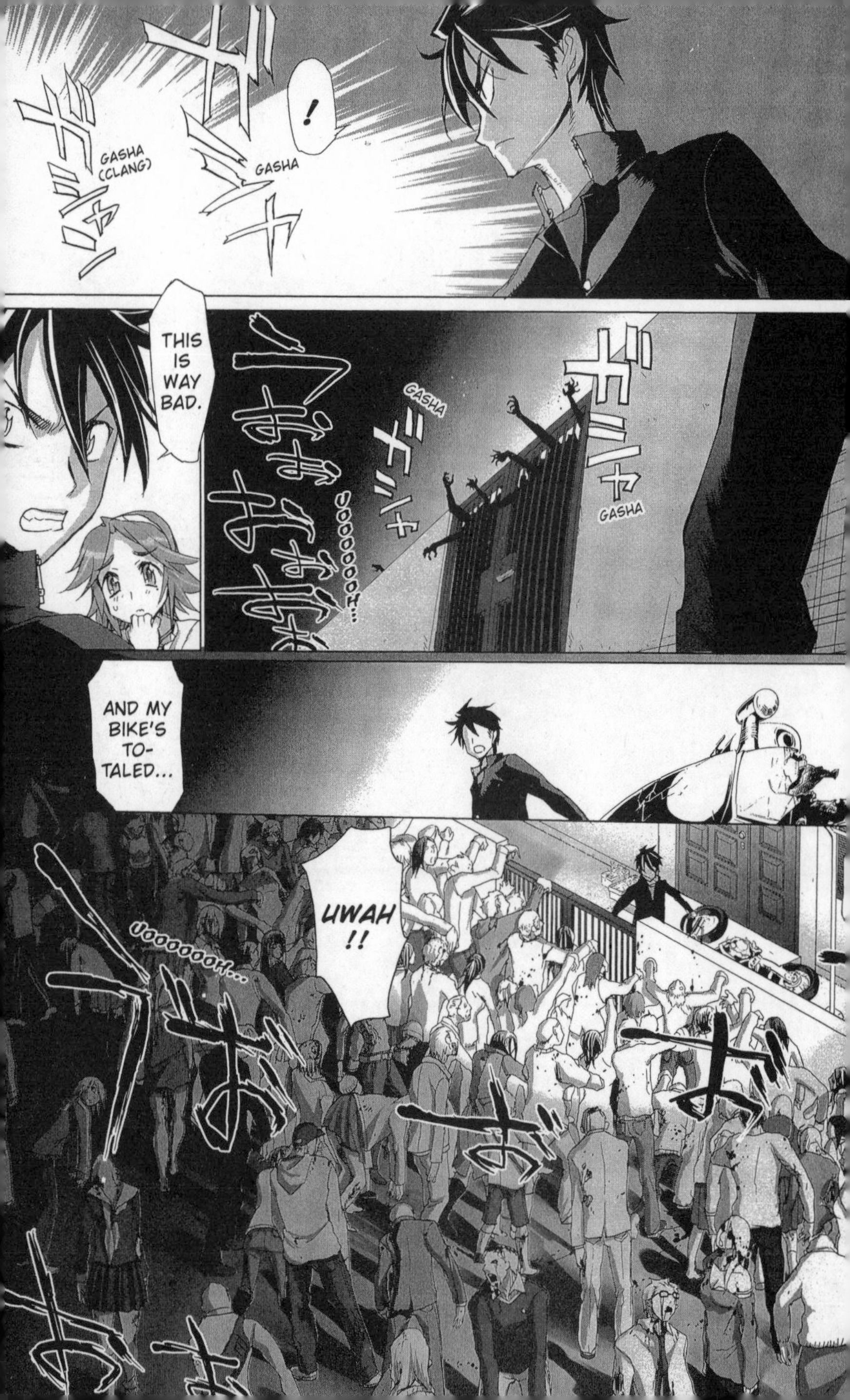
!
GASHA
GASHA (CLANG)
GASHA
GASHA
UOOOOOOOH...
THIS IS WAY BAD.
AND MY BIKE'S TO-TALED...
UWAH !!
UOOOOOOOH...

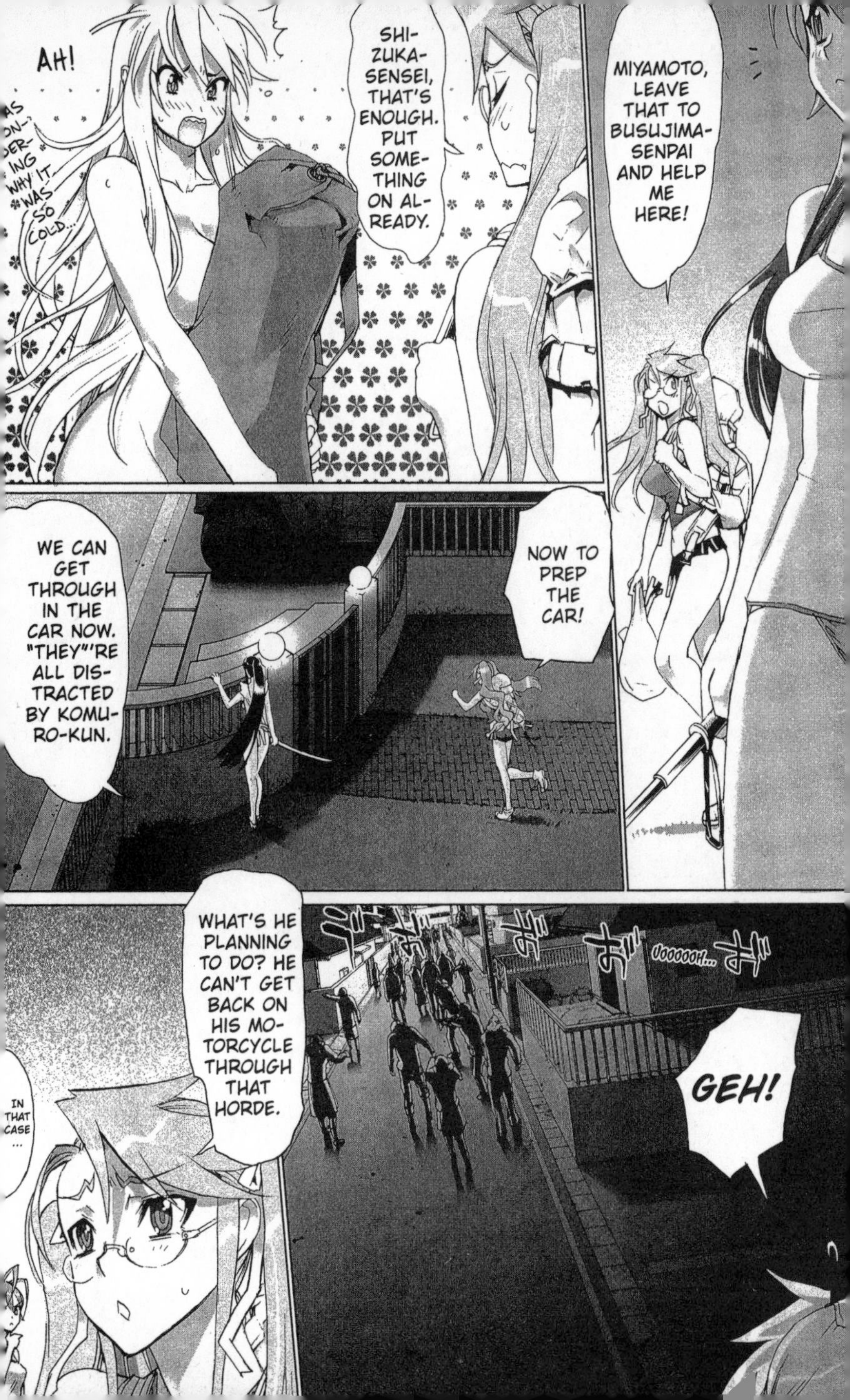
MIYAMOTO, LEAVE THAT TO BUSUJIMA-SENPAI AND HELP ME HERE!
SHI-ZUKA-SENSEI, THAT'S ENOUGH. PUT SOME-THING ON AL-READY.
AH!
AS ON-DER-ING WHY IT WAS SO COLD...
NOW TO PREP THE CAR!
WE CAN GET THROUGH IN THE CAR NOW. "THEY"'RE ALL DIS-TRACTED BY KOMU-RO-KUN.
UOOOOOH...
GEH!
WHAT'S HE PLANNING TO DO? HE CAN'T GET BACK ON HIS MO-TORCYCLE THROUGH THAT HORDE.
IN THAT CASE ...

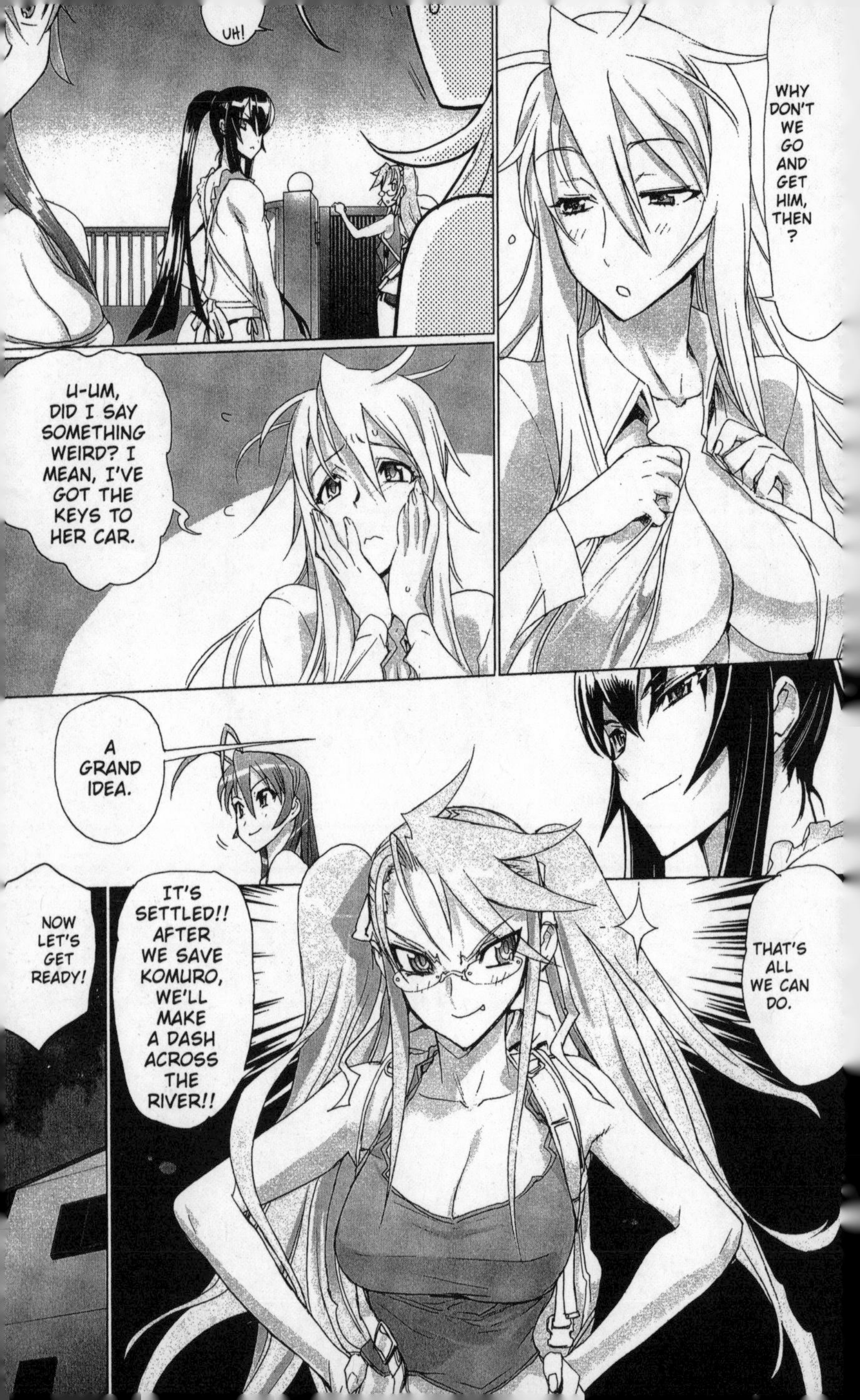
WHY DON'T WE GO AND GET HIM, THEN?
UH!
U-UM, DID I SAY SOMETHING WEIRD? I MEAN, I'VE GOT THE KEYS TO HER CAR.
A GRAND IDEA.
THAT'S ALL WE CAN DO.
IT'S SETTLED!! AFTER WE SAVE KOMURO, WE'LL MAKE A DASH ACROSS THE RIVER!!
NOW LET'S GET READY!

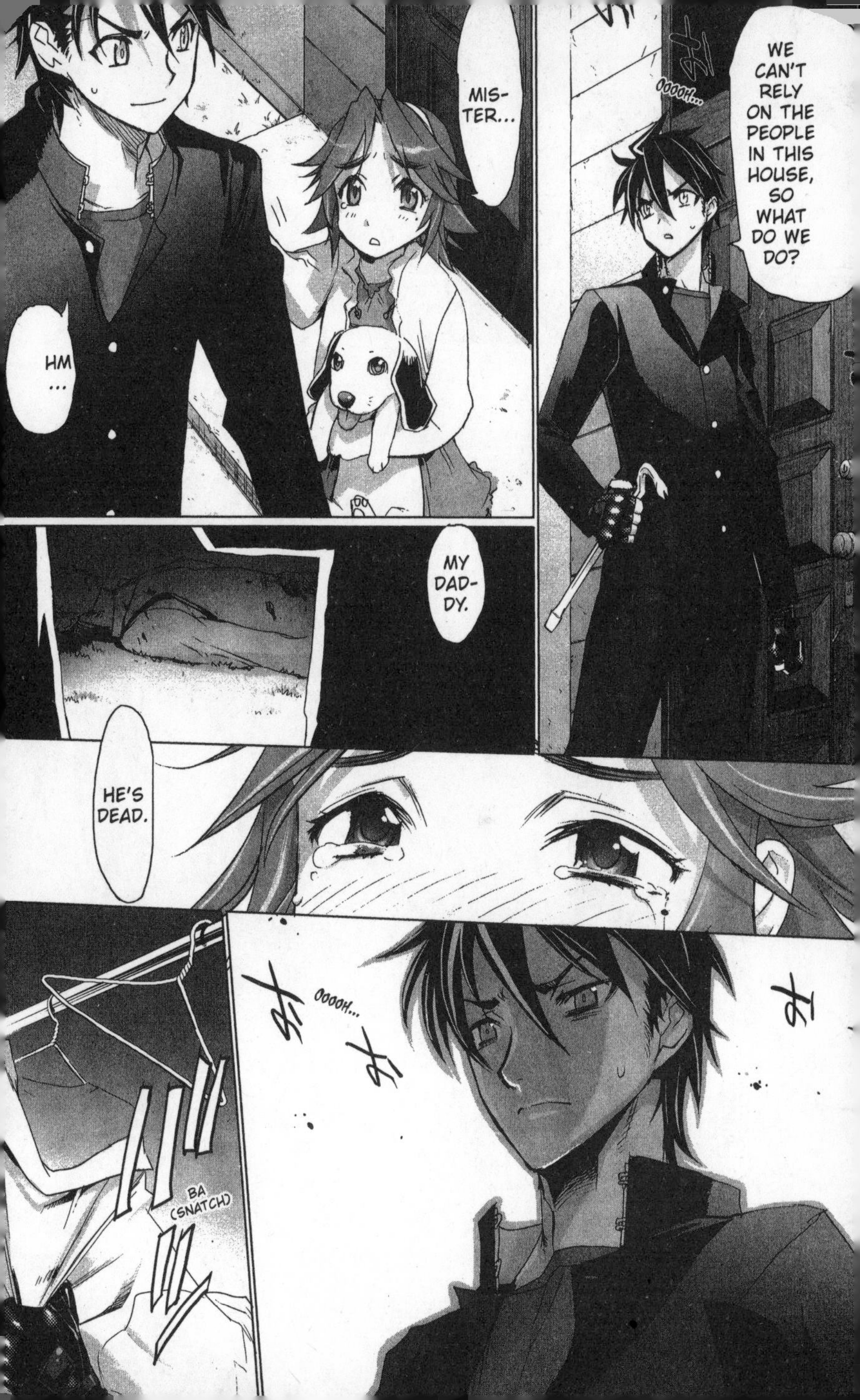
OOOOH...
WE CAN'T RELY ON THE PEOPLE IN THIS HOUSE, SO WHAT DO WE DO?
MIS-TER...
HM ...
MY DAD-DY.
HE'S DEAD.
OOOOH...
BA (SNATCH)

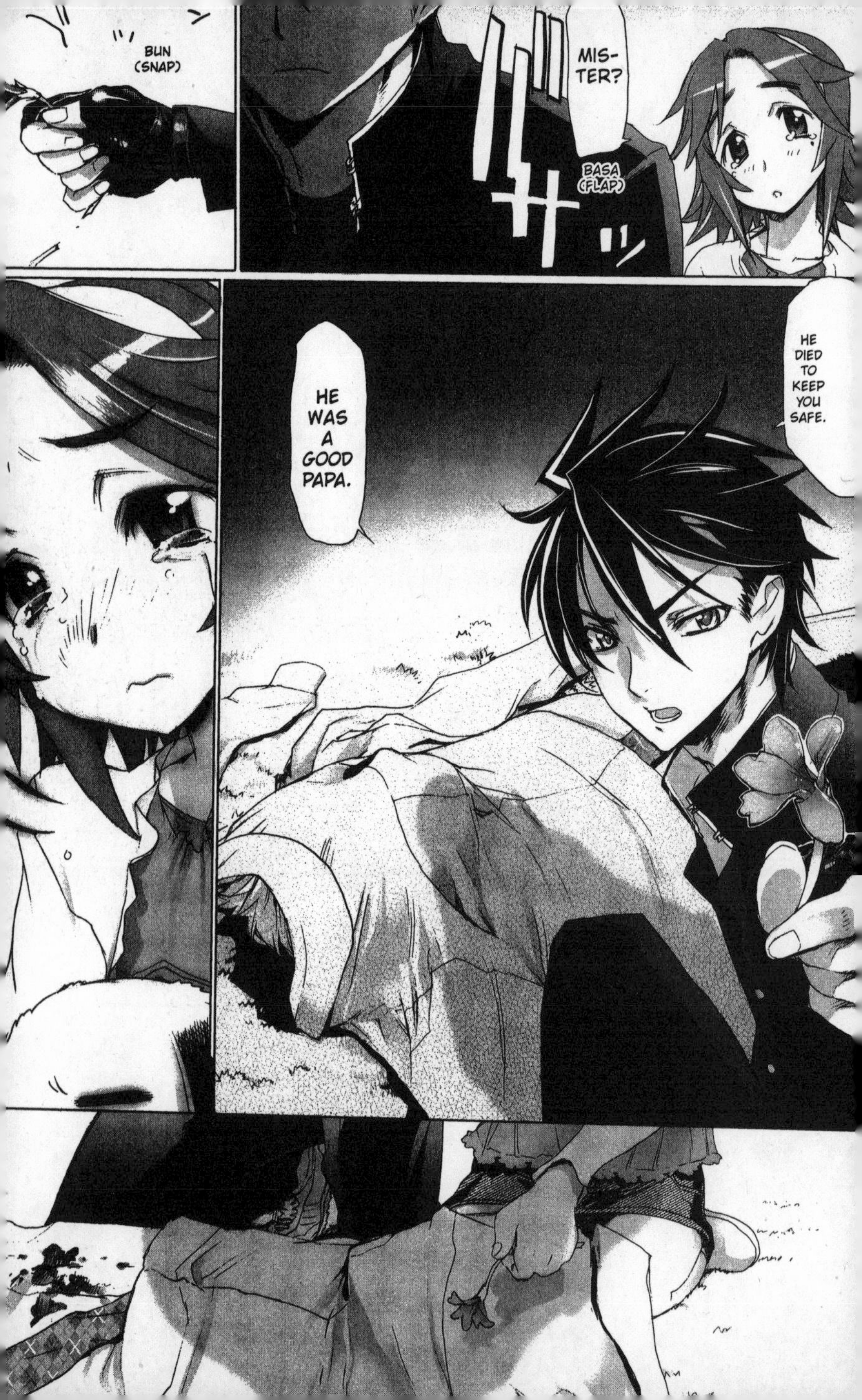
MISTER?
BASA (FLAP)
BUN (SNAP)
HE DIED TO KEEP YOU SAFE.
HE WAS A GOOD PAPA.

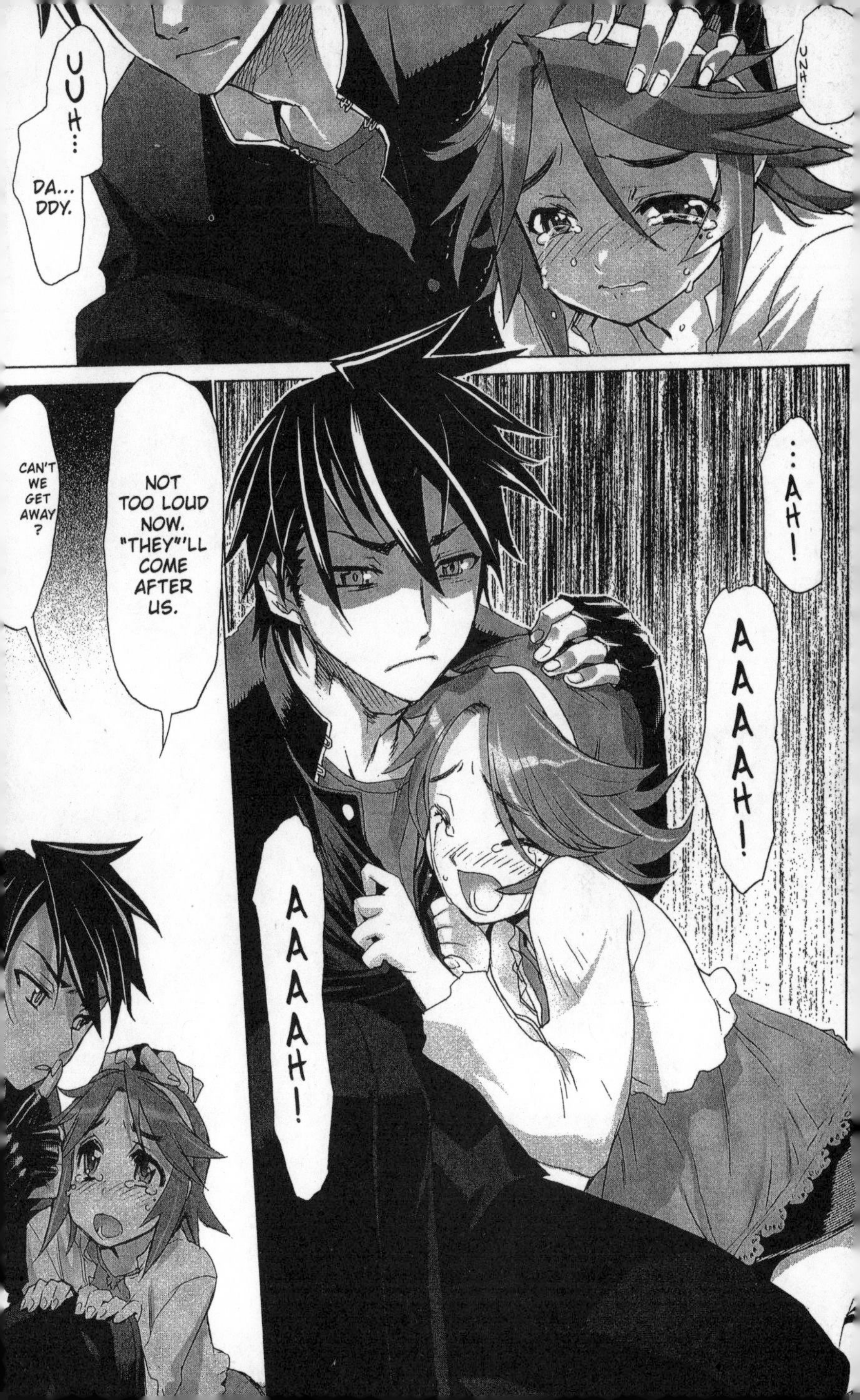
UNH...
UUH... DA... DDY.
...AH!
AAAAAH!
AAAAAH!
NOT TOO LOUD NOW. "THEY"'LL COME AFTER US.
CAN'T WE GET AWAY?

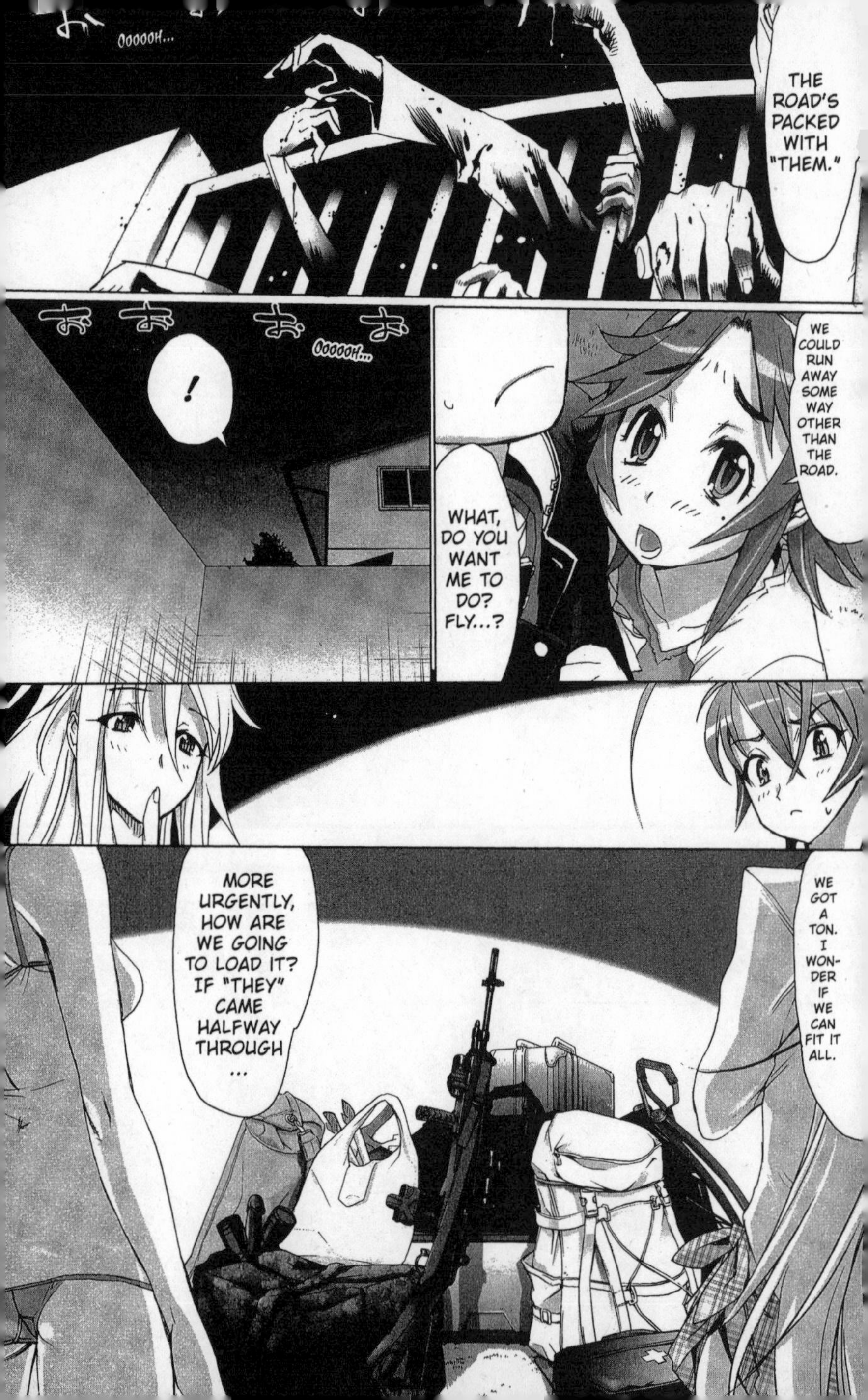
THE ROAD'S PACKED WITH "THEM."
OOOOOH...
WE COULD RUN AWAY SOME WAY OTHER THAN THE ROAD.
WHAT, DO YOU WANT ME TO DO? FLY...?
おおおお
OOOOOH...
!
WE GOT A TON. I WONDER IF WE CAN FIT IT ALL.
MORE URGENTLY, HOW ARE WE GOING TO LOAD IT? IF "THEY" CAME HALFWAY THROUGH...

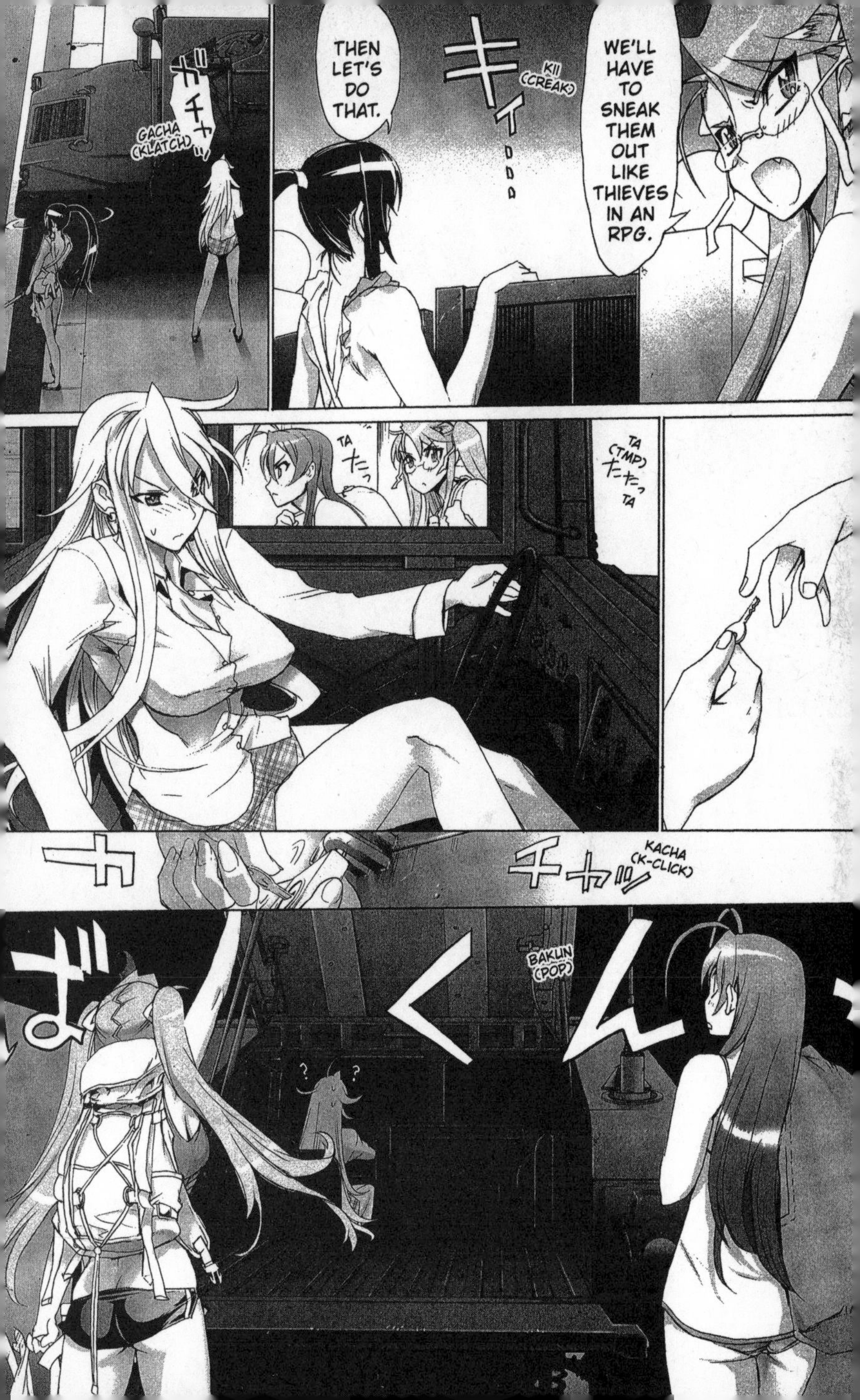
WE'LL HAVE TO SNEAK THEM OUT LIKE THIEVES IN AN RPG.
KII (CREAK)
THEN LET'S DO THAT.
GACHA (KLATCH)
TA (TMP)
TA
TA
KACHA (K-CLICK)
BAKUN (POP)

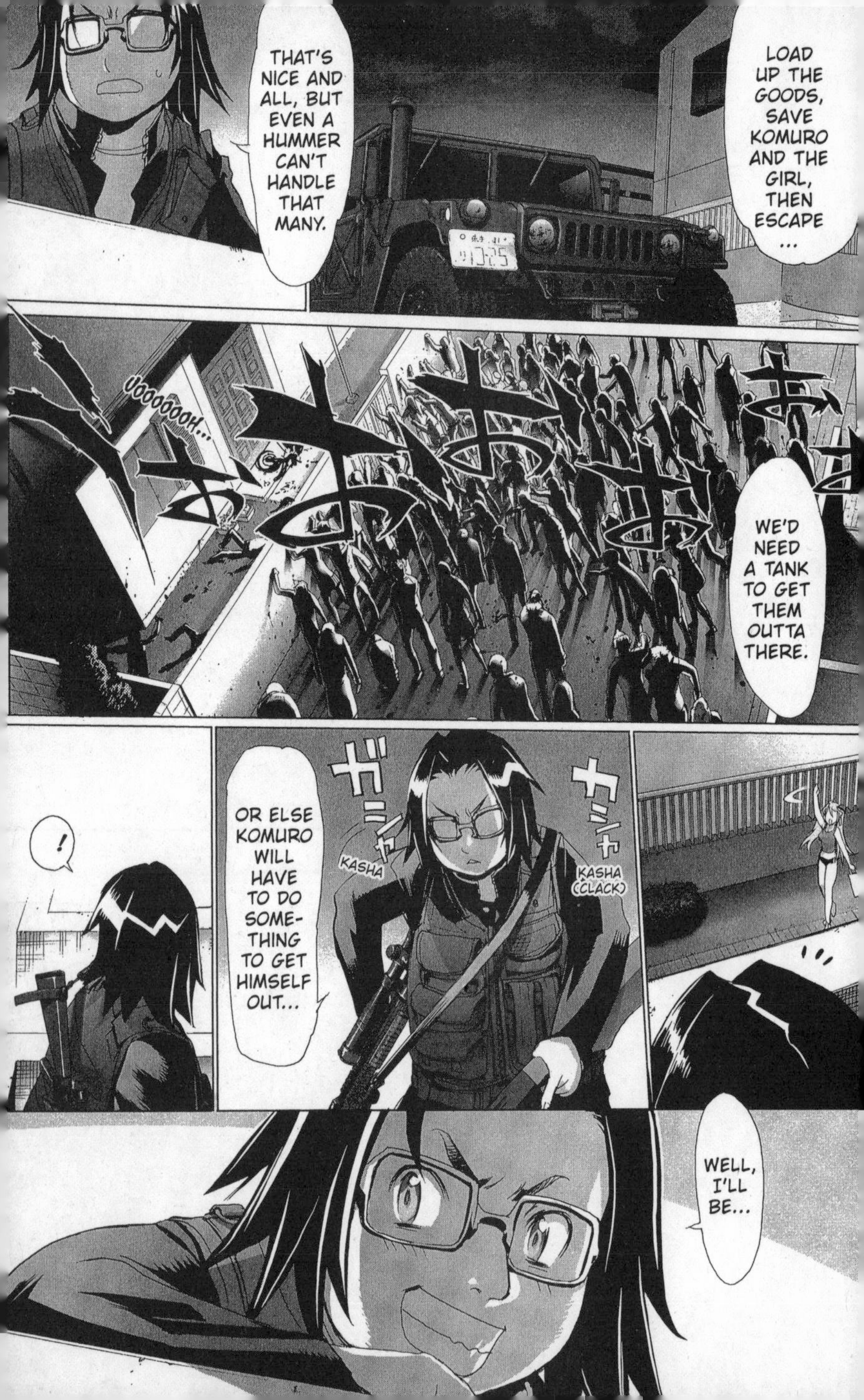

LOAD UP THE GOODS, SAVE KOMURO AND THE GIRL, THEN ESCAPE...
THAT'S NICE AND ALL, BUT EVEN A HUMMER CAN'T HANDLE THAT MANY.
WE'D NEED A TANK TO GET THEM OUTTA THERE.
VOOOOOOH...
KASHA (CLACK)
OR ELSE KOMURO WILL HAVE TO DO SOME-THING TO GET HIMSELF OUT...
KASHA
!
WELL, I'LL BE...

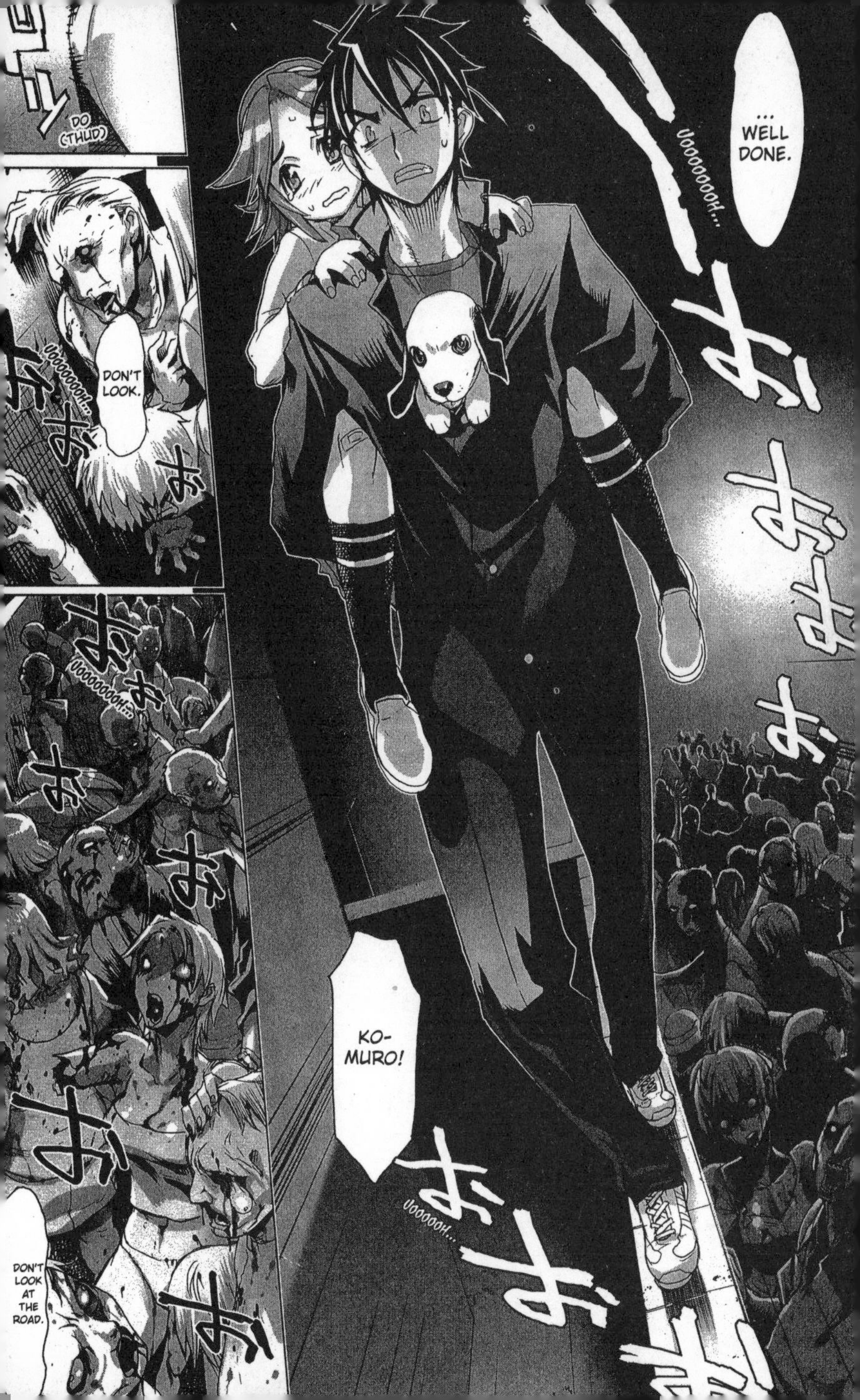
...WELL DONE.
UOOOOOOOOH...
KO-MURO!
UOOOOOH...
DO (THUD)
UOOOOOOOOH...
DON'T LOOK.
UOOOOOOOOH...
DON'T LOOK AT THE ROAD.

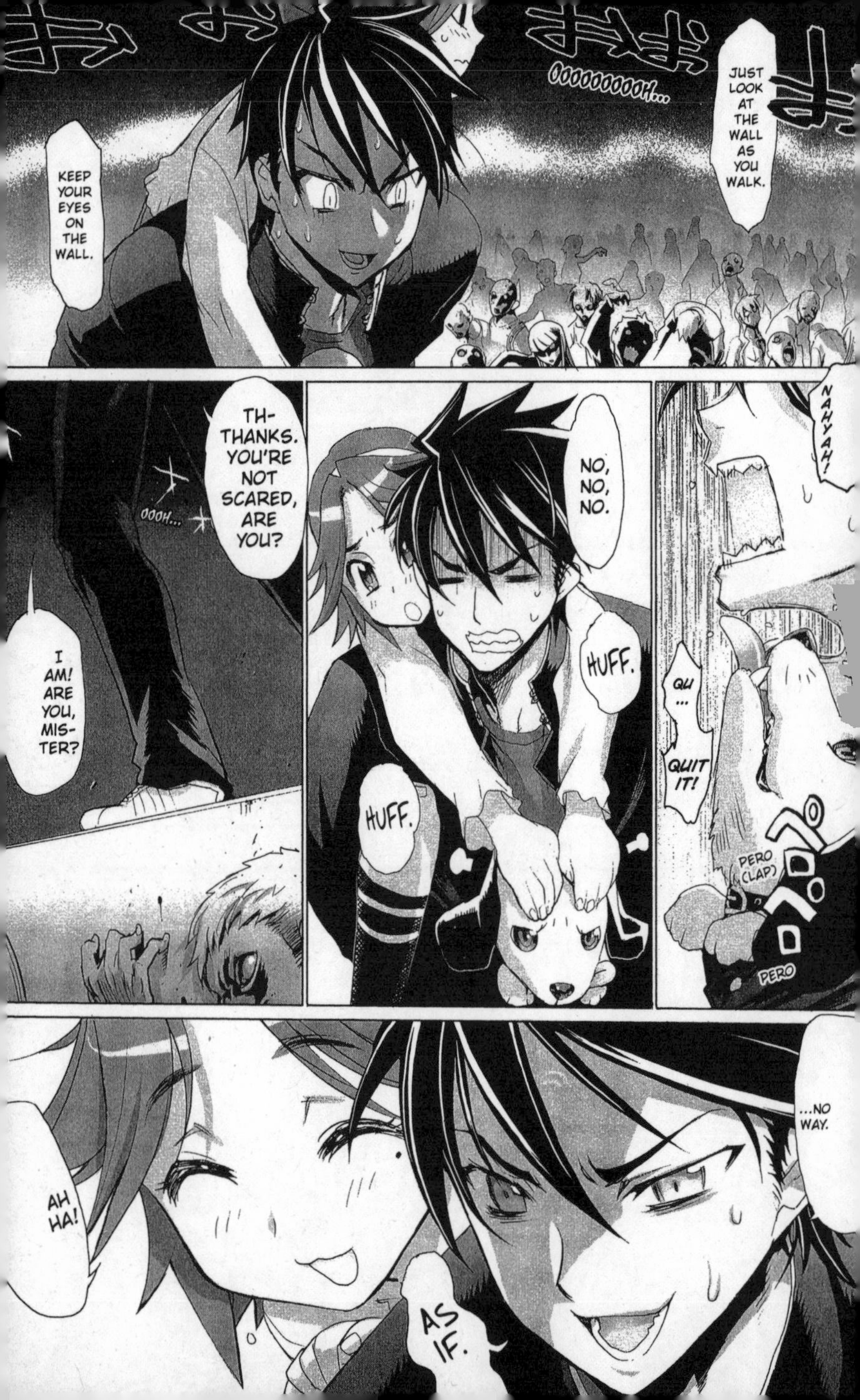
OOOOOOOOOOH...
JUST LOOK AT THE WALL AS YOU WALK.
KEEP YOUR EYES ON THE WALL.
NAHYAH!
QU... QUIT IT!
PERO (LAP)
PERO
NO, NO, NO.
HUFF.
HUFF.
TH-THANKS. YOU'RE NOT SCARED, ARE YOU?
OOOH...
I AM! ARE YOU, MISTER?
...NO WAY.
AH HA!
AS IF.

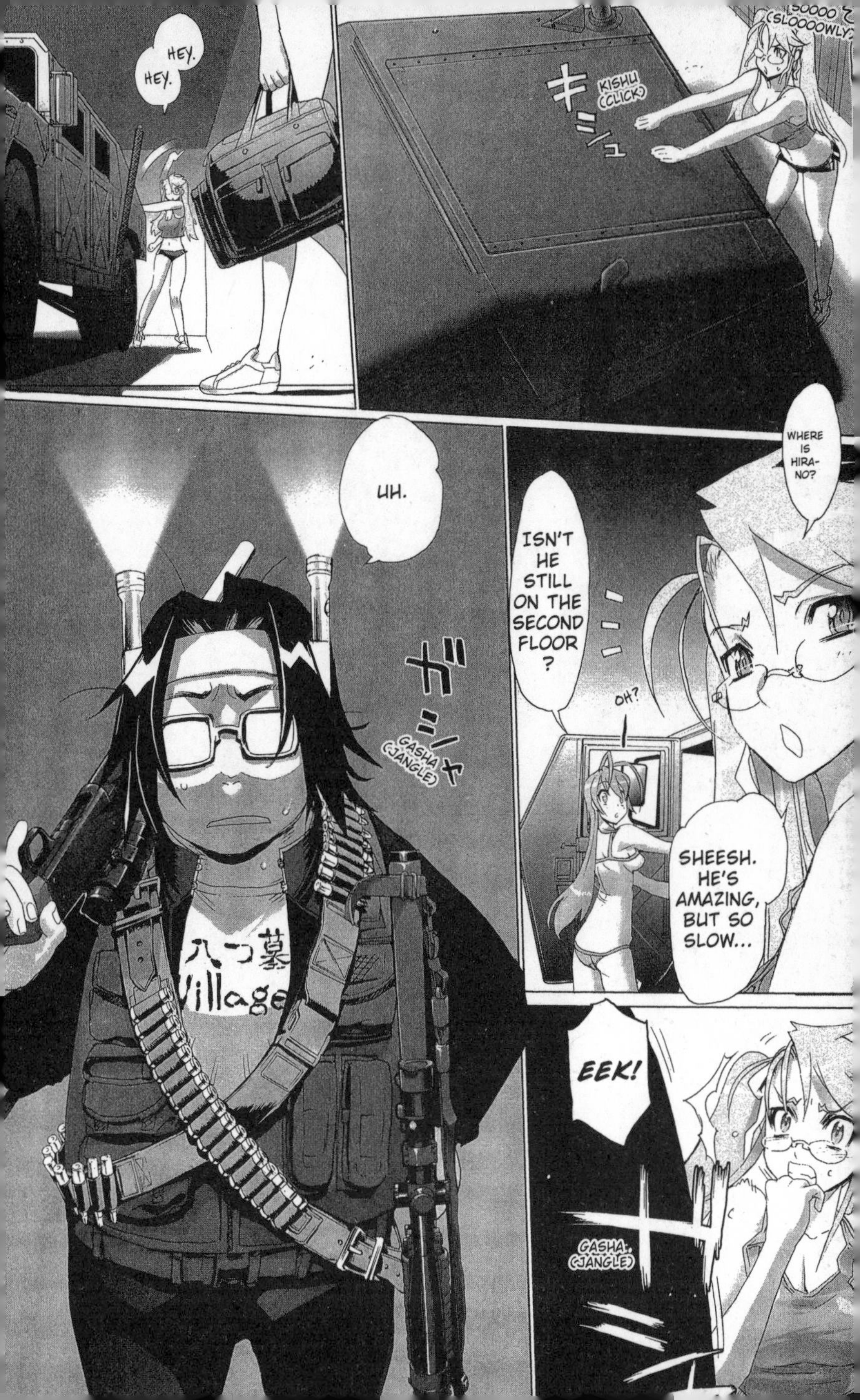
SOOOO
(SLOOOOWLY)
キシュ
KISHU (CLICK)
HEY.
HEY.
WHERE IS HIRA-NO?
ISN'T HE STILL ON THE SECOND FLOOR?
OH?
SHEESH. HE'S AMAZING, BUT SO SLOW...
EEK!
GASHA (JANGLE)
UH.
ガシャ
GASHA (JANGLE)
八つ墓 Village

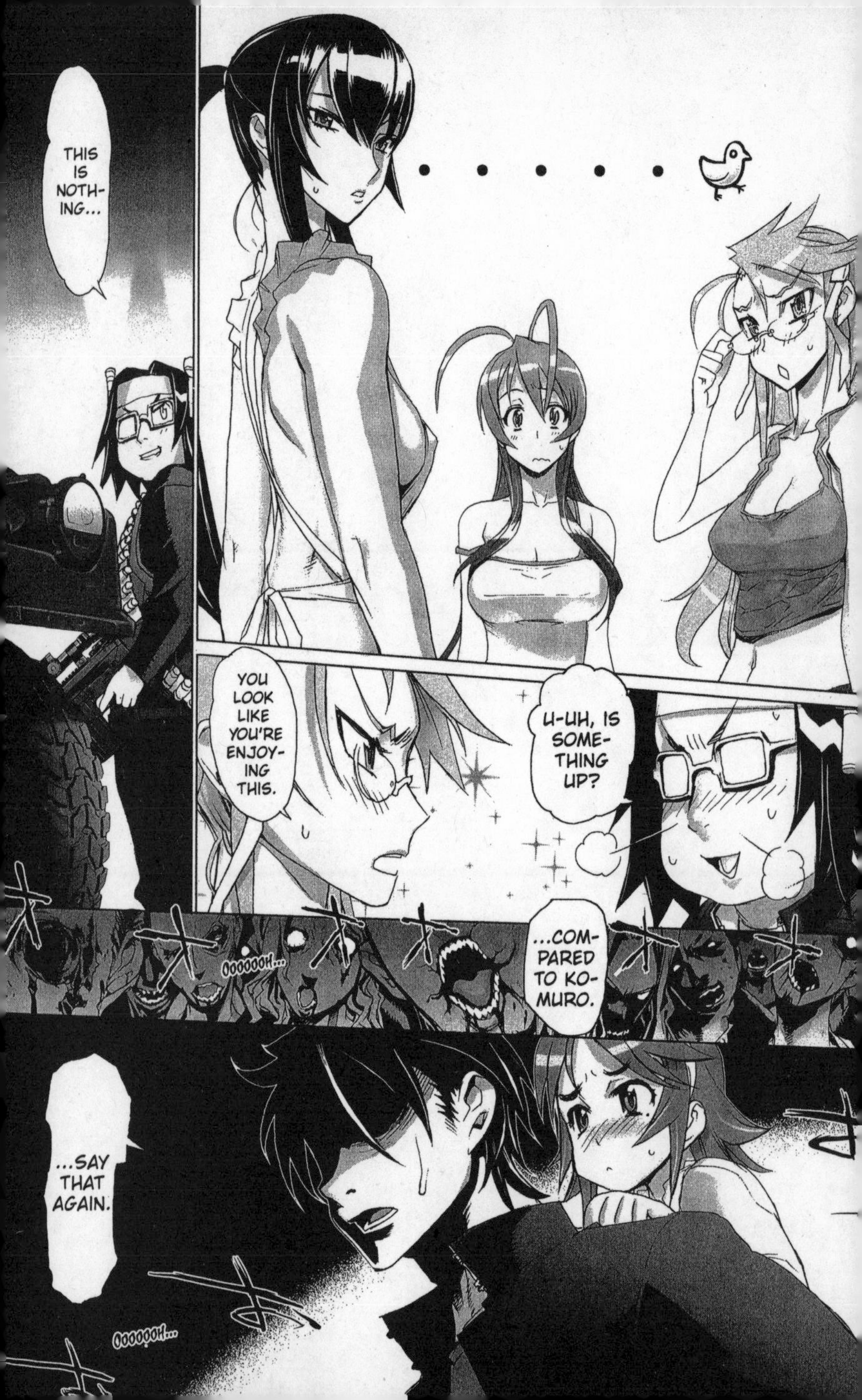
. . . . .
U-UH, IS SOME-THING UP?
YOU LOOK LIKE YOU'RE ENJOY-ING THIS.
THIS IS NOTH-ING...
...COM-PARED TO KO-MURO.
OOOOOOH...
...SAY THAT AGAIN.
OOOOOOH...

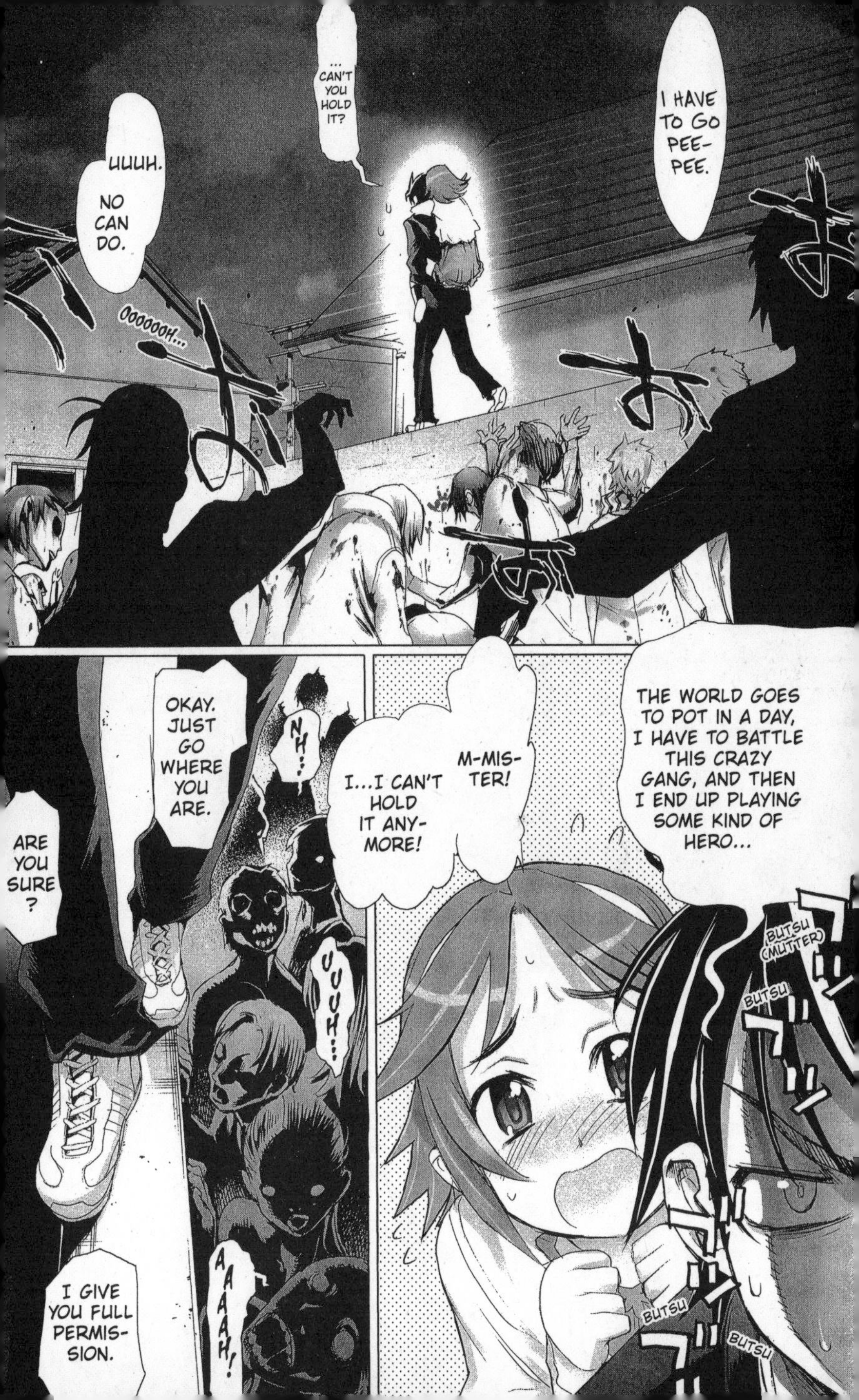
I HAVE TO GO PEE-PEE.
...CAN'T YOU HOLD IT?
UUUH. NO CAN DO.
OOOOOOH...
THE WORLD GOES TO POT IN A DAY, I HAVE TO BATTLE THIS CRAZY GANG, AND THEN I END UP PLAYING SOME KIND OF HERO...
BUTSU (MUTTER)
BUTSU
BUTSU
BUTSU
M-MISTER!
I...I CAN'T HOLD IT ANYMORE!
OKAY. JUST GO WHERE YOU ARE.
NH...
ARE YOU SURE?
UUUH...
AAAAH!
I GIVE YOU FULL PERMISSION.

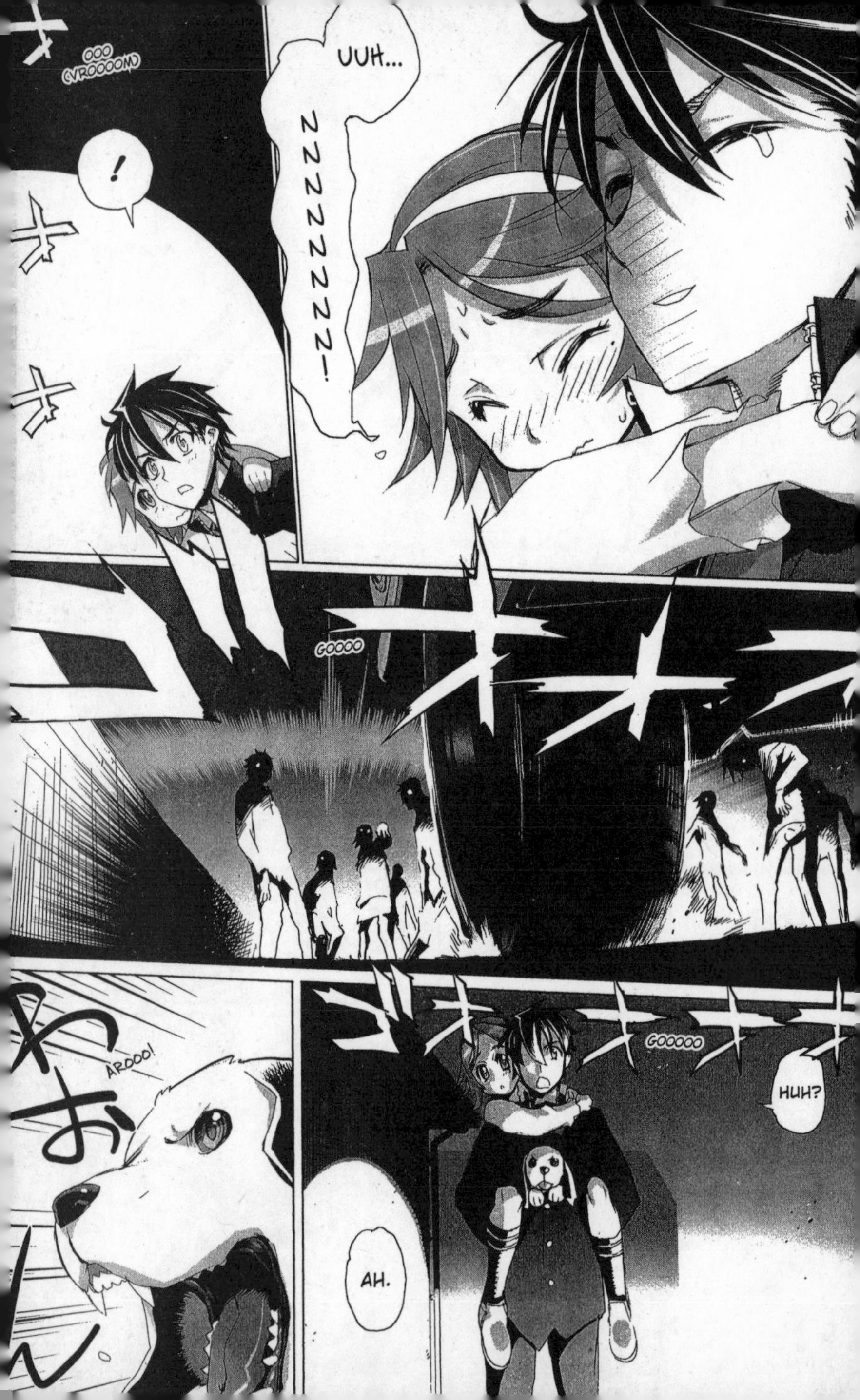
UUH...
ZZZZZZZZZ!
OOO (VROOOOM)
!
GOOOO
GOOOOO
HUH?
AH.
AROOO!

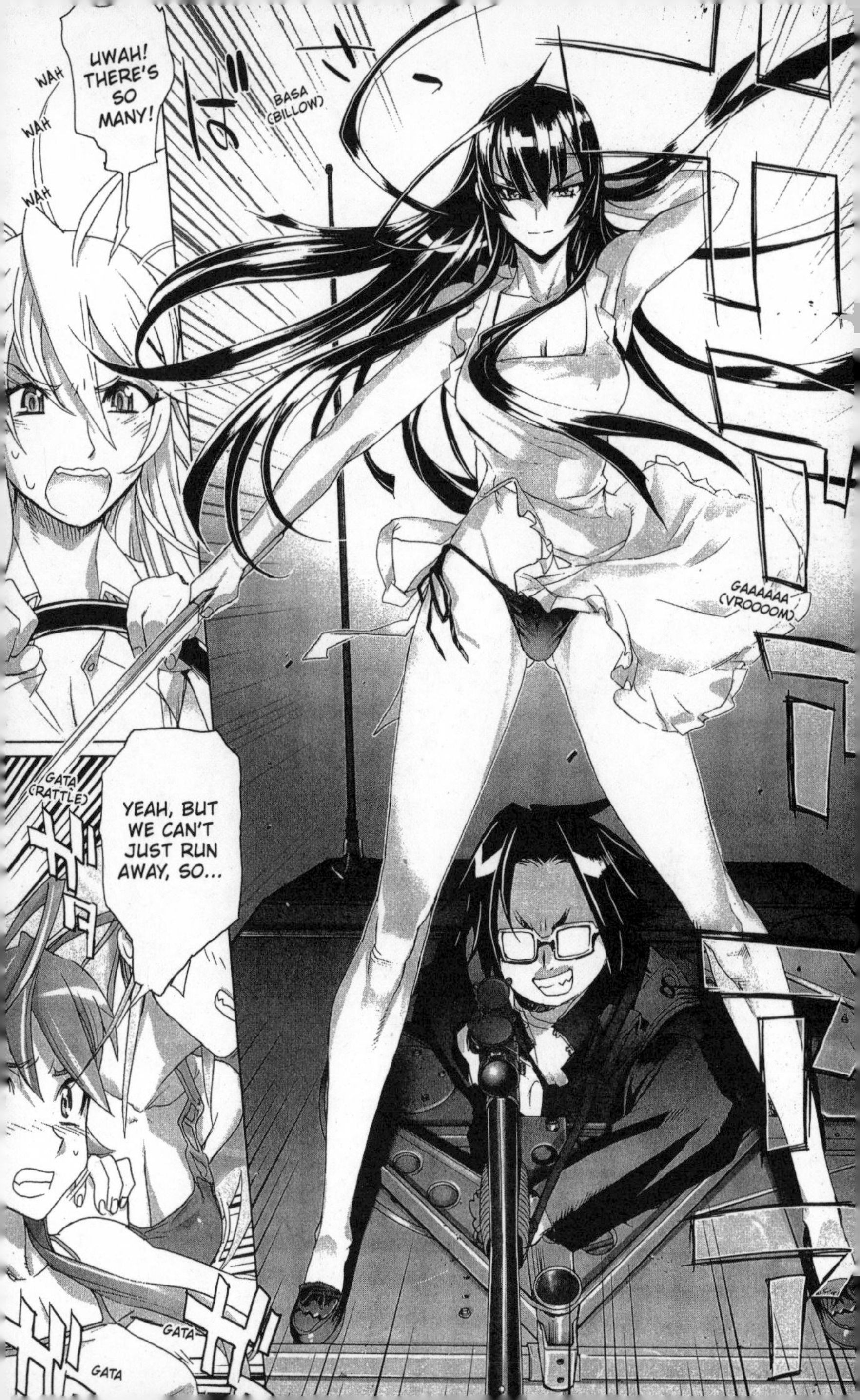
BASA (BILLOW)
GAAAAAA (VROOOOM)
WAH
WAH
WAH
UWAH! THERE'S SO MANY!
GATA (RATTLE)
YEAH, BUT WE CAN'T JUST RUN AWAY, SO...
GATA
GATA

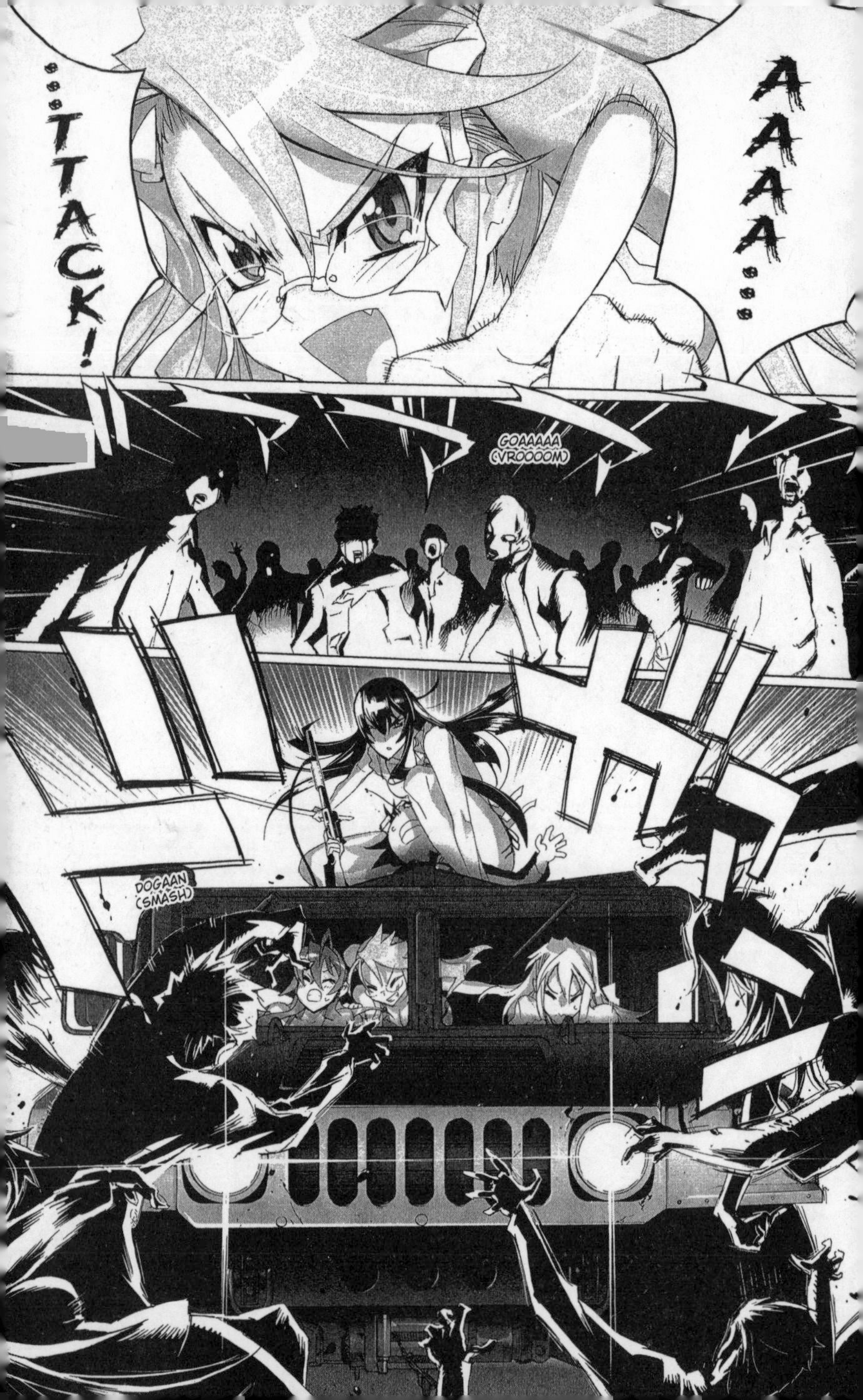
AAAA...
...TTACK!
GOAAAAA
(VROOOOM)
DOGAAN
(SMASH)

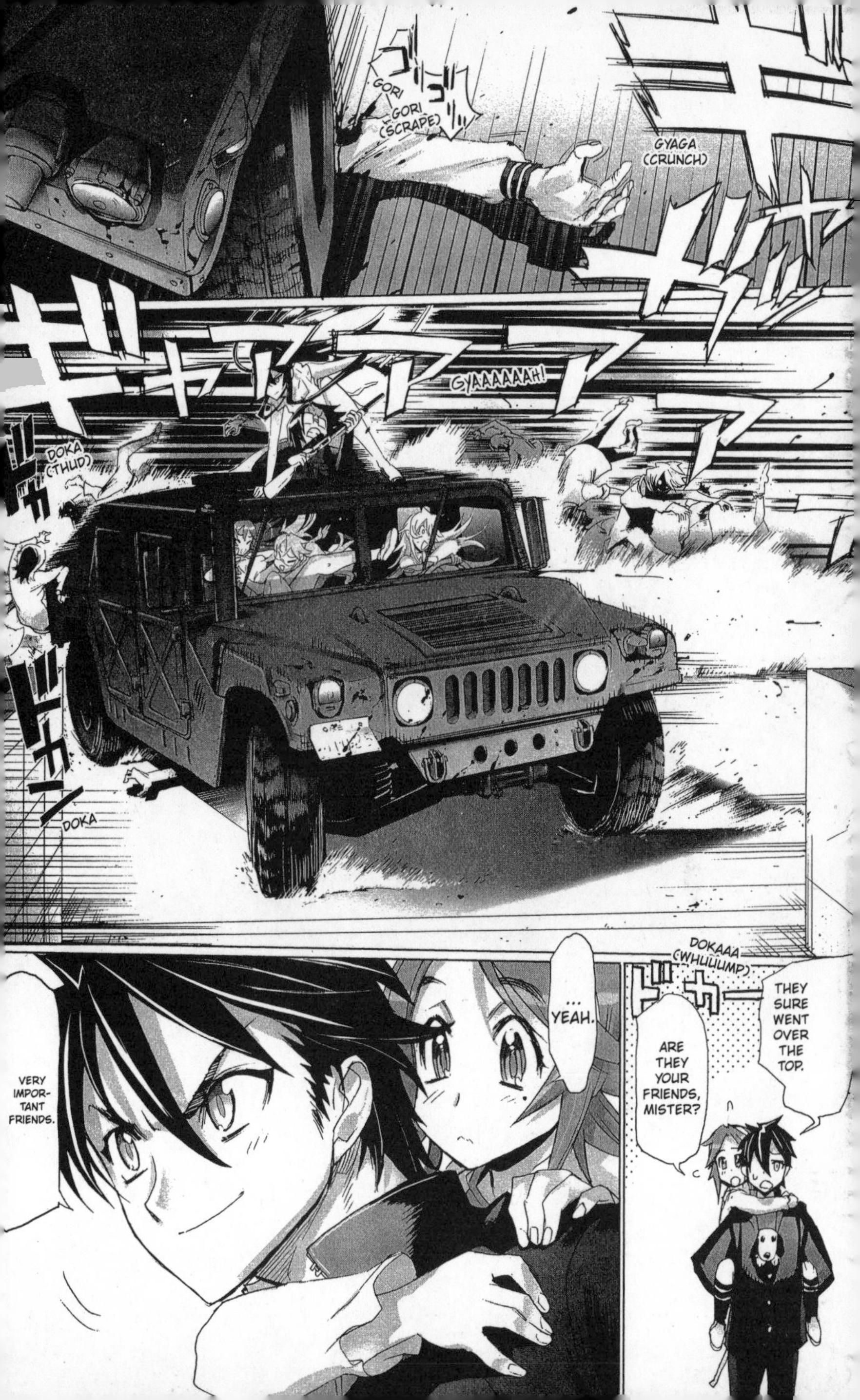
GYAGA (CRUNCH)
GORI GORI (SCRAPE)
GYAAAAAAH!
DOKA (THUD)
DOKA
DOKAAA (WHUUUMP)
THEY SURE WENT OVER THE TOP.
ARE THEY YOUR FRIENDS, MISTER?
... YEAH.
VERY IMPORTANT FRIENDS.

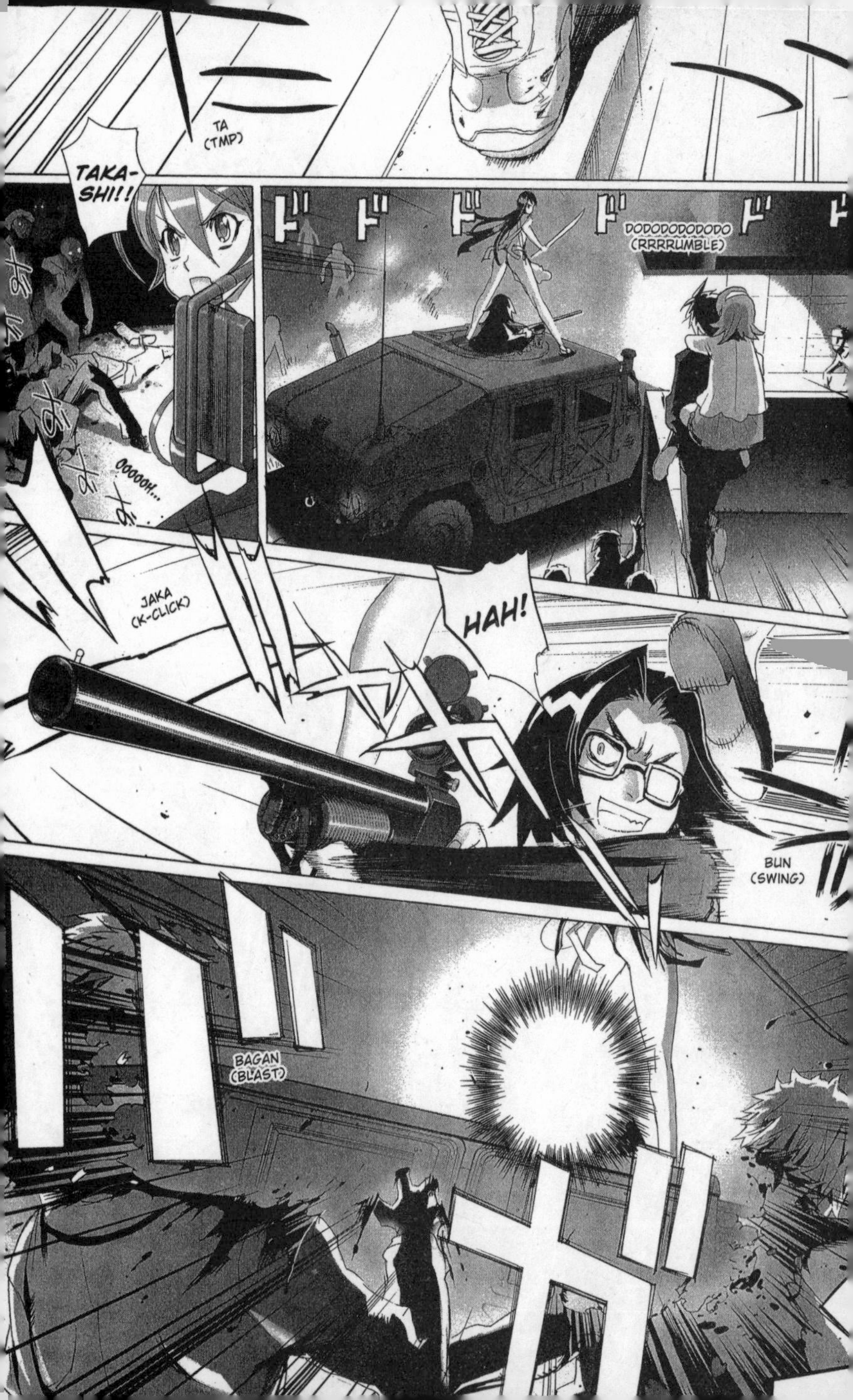

TA
(TMP)
DODODODODODODO
(RRRRUMBLE)
TAKA-SHI!!
OOOOOH...
HAH!
JAKA
(K-CLICK)
BUN
(SWING)
BAGAN
(BLAST)

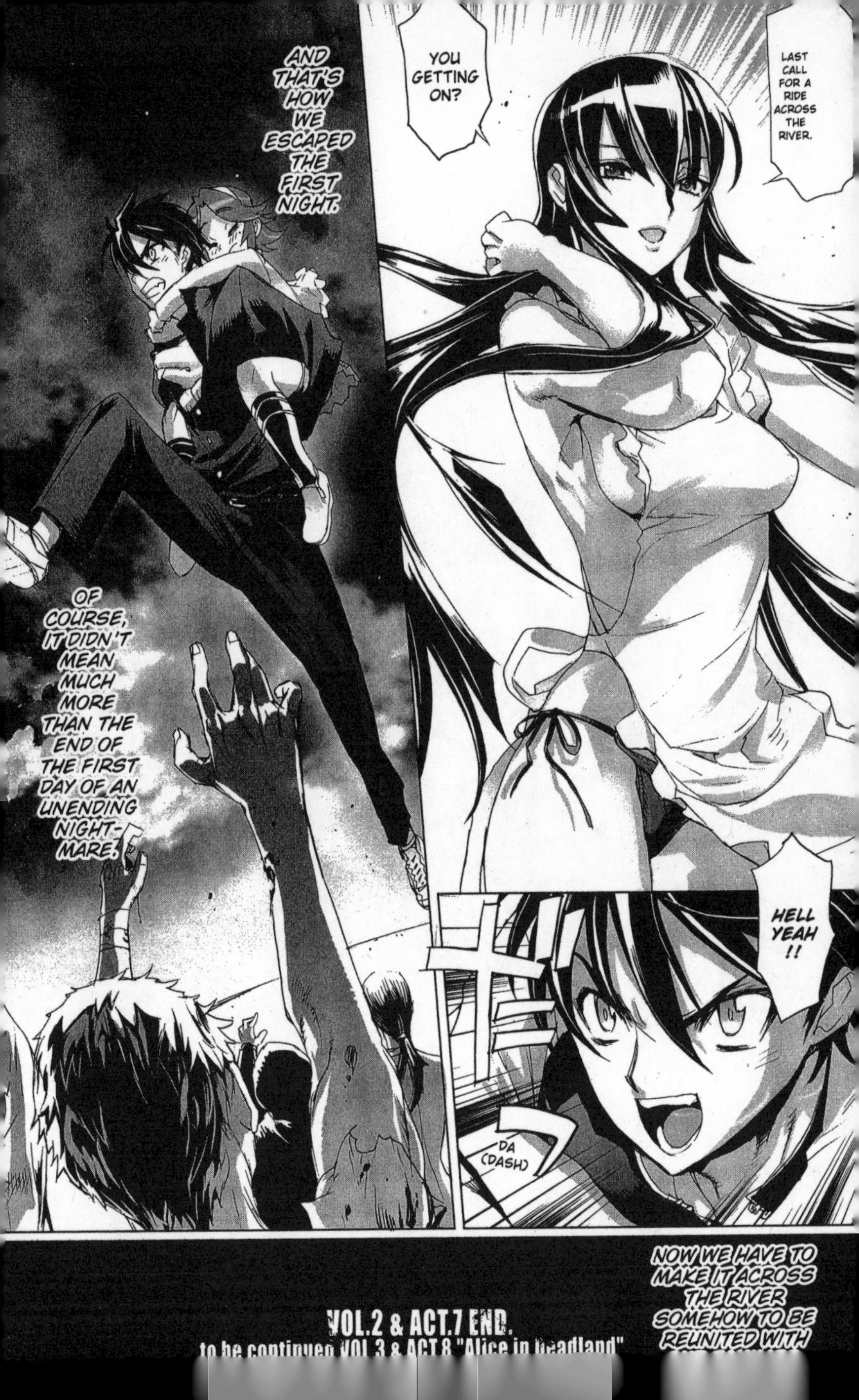
LAST CALL FOR A RIDE ACROSS THE RIVER.
YOU GETTING ON?
HELL YEAH!!
DA (DASH)
AND THAT'S HOW WE ESCAPED THE FIRST NIGHT.
OF COURSE, IT DIDN'T MEAN MUCH MORE THAN THE END OF THE FIRST DAY OF AN UNENDING NIGHT-MARE.
NOW WE HAVE TO MAKE IT ACROSS THE RIVER SOMEHOW TO BE REUNITED WITH
VOL.2 & ACT.7 END.
to be continued VOL.3 & ACT.8 "Alice in Deadland"

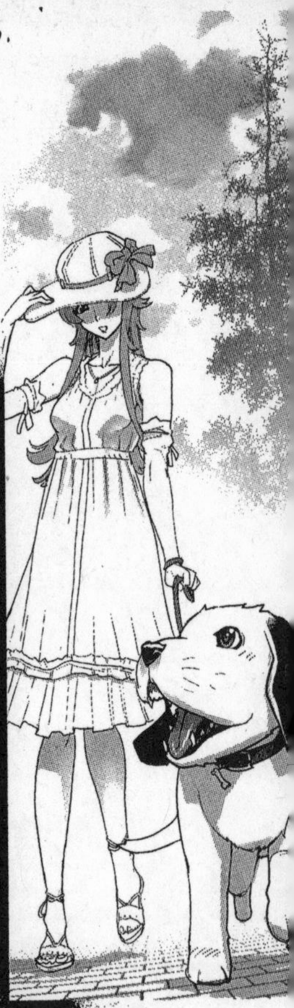

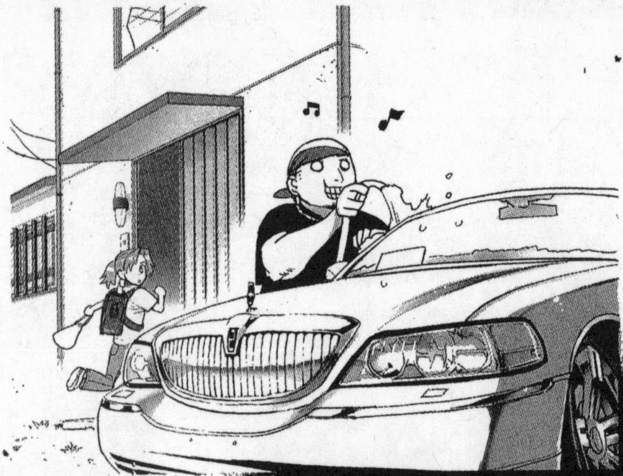

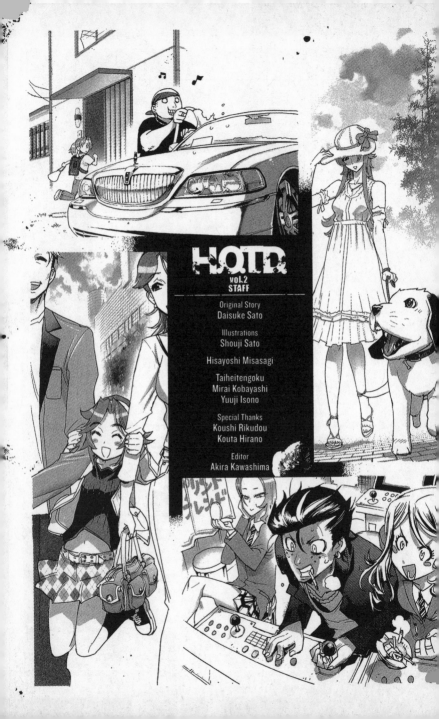

# H.O.T.D.

**vol.2**
**STAFF**

Original Story
Daisuke Sato

Illustrations
Shouji Sato

Hisayoshi Misasagi

Taiheitengoku
Mirai Kobayashi
Yuuji Isono

Special Thanks
Koushi Rikudou
Kouta Hirano

Editor
Akira Kawashima

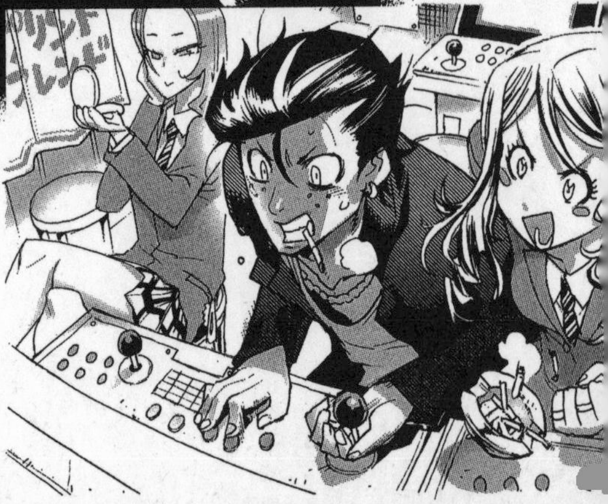

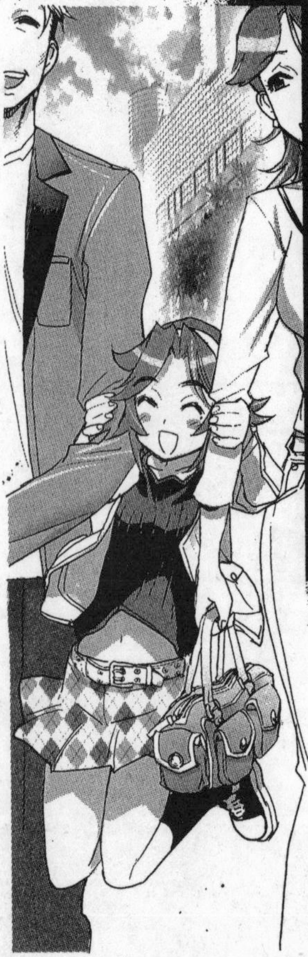

# Special Appendix: List of Weapons [Volumes 1 & 2]

A multitude of weapons to use against "them" appears throughout this series. As a special appendix in volume 2, we now present to you the list of said weapons along with explanations and commentary from the author, Daisuke Sato.

## MOP HANDLE

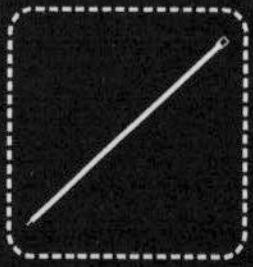

The remains of your typical mop used for classroom clean-up with the head removed. Made of aluminum. Approximately 120 cm long. Rei's primary weapon during the school arc.

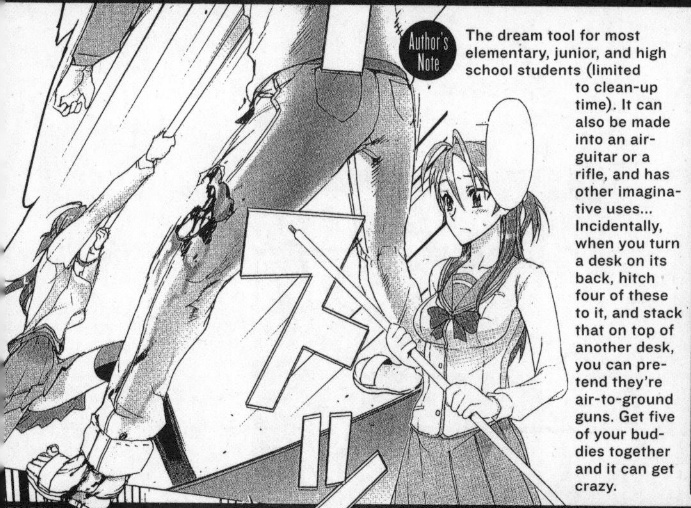

Author's Note

The dream tool for most elementary, junior, and high school students (limited to clean-up time). It can also be made into an air-guitar or a rifle, and has other imaginative uses... Incidentally, when you turn a desk on its back, hitch four of these to it, and stack that on top of another desk, you can pretend they're air-to-ground guns. Get five of your buddies together and it can get crazy.

## METAL BAT

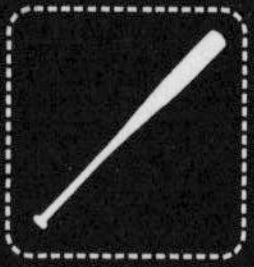

Borrowed without permission from the baseball team. Made of an alloy. 84 cm long and weighs over 900 grams (following official baseball rules). Used by Takashi and Hisashi. Excellent destructive force.

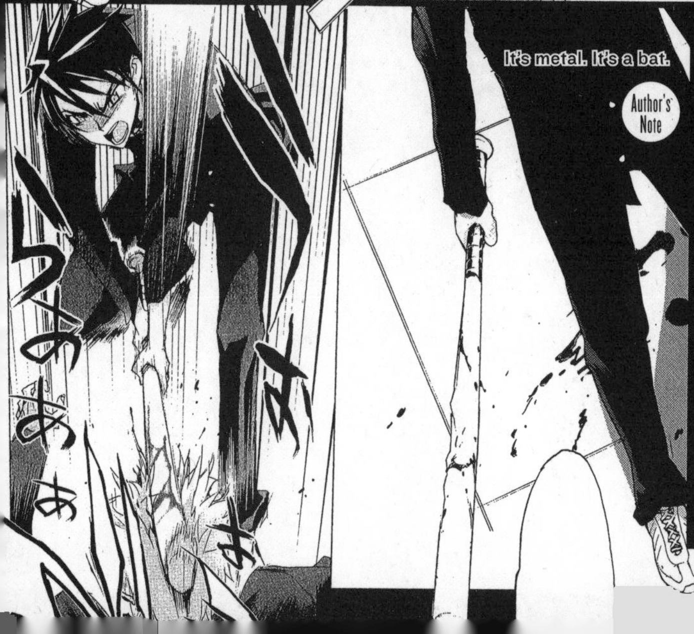

Author's Note

It's metal. It's a bat.

## WOODEN SWORD

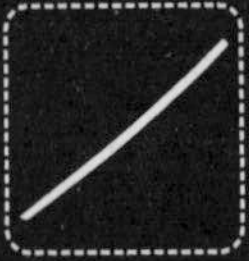

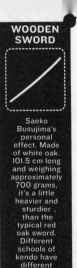

Saeko Busujima's personal effect. Made of white oak. 101.5 cm long and weighing approximately 700 grams, it's a little heavier and sturdier than the typical red oak sword. Different schools of kendo have different designs for it.

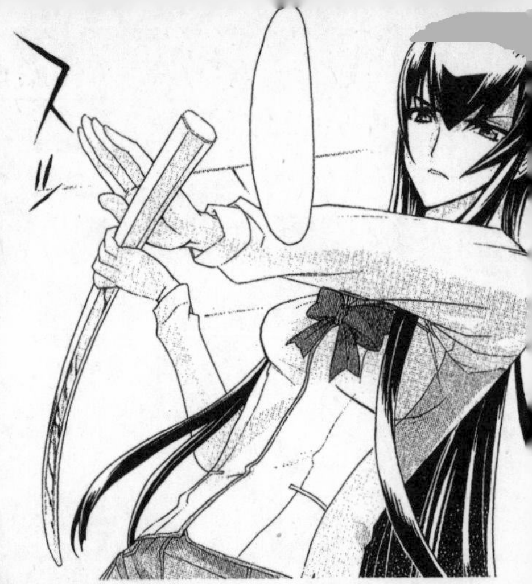

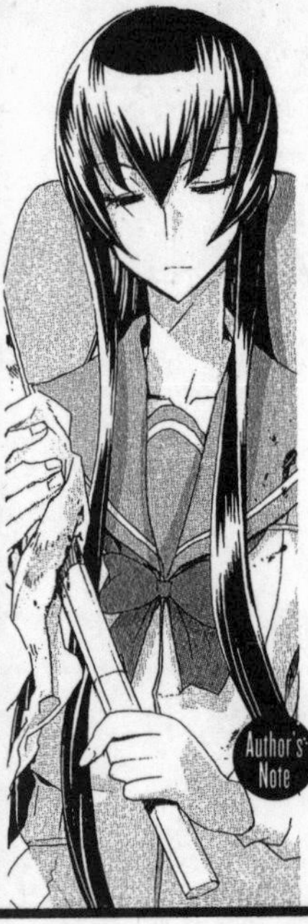

Author's Note

This sword actually has sealed in it a secret that could dispel all of the mysteries of the Yamato Chotei and the entire Japanese race, and the Busujima family, descendents of the poison unit that served under Chotei since ancient times, has fought through the ages to protect that secret. However, that has nothing to do with this series, *Highschool of the Dead*.

## NAIL GUN

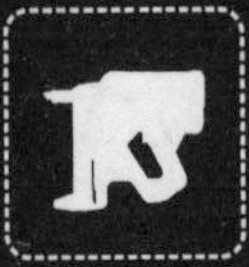

A tool from shop class. Within its internal combustion chamber, a gas is ignited that thrusts the nail out. It's 317 mm long and 403 mm high with a weight of 3.9 kg (not including the T square taped to it for support).

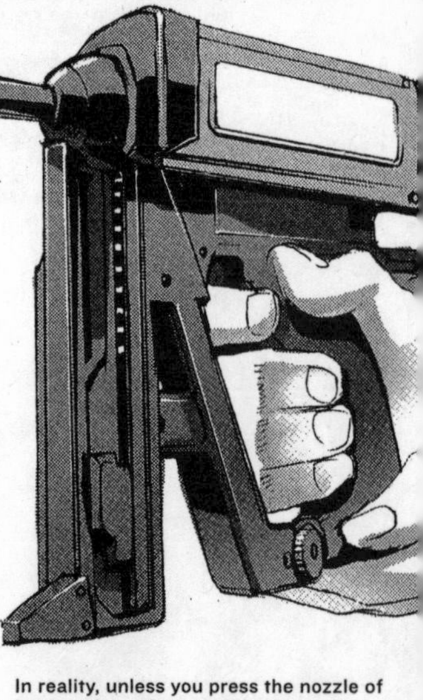

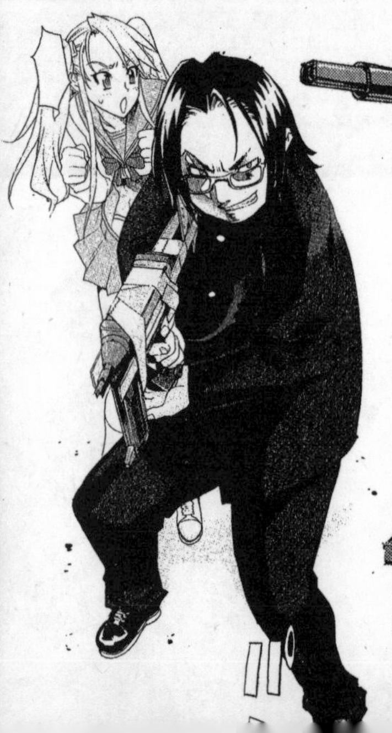

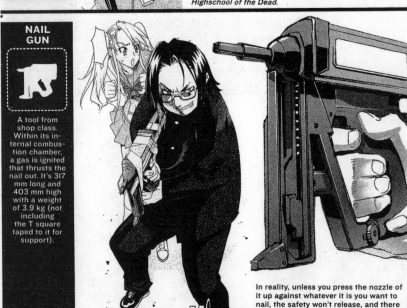

In reality, unless you press the nozzle of it up against whatever it is you want to nail, the safety won't release, and there are a number of things about it that make it tricky to use. But hey, Kouta-chan can make it work, so go figure.

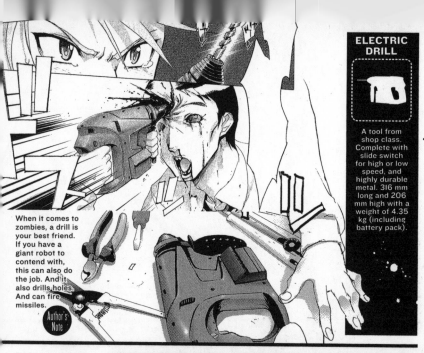

## ELECTRIC DRILL

A tool from shop class. Complete with slide switch for high or low speed, and highly durable metal. 316 mm long and 206 mm high with a weight of 4.35 kg (including battery pack).

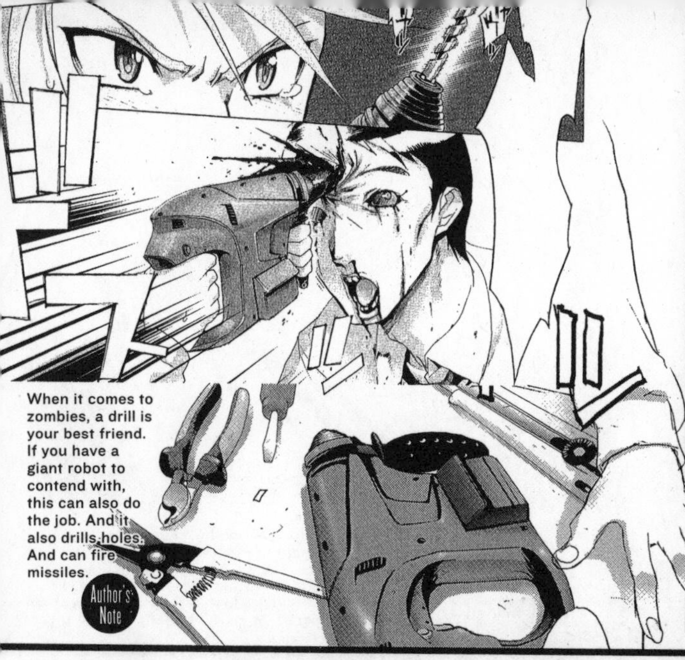

When it comes to zombies, a drill is your best friend. If you have a giant robot to contend with, this can also do the job. And it also drills holes. And can fire missiles.

Author's Note

## SMITH & WESSON M37 AIRWEIGHT

Borrowed without permission from a deceased cop. 194 mm long. Caliber: 38 mm x 5. Made in the USA. Its M36 chief's special frame was traded out for an aluminum alloy, making it lighter.

Back in the day, the Nanbu M60 revolver was almost the only gun carried by police, but apparently there are many different ones used now. Still, I wanted to pay homage to the classics, hence what you see here.

Author's Note

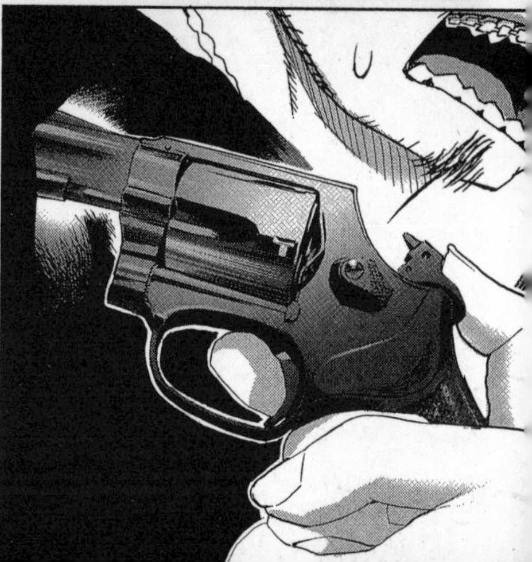

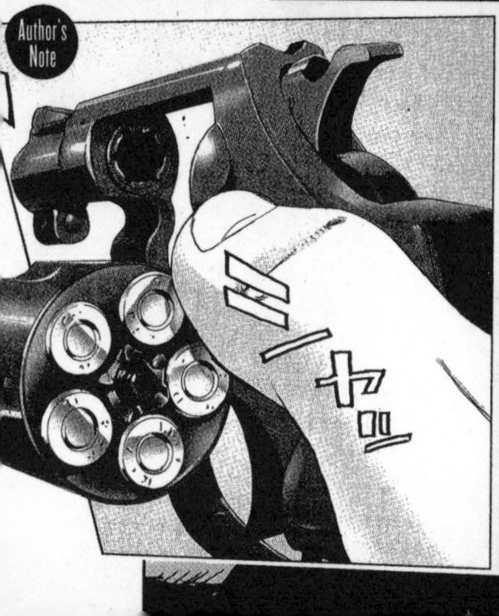

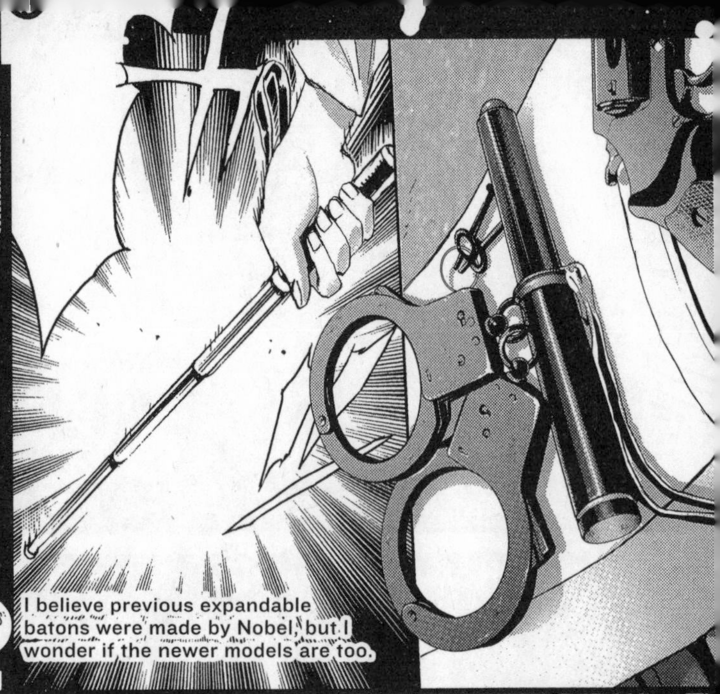

## BATON

Second item borrowed without permission from the deceased officers. 65 cm long, it weighs approximately 430 grams and has a special alloy body. Can expand to three lengths. Made in Japan.

Author's Note

I believe previous expandable batons were made by Nobel, but I wonder if the newer models are too.

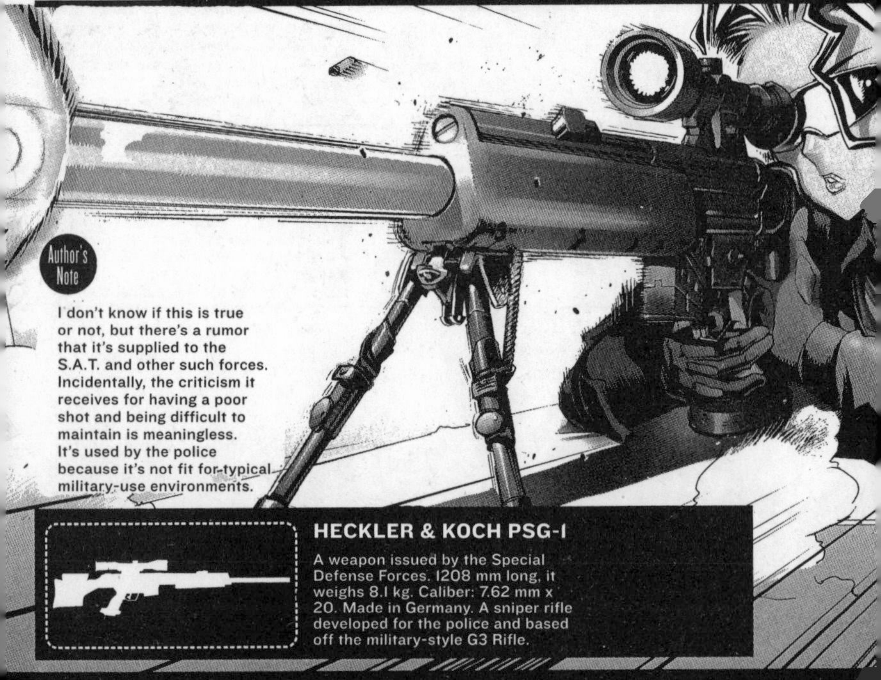

Author's Note

I don't know if this is true or not, but there's a rumor that it's supplied to the S.A.T. and other such forces. Incidentally, the criticism it receives for having a poor shot and being difficult to maintain is meaningless. It's used by the police because it's not fit for typical military-use environments.

## HECKLER & KOCH PSG-1

A weapon issued by the Special Defense Forces. 1208 mm long, it weighs 8.1 kg. Caliber: 7.62 mm x 20. Made in Germany. A sniper rifle developed for the police and based off the military-style G3 Rifle.

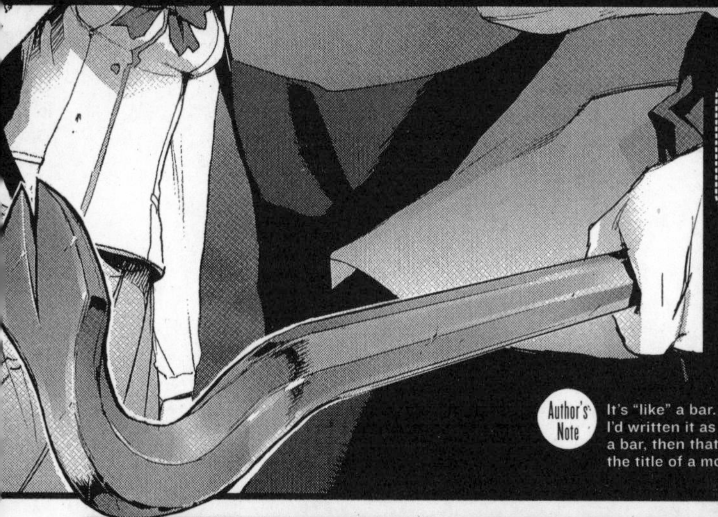

## CROW BAR

A tool from shop class that Takagi procured. 560 mm long. Excellent destructive force.

Author's Note

It's "like" a bar. But if I'd written it as "Like..." a bar, then that'd be the title of a movie.

## SPRINGFIELD MIAI SUPER MACH

Rika Minami's personal effect. The result of many a modification. 1118 mm long, it weighs 4.5 kg. Caliber: 7.62 mm x 20. Made in the USA. The fully-automated function of an army-issued MI4 was removed, and now it's used for consumer use.

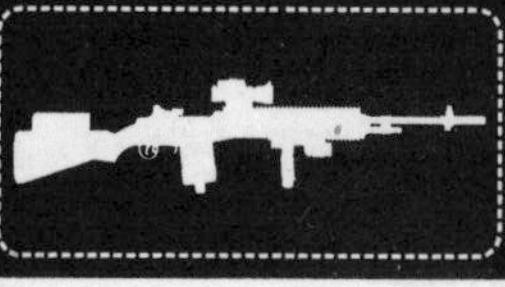

Author's Note

**Apparently, even the MI4s used by the U.S. Marines have had their rapid-fire functions ceased. It seems they didn't realize that when a gun is fully automated, the shots kick the gun back and the nozzle reflexively pops up, spraying the bullets every which way; hence their removal. Also, when the fully automated functions are left intact, soldiers with little training only end up wasting bullets when they use it, so there's that reason too. Incidentally, the modern types being revived by special units and the like have also had their fully automatic functions removed.**

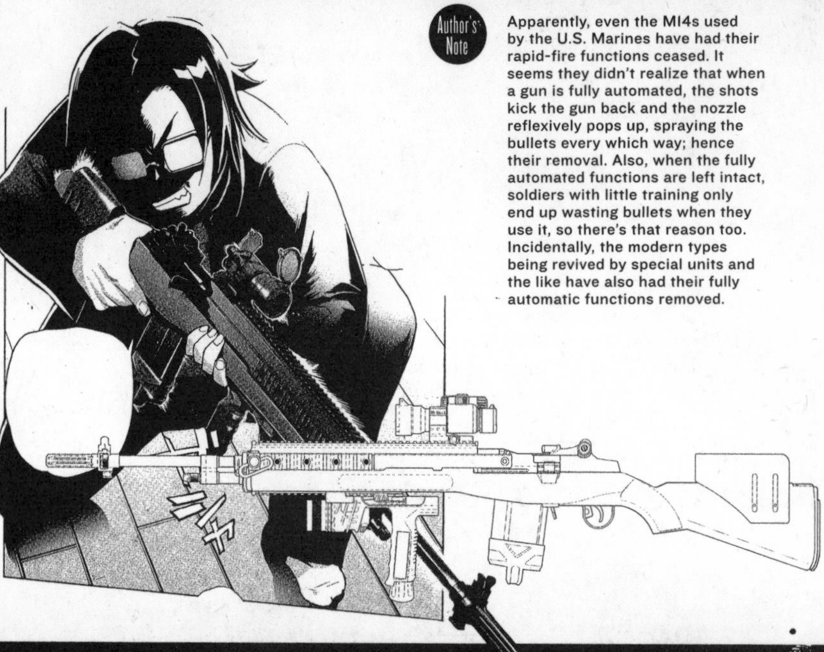

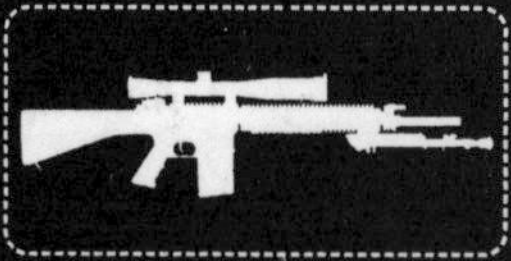

## KNIGHT'S SR-25 TYPE ARMALITE AR-10 V.

From Rika Minami's personal collection. Kouta's favorite gun (heh). 1118 mm long, it weighs 4.88 kg (minus the scope). Caliber: 7.62 mm x 20. Made in the USA. One part from an AR-10 was issued for consumer use without the fully automated function, but Rika imported some parts through the black market (so far, legal) and incorporated them into it (illegal).

Author's Note

**Kouta's imagination is considerably different from the truth (heh). In reality, Rika gunsmithed an Armalite AR-10A4 law enforcement carbine (very different from the original one from the 1950s) that she bought from an American soldier, fashioning it to be an SR-25 type. She then smuggled it into Japan through an American army transport. Some women can be very scary.**

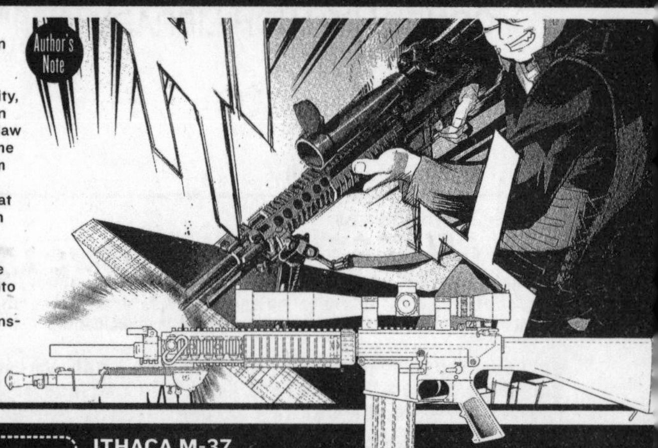

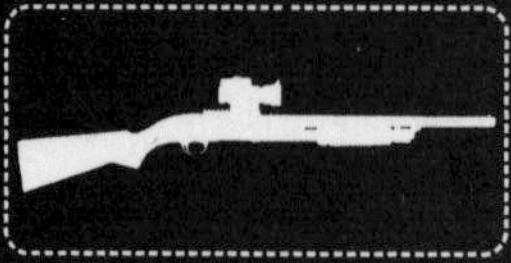

## ITHACA M-37

Rika Minami's personal effect. Equipped with a sight on top. 1017 mm long, it weighs 2.3 kg (with sight installed). Caliber: 12-gauge x 4. Made in the USA. The best selling shotgun for its light handling and superior shot.

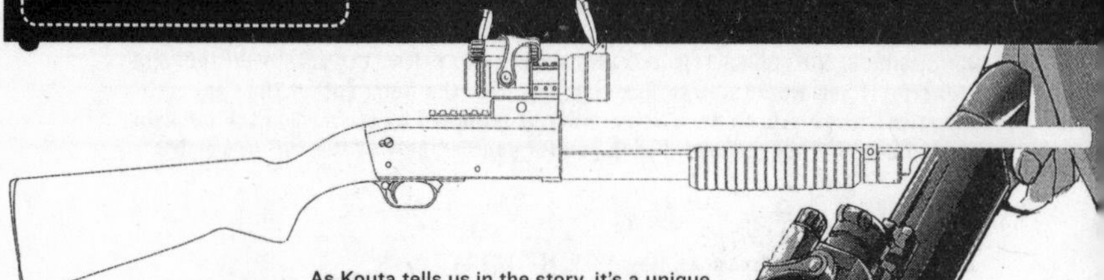

Author's Note

**As Kouta tells us in the story, it's a unique pump-action style shotgun. When I hear the name "Ithaca M-37", what comes to mind is the war in Vietnam with American soldiers pumping these while smoking a joint.**

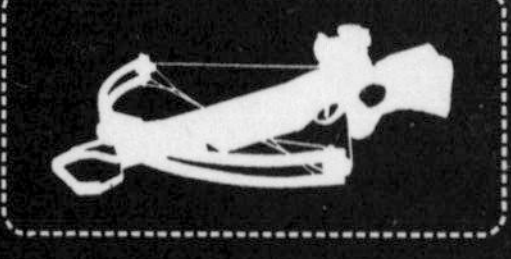

## BARNETT WILDCAT C5

Rika Minami's personal effect. Was stored in the locker disassembled. 150 pounds of draw force. Weighs 2.8 kg. Made in England. Takes considerable strength to set the bow string, even for a man. Will be making a debut later in the series.

Author's Note

**I've actually held one of these in real life. It requires know-how and strength to pull the string. Incidentally, the targets for this kind of crossbow are deer and bears, and in Japan it can be purchased without any restrictions or registration required. Either way, they're expensive and places where you can fire them are limited.**

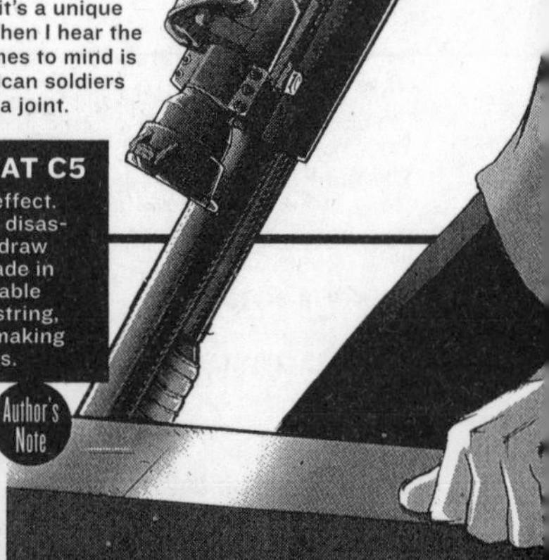

# HIGHSCHOOL OF THE DEAD ❷

**DAISUKE SATO**
**SHOUJI SATO**

Translation: Christine Dashiell

Lettering: Chris Counasse

This book is a work of fiction. Names, characters, places, and incidents are the product of the author's imagination or are used fictitiously. Any resemblance to actual events, locales, or persons, living or dead, is coincidental.

GAKUENMOKUSHIROKU HIGHSCHOOL OF THE DEAD Volume 2 ©2007 DAISUKE SATO ©2007 SHOUJI SATO. Edited by FUJIMISHOBO. First published in Japan in 2007 by KADOKAWA CORPORATION, Tokyo. English translation rights arranged with KADOKAWA CORPORATION, Tokyo, through TUTTLE-MORI AGENCY, INC., Tokyo.

Translation © 2011 by Hachette Book Group, Inc.

Yen Press
Hachette Book Group
1290 Avenue of the Americas, New York, NY 10104

www.HachetteBookGroup.com
www.YenPress.com

Yen Press is an imprint of Hachette Book Group, Inc.
The Yen Press name and logo are trademarks of Hachette Book Group, Inc.

First Yen Press Edition: April 2011

ISBN: 978-0-316-13239-8

20 19 18 17 16 15 14 13 12 11

BVG

Printed in the United States of America

MAY 2017